Southern Literary Studies
Louis D. Rubin, Jr., Editor

The Major Fiction of William Gilmore Simms

William Gilmore Simms

James Grant Wilson and John Fiske (eds.), *Appletons' Cyclopædia of American Biography* (New York, 1888), V, facing p. 533.

The Major Fiction of William Gilmore Simms

CULTURAL TRADITIONS AND LITERARY FORM

Mary Ann Wimsatt

LOUISIANA STATE UNIVERSITY PRESS
Baton Rouge and London

98 97 96 95 94 93 92 91 90 89 5 4 3 2 1

Designer: Laura Roubique Gleason
Typeface: Sabon
Typesetter: G&S Typesetters, Inc.
Printer: Thomson-Shore, Inc.
Binder: John H. Dekker & Sons, Inc.

Library of Congress Cataloging-in-Publication Data

Wimsatt, Mary Ann, 1934–
The major fiction of William Gilmore Simms: cultural traditions and literary form / Mary Ann Wimsatt.
p. cm. — (Southern literary studies)
Bibliography: p.
Includes index.
ISBN 0-8071-1459-6
1. Simms, William Gilmore, 1806–1870—Criticism and interpretation. 2. Southern States in literature. I. Title. II. Series.
PS2853.W56 1989
813′.3—dc19 88-23139
CIP

The paper in this book meets the guidelines for permanence and durability of the Committee on Production Guidelines for Book Longevity of the Council on Library Resources. ∞

For Jim
and also
to the memory of Arlin Turner

Do not, however, suppose me insensible to the sweet solicitings of fame. It has been the dream of my life, the unnamed inspiration of my boyhood—dearer than life, for which I take cheerfully to toil, and toil on, though I see not the reward.

—William Gilmore Simms to Rufus Wilmot Griswold, June 20, 1841

Contents

Illustrations

Acknowledgments

Jared Bunce, the Yankee peddler who swindles his way through Simms's first novel, *Guy Rivers,* inveigled me into writing this book. Some years ago, when I was studying the variety of native humor that Simms uses in his fiction, I grew interested in Jared and the possible sources for him—a puzzle that previous critics had tried in vain to solve. My search for sources took me from the East Coast to the West Coast and from South Carolina to Harvard and beyond; meanwhile, I had started to analyze Simms's literary structures and the various conventions behind them, and I had also started to investigate the way in which Simms managed, often quite deftly, to give elements of southern culture a literary shape. After studying that culture in some detail while examining theoretical formulations about his principal literary genre, romance, I began to see how cultural traditions and literary form converge at almost every level of his fiction.

The result is this book, an analysis and interpretation of Simms's major fiction against the background of his long literary career and with glances at his poetry, orations, criticism, and historical writing. The study as it stands is different in conception and design from the one I originally set out to write. And so Jared Bunce, the "shadow-skinning Yankee" whom I had planned to dispose of briefly but whose immediate literary antecedents I could never succeed in pinning down, may number me among his victims.

In the course of so varied an inquiry, I have accumulated a great many debts that it is now a pleasure to acknowledge. I am grateful to Duke University librarians Florence Blakely, Albert Nelius, Elvin Strowd, and Mattie Russell for their help with various stages of the project; to John Chalmers, head of the rare-books division in the Harry Ransom Center, University of Texas; to James Thorpe and the late Ray Billington of the Huntington Library, San Marino, California; to E. L.

Inabinett, director of the South Caroliniana Library, University of South Carolina; and to librarians at the University of Kentucky, the University of North Carolina at Greensboro, Harvard University, and the British Museum, who helped unearth various rare materials.

I am also extremely grateful to Simms's granddaughter, Mary C. Simms Oliphant of Greenville, South Carolina, for extended conversations about Simms and for her many letters answering questions or providing factual information; and to John C. Guilds of the University of Arkansas, to Miriam J. Shillingsburg of Mississippi State University, to James E. Kibler, Jr., of the University of Georgia, and to Betty Jo Strickland of Brunswick Junior College for their help with the project and their own substantial scholarship on Simms. I owe thanks to Rosalyn Rossignol, my expert research assistant at the University of North Carolina, who checked sources and references untiringly; to Joseph M. Flora and Robert Bain of the same university, who sustained me with help and humor; to Louis J. Budd of Duke University, who answered dozens of questions on several dozen matters; and to my fellow editors of *The History of Southern Literature*, especially Rayburn S. Moore, Lewis P. Simpson, and Louis D. Rubin, Jr., who provided aid and encouragement at several stages of the study. Louis Rubin read the entire manuscript with his usual astute eye; Louise Y. Gossett of Salem College and Eugene D. Genovese of the University of Rochester also read the manuscript and offered detailed suggestions for its improvement. Beverly Jarrett and Catherine Landry of Louisiana State University Press guided it through the publication process with sure hands.

Early in the study I incurred great obligations to two scholars now dead, Arlin Turner of Duke University and C. Hugh Holman of the University of North Carolina at Chapel Hill. Both gave generously of time, advice, and information, and one of my keen regrets is that neither lived to see the completion of the project. Like most other Simmsians, I have made frequent use of Holman's own extensive work on Simms, which, along with the six volumes of the Simms letters edited by Mrs. Oliphant and the late T. C. Duncan Eaves, forms the foundation of modern scholarship on the author. I have also profited from William Charvat's work on the economics of professional authorship, from studies by James Hart and Jane Tompkins of popular fiction and its cultural milieu, and from the insights of several students and theoreticians of romance—among them Richard Chase, Joel Porte, Michael

Bell, Gillian Beer, and particularly Northrop Frye, whose observations on the genre in *Anatomy of Criticism* and *The Secular Scripture* furnish striking congruences with Simms's procedures.

I owe a double debt of gratitude to the National Endowment for the Humanities for the grant under which I began *The Major Fiction of William Gilmore Simms* and the grant under which I completed it: the project was literally made possible by the generous financial support of that agency. My thanks also to my colleagues at Southwest Texas State University, Michael J. Hennessy, Martha L. Brunson, and G. Jack Gravitt, for help of various kinds and to officials of the university for financial assistance through several types of research grants. Finally, I am exceedingly grateful to my husband Jim, who read and commented carefully on the manuscript—and to our children, Andrew and Alison, who endured its various metamorphoses and who asked, while watching me compose draft after draft, "Why can't you get it right the first time?"

Abbreviations

BB	*Border Beagles*
C	*The Cassique of Kiawah*
E	*Eutaw*
F	*The Forayers*
GR	*Guy Rivers*
HH	*Helen Halsey*
K	*The Kinsmen*
KW	*Katharine Walton*
L	*The Letters of William Gilmore Simms*
M	*Mellichampe*
P	*The Partisan*
RH	*Richard Hurdis*
W	*Woodcraft*

The Major Fiction of William Gilmore Simms

Introduction

During his lifetime, which spanned the antebellum period, William Gilmore Simms was the leading exemplar of literary activity in the South. In more than thirty years of a crowded career, he produced or had a hand in producing over eighty volumes and enough uncollected writing to fill perhaps twenty volumes more.[1] He wrote essays and book reviews, ran magazines and edited newspapers, published orations on political and social topics, and composed poetry, plays, novels, tales, sketches, novelettes, biographies, a history, and a geography, meanwhile conducting a correspondence so heavy and varied that he sometimes seems like several people instead of a single individual. A planter, a politician, and an outspoken advocate of regional concerns, he became, through his many activities, the intellectual and cultural symbol of antebellum southern civilization: the story goes that when the Southern Convention met in Savannah in 1856 it recommended that "there be a Southern literature" and that Simms "be requested to write this literature."[2] "The judgment of an impartial and enlightened criticism must assign him a proud and elevated niche in the Pantheon of American letters," declared a contemporary reviewer; "time, alone, can complete the fulness of his fame."[3]

1. Such is the estimate of C. Hugh Holman in his essay on Simms in Robert Bain, Joseph M. Flora, and Louis D. Rubin, Jr. (eds.), *Southern Writers: A Biographical Dictionary* (Baton Rouge, 1979), 405.

2. This story, which may be apocryphal, originated in the anonymous essay "Southern Literature," in *Putnam's Monthly: A Magazine of Literature, Science, and Art,* IX (February, 1857), 207–208. It is quoted in William P. Trent, *William Gilmore Simms* (Boston, 1892), 247–48*n*2. It is also quoted in C. Hugh Holman, "William Gilmore Simms and the 'American Renaissance,'" in *The Roots of Southern Writing: Essays on the Literature of the American South* (Athens, Ga., 1972), 78.

3. [J. Quitman Moore], "William Gilmore Simms," *De Bow's Review,* XXIX [n.s., IV] (December, 1860), 702, 712. Moore is identified as the author of this review in

But time has *not* completed the fullness of Simms's fame; it has, instead, diminished the luster of his once-proud literary reputation. No one has yet produced a satisfactory study of his life or a comprehensive critical examination of his writing, and as a result his work has gradually faded from public view. The neglect of his writing has had disastrous consequences for his reputation in the late twentieth century: for the most part, he has been relegated to the corners of literary histories, and his tales and poems have nearly vanished from anthologies. Ironically enough, moreover, the few books that have been written about him have not materially advanced our knowledge of his role in American and southern letters. The one existing full-length biography, for instance—produced by William Peterfield Trent in 1892 for the American Men of Letters Series—has damaged his reputation rather than aided it. More than any other document, Trent's little volume is responsible for the misconceptions still current about Simms.

Trent, who was barely twenty-eight when he began the book, approached his task professionally: he visited Simms's native city, Charleston, interviewed Simms's friends and relatives, and drew upon important family papers given to him by Simms's oldest daughter, Augusta. But his biography—whose 350-odd octavo pages were produced in only seven short weeks—is one of the least balanced and judicious treatments ever accorded an important author. A scion of the New South, Trent disliked the culture of the Old South that receives such affectionate portrayal in Simms's pages, and he scorned the genre of romance that had been Simms's dominant literary form throughout his life. Although Trent had ample sympathy for Simms the man, he viewed Simms's writing, in the main, with amused condescension, mocking its sometimes careless style and unfairly deprecating its abundant humor. Because Trent lacked access to the full range of Simms's correspondence, his book is limited in biographical information; and though it is fairly accurate in its factual material, it is unreliable in critical judgments and unfortunately facetious in tone. In the absence of other full-scale biographies, however, it remains the standard treatment of the productive southern author—despite the fact that it has

---

Mary C. Simms Oliphant, Alfred Taylor Odell, and T. C. Duncan Eaves (eds.), *The Letters of William Gilmore Simms* (Columbia, S.C., 1952–56, 1982), IV, 152*n*137, hereafter cited as *L*, where possible within the text, by volume and page number.

received, as a recent scholar says, an "almost constant drumbeat of criticism . . . at least in the South, since 1892."[4]

In his book Trent echoed attitudes common to the postbellum era, when the increasing hegemony of northern writers together with the vogue of realistic fiction had begun to obscure Simms's substantial achievement in letters. Simms himself, through the very talents that enabled him to write so fluently, has operated to impede scholarly investigation of his oeuvre: the Irish eloquence that his contemporaries often praised, his *cacoëthes scribendi* as he aptly termed it, has resulted in a volume of work so large that it has kept all but a few of his students from making their way through it. Compounding the problem is the fact that to set forth the essential outlines of his writing—and particularly of his long fiction, on which his reputation chiefly rests—is a fairly demanding intellectual task. For that fiction, nurtured by personal experience and grounded in the history and culture of the South, needs to be viewed against the background of his times and in the context of his public and private activities. It should also be viewed alongside his poetry, history, essays, and speeches, with which it shares a number of concerns. The breadth of this enterprise, however, gives even dedicated Simmsians pause: it seems easier, at the outset, to sink than swim. And so matters have remained—sunk, more or less—since Simms's death more than a century ago.

Yet Simms's fairly secure position as the antebellum South's principal man of letters, coupled with the still uncertain assessment of his literary ranking, suggests the need for a detailed study of his long fiction that takes into account both the literary and the cultural influences upon it. And his own plaint that despite unceasing efforts he had left all his better works undone—uttered in a period of despair when he realized he could never fulfill the ambitions of his youth—invites us to look again at what he *had* been able to accomplish.[5] The time seems right for such an enterprise: the Revolutionary War volumes and the Border Romances are again in print; *Woodcraft,* one of his best books, has been newly edited; a sixth volume of his invaluable letters has been

4. Conversation of Mary C. Simms Oliphant and author, August 17, 1972; John McCardell, "Trent's *Simms:* The Making of a Biography," in William J. Cooper, Jr., Michael F. Holt, and John McCardell (eds.), *A Master's Due: Essays in Honor of David Herbert Donald* (Baton Rouge, 1985), 200.

5. Simms's remarks are quoted in Trent, *William Gilmore Simms,* 323–24.

issued; an important bibliographical study of his poetry has been published; and at least two scholarly accounts of his life are well under way.[6] Moreover, the active concern of scholars with revising and expanding the literary canon makes it feasible to suggest that an author who once occupied so commanding a position in the minds of his contemporaries be once again accorded serious and thoughtful attention. To grant him such attention is the object of the present study.

The Major Fiction of William Gilmore Simms is not a biography, though it employs biographical material as a fundamental part of the literary record; nor is it solely a historical account, though the story of Simms's accomplishments and defeats forms an important part of the picture. It is chiefly a critical study making use of biographical and historical information and also of modern formulations about romance. One of its purposes is to examine Simms's use of the romance tradition and suggest some ways of viewing his novels in the light of twentieth-century literary theory. The other is to stress the major, in fact the crucial, role that the South played in providing material for his writing. Simms knew at first hand the three great southern regions described by such scholars as Howard Odum, C. Hugh Holman, and Randall Stewart: the southeastern low country, or tidewater; the Piedmont and the Appalachian mountain ranges; and the Gulf, Deep, or lower South in its pioneer and settlement stages. He drew on these regions as the basis for the three main groups of his novels—colonial and Revolutionary War romances, from *The Yemassee* to *The Cassique of Kiawah,* set in the low country and tracing its development from the founding of the Carolina colony in the late seventeenth century through the Indian wars and the Revolution; Border Romances like *Guy Rivers,* set in the Gulf South and describing its rowdy, crime-ridden frontier; and mountain tales and romances such as *Voltmeier,* portraying the rugged society of the upland South. The record of the cultural traditions behind his fiction derives from his contacts with these three great southern regions and the types of literature historically associated with them.

Simms grew up in the low country and was steeped in its traditions;

6. The AMS Press brought out the Border Romances; James B. Meriwether and Stephen E. Meats edited *The Revolutionary War Novels of William Gilmore Simms,* with annotations by various contributors (Spartanburg, S.C., 1976); Charles S. Watson edited *Woodcraft: Or Hawks About the Dovecote. A Story of the South at the Close of the Revolution* (New Haven, 1983); James E. Kibler, Jr., wrote *The Poetry of William Gilmore Simms: An Introduction and Bibliography* (Spartanburg, S.C., 1979); and both John C. Guilds and John McCardell are at work on biographies.

he visited the Gulf South or Old Southwest as he was on the verge of committing himself to a life of writing. The fact that he knew these two major regions of the South, tidewater and frontier, from before the beginning of his work as a professional author and that he drew upon them from his earliest writing makes possible a study of the development of his fiction along chronological lines. To approach it in this manner is to construct a painful account of his literary fortunes as we witness his exuberant hopes for wealth and fame gradually fade before economic and social factors over which he had little control. He began his career in the 1820s with volumes of poetry and works of short fiction; by the middle 1830s, he had settled on long fiction—especially on the romance, then at its zenith—as the surest way to popular renown. Sparking his ambition was the enthusiastic response to his first novels, *Guy Rivers, The Yemassee,* and *The Partisan:* reviewers claimed that his reputation was permanently established, announced that his name guaranteed the quality of his books, and declared, in a fairly typical statement, that "he must take rank at once as the first American novelist of the day."[7] Convinced on the basis of this praise that he could succeed as a professional author, in the 1830s he poured forth books about the Revolution, the Gulf South, Spain, and Spanish America, meanwhile collecting his poetry and short fiction and beginning his propaganda for slavery. Eager for renown, he wrote too much and too hastily, even by contemporary standards; but his books sold well, his reviewers continued enthusiastic, and by the end of the decade his plans for literary glory seemed secure.

Simms's prospects would be dimmed, however, by the panic of 1837, the economic recession that altered the course of several promising literary careers and helped to change the complexion of fiction in antebellum America. In connection with other factors, the recession seriously injured the sales of the long fiction on which he had established his early reputation. Bitterly denouncing those "sad days for authordom," between 1842 and 1850 he quit writing novels and turned to other genres, chiefly history, biography, poetry, and criticism (*L,* I, 421). He also became a diligent and an influential editor of several southern magazines, reading and reviewing important contemporary books. His labors in these areas amplified his knowledge of southern

7. Review of *The Yemassee,* New York *Times,* April 16, 1835; Review of *The Partisan, Southern Literary Journal,* I (January, 1836), 347; Review of *Martin Faber, American Monthly Magazine,* IV (February, 1835), 358.

culture and enriched the novels he would write after midcentury, but they took him away from his major genre at an important point in the development of his reputation and the maturation of his talent.

Between 1850 and the Civil War, Simms produced his most vigorous and effective work—four Revolutionary War Romances, an important satiric novel about the founding of South Carolina, saucy studies of patrician manners, and short pieces making obvious use of southern backwoods humor. These works, however, which were issued during a turbulent period in national history and in an economic climate still unfavorable for belles-lettres, brought him neither the income nor the popularity of his youth; and meanwhile, his growing involvement in the politics of secession tended to deflect him from imaginative writing. The war itself virtually ended his career, for when he returned to fiction after 1865, literary taste had shifted in the direction of realism. He tried to accommodate himself to the new mode in his Mountain Romances, also producing two fine tall tales that put him in the first rank of backwoods humorists. But he never again attained the heights of his youth, and the final picture of his literary fortunes is as of a dream fondly cherished but only imperfectly realized.

Hugh Holman, describing the shift from romance to realism that began in the 1840s, observes that rarely has a historical event divided literary movements with such precision as the panic of 1837.[8] It caused an equally sharp division in Simms's literary production, and hence his career as a novelist falls into two phases—the period from 1825 through 1842, when he established himself as an author but then was temporarily forced away from long fiction, and the period between 1850 and 1870, when he returned to long fiction only to be interrupted again by the Civil War. The first stage of his fiction is characterized by his careful attention to romance structures and his use within these structures of episodes and settings deriving from Gothic romance. Inspired by his travels in the Old Southwest, he also started to weave vivid sequences of backwoods humor into his writing, sprinkling tall talk throughout his letters and tales and portraying outrageous frontier antics in his novels about the formative stage of the lower South. The reviews he wrote in the 1840s increased his interest in southern humor and also in another mode that would influence his mature fic-

8. Holman, "William Gilmore Simms and the 'American Renaissance,'" in *The Roots of Southern Writing*, 75–86 (see particularly p. 79).

tion, that of the novel of manners. As a result, when he started publishing novels again in 1850, he replaced the Gothic elements of his early work with satiric passages of social comedy and increasingly raucous backwoods humor. His use of these strains connects him centrally to traditions in southern literature from the colonial period through the twentieth century. For polite mockery of aristocratic social customs has been a concern of tidewater writing from William Byrd II to Ellen Glasgow, while frontier or backwoods humor animates the work of authors otherwise as different as Robert Bolling, Eudora Welty, and William Faulkner.

Obscuring Simms's achievements for many of his readers have been the flaws apparent in his writing, which have occasioned far too much unenlightened criticism of it. There is no point in ignoring these flaws and in fact some merit in examining them, since they illuminate certain personal qualities of the man that influenced his characteristic methods of composition. His books are verbose and in places overblown or awkward; they are sometimes melodramatic and sentimental; they are often poorly constructed; and their occasionally strident southern sectionalism grates harshly on twentieth-century ears. Such drawbacks stem, in a curious way, from some noteworthy personal traits of the author that have kept the memory of his exuberant personality alive even though the knowledge of his work has faded. By his own testimony and the recollections of those who knew him, he was broad-gauged, spontaneous, and generous, open and uninhibited, rebellious, outspoken, and articulate. But he was also careless and disorganized, and he kept far too busy with one or another project to spend much time refining or perfecting his style.

Schooled from an early age in British and American literature, Simms was determined to establish himself as a popular professional author through the employment of established literary conventions; and he poured forth book after book that demonstrates his command of these conventions but that also shows little discrimination between the really good and the trite or second rate. He was driven, absolutely compelled, to write, to produce, to put words onto paper; as he himself remarked to a favorite correspondent, "If I wander, I muse; if I muse, I compose; if I compose, I am feverish, 'till I can grasp the pen & make the record" (*L*, III, 173). Trent tells the story of Simms's visit to New York in 1835, when he took his publisher, Harper Brothers, the uncompleted manuscript of *The Partisan*. The portions he had finished were immediately sent to press and were soon printed. He meanwhile told the Harpers that he was going on vacation and would be away from New York for a week. "But," said James Harper, "we are out of copy, and unless you can furnish more, we shall have to suspend work on your novel until you return." The author replied, "That will never do . . . give me pen, ink, and paper, and I'll go upstairs and find a place to write." In "less than half an hour," Trent continues, Simms "came down again with more manuscript than would be required during his absence." James Harper, who told the story in later years, said that Simms "had the most remarkable talent for writing he had ever known." But as Trent comments, "[C]ould any talent neutralize the effects of such methods of composition?"[9]

Also operating to obscure Simms's achievements in letters have been the demands of the romance tradition in which he worked: in fact, it is not too much to claim that a general misunderstanding of this tradition coupled with ignorance of his work is in large measure responsible for the neglect or misinterpretation of his writing. The fascination of scholars with realism and their gradual loss of ability to understand romance has functioned to eclipse his accomplishments in the genre. One can see the typical misunderstandings emerging as writer after writer in the twentieth century tries to excuse or explain away Simms's attachment to the romance form. Fostered by Vernon L. Parrington, the dominant critical attitude toward Simms maintains that he was essentially a failed realist instead of the romancer he consistently claimed to be. Parrington, a great admirer of Simms, believed that Charleston's social and economic romanticism had stifled the author's impulses toward realism and that although in taste and temperament Simms was "a pronounced realist . . . his career took shape from a generation given to every romantic excess." From Parrington the argument passes to Hampton M. Jarrell, whose 1932 Duke University dissertation is entitled "William Gilmore Simms: Realistic Romancer"; to Edd Winfield Parks, who in *Ante-Bellum Southern Literary Critics* subtitles his chapter on Simms "Realistic Romanticist"; to Van Wyck Brooks, who states "it was his realism that kept the work of Simms alive"; and to Clement Eaton, who—in a virtual reprise of Parrington—says "the popular taste of the period, both North and South, forced [Simms]

9. Trent, *William Gilmore Simms,* 111.

to compose in the romantic style, but his natural bent was toward realism."[10]

To such remarks, however, the repeated pronouncements of the author himself are opposed. Throughout his life, Simms insisted that his works were "*romances,* not novels," and begged that they be read in the light of the genre's conventions (*L,* III, 388). Those conventions, as described by twentieth-century literary theorists, include a dialectic structure, a commitment to ideals, a strong pastoral element, and happy or providential endings. If Simms's use of these elements and his innovations in them are sympathetically viewed, it is possible to see the skill with which he wove backwoods humor and manners comedy into his romance framework and therefore to appreciate his contributions, which have been almost entirely overlooked, to these emerging strains of nineteenth-century fiction.

I attempt throughout this study to stress Simms's achievements in these areas, and I also devote proportionately more attention to lesser-known but skillful novels like *The Cassique of Kiawah* in which such elements appear than to more familiar ones like *Woodcraft* and *The Partisan*. Because it is important to trace the evolution of Simms's talent in satire and humor, I use where feasible the first editions of his books and indicate as necessary the revisions he made in other editions that enhance his contribution to these modes. When citing later editions, I use the Author's Uniform Edition issued in the 1850s by J. S. Redfield since it or the sets reprinted from it are available in most college and university libraries. In the course of the book, I address where possible major issues in the history of Simms criticism, and I also try to give a comprehensive picture of that criticism through the footnotes. Finally, I quote freely from Simms's magnificent letters, both because they are vital documents for the study of antebellum civilization and because they give, better than any other single source, a compelling picture of Simms the man.

Fortunately for scholars intrigued by legends of his lively personality, that man, as he himself observed, wore his character "pretty

10. Vernon L. Parrington, *The Romantic Revolution in America, 1800–1860,* vol. II of *Main Currents in American Thought* (New York, 1927–30), 136, 126; Edd Winfield Parks, *Ante-Bellum Southern Literary Critics* (Athens, Ga., 1962); Van Wyck Brooks, *The World of Washington Irving* (New York, 1944), 314; Clement Eaton, *The Mind of the Old South* (Rev. ed.; Baton Rouge, 1967), 252.

much out of door [*sic*], & possibly somewhat out at the elbows" (*L*, III, 191). Frank, ingenuous, and unselfish, Simms was also overbearing and imperious: one of his closest friends admitted that he "*declaimed* rather than conversed," and another friend less charitably complained, "I wonder how he knows anybody; he listens so little."[11] A convivial host and companion, he loved to revel and carouse: "We drank your health in joyous bumpers," he told one friend, and he affectionately cried to another, "I long to gripe [*sic*] you by the fist! To have a bout in your sanctum, and with a cigar & over a bottle of old Madeira, to say—'Sessa! Let the world slide!'" (*L*, III, 10, 360–61).[12] His love of fun and mimicry, his energy and robustness, are well described by Paul Hamilton Hayne, who says that he kept, "into mature manhood, and beyond . . . all the enthusiasm, the animal vigor, and high spirits of the boy."[13]

Tall, stalwart, handsome, Simms possessed great strength of character; during a lifetime marked, as he said, by the shafts of "the insatiate archer Fate," he endured disappointments and defeats with faith and staunchness (*L*, IV, 402). The record of his life and work is the record of the trials of a professional man of letters living in the South in the antebellum period; but it is also a story of fortitude and courage sustaining him in periods of grave despair. He himself forecast the possible demise of his hopes when he wrote:

> The spirit was within him, & he strove,
> Unqualified by base desire or deed,
> Most nobly though perchance he never won,
> The golden goal he sought.[14]

In 1860, a writer in *De Bow's Review* declared that Simms reflected, "in sentiment and character, the moral and intellectual attributes that distinguish the spirit and temper of Southern civilization; announces its opinions, illustrates its ideas, embodies its passions and prejudices, and betrays those delicate shades of thought, feeling, and

11. [Paul Hamilton Hayne], "William Gilmore Simms," *Appletons' Journal*, IV (July 30, 1870), 139; Henry Timrod to Paul Hamilton Hayne, June 4, [1867], in Jay B. Hubbell (ed.), *The Last Years of Henry Timrod, 1864–1867* (Durham, N.C., 1941), 84.

12. In the second passage, Simms is paraphrasing the Induction to *The Taming of the Shrew*, i, 6.

13. Hayne, "William Gilmore Simms," 139.

14. These lines from a manuscript poem are quoted in *L*, IV, under the engraving of Simms facing 487.

conduct, that go to form the character, and stamp the individuality of a people." Hugh Holman said much the same thing when he remarked that Simms's career is of major importance in the degree to which he embodied the attitudes and crystallized the assumptions of antebellum southern society.[15] The unity and sense of purpose that both writers found in Simms's career is found also in his fiction; and it is finally my principal concern in this book that a coherent account of his achievement in that fiction within the context of his personal life and literary career be fully and firmly set forth.

15. [J. Quitman Moore], "William Gilmore Simms," 708; C. Hugh Holman, "The Status of Simms," *American Quarterly,* X (Summer, 1958), 181.

1
Soundings

William Gilmore Simms was born on April 17, 1806, in Charleston, a city that figures memorably in his writing and one that he would alternately praise and revile throughout his life. Although well past the days of its eighteenth-century glory, Charleston during his boyhood was an elegant, pleasant, breezy seacoast town already fixed in the habits of patrician snobbery fostered by its origins as the center of a rich proprietary colony, its ties to British and Barbadian aristocracy, and its connection with plantation gentry. The colonial capital of South Carolina, it had played a major role in the state's early political development; and it was still the social, as to some extent the political, center of low-country civilization—the place to which people of wealth and fashion gravitated, "the city 'par excellence' of American society and luxury," as Prince Achille Murat, touring the South in the early nineteenth century, observed. One of the most delightful places in America, it was situated between the Ashley and the Cooper rivers, its broad straight streets virtually connecting them; the summer home of rich families from nearby plantations, it abounded in graceful town dwellings whose gardens and piazzas, redolent of their origins in West Indian architecture, charmed the stream of visitors who flocked to the city. In the eighteenth century "the hub of the Low Country universe," in the nineteenth the center of southern sophistication, it epitomized both the polish and the haughtiness of low-country living. To this lively, proud, provincial little town Simms's earliest affectionate notions of place were attached, and the story of his career is in part the story of his vexed relationship with Charleston.[1]

1. Carl Bridenbaugh, *Cities in the Wilderness: The First Century of Urban Life in America, 1625–1742* (Rev. ed.; New York, 1955), 99, 255, 417–18; Lawrence Henry Gipson, *The British Isles and the American Colonies: The Southern Plantations 1748–1754* (New York, 1960), 144–47, vol. II of *The British Empire Before the American*

Simms was not of old Charleston stock, though his forebears had played honorable roles in the eighteenth-century city. His maternal ancestors were the Singletons, Virginia gentlefolk who had moved to Charleston before the Revolution. Particularly noteworthy in family annals was his great-grandfather, Thomas Singleton, inspector general of tobacco for the province and a gentleman noted for his elegance, independence, patriotism, and wit. Too old to fight in the Revolution, he bedeviled the British garrison with his gibes—costuming, so the story runs, his pet baboon in the garb of a British general officer and styling him "Colonel Balfour" after the Scottish commandant of Charleston. For this prank he was confined for the better part of three years to a prison ship anchored off St. Augustine, where his resolution, like that of his fellow captives, proved "more than a match," Simms says, for "the brutal & ungenerous" actions of the British (*L*, I, 159). It was in part to this redoubtable old patriot that Simms owed his own ability for mockery, his considerable bent for mischief, and his astringent wit.[2]

The British military power in South Carolina was menaced more directly by Simms's maternal grandfather, John Singleton, and his great-uncles Bracey and Ripley, who had fought in Francis Marion's militia brigade and whose exploits form one source for Simms's writing about the war in South Carolina. In a letter of 1841, he proudly maintained that all his mother's male relatives "bore arms in the defence of Charleston," and from their deeds he drew names, accounts of battles, characters, descriptions, and anecdotes (*L*, V, 359). Through the stories of these men that he heard as a boy, he imbibed both a strong national patriotism and a fierce southern pride; later, he would passionately recall in his writing an era when the South furnished political leadership to the nation and when America's first international war was won on southern soil.

Simms's father, William Gilmore Simms the elder, was a dashing, mercurial Irishman who during boyhood had emigrated to South

---

Revolution; Thomas R. Waring, "Charleston: The Capital of the Plantations," in Augustine T. Smythe *et al., The Carolina Low-Country* (New York, 1931), 131–46; Prince Achille Murat, *America and the Americans,* trans. Henry J. S. Bradfield (Buffalo, 1851), 247; Carl Bridenbaugh, *Myths and Realities: Societies of the Colonial South* (Baton Rouge, 1952), 59.

2. Trent, *William Gilmore Simms,* Chaps. 1–2; Alexander S. Salley, "William Gilmore Simms," in *L*, I, lix–lxxxix; letters from Mary C. Simms Oliphant to author, May 19, 1976, July 4, 1976.

Carolina and, after settling in Charleston, had set up as a merchant in King Street. His marriage in May, 1804, to Harriet Ann Augusta Singleton, the daughter of John and Jane Miller Singleton, was a fortunate match for him, as it connected him with an established family in the city; and the union seems to have been, for its brief duration, happy. But the troubles that would plague the Simms family began with the death of the first son when the second, Simms himself, was only six months old. Then the elder Simms's business faltered; and when his wife died in 1808 at the birth of her third son, who also died, Simms's father left Charleston in a frenzy, later declaring in a memorable phrase that the city was for him "*a place of tombs*." He went first to Tennessee and then on to Louisiana, where he served under Andrew Jackson in the Battle of New Orleans; he fought also under Jackson in the Florida campaign. He settled finally in Mississippi, acquiring a plantation between Georgeville and Hattiesburg where he lived with his brother James for the rest of his life.[3]

Simms, who was reared by his maternal grandmother, saw his father infrequently; but the elder Simms made a lasting and vital impression on his son. Celtic to the core, he was—by family testimony and the evidence of his actions—rash, courageous, bold, and resolute; he was also, in the words of his son, "a man of great energy & enthusiasm of character, a lively & playful temper—full of humour, and no small poet in the acceptation of those days" (*L,* I, 160). From his father Simms apparently inherited his own playfulness of temper, his high spirits, rashness, and impetuosity, his abundant humor, his capacity for melancholy, his winning spontaneity of manner, his enormous verbal fluency, and his flair for many kinds of literary expression. He also seems to have derived from his father impatience, argumentativeness, a tendency toward restless dissatisfaction with his circumstances, and perhaps an inability to judge his talents or his prospects wisely. He described the darker side of his nature in letters of the 1830s in which he castigated his "wholesale & unwholesome" discontent and observed that he was "too ambitious & too sensitive a man not to suffer frequent touches of despondency & gloom" (*L,* I, 54, 92). And he caught the essence of his character when he told a correspondent in 1841, "I am a very unconventional sort of person; very ardent in my temperament, very earnest in my object; express myself usually in the first

3. Trent, *William Gilmore Simms,* 17, 4; Salley, "William Gilmore Simms," in *L,* I, lx; *L,* I, 160.

words that come uppermost; write usually as I talk; and as the world goes, am accounted a somewhat rude, blunt man" (*L,* VI, 27).

When his father fled from Charleston, Simms was left in the care of his grandmother, Jane Miller Singleton Gates, who, after John Singleton's death, had married Jacob Gates and was apparently again a widow. Mrs. Gates, whose personality and convictions strongly influenced Simms, played a leading role in heading her young charge toward authorship. She showered him with affection, and she kindled his imagination by telling him rousing stories of colonial Charleston, pirates, ghosts, Indians, and the Revolutionary War. In later years, Simms remembered his grandmother as "a stern though affectionate parent," but he also complained that she mismanaged his inheritance and stinted his education—which was, he lamented, "almost wholly nominal & . . . wretchedly neglected" (*L,* I, 161).

From his upbringing in Charleston, and particularly from his grandmother, Simms acquired a strong sense of tradition, an intense devotion to the South, an abiding commitment to low-country or tidewater values, and an overwhelming interest in the Revolutionary War. From Mrs. Gates he also apparently inherited an imperious disposition, an overbearing manner, and perhaps a certain obtuseness in personal relationships that would cause him a good deal of trouble in later life. These qualities, when crossed with the traits inherited from his father, resulted in a personality that was colorful, carefree, and contradictory, the Celtic strain predominating—alternately haughty and tender, sensitive and impulsive, ambitious, energetic, headstrong, and obstinate. To this mixture of personal qualities we may trace some origins of his problems in professional life and perhaps some bases for the diversity of his writing in types and texture.

Simms's biographers say that he was lonely, that he spent many hours wandering by the sea, that he liked to hang around taverns and talk with wagoners in a city which, despite its considerable aura of sophistication, still maintained close contacts with the wilderness and frontier.[4] As a child he was timid, imaginative, contemplative, and surprisingly sickly for a man who in later life was aggressive and robust; he read a great deal and was only sporadically educated—he attended the city schools for about four years and the College of Charleston for two. At the latter institution, he picked up a smattering of languages,

4. Trent, *William Gilmore Simms,* Chap. 1; Salley, "William Gilmore Simms," in *L,* I, lxii–lxiii; Donald Davidson, Introduction to *L,* I, xxxvii–xl.

including French, Italian, and German, that spurred his interest in foreign literature and enabled him to draw upon it throughout his life. The family, though comfortable, was not wealthy; and Mrs. Gates took him out of school when he was twelve to apprentice him to a druggist, hoping thereby to prepare him for a career in medicine.

In this hope she was destined to disappointment, for, from childhood on, Simms was captivated by the written word. He was, he told correspondents, "an insatiate reader" who "soon emptied all the bookcases" of his friends; he "got books," he said, and "devoured them . . . and probably, in this way, acquired a thousand times more" than he could have done "under the ordinary school advantages" (*L*, I, 161, V, 357). He was also an energetic young writer who had early begun to produce poetry and drama. At age twelve he wrote a play about Indians that was full of "red paint"; shortly thereafter he composed odes, stories, and romantic sketches; he translated works from several languages; and before he was twenty-one, he had written and destroyed two tragedies from which he salvaged a series of poems that he later included in a collection of his early verse.[5] While still in his teens, in other words, Simms was a budding professional author who needed only to find his voice and his readership to enter the ranks of established popular writers.

In this effort he was helped, inadvertently, by contacts with his father. At the time the elder Simms left Charleston, he had made Mrs. Gates promise to bring Simms to him when he had found a new home—an arrangement that would cause some friction a few years later. When the elder Simms sent for his son, Mrs. Gates refused to let him go; and hence about 1816, when Simms was ten, his father tried to get custody of him, sending emissaries, so the story goes, to seize him and convey him to Mississippi. After these attempts failed, the elder Simms visited the boy and his grandmother in Charleston, where he poured forth tales of his exploits with the Seminoles and on the Mississippi frontier.

The youth was no doubt enthralled by his father's adventures, and after concluding his apprenticeship with the druggist, he accepted the elder Simms's invitation to visit the Old Southwest. In 1824, at the impressionable age of eighteen, he made his way to Mississippi by boat, stagecoach, and horseback, joining his father and uncle on their plan-

5. Salley, "William Gilmore Simms," in *L*, I, lxv.

tation and remaining with them until 1825. With his father he traveled into Indian territory and heard stories of the early Spanish explorations that he would later weave into his fiction and verse. He returned to the Gulf South the following year, and shortly afterwards he described, in tones laced with low-country condescension, the society that settlement was spawning—the towns with tree stumps still in the streets, the makeshift theaters, and the fumbling attempts at culture. In a statement whose justice he would later concede, his father denounced Charleston and urged him to remain in Mississippi.

> Return to Charleston! Why should you return to Charleston, where you can never succeed in any profession, where you need what you have not,—friends, family, and fortune; and without these your whole life, unless some happy accident should favor you, will be a mere apprenticeship, a hopeless drudging after bread. Ho! do not think of it. Stay here. Study your profession here, and pursue it with the energy and talent which you possess, and I will guarantee you a future, and in ten years a seat in Congress. Do not think of Charleston. . . . Charleston! *I know it only as a place of tombs.*[6]

But Simms, who was already engaged to Anna Malcolm Giles, a young Charleston woman he had apparently known for some years, stubbornly made his way back to the seaboard city, where he married in 1826. From that time forward, though he made at least two more visits to the lower South and several memorable trips to the Appalachian Mountains, where spartan backwoods conditions revived for him some memories of the Old Southwest, his literary fortunes were bound up with his life in the low country and his participation in the literary circles of the East.

Yet, perhaps without fully realizing it, by his early twenties Simms had accumulated a store of material for his writing on which he would draw for the rest of his life. For he had come to know in some detail two great historic regions of the South—the low country or tidewater, civilized, patrician, elegant; and the wilder Gulf or lower South in its Indian and pioneer phases.[7] His exposure to the South in its historical

6. *Ibid.*, lxi–lxii; Trent, *William Gilmore Simms*, 11–12, 14, 16–17, 4, 47; Salley, "William Gilmore Simms," in *L*, I, lxv; *L*, I, 10–38, V, 398; W[illiam] Stanley Hoole, "Alabama and W. Gilmore Simms," *Alabama Review*, XVI (April, July, 1963), [83]–107, 185–99, rpr. without footnotes in *According to Hoole: The Collected Essays and Tales of a Scholar-Librarian and Literary Maverick* (University, Ala., 1973), 134–60.

7. On the subject of southern regional diversity, see Howard W. Odum, *Southern Regions of the United States* (Chapel Hill, 1936), 1–244; Rupert B. Vance, *Human Geography of the South: A Study in Regional Resources and Human Adequacy* (2nd ed.;

and geographical diversity, which laid the groundwork for his mature view of southern culture, also provided the basis for his most deeply felt and solidly imagined writing. It sinewed his histories, biographies, poems, essays, and orations, and it gave rise to the major branches of his fiction—short novels, tales, and romances set in the low country and treating its evolution from the seventeenth century into the antebellum period, and fiction picturing the settlement stages of the Gulf and mountain South.

If the low-country South gave Simms his social values, his political allegiances, his sense of caste, class, profession, ambition, personal status, and literary aspiration, and if it coincided in a measure with all that was "Singleton" in his blood, the Gulf and border South chimed heartily with what was Celtic, carefree, rebellious, earthy, and "Simms" in his nature—the lusty, daring, foolhardy streak traceable to his father and abounding in the men who settled frontier Mississippi. These strains in his nature and experience lie behind two vibrant, persistent elements in his writing that help explain the complex response it has elicited to the present day. The "Charleston" and "Singleton" strain—in other words, the genteel, conservative element—led him to employ traditional literary forms like the historical romance, a highly conventionalized and public genre, as his dominant mode in fiction. His choice of this genre bound him to the stylized patterns already fixed in it and led him to employ the sentimental, Gothic, and melodramatic strains that were rampant in popular writing of the time as part of its legacy from romance.

At the same time, these elements of Simms's literary and cultural experience involved him with traditions that historically have characterized the literature of his native region. For the southern seaboard or tidewater, with its pervasive sense of the past and the passage of time, encouraged the development of historical romance: it is no accident that in the antebellum era Simms, John Pendleton Kennedy, William A. Caruthers, and John Esten Cooke all wrote in this mode or that, a century later, Margaret Mitchell in *Gone With the Wind* chose it too. Moreover, this society of fixed classes with its fondness for gracious living lent itself to the themes of the novel of manners, which thrives

---

Chapel Hill, 1935), 3–76; Randall Stewart, "Tidewater and Frontier," in George Core (ed.), *Regionalism and Beyond: Essays of Randall Stewart* (Nashville, 1968), 219–33; and C. Hugh Holman, *Three Modes of Modern Southern Fiction: Ellen Glasgow, William Faulkner, Thomas Wolfe* (Athens, Ga., 1966), Chap. 1.

on a stable, caste-conscious society concerned with the outer forms of conduct and jealous of its hereditary privileges. Over more than a century, novels as different as Kennedy's *Swallow Barn* and Ellen Glasgow's *They Stooped to Folly* suggest the congeniality of the tidewater with the novel of manners mode.

On the other hand, the "Gulf South" and the "Simms" strain in the author's background turned him early in life toward the traditions of southern or southwestern humor, whetting his interest in writers like Joseph Glover Baldwin and Augustus Baldwin Longstreet, whom in outlook and experience he resembled. This strain also contributed to the earthy realism of his writing and the undercurrent of energy that courses beneath its stylized structures, giving strong indication of his personal enthusiasm and charm. The elements of southern humor in his work connect it with the literary traditions of the Gulf South, whose writing historically has reflected the violence and social instability recorded in that humor and associated with the influence of the frontier.[8]

Logically enough, therefore, the low-country South is the setting for Simms's historical fiction, which is crossed, in his midcentury writing, by astringent social comedy in the novel of manners vein. The Gulf South and mountain South are the settings for his writing about the backwoods, which is streaked with violence and leavened by elements from folklore and southwestern humor. The "manners" and "humor" strands in his fiction are nineteenth-century versions of literary realism which he carefully fitted into the romance structures that remained the dominant literary patterns of his writing and that history on the one hand and his frontier travels on the other had encouraged. Viewed in this fashion, the most noteworthy currents in his long fiction result from its grounding in literary and cultural traditions that accord with qualities in his temperament, upbringing, and experience.

Finally, since the matter of Simms and Charleston will be an issue at points throughout this book, it is worth noting that his complex temperament and his exposure at an early age to both the backwoods and the civilized South help account for his stance toward Charleston and Carolina, which was that of an outsider and insider simultaneously. For although through the Singleton branch of his family he had strong, proud roots in Charleston, from his father he inherited a considerable

8. On these qualities in the literature of the Gulf South, see Holman, *Three Modes*, 28–30.

degree of suspicion toward the city. The older Simms, who inveighed against Charleston to the end of his life, bequeathed to his son a deep-seated bitterness that Simms, offended on his own by the town, would translate into highly wrought and imaginative disquisitions on what he thought was Charleston's neglect of him and his books.

The myth of Simms's abuse by Charleston, fed by colorful writers such as William P. Trent and Vernon L. Parrington, is nourished by Simms's earliest extant correspondence and appears in his letters to the end of his life, so that they, on this count, cannot be fully trusted. From the outset of his career, this sensitive and vulnerable young Southron was apparently bent on proving that "my birthplace is . . . the most reluctant community in the country to acknowledge my claims; and I walk the streets of my native city, very much as if I were a stranger" (*L*, V, 383). It mattered not to him that Charleston publishers issued many of his books and that Charleston readers praised them, nor that it was Charleston and the rest of South Carolina that took up his cause when the North began to cavil at his writing. He was convinced, from an early period in his life and on the partial strength of his father's example, that the town ignored or ridiculed him. And this unshakable conviction says a good deal about the self-preoccupation and the tendency to obsession of the man.

These traits were soon to be submerged, however, under the pressure of responsibilities after Simms returned to Charleston from Mississippi. Even for one who habitually thrived on overwork, he was an exceptionally busy person from 1825, the date of his return, to the publication of his short novel *Martin Faber* in 1833—the point at which his career as a serious writer of prose fiction may properly be said to begin. Much of what we know about his life in these years comes from detailed biographical accounts he drew up in letters of the late 1830s and the early 1840s, when as an established author he was beginning to review the events of his youth. Two of these letters went to James Lawson, the New York marine insurance agent and littérateur who was Simms's closest northern friend; another was sent to Rufus Wilmot Griswold, who was preparing *The Poets and Poetry of America* and had asked Simms for facts about his personal life and writing. There are some slight discrepancies of fact in these letters; but together they give a comprehensive description of the energetic author's many interests from boyhood on—especially his commitment to poetry and his efforts to establish periodical literature in the South.

"At the close of the war of 1815," Simms wrote Lawson, "I was somewhere between 8 & 9 and busied myself in versifying the events of the war. The battles of New Orleans—the affairs between the Hornet & Peacock—Constitution & Guerrière were all put into verse, and actually stitched into a little book which I devoted to this purpose" (*L*, I, 285). "At 15," he said to Lawson in another letter, "I commenced to publish in the newspapers, and at 16, 17 & 18 I was a regular contributor to the Charleston Courier, Gazette, &c. A little after this I began to make books, a vocation which, at 30 has accumulated no small number on the shelves of the Booksellers. At 18 I began to read law, at 19 I entered a Lawyer's office, at 21 I was admitted to practice, and was a married man." In an afterthought that is also something of an understatement, he added, "I was evidently living fast" (*L*, I, 162).

"During these latter periods," Simms continued, "I was more or less constantly concerned in or connected with literary periodicals, monthly, semi-monthly, & weekly" (*L*, I, 162). More specifically, between 1825 and 1833 he served as editor or coeditor of three magazines and a newspaper issued in Charleston: the *Album* (1825–1826), which he conducted in company with other Charlestonians styling themselves a "Society of Young Gentlemen"; the *Southern Literary Gazette*, which he edited during 1828 and early 1829 in conjunction with his friend James Wright Simmons and then, for a few months, carried on alone; the Charleston *City Gazette*, a newspaper that he purchased with another friend and issued from 1830 to 1832; and the *Cosmopolitan: An Occasional*, which he edited with his long-time companions Charles and Edward Carroll in 1833. The *City Gazette* is less important for his work in belles-lettres than for an understanding of his social and political attitudes; but the other periodicals, which he served as editorial writer, reviewer, and contributor, tell a good deal about his literary policies and practice.

Taken together, the journals reveal Simms's dual allegiance to American and southern culture, his wide acquaintance with contemporary writing, his strong support of native authors, and his determination to make a place for himself in the national literary scene. They also show his concern for the development, in literary matters as in other ways, of his region. The main goal that Simms worked diligently toward in his magazines, as John C. Guilds aptly remarks, was the advancement of the literature of the South.[9] Hence Simms said in the *Album* that he

9. John C. Guilds, "Simms's Views on National and Sectional Literature, 1825–1845," *North Carolina Historical Review*, XXXIV (July, 1957), 394. For detailed con-

hoped to provide the region with "a general mart for intellect," and in the *Southern Literary Gazette* he commended the novel *Edgehill,* issued anonymously as "By a Virginian," announcing, "This looks well; the South is not asleep, merely dozing, perhaps; we hope her nap will shortly be concluded."[10] At the same time, as Guilds also notes, Simms joined forces where necessary with northern critics in deploring British hegemony in letters. Thus he said, for example, in the lengthy introduction to the *Southern Literary Gazette,* "The first remark that suggests itself, on taking a survey of the actual state and prospective advancement of our literature, is, the unfortunate relation in which we stand, and seem almost unavoidably to have been placed, with regard to the 'Mother Country.'"[11]

Important features of the magazines Simms would head in mid-career—the *Magnolia,* the *Southern and Western,* and the *Southern Quarterly Review*—were anticipated by the *Album* and the *Southern Literary Gazette.* Under Simms, the *Gazette* contained three departments—"Critical Notices of New Publications," "Original Poetry," and a "General Miscellany" comprising, in his words, "Essays, Tales, Sketches, Anecdotes, &c." The "Critical Notices" section was repeated, after a fashion, in the "A Chat in the Symposium" part of the *Cosmopolitan,* in which Simms and his fellow editors conducted leisurely discussions of current literary modes and reigning reputations. The existence early in Simms's career of substantial review departments in his journals shows that his activity as a critic was already well advanced and prepares for the important criticism he would produce near midcentury. As he would later do in *Views and Reviews in Ameri-*

---

sideration of Simms's work as editor, see the following studies by Guilds: "Simms's First Magazine: *The Album,*" *Studies in Bibliography,* VIII (1956), [169]–83; "William Gilmore Simms and the *Southern Literary Gazette,*" *Studies in Bibliography,* XXI (1968), [59]–92; "The 'Lost' Number of the *Southern Literary Gazette,*" *Studies in Bibliography,* XXII (1969), 266–73; "William Gilmore Simms and the *Cosmopolitan,*" *Georgia Historical Quarterly,* XLI (March, 1957), [31]–41.

10. The *Album* came out in fifty-one numbers comprising two volumes. The second volume was discovered by James E. Kibler, Jr.; see "*The Album* (1826): The Significance of the Recently Discovered Second Volume," *Studies in Bibliography,* XXXIX (1986), [62]–78. The quotations in the text are from [William Gilmore Simms], *Album,* I (August 20, 1825), 61, and from [Simms], "Edgehill," *Southern Literary Gazette,* n.s., I (June 1, 1829), 33. Guilds in "Simms and the *Southern Literary Gazette,*" 81*n*36, identifies the author of the novel *Edgehill* as James E. Heath.

11. Simms, Introduction, *Southern Literary Gazette,* I (September, 1828), 1; on the general point, see Guilds, "Simms's Views on National and Sectional Literature," 393–405.

can Literature, History and Fiction (1845), for example, he commended in the *Cosmopolitan* the new "romantic resources of the West" and earnestly recommended that they be tapped; he would tap them himself in the Border Romances, in which he anticipates A. B. Guthrie, Louis L'Amour, and dozens of other chroniclers in fiction of the West. His comments on contemporary authors are often acute, agreeing in the main with standard views: he deplores Washington Irving's lack of inventiveness, charges that Walter Scott and James Fenimore Cooper wrote too much and too fast, and complains that Cooper in particular was "lamentably deficient in his efforts at the description of the female character"—a remark that anticipates by about fifteen years James Russell Lowell's comment in *A Fable for Critics* that Cooper's women are "sappy as maples and flat as a prairie."[12]

Simms's extensive work as editor bears directly on his development as a professional author, since it demonstrates that, as he gradually moved from law to letters, he was exposed on a regular basis to the writing of men a little older than he who had consciously chosen the literary vocation. To some extent he modeled his career on the example of the authors, British and American, who dominated the literary marketplace in the 1820s. But as he would later learn to his cost, Irving, William Cullen Bryant, and Cooper, northern writers born in the eighteenth century, had established their reputations under markedly different conditions from those that obtained for him—a southern writer born in the nineteenth century, lacking ready access to major publishing centers, and beginning his career in earnest only a few years before the panic of 1837 curtailed the production of the long fiction on which he had fixed his hopes for wealth and fame.

Despite Simms's heavy involvement with editing, however, his main commitment, as he told Rufus Griswold, was to his own imaginative writing—to poetry and after it to prose. During the same years he was helping to start various journals, he was also turning out poetry in profusion—so much poetry that he might have said, with his early idol Byron, "I pour'd along the town a flood of rhyme."[13] What he did say,

12. [William Gilmore Simms], "Prospectus," *Southern Literary Gazette,* n.s., I (May 15, 1829), and *Cosmopolitan: An Occasional,* I (1833), 23, 19–20. Guilds, "Simms and the *Cosmopolitan,*" 32, states that the journal should actually be considered a book because it appeared at irregular intervals and its three editors were apparently its sole authors. On 38*n*22, Guilds suggests that Simms was the chief author of the "Chat in the Symposium" section of the *Cosmopolitan.*

13. George Gordon, Lord Byron, *English Bards and Scotch Reviewers,* line 48.

in fact, is similar: "I commenced doggrelizing," he wrote Griswold, "at 8 or 9, began to accumulate my doggrel in books even at that early period, and at 15 was printing it in newspapers whenever a good-natured Editor could be found" (*L,* V, 356). He channeled much of his verse into his journals and collected it in six volumes published in swift succession between 1825 and 1832: *Monody, on the Death of Gen. Charles Cotesworth Pinckney* (1825), his first published book, composed of a stately poem in heroic couplets about a South Carolina Revolutionary War hero; *Lyrical and Other Poems* (1827), an important volume of lively verses on history, nature, and love; *Early Lays* (1827), containing many of his light or humorous poems together with stanzas on southern themes; *The Vision of Cortes, Cain, and Other Poems* (1829), in which, in Byronic vein, he develops hero-villain figures from Spanish history or the Bible; *The Tri-Color; or The Three Days of Blood, in Paris* (1830), a spirited compound of verse and prose describing the July Revolution of 1830; and *Atalantis. A Story of the Sea* (1832), a graceful blank-verse poetic drama influenced by the masque form and in debt, as Simms indicated, to Milton and Shakespeare.[14]

Simms's early poetry, in general, displays verbal fluency, metrical sensitivity, and a great range of topics, moods, and tones. Since much of it, as he says in the preface to *Lyrical Poems,* was written before his nineteenth year, it is not verse of great profundity, but neither is it a poetry consisting entirely of surfaces, as critics have commonly supposed. It is spirited, graceful, bold, and moving; it is also more introspective than one might expect from a person of his temperament, though this feature is often concealed by its conscious use of poetic conventions. Much of his early poetry gives evidence of the energy and ardor that were fundamental to his personality—while, viewed as a whole, it indicates that at a fairly young age he was steeped in the literature of the Anglo-American tradition and was deliberately making use of that tradition in his efforts to establish himself as a literary figure.

14. The first four of these early Simms volumes were published in Charleston: *Monody* by Gray and Ellis; *Lyrical and Other Poems* by Ellis and Neufville; *Early Lays* by A. E. Miller; and *The Vision of Cortes* by James S. Burges. The title page of *The Tri-Color* indicates that it was issued in London by Wigfall and Davis; according to James E. Kibler, Jr., however, it was probably published in Charleston in 1830 or 1831. See Kibler, *Poetry of Simms,* 61–62. *Atalantis* was brought out in New York by J. and J. Harper. *Lyrical and Other Poems* is hereafter called *Lyrical Poems.*

Simms's first volumes of verse also show that he was trying to reach a national rather than a strictly southern audience and had no qualms about imitating established authors, northern or British, in order to do so. He therefore gave the kind of treatment that such writers had developed for their poetry to topics he would later view from a southern slant. His poems about the Revolution, for example—surprisingly few in number for one who would virtually become the literary custodian of the war—stress figures associated with the northern phase of the conflict, such as Benedict Arnold and John André, more than the heroes of the war in the South. His poems about Indians have also a national rather than a regional cast: they stress generic Indian qualities such as staunchness and bravery rather than local or regional peculiarities. Like Irving and others, for instance, he wrote about the fierce seventeenth-century New England chieftain King Philip, who was then a popular literary subject in the North. Two poems near the beginning of *Lyrical Poems,* "Death of King Philip" and "Song of Philip," reveal his sympathetic interest in the Indian's courage and determination. His poems about southern Indians generally stress the same qualities; such, at least, is the case with the first piece in the volume, "The Broken Arrow," an elegiac treatment of William McIntosh, the controversial Creek leader who had been shot in Georgia by fellow Creeks for illegally ceding tribal lands to whites. Simms had heard tales of McIntosh on his travels in the 1820s through the Gulf South and might therefore have been expected to give the poem a specifically southern setting. But instead the stanzas, spoken by an unnamed member of McIntosh's tribe, eulogize the slain leader in general terms appropriate for readers throughout the country, most of whom were probably unfamiliar with the southern Indian's plight.

> Ye warriors, who gather the brave to deplore,
> And repine for the Chief, ye shall witness no more,
> Let the hatchet of fight still unburied remain,
> Whilst we joy in the glory of him that is slain.
>
> Unbounded in soul, as unfearing in fight,
> Yet mild as the dove, when untempted to smite,
> His arm was resistless, his tomahawk true,
> And his eye, like the eagle's, was lightning to view.
>
> (*Lyrical Poems,* [7])

Perhaps even more than such verses, Simms's nature poetry smacks strongly of British and native authors. Wordsworth lies behind the meditative blank-verse stanzas such as "Summer Night-Wind" that went into the "Miscellaneous Poems" section of *The Vision of Cortes;* Keats influenced one of Simms's earliest pieces, called simply "Autumn"; and Bryant, his mentor and long-time friend, inspired poems as different as "Vive Memor Lethi," with its echoes of "Thanatopsis," and "To a Bird at Sea," which deliberately follows "To a Waterfowl" in subject and stanza form.[15]

Byron, however, formed the single most potent influence on the young Simms, inspiring more poems and affecting them in more ways than anyone so far has indicated, though a beginning has been made by James O. Hoge and a few other writers.[16] Byron's love lyrics gave birth to many of Simms's; Byron's "Cain" lies behind Simms's "Cain"; Byron's devotion to the cause of Greek liberty spurred a string of Simms poems on the subject like "The Greek Song of Triumph"; and *Childe Harold's Pilgrimage* influenced many of Simms's poems about the sea—perhaps most obviously "Apostrophe to Ocean," with its narrator who sensitively responds to the power of the waves.

Waters, dark waters of the boundless sea,
  Whose march by human effort is unstay'd,
Now could I bow a worshipper to thee,
  As, with a living energy array'd,
  Thou leap'st in mountains far above my head:
And I, in the frail bark, in which I ride,
  Within thy undulating bosom's shade
Am scarcely seen, while, in thy might of pride,
Thou art the only life, in thy vast world beside.
(*Early Lays,* 24)

Yet despite their echoes of "Englishmen and Northernmen" and their emphasis on topics of national concern, these same volumes of verse show Simms beginning to draw on the South as a significant sub-

15. Kibler, *Poetry of Simms,* 15, attributes the unsigned poem "Autumn," which appeared in the New York *Mirror* of October 21, 1826, to Simms and notes Keats's influence upon it. The poem is also in debt to Bryant's "Thanatopsis," particularly in its closing stanza.

16. James O. Hoge, "Byron's Influence on the Poetry of William Gilmore Simms," *Essays in Literature,* II (Spring, 1975), 87–96. See also Edd Winfield Parks's comments on Simms and Byron in *William Gilmore Simms As Literary Critic* (Athens, Ga., 1961), 49–50.

ject for his writing.[17] Major themes of his mature work appear in embryo here—southern landscape and seasons, developed by both Romantic and Augustan methods; southern history; southern Indians and their tragic struggle with whites for land; Charleston, viewed humorously or satirically; and the Gulf South or Old Southwest, presented for the most part in a lush descriptive manner. "Ashley River," a long poem in couplets in the eighteenth-century topographical vein, which was printed in the *Southern Literary Gazette* and revised for *The Vision of Cortes*, has some fine passages that nicely describe the limpid river forming Charleston's western boundary. "The Last of the Yemassees," which first saw print in *Early Lays,* poignantly portrays the Indian heroism also shown in *The Yemassee* that has helped to keep it Simms's best-known novel. "The Carolana Maid," also in *Early Lays,* gives patriotic treatment to a familiar point of southern pride, the Revolutionary battle at Eutaw Springs that helped drive the British from South Carolina. The stanzas titled "Carolinians!" in the same volume laud local partisan militia leaders Francis Marion, William Moultrie, and Thomas Sumter in much the same manner as Simms's fiction about the war. And his important poems dealing with the Gulf South, such as "To a Winter Flower, *Written in the Creek Nation,*" and "Summer, *Written in the Choctaw Nation,*" show him taking note of Indian customs or describing Mississippi scenery while fondly recalling the seaboard South. Hints of his work-to-be in southern humor are evident in his early volumes of poetry: some stanzas in *Lyrical Poems* called "Written in Mississippi," for instance, treat a bee-tree, prime element in writing about the frontier from Cooper through the antebellum humorists, and "Camp Meeting," culled from the *Album* for *Lyrical Poems,* encroaches on territory that the humorists would shortly claim as their own. Simms's use of the South, particularly in this group of poems, suggests that he was already moving, somewhat tentatively, in the direction that would lead him in the next decade to fame.

Finally, since buoyant humor is one element, though a neglected one, in all Simms's most successful writing, it is worth noting here that a surprisingly large number of his early poems are comic. Notable among these are "To Fortune, On [P]urchasing a Lottery Ticket," which calls the blind goddess "Coy damsel"; "To Time, On New

17. [Simms], "Edgehill," *Southern Literary Gazette,* n.s., I (June 1, 1829), 33.

Year's Day," which calls the Grim Reaper "old Codger"; and the four-line stanza entitled simply "Epigram," written (as the subtitle says) after Simms had read an obviously boring "Fourth of July Address to Freedom."[18]

Of Freedom, I would ask one favor,
  Some future moment I'd requite her,
To use her greatest, best endeavor,
  And free me from this Tyrant writer!

In his early fiction, as in his verse, Simms treats a wide variety of subjects, including the South, with humor and charm. The stories, sketches, whimsies, and philosophical musings that he published in his journals and collected in the 1830s are important in their own right as the youthful work of a leading American author; they also foreshadow, often quite plainly, the varied directions his mature productions in prose would take. His categories are those of popular fiction, that is, of magazine fiction, of the time: sensational Oriental narratives, material imitated from German sources, stories of the supernatural, sketches of the Revolution, and work in the vein of southern humor, which he had heard in oral form in the Gulf South and which by the 1820s was cropping up in newspapers throughout the country. He produced less fiction than poetry in the twenties and was somewhat less technically adept in constructing it; yet precisely because his occasionally careless methods lay bare his underlying scheme, one can see with some clarity the materials of his fiction emerging.

Simms's interest in melodramatic treatments of the Orient, a legacy from the eighteenth century by way of the Romantics, is shown in "Zamor and Zuelieme—An Arabiam [*sic*] Tale," a short piece faintly reminiscent of *Rasselas,* and at greater length in "The Robber," an "Eastern Tale" replete with ghouls, buzzards, criminals, and rotting corpses. In its stress on the Moorish cast of Middle Eastern life, "The Robber" foreshadows Simms's novels like *Count Julian* about the Moors in medieval Spain; and "Zamor and Zuelieme," as John Guilds notes, employs a name (respelled "Zulieme") that Simms would use in one of his last novels, *The Cassique of Kiawah,* for a heroine of Spanish and Moorish extraction.[19] Stories like "The Dead Lover," whose

18. These poems appear in Simms, *Early Lays,* 48–51, 36–40, and 95.

19. [William Gilmore Simms], "Zamor and Zuelieme," in *Album,* I (December 10, 1825), 191–94; and "The Robber," in *Album,* I (July 2, 9, 16, 23, 30, August 6, 13, 1825), 6–7, [9]–10, [17]–18, [25]–26, [33]–34, [41]–42, [49]–50, respectively. On "Zamor and Zuelieme," see Guilds, "Simms's First Magazine," 180.

later version, "The Spirit Bridegroom," carried the open admission that it was imitated "from the German," point to Simms's knowledge of German literature that would appear again in *Voltmeier.*[20] The three pieces entitled simply "Sketches," reworked from a verse in *Lyrical Poems* called "A Sketch," depict a mercenary narrator who deserts his young sweetheart and thereafter lives a gloomy life, part of which he spends in the "uncultivated wilds" of what appears to be the Old Southwest.[21] By emphasizing the narrator's morbid introspectiveness, Simms in "Sketches" opens the vein of the criminal confession that he would mine with some success in *Confessions of a Murderer,* published in the last issue of the *Southern Literary Gazette;* in *Martin Faber,* which derives from *Confessions of a Murderer;* and in the Border Romances, of which "Sketches" are perhaps the earliest extant forerunners in his writing.

Among Simms's other fiction in the three periodicals, "Not At Home" is a whimsy based on essays of the *Spectator* type, while "The Vision" is a fable about the connection between virtue and happiness. "Omens of War" and "Battle of Fort Moultrie," later revised as "A Passage of Arms in '76," give evidence of his interest, already running high, in the American Revolution; "Battle of Fort Moultrie," in addition, shows his fondness for the dream-vision narrative, a form he would employ at intervals throughout his career. "Indian Sketch," a prose reworking of material in the poem "At Midnight" in *Lyrical Poems,* derives from his first-hand experience on the 1820s trips and serves as the base story for tales ranging from "The Choctaw Criminal" in *The Book of My Lady* (1833) to "Oakatibbe" in *The Wigwam and the Cabin* (1845).[22] "The Poet Chatelard," involving Mary, Queen

20. "The Dead Lover" appeared in *Southern Literary Gazette,* I (February, 1829), 282–86. It was later published as "The Spirit Bridegroom" in New York *Mirror,* December 15, 1832, [185]–86. Simms revised and republished it several additional times. For a listing of its versions, see Betty Jo Strickland, "The Short Fiction of William Gilmore Simms: A Checklist," *Mississippi Quarterly,* XXIX (Fall, 1976), 597–98.

21. The quotation is from [William Gilmore Simms], "Sketches.—No. 2," *Album,* I (July 23, 1825), 31. "Sketches.—No. 1" appeared in the *Album,* I (July 16, 1825), 19–21; "Sketches.—No. 3," in I (July 30, 1825), 36–37. The poem corresponding to these pieces appears in Simms, *Lyrical Poems,* 117–20. For full discussions of these and other of Simms's youthful tales, see Betty Jo Strickland, "The Short Fiction of William Gilmore Simms: A Critical Description and Checklist" (Ph.D. dissertation, University of Georgia, 1975), and Guilds's articles on Simms's magazines.

22. Simms's successive revisions of "Indian Sketch," culminating in the tale "Oakatibbe," have been analyzed by Miriam J. Shillingsburg in "The Maturing of Simms's Short Fiction: The Example of 'Oakatibbe,'" *Mississippi Quarterly,* XXXVIII (Spring, 1985), [99]–117.

of Scots, and "La Pola," treating Simon Bolivar, which appear in other versions in magazines or collections, show his concern, also evident in later volumes, with exotic episodes in foreign history. "Country Comforts," about two southern bloods forced to spend some unpleasant days in a rural inn, and "The Fisherman," a tale of a lazy, improvident planter who vainly fishes for sunken treasure, anticipate his important work in southern humor. But of these early stories, the most important for his mature work in fiction are "Moonshine," a narrative of the Revolution in South Carolina that was published serially in the *Album,* and "Chronicles of Ashley River," a series of sketches about an Indian uprising in the Charleston area that appeared in installments in the *Southern Literary Gazette.*[23]

"Moonshine" begins as a whimsical, digressive first-person narrative somewhat in the manner of *Tristram Shandy,* but it soon becomes a full-blown story of action about the impact of the Revolutionary War on an aristocratic South Carolina family. It depicts the fortunes of wealthy Colonel Walton, a Tory whose daughter Charlotte falls in love with a partisan, Edward Manning. That the Colonel Walton of "Moonshine" is a forerunner of the character with the same name in *The Partisan* and *Katharine Walton* is suggested by his situation as the widowed father of a single daughter and the fact that he, like the later Walton, is modeled in part on South Carolina patriot Isaac Hayne, as the detail of a wife who died of smallpox indicates. More general elements in the tale that foreshadow Simms's Revolutionary War Romances are the emphasis on the British occupation of Charleston and the movement of central characters to the city late in the story.

23. Publication details for the Simms stories mentioned in this paragraph are as follows: "Not At Home," *Album,* I (December 24, 1825), [203]–205; "The Vision," *Album,* I (October 1, 8, 15, 1825), [105]–106, 116–17, 122–23, respectively; "Battle of Fort Moultrie," *Southern Literary Gazette,* n.s., I (August 1, 1829), 137–42; "Omens of War—A Recollection," *Southern Literary Gazette,* n.s., I (September 1, 1829), 179–81; "Indian Sketch," *Southern Literary Gazette,* I (November, 1828), 142–49; "The Poet Chatelard," *Cosmopolitan,* I (1833), [25]–39; "La Pola," *Cosmopolitan,* II (1833), [169]–81; "Country Comforts," *Album,* I (December 17, 1825), [195]–98; "The Fisherman—A Fact," *Southern Literary Gazette,* n.s., I (October 15, 1829), 242–46; "Moonshine," *Album,* I (August 6, 20, September 3, 10, 24, October 1, 15, 29, November 12, 26, December 3, 10, 24, 1825), 46–47, [57]–58, [73]–75, 85–87, 100–102, 106–108, 123–25, 140–42, 160–61, 174–76, 180–82, 189–91, 206–208, respectively; "Chronicles of Ashley River, Nos[.] 1–6," *Southern Literary Gazette,* n.s., I (July 15, August 1, September 1, September 15, October 15, November 1, 1829), 115–16, 129–30, 176–78, 208–10, 247–52, 278–80, respectively. The final issue of the last magazine was titled *Pleiades, and Southern Literary Gazette.* Each of these stories is either anonymous or pseudonymous.

"Chronicles of Ashley River," Simms's other important early story that looks forward to his mature fiction, bears something of the same relationship to *The Yemassee* that "Moonshine" does to *The Partisan* and other Revolutionary War Romances. Published in six installments in the *Southern Literary Gazette* after Simms became the sole editor, it is a tale of the first settlement of Charleston on the western bank of the Ashley River and of the settlers' removal, after Indian attack, across the river to their permanent location on Oyster Point. Like "Moonshine," "Chronicles of Ashley River" begins humorously, using mock-heroic methods to poke fun at ponderous colonial annals and chronicles; like "Moonshine," it mingles history and fiction, though with greater success; and as in "Moonshine," the story changes in midstream from parody to an exciting narrative of action that centers on a bloody battle between the white settlers and the Yemassee Indians, led by sly Chief Redfoot. In *The Yemassee,* Simms would emphasize the combination of plebeian and patrician elements in early South Carolina, the patrician dominating. Here, in one of his earliest attempts to mortify the vanity of antebellum Charleston, he stresses its plebeian origins, as he would do again in *The Cassique of Kiawah.*

"Chronicles of Ashley River" displays the typical mixture of national types that Simms would use in much of his later writing—vociferous pioneers, a heroic Negro, a humorous drunken Irishman, and rampaging Indians. The sketches also show his skillful use of such comic methods as counterpointed dialect to relieve the tension of his narrative. Hence, in the kind of humorous exchange in dialect at which he excelled, he has an Irish sergeant belabor Redfoot, who has knocked at night on the tavern door: " [W]hat will ye be after seeking, this blessed night of the Lord; breaking up the rest and reposed comfort of the good peoples, with your obstropolous tantarraras." Redfoot, who plans to attack the inhabitants of the building, unctuously and hypocritically replies: "Brother, I have done you a wrong, which I would undo, for the kindness that is betwixt us. Let me in therefore, brother, I pray, that the evil spirit may not stand betwixt us, making noises and hissing."[24]

By the late 1820s, therefore, Simms was beginning to explore the topics he would develop in his mature fiction and verse, and he was tending more and more to gravitate toward southern subjects. His ex-

24. [William Gilmore Simms], "Chronicles of Ashley River—No[.] 3," *Southern Literary Gazette*, n.s., I (September 1, 1829), 177.

periences in the low-country South of his childhood and the Gulf South on his trips to see his father gave rise to the most noteworthy writing of his apprentice period and anticipate the paths he would shortly explore. He would turn these experiences to even better account in the 1830s, as, in novels about the Yemassee War, the Revolution, and the Old Southwest, he would stake out his claims as a writer to be reckoned with on the national literary scene.

2
An Old Tribe in Carolina: Popular Romance, the Low Country, and The Yemassee

The 1820s had ended well for Simms, who had several volumes of poetry to his credit and substantial editorial experience under his belt. But the 1830s opened sadly, with a series of family and other tragedies that caused him strain and grief. In March of 1830, his father died in Mississippi, and during the spring of the following year Simms traveled to the Gulf South to settle the estate. Shortly after he returned to Charleston, his grandmother died; then, in February, 1832, his wife Anna, long tubercular, died also, leaving him with their daughter, Augusta, to rear. As the outspoken young editor of the Charleston *City Gazette,* he had lost standing in the city by taking the Union side in the nullification controversy and writing fiery editorials supporting his position. Angry citizens had menaced him at the *City Gazette* office, he bravely fending them off; but when his partner E. S. Duryea died in March, 1832, he was forced to sell the newspaper, whose subscriptions had steadily declined.[1] Describing the situation with considerable feeling to Lawson, he wrote that, after selling the paper, "sick, sad and desolate, I for the first time proceeded to the North. Never was loneliness much more complete than mine on that first visit to a land of strangers. I had lost all—almost everything" (*L,* I, 165).

In New England and New York, where Simms spent the summer and early fall of 1832, his fortunes began almost immediately to improve. He prepared his poem *Atalantis* for the press; issued late in the year to warm acclaim, it was the first of his books (except possibly *The Tri-Color*) to be published outside of Charleston. He had meanwhile made friends with a group of New York literary men, among them

1. Trent, *William Gilmore Simms,* 58–68; Salley, "William Gilmore Simms," in *L,* I, lxvi–lxviii; [Mary C. Simms Oliphant, Alfred Taylor Odell, and T. C. Duncan Eaves], "The Family Circle," in *L,* I, cxlviii. On the *City Gazette,* see Jon L. Wakelyn, *The Politics of a Literary Man: William Gilmore Simms* (Westport, Conn., 1973), Chap. 1.

William Cullen Bryant, poet and editor of the New York *Evening Post*, and Robert Charles Sands, an author and journalist. He had solidified his friendship with Lawson, who would act henceforward as his informal literary agent, and had joined him in courting attractive young women in the city. And he had formed an acquaintance with Willis Gaylord Clark of Philadelphia, who with his brother Lewis would shortly begin to edit the influential *Knickerbocker Magazine*, which published some of Simms's early short fiction and verse.[2]

Simms's first visit to the North, filled as it was with new social and literary experiences, marked a definite turn in his fortunes. It distracted him temporarily from his regional and family preoccupations, introduced him to the cosmopolitan life of letters in the nation's foremost publishing center, and increased his determination to pursue a literary career. Through his contacts with New York, which he visited almost yearly in the 1830s, he virtually became, as Trent remarks, a Knickerbocker author—a status he was not to lose until his intense involvement with southern sectional politics after midcentury.[3] He also became a popular national author whose books, until the early 1840s, were issued by important publishers in the North like Harper Brothers or Carey and Hart. From his first lonely visit to this land of strangers we may date his introduction to the professional life of letters in antebellum America.

Simms's writing between 1830 and 1842, which represents the first phase of his efforts as a serious professional author, displays his awareness of the literary marketplace and his determination to use his varied talents to advantage in it. During this period, he brought out both prose and poetry, concentrating on the former as the surest way to popular renown. In *The Book of My Lady* (1833), he reprinted some of his early fiction and verse, and in *Carl Werner* (1838) he collected additional stories and tales. In the short novel *Martin Faber* (1833), expanded for *Martin Faber, The Story of a Criminal; and Other Tales* (1837), he mined the vein of the criminal confession that he had already opened in "Sketches," and in *Southern Passages and Pictures* (1839), an important volume of poetry, he continued the emphasis on

2. Salley, "William Gilmore Simms," in *L*, I, lxviii; Trent, *William Gilmore Simms*, 69–72; Thomas L. McHaney, "An Early 19th-Century Literary Agent: James Lawson of New York," *Publications of the Bibliographical Society of America*, LXIV (Second Quarter, 1970), 177–92.

3. Trent, *William Gilmore Simms*, 72.

southern traditions and landscape that had emerged in his poems of the preceding decade.[4] But his major work during the period was his long fiction, and the principal categories of that fiction show clearly his desire for acclaim as an author through the exploitation of popular literary traditions.

Like his northern contemporaries Fenimore Cooper, James Kirke Paulding, and Robert Montgomery Bird, Simms energetically produced novels in several fields: historical fiction about the American past—*The Yemassee* and *The Partisan* (1835), *Mellichampe* (1836), and *The Kinsmen* (1841); books about the American frontier that have a loosely contemporary setting—*Guy Rivers* (1834), *Richard Hurdis* (1838), and *Border Beagles* (1840); and novels set in Spain or Spanish America—*Pelayo* (1838) and *The Damsel of Darien* (1839). Because these works, as he insisted, are romances, and because the romance is the form he would use for his long fiction throughout his life, we will do well to pause here and take a look at the background and traditions of the genre, since an enlightened understanding of his procedures in it will aid greatly in our subsequent examination of his fiction.[5]

4. Kibler, *Poetry of Simms*, 67, says that *Southern Passages and Pictures* was actually issued late in 1838.

5. Simms's most important theoretical statement about the romance as a literary form occurs in the advertisement to *The Yemassee. A Romance of Carolina* (New York, 1835), I, vi–vii. There he says:

> Modern romance is the substitute which the people of to-day offer for the ancient epic. Its standards are the same. . . . It invests individuals with an absorbing interest—it hurries them through crowding events in a narrow space of time—it requires the same unities of plan, of purpose, and harmony of parts, and it seeks for its adventures among the wild and wonderful. It does not insist upon what is known, or even what is probable. It grasps at the possible; and, placing a human agent in hitherto untried situations, it exercises its ingenuity in extricating him from them, while describing his feelings and his fortunes in their progress.

Unless otherwise indicated, all further references to the novel are to this edition, cited by volume and page number within the text. (Simms changed the advertisement slightly for *The Yemassee: A Romance of Carolina* [Rev. ed.; New York, 1853].)

On the subject of the romance, see also Simms's comments in *L*, III, 388: "The Yemassee, & in fact most of my works are *romances*, not novels. They involve sundry of the elements of heroic poetry. They are imaginative, passionate, metaphysical; they deal chiefly in trying situation, bold characterization, & elevating moral. They exhibit *invention* in large degree, & their progress is dramatic; the action being bold[,] salient, & with a regularly advancing convergence to the catastrophe."

In books and correspondence, Simms insisted that his fiction should be judged by the standards he set for it—a statement that his twentieth-century readers have seldom heeded.

Historical and contemporary romance, the forms Simms used for his fiction about the low country and the Gulf South respectively, are versions of the popular or bourgeois romance that had emerged with the spread of literacy and print in the eighteenth century; and it, in turn, is a descendant of the aristocratic romance that had flourished since the Middle Ages. As his letters and literary criticism reveal, Simms theorized about romance throughout his life, and he was steeped in its traditions through the work of many authors: Chaucer, Malory, Sidney, Shakespeare, and particularly his master Walter Scott, whom he called "more perfect, more complete and admirable, than any writer of his age."[6] Scott himself was steeped in the traditions of romance, and he used its organizing patterns in the format of the Waverley novels. He used, in other words, a dialectic structure, visible clearly at the historical level of the books, that displays forces in conflict and that also dictates his construction of the fictional narratives, which are love stories whose strong symbolic element gives his statement about history the shape of romance.

Scott's vision of Britain's history, the focus of much twentieth-century scholarship, was heavily influenced by the symbolizing, reconciling tendencies inherent in romance.[7] In studying the British past, he saw that a middle way had emerged from the clashes and reconciliations of two extremes, portrayed in his novels: Scottish Jacobites and British Hanoverians in *Waverley* (1814), Covenanters and Anglicans in *Old Mortality* (1816), Normans and Saxons in *Ivanhoe* (1819), Puritans and Cavaliers in *Woodstock* (1826). In his works he tends to represent the opposing extremes through historical figures like Charles II or Grahame of Claverhouse and to use the main fictional characters, the Waverleys, Ivanhoes, Roses, and Rowenas, to epitomize major elements in the society of their eras while communicating his vision of the emerging middle way. His heroes, though differentiated in time and

6. [William Gilmore Simms], "Modern Prose Fiction," *Southern Quarterly Review*, XV (April, 1849), 83. The system of volume numbering used on the covers of the *Southern Quarterly Review* is inaccurate. I have followed the volume numbers used in the Duke University William R. Perkins Library file of the journal and have supplied the numbers of the new series in hopes of clarifying my references to the periodical. The new series began in April, 1850.

7. See, for example, Georg Lukács, *The Historical Novel*, trans. Hannah and Stanley Mitchell (1962; rpr. Atlantic Highlands, N.J., 1978), Chap. 1; David Daiches, "Scott's Achievement as a Novelist," in A. Norman Jeffares (ed.), *Scott's Mind and Art* (New York, 1970), 21–52; Daiches, "Scott and Scotland," in Alan Bell (ed.), *Scott Bicentenary Essays* (New York, 1973), [38]–60.

class, are moderate spokesmen for one side at the historical level, while their female counterparts usually are equally moderate spokeswomen for the other side.

Hence in *Old Mortality,* a novel about the clash of Anglican Royalists and Scottish Covenanters in late seventeenth-century England, hero Henry Morton, a low-keyed Presbyterian, and heroine Edith Bellenden, a temperate Anglican, reflect the conflict of religious views that is settled only when the tolerant William III ascends the throne. In *Redgauntlet* (1824), a book about a Jacobite uprising some years after the battle of Culloden, hero Darsie Latimer and his sister Lilias—the children of an English noblewoman with Whig relatives and a Scottish nobleman with Jacobite connections—symbolize the struggles between England and Scotland, Protestants and Catholics, and Hanoverians and Jacobites in the middle eighteenth century. And in *Ivanhoe,* which depicts the hostility between Normans and Saxons in the decades following the Norman Conquest, the heroine, a stately Saxon princess, and the hero, a Normanized Saxon loyal to both Saxon father and Norman king, are shaped to signify the gradual rapprochement of the groups Scott represents as "two hostile races."[8] Thus their wedding, which is attended by nobles of both parties, figures forth the eventual amalgamation of the groups—just as Ivanhoe's attraction to the beautiful Jewish woman Rebecca, nourished in secret and eventually abandoned, reflects the unhappy fact that the Jews were not assimilated into the society of twelfth-century England. Through the marriage of his typical hero and heroine, Scott makes use of the symbolizing impulse in romance to emphasize the compromises that contending elements in British history, in his view, had already made.

Scott influenced dozens of American novelists, but the story of his popularity in antebellum America does not need to be told in detail here. What does need to be emphasized, however, since it has apparently never been remarked, is the degree to which American novelists, working from a different set of cultural conditions, modified Scott's romance patterns in order to make distinctive historical statements of their own. In this regard the practice of Cooper and Simms, Scott's most important American followers, is instructive. They employed his basic structures but made changes in them that reflect their perceptions of their country's history, which was different in fundamental ways from that of Britain.

8. [Sir Walter Scott], *Ivanhoe; A Romance* (Edinburgh, 1820), I, 4.

The development of American civilization, viewed historically, had involved the extinction or expulsion of the enemy rather than reconciliation and compromise with him as a fundamental condition of cultural advance. Therefore, although Cooper and Simms followed Scott in using history for thematic statement and in making their chief fictional narratives symbolize elements at the historical level of their books, their fictional plots do not represent quite the same things as Scott's. Cooper in *The Spy* (1821) and such novels of the Leatherstocking series as *The Last of the Mohicans* (1826) developed plots that show the traditional romance lovers, hero and heroine, struggling to destroy or expel the enemies—Britons, French, or Indians—threatening the development of American civilization. At the same time, he symbolized another important element in American culture, the pioneering spirit, through the massive, poignant figure of Natty Bumppo. The evidence of Simms's fiction suggests that he understood the procedures of both Scott and Cooper, and he utilized their literary patterns for his fictional design.[9] But he modified these patterns, sometimes in striking ways, in order to make plain the peculiar conditions of southern culture.

Like those of his predecessors, Simms's works employ the central conventions of popular fiction; they show a keen awareness of romance traditions; and they convey a statement about history through literary terms. They express the ideals of the ruling class, which in Simms's work is the planting class of the colonial and antebellum South. They dramatize the conflicts of these ideals with forces threatening them by a two-sided or dialectic structure revealed most obviously through their main narratives—symbolic constructions in which attractive heroines and heroes representing antebellum cultural ideals battle villains representing the anti-ideals that, if successful, would destroy southern civilization. They resolve this conflict through persistently happy or providential endings in which heroes defeat villains and marry heroines, in an action that emphasizes the victory of southern ideals. And they use as their most characteristic setting the natural domain, represented in its pastoral dimension by the plantation and in its wilder aspect by the forest from which southern plantations developed. They also exhibit the central romance procedure of

9. For another view of Simms's relationship to his literary predecessors, see C. Hugh Holman, "The Influence of Scott and Cooper on Simms," in *The Roots of Southern Writing*, 50–60.

slanting or weighting the dialectic structure in favor of the side that Simms as author perceives as "right"—a feature that is expressed, in part, through a system of character pairing in which figures who are moral opposites or doubles confront each other.[10]

All Simms's long romances, like Scott's and Cooper's, have an additional dimension, a framing or an enveloping action that constitutes the public side of the narration and that is grounded in the history of a society and an epoch. The framing action, which in the books about the low country is the colonists' successful prosecution of war and in those about the Gulf South is the region's gradual assimilation of elements from tidewater civilization, makes evident a basic element of his design. That element is the time perspective, the vantage point that develops out of the passage of time between the era shown in the novel and his own period. By means of this vantage point, he is able to impose the interpretation of his age upon the events of the past and thus to convey his sense of a providential movement in history by reference to an action whose shape is completed and whose pertinence to the present is clear. The time perspective, an extremely valuable element for his fiction, enables him to create the happy endings typical of romance, which give it, as is sometimes remarked, a Hegelian literary shape.[11]

The framing action and time perspective make possible the symbolic dimension, which has been a generally overlooked dimension, of Simms's central story lines. In constructing his plots, he carefully observes the conventions of his genre: with few exceptions, his main narratives (usually love stories) show a brave, virtuous hero and heroine contending with a villain who wants to destroy the hero and marry the heroine. At the end of a book or its sequel, however, the lovers have defeated their enemies and are about to marry each other. The situation in the love story echoes the situation in the framing action where, either actually within a novel or implicitly in its references to history completed, the southern civilization represented by the lovers has like-

10. For theoretical descriptions of romance that shed light on Simms's procedures, see Northrop Frye, *Anatomy of Criticism: Four Essays* (Princeton, N.J., 1957), 186–203, 304–307, and *The Secular Scripture: A Study of the Structure of Romance* (Cambridge, Mass., 1976). See also Robert Scholes and Robert Kellogg, *The Nature of Narrative* (New York, 1966), 66–69, 226–29, 248–50, and Gillian Beer, *The Romance* ([London], 1970), no. 10 of John D. Jump (ed.), *The Critical Idiom*.

11. C. Hugh Holman, *The Immoderate Past: The Southern Writer and History* (Athens, Ga., 1977), Chap. 1; Lukács, *The Historical Novel*, Chap. 1.

wise overcome the obstacles confronting it. Simms's main plots are conventionalized in accordance with the relatively bourgeois and romantic tastes of his readers; but because in the century since his death literary taste has shifted toward realism, his practice in plotting has often puzzled or annoyed critics who do not understand or do not sympathize with what he was trying to do. Simms constructed his narratives to meet the requirements of an abstract design that was as essential to him as it was to Kennedy, Cooper, John Esten Cooke, and other popular writers of the antebellum period, whose plots are central, not peripheral, to their purposes in art.[12]

Simms's substantial achievement in his long fiction—and one that warrants some emphasis, as it has been almost entirely ignored—was to blend elements from both history and literary tradition in shaping his romance structures while drawing on many of the same elements for numerous realistic details. It is somewhat easier at this point, concentrating on his fiction set in the low country, to show how he employed history than to analyze his use of literary traditions, since his procedures in that regard are highly complex. He chose the conflicts that marked the South Carolina past, for instance, as the source of the dialectic structure of his novels, centering *The Yemassee* on the colonists' tragic clash with a formerly friendly Indian tribe and the Revolutionary War Romances on their protracted bloody struggle with Britain. He used the outcome of these conflicts, which he felt that history (perceived through the time perspective) had decreed was "right," as the foundation for his happy endings, which express his sense of a providential movement at work on the settlers' behalf. He used the strong patrician element in the colony, fostered by the conditions of its founding and its emigration patterns, as the basis for his portrait of its persistent aristocratic traditions. He made the great plantations carved from the South Carolina swamplands the pastoral part of his romance green world and the dense forests where colonial wars were fought the untamed or wilder side, while he used the gloom of the same forests, together with the savage emotions that war helped generate, for the

12. A similar point about the conventionalized narratives in antebellum fiction is made by Jane Tompkins, *Sensational Designs: The Cultural Work of American Fiction, 1790–1860* (New York, 1985), 113. Stereotyped plots and characters, Tompkins says, "convey enormous amounts of cultural information in an extremely condensed form. As the telegraphic expression of complex clusters of value," such stereotypes are "*essential* to popularly successful narrative" (xvi).

Gothic effects that bulk large in his long fiction of the 1830s. Finally, he found in such figures as South Carolina governor Charles Craven in the Yemassee War and Francis Marion during the Revolution the heroes of the colonial era to whom eighteenth-century American historians had already accorded mythical status—a measure that encouraged him to paint them larger than life when he transferred them to his romance canvas.

The history of the low country reveals in copious detail how cultural traditions reinforce literary conventions at almost every level of Simms's books. The region had, for example, a series of conflicts marking its past that made it, as Simms indicated in *Views and Reviews,* a field ripe for the historical romancer.[13] These included the strife, beginning in the fifteenth century, between England and Spain for mastery of the coast. This struggle, which Simms uses as the backdrop for *The Yemassee* and *The Cassique of Kiawah,* was only superficially resolved by the planting of the first permanent English colony near the present site of Charleston in 1670, since the Spaniards in St. Augustine continued to menace the infant province for years. As English settlement gradually expanded, there were recurrent battles between pioneers and Indians—the Westo War of 1673, the Stono War of 1674, and of course the Yemassee War in 1715. There were also, in the early colonial period, clashes between citizens and pirates and among various social groups; there was finally the climactic battle with Britain, in which South Carolina played an important part. In addition to using these conflicts for the framing action and dialectic construction of his novels, Simms draws upon them for numerous authentic details—the statistics, events, and actual figures from history that lend credibility to his presentation while grounding it firmly in a particular place and era.[14]

13. William Gilmore Simms, *Views and Reviews in American Literature, History and Fiction,* ed. C. Hugh Holman, 1st ser. (Cambridge, Mass., 1962), 77–78. Unless otherwise indicated, further references to this work are to this modern scholarly edition.

14. M. Eugene Sirmans, *Colonial South Carolina: A Political History, 1663–1763* (Chapel Hill, 1966), Chaps. 1–10; David Duncan Wallace, *South Carolina: A Short History, 1520–1948* (Columbia, S.C., 1961), Chaps. 1–17; Bridenbaugh, *Myths and Realities,* Chap. 2; Edward McCrady, *The History of South Carolina Under the Proprietary Government, 1670–1719* (New York, 1897); Samuel Gaillard Stoney, "The Country and the People," in Albert Simons and Samuel Lapham, Jr. (eds.), *Plantations of the Carolina Low Country* (Rev. ed.; Charleston, 1964), 11–43; Verner W. Crane, *The Southern Frontier, 1670–1732* (1929; rpr. Ann Arbor, 1956), Chaps. 1–6; and Chapman J. Milling, *Red Carolinians* (Chapel Hill, 1940), 52–53, 72–83.

For the aristocratic values that are fundamental to his romances and that play a central part in the construction of his fictional narratives, Simms found material in the original plans for the colony, in its Fundamental Constitutions, and in its settlement patterns. Low-country South Carolina had from its beginnings a pronounced patrician cast stemming from its origins as a proprietary colony governed by eight British noblemen, led by Anthony Ashley Cooper, Earl of Shaftesbury, who wanted to foster a landed gentry as a way of assuring aristocratic rule in the province. Hence there was created, in the Fundamental Constitutions that he helped draw up, a resident nobility, the landgraves and cassiques who assisted the lords proprietors in running the colony and who, with their titles, were granted enormous tracts of land—48,000 acres for each landgrave and 24,000 for each cassique (a title borrowed from the Indians that sometimes appears in Simms's writing). Although this scheme proved impractical and was abandoned, it helped give South Carolina its patrician tone, the foundation of its great plantation system, and its preference for rule by a landed gentry.[15] Increasing the aristocratic tenor of the province were its emigration patterns—its attraction of royalist refugees from the English civil wars and its appeal to wealthy planters from Barbados, the latter congregating in the area north of Charleston known as Goose Creek. Simms used these facts from the colony's early history in creating an aristocratic lineage for the heroines and heroes of his low-country fiction, and he also used them as a bridge to the dominant values of his readers, who were largely middle class or upper middle class and genteel.[16]

Besides aristocrats, the Carolina province exhibited what one scholar calls "a yeasty mass of divergent peoples"—French Huguenots, Scots settlers at Port Royal, Sephardic Jews, Irish Catholics, and Quakers.[17] These settlers made provincial life vibrant, colorful, and explosive, increased the political complexity of the colony, and contributed to Simms's detailed depiction of its social life. The landgraves and cassiques created by the Fundamental Constitutions and their

15. Sirmans, *Colonial South Carolina,* 10; McCrady, *The History of South Carolina Under the Proprietary Government,* Chap. 4.

16. On the social level of readers in the antebellum period, see William Charvat, *Literary Publishing in America, 1790–1850* (Philadelphia, 1959), 60, and James D. Hart, *The Popular Book: A History of America's Literary Taste* (New York, 1950), 85–86.

17. Stoney, "The Country and the People," in *Plantations of the Carolina Low Country,* 15, 17–18.

high-born, tradition-loving descendants are central to his picture of upper-class rule, while the great admixture of people in the other classes and the friction that existed among various ethnic and religious groups encouraged his emphasis, which has both a realistic and a romance slant, on the intricate social system of South Carolina. Simms also used a lively throng of woodsmen, farmers, and sailors to provide the yeoman element, which has generally been seen as a realistic element, in his fiction, and to render in literary terms the cultural fact that there were substantial numbers of plain people inhabiting the province.

Beneath such people on the social ladder were the slaves, who in many cases had accompanied their Barbadian masters to the colony and whose presence there underscored the fact that provincial social patterns were influenced by West Indian prototypes. Although slaves existed in the province from an early date, they were not imported in large numbers until the 1690s, when the expansion of rice cultivation necessitated a large, cheap labor force; and they did not greatly outnumber whites in Carolina until after 1710.[18] Simms's depictions of his black characters reflect his broad knowledge of historical fact, and they also reveal, somewhat more directly, his awareness of literary convention and his determination to use both it and social history to implement political propaganda as the antebellum sectional crisis grew worse. In his fiction he is less concerned, in other words, to trace the evolution of slavery as an institution than to show it as an established, beneficent part of southern life and to use it as a vehicle for his forthright sectionalist views. Influenced by stereotypes of blacks in fiction and drama, his Negroes are sometimes lazy, sensual, or improvident, but they are also loyal, brave, and clever; and they function for the most part to reinforce the "right" side of the dialectic structure in his major fiction. They thwart enemies of their white owners, rescue the same owners from danger, and perform courageous, self-sacrificing acts on behalf of the stratified social system that they, like their masters, uncompromisingly uphold.

The most basic of South Carolina's features, its terrain, provided abundant, striking elements for Simms's literary scheme. Geographically, low-country South Carolina occupies a broad coastal plain stretching inland about one hundred miles, penetrated by rivers,

18. Sirmans, *Colonial South Carolina*, 4, 14, 24; Wallace, *South Carolina: A Short History*, [183].

creeks, inlets, and salt marshes and protected from the ocean by the sea islands, which form an almost unbroken chain along the coast from a point north of Charleston to Savannah.[19] In colonial times the mainland was thickly wooded, blooming, and beautiful; and there was a tendency in writing before Simms's era to portray it in idealized terms that accord well with the idealizing propensity of romance. John Archdale, for example, a former governor of the colony whom Simms loved to quote, proclaimed that "the Land . . . is beautified with odoriferous and fragrant Woods, pleasantly green all the year," and the sixteenth-century French explorer René Laudonnière, whom Simms cites in *The History of South Carolina,* described "cedars, palmes, and bay trees, of so sovereign odor, that balme smelleth nothing in comparison." At a practical level, the forests and their game furnished the lumber, skins, and furs on which colonial trade depended, while the flowers, trees, and grasses of the region, its fox, hare, deer, and other animals, form an authentic backdrop for the scenes of peace or conflict Simms portrays there.[20]

The soil and climate of the low country, which likewise drew praise from early commentators, invited agriculture and hence, like the landscape, lent themselves to the romance mode. With its tidal rivers, its humid, temperate climate, and its rich soil, the region proved suitable for the cultivation of rice, which soon became the great colonial staple. The conditions of its growth encouraged the development of large plantations and fastened them firmly to the rivers needed for irrigation and transportation of the precious grain to market; fittingly, the river swamplands where much rice was cultivated were called "the Golden Mines of *Carolina*" by an eighteenth-century writer.[21] They proved

19. Wallace, *South Carolina: A Short History,* Chap. 1; William A. Schaper, *Sectionalism and Representation in South Carolina* (1901; rpr. New York, 1968), 17–22. The term *low country,* while commonly used to describe the entire area below the fall line, more accurately designates the sea islands and the coastal region. On this point, see Schaper, 17–18.

20. John Archdale, *A New Description of That Fertile and Pleasant Province of Carolina. . . .* (1707); rpr. in B. R. Carroll (comp.), *Historical Collections of South Carolina. . . .* (New York, 1836), II, 95; William Gilmore Simms, *The History of South Carolina. . . .* (Charleston, S.C., 1840), 29; James E. Kibler, Jr., "Simms as Naturalist: Lowcountry Landscape in His Revolutionary Novels," *Mississippi Quarterly,* XXXI (Fall, 1978), [499]–518.

21. George Milligen-Johnston, *A Short Description of the Province of South-Carolina, With An Account of the Air, Weather, and Diseases, at Charles-Town* (1770); rpr. in Chapman J. Milling (ed.), *Colonial South Carolina: Two Contemporary Descriptions* (Columbia, S.C., 1951), 119. See also Bridenbaugh, *Myths and Realities,* 56.

equally valuable for the literary conventions of Simms's fiction. The circumstances of South Carolina agricultural history enabled him to connect the swamps where rice was grown to the manors that planters' wealth created through the forested tracts common to both. The estate Holly Dale in *The Forayers,* for example, is approached "through long, dark, silent avenues of the natural forest," and the Oaks in *Katharine Walton* has "a continuous wall of thicket almost encircling" the dwelling. Typically, moreover, "a noble colonnade" of trees that are common to a particular region gives access to the manor house.[22] As an extension of the natural landscape, the plantation usually represents its ideal features. Simms's estates are therefore powerful symbols of the pastoral and the patrician—of what he saw as best in low-country living and of what he had imbibed from both the literary and the cultural traditions behind his work.

The history of the low country inspired Simms to forge through his fiction an optimistic statement about the region's proud past—a statement that is predicated on his ardent belief in its equally proud future and that takes shape through the generic plot he constructed for his novels about the region. This plot says a good deal about his involvement with the past of the low country, his hopes for its successful future, and his fundamental allegiances in art. It shows his typical combination of romance structures with realistic cultural content, and it also makes some points about specific conditions in low-country history that are basic to his purposes in fiction. It reveals, for example, the heartfelt national and southern patriotism that marks most of his writing with a historical slant and that particularly inspires his notable body of work about the Revolution. It communicates too his belief, as commentators interested in the sociocultural implications of his fiction have sensed, that the values engendered by South Carolina's patrician heritage and the wars it had fought and won augured well for the

22. W[illiam] Gilmore Simms, *The Forayers: Or The Raid of the Dog-Days* (New York, 1855), 274, *Katharine Walton: Or The Rebel of Dorchester* (Rev. ed.; New York, 1854), 128, and *The Forayers,* 187. Unless otherwise indicated, all further references to these novels are to these editions, cited by page number within the text (as *F* and *KW* where necessary for clarity). Simms may have been reflecting a tendency of his own time in his descriptions of plantations in the Revolutionary period. In *The Civilized Wilderness: Backgrounds to American Romantic Literature, 1817–1860* (New York, 1975), 55, Edward Halsey Foster describes antebellum America's effort "to represent civilization and wilderness simultaneously in the same environment—notably *in a sympathetic linking of architecture with wilderness landscapes*" so that "together house and setting formed . . . a civilized wilderness."

struggles it was bracing itself to confront during his own lifetime.[23] And, viewed aesthetically, it conveys his adherence to romance methods as the best way of making these statements.

As it takes shape in *The Yemassee* and the Revolutionary War novels, this plot shows the familiar heroine and hero of romance overcoming threats to their region posed by several kinds of enemies—pirates, Indians, and Spaniards in *The Yemassee,* Britons from several social orders, lower-class loyalists, and lukewarm patriots in the books about the Revolution. Such narrative structures echo definite elements at the historical level of the novels. It might well be claimed, in fact, that the convergence of love story and framing action to create an optimistic statement that Simms felt history had already ratified is perhaps the most fundamental part of his rhetoric in these volumes as narrative structures express it. Through this convergence, he urges us to agree that what happened should have happened: that the lovers who married should have married; that the rivals they defeated deserved to lose; that the social system they protected should have persisted; and that the wars they and other colonists fought were rightly won. He also urges us, though more subtly, to accept his conviction that the class system established in the antebellum South as a result of these events in the past should continue to endure and that the political problems South Carolina was facing in the antebellum period should be handled as boldly as comparable problems had been handled in the colonial era.

Simms's most popular and enduring work of fiction, *The Yemassee,* is particularly useful in illustrating these concepts because in it he threads many elements of colonial Carolina history through his framing action and fictional narratives. Set in the South Carolina low country of the early eighteenth century, the book was influenced, like all his important writing, by a mixture of personal and literary elements: the tales of his grandmother, his contacts with Indians in South Carolina and the Gulf South, his reading of Cooper's *The Last of the Mohicans,* and his knowledge, gained from visits in 1833 and 1834 to the North, of the commanding position that historical fiction occupied in the national marketplace.[24] In the summer of 1834, he wrote Lawson, "I am

23. Among the scholars who stress the sociocultural elements in Simms's fiction is William R. Taylor, *Cavalier and Yankee: The Old South and American National Character* (New York, 1961), Chap. 8.

24. William Gilmore Simms, *The Yemassee: A Romance of Carolina,* ed. C. Hugh Holman (Boston, 1961), xii–xix. Simms had already drawn on *The Last of the Mohi-*

doing nothing, but thinking much, and digesting the plan of an Indian Tale—a story of an early settlement and of an old tribe in Carolina." As usual, he worked rapidly; "[t]he story advances with haste," he said to Lawson in November, "and I may be able to have it ready for the publishers by January" (*L,* I, 61, 63). The book was issued in April, 1835, to a chorus of praise: reviewers commended its "bold and original" design, styled it "the Romance of the Season," and insisted that no work of American fiction was superior to it.[25] It was in fact so popular that two editions were published within a month and a third before the end of the year, Simms revising it slightly for the second printing.[26]

The Yemassee has ties to several literary traditions, as is shown by its two main narrative strands—one involving white settlers and conveyed through standard romance structures that communicate the conventional attitudes of Simms's culture toward Indian-white conflicts, the other centering on the Indians and containing epic and tragic elements inherent in the spectacle of a gallant race defeated. In their different tone and literary derivations, the two narratives reflect the division between Simms's public conviction, as a southerner writing in the nineteenth century, that the course history had taken in defeating the Indians had enabled white civilization to prosper, and his private sense that the Indians were a noble people who deserved better treatment than they got from their white opponents. His complex attitude,

---

cans for the early poem "The Last of the Yemassees." He used the novel again in *The Yemassee* for his picture of a drunken Indian corrupted by the whiskey of the white settlers, his semihumorous portraits of psalm-singing Puritans, and his presentation of the noble Indian whose death at the end of the book signifies the defeat of the tribe. On correspondences and divergences between the books, see Louis D. Rubin, Jr., "The Romance of the Colonial Frontier: Simms, Cooper, the Indians, and the Wilderness," in J. Gerald Kennedy and Daniel Mark Fogel (eds.), *American Letters and the Historical Consciousness: Essays in Honor of Lewis P. Simpson* (Baton Rouge, 1987), [112]–36.

25. [Charles Fenno Hoffman], Review of *The Yemassee,* New York *American,* April 18, 1835; Review of *The Yemassee,* New York *Times,* April 16, 1835; Review of *The Yemassee,* New York *Commercial Advertiser,* April 18, 1835. A few reviewers noted marks of haste and carelessness in the book. See, for instance, [Lewis Gaylord Clark], "Literary Notices," *The Knickerbocker, or New-York Monthly Magazine,* V (April, 1835), 343. Although they are anonymous, the "Literary Notices" in the *Knickerbocker Magazine* have traditionally been ascribed to Clark. On this point, see Perry Miller, *The Raven and the Whale: The War of Words and Wits in the Era of Poe and Melville* (New York, 1956), *passim.*

26. *L,* II, 226*n*279; Holman, "A Note on the Text," in Simms, *The Yemassee,* [xxiii], and Introduction to Simms, *The Yemassee,* viii.

observable throughout the novel, leads him to fashion a dialectic system in which his sympathy is almost equally divided between the two sides. It is this implicit recognition that the fall of an enemy can be tragic that allies his work to the epic and results in a novel in which tragic elements offset or qualify the comic, realistic, and romantic features of his presentation.[27]

The Yemassee shows the Carolina colony only forty-five years after its founding, when it sprawled precariously along the South Atlantic coast, with Indian tribes to its north and west and Spanish settlements southward. Despite the spread of plantations and the rapid growth of Charleston as an urban center, much of the province was still in the pioneer phase. The Indians who are the center of interest in the story had once been a subject nation of Spain. By the late seventeenth century they had begun to penetrate the territory north of the Savannah River, and by the early eighteenth century they were intermingled with white settlers in the so-called Ten Towns in southeastern Carolina. They had originally been on good terms with their British neighbors; but in 1715, infuriated by white abuses and possibly incited by Spain, they massacred the settlers in Pocotaligo, the largest of the towns, and then, killing and burning as they went, drove the war to the gates of Charleston. The whites, led by the popular governor Charles Craven, beat them back at the Salkehatchie (or Combahee) River, while a detachment of colonists captured Pocotaligo; but the war dragged on for two years before peace was concluded.

The war was made more difficult for the white settlers by social and political friction in the colony resulting from changes in proprietary rule. At the establishment of Carolina in the 1670s, its lords proprietors had espoused a policy of religious toleration in hopes of encouraging emigration to the province. But the rise of political conservatism and High-Church Anglicanism in early eighteenth-century England caused some changes in the standards of the proprietors that increased internal strife in Carolina and widened the gap between Charleston and the settlements. Led by John Carteret, Lord Granville, the proprietors dropped the policy of religious toleration and supported the establishment of the Anglican church in the province. This move, which caused friction between the large numbers of Anglicans and dissenters in Carolina, added to Craven's burdens in uniting his

27. Holman, Introduction to Simms, *The Yemassee,* xix.

people—but it gave Simms rich material for portraits, both serious and comic, of provincial political alignments.[28]

Simms's historical framing action for the novel, rendered through commentary and narrative structures, shows his broad grasp of these and similar issues in the colony. In it he discusses Lord Granville in some detail, portrays a prominent dissenter in the province, Landgrave Edmund Bellinger, and develops Charles Craven as his chief historical figure. He makes much of the possible league between Spain and the Yemassee Indians, using details gleaned from his chief printed source, the eighteenth-century historian Alexander Hewatt, about the "good" Yemassee Indian Sanuté, or Sanutee, and the "bad" one Ishiagaska, who took, says Hewatt, Spanish talk of conspiracy to his Indian tribe.[29] Simms emphasizes the pirate menace to the young colony in the person of the villain, Richard Chorley, who is in league with Spain and Ishiagaska; the alliance of the Yemassee with sister tribes in the war; the friction, which he portrays humorously, between Anglicans and dissenters; the contacts among various social groups in the province, including patricians, blacks, and pioneers; and the frontier conditions along the Carolina coast. From these elements he fashions his main narrative, a many-sided story whose effects range from satirical and humorous to Gothic, melodramatic, and tragic.

This narrative, when centering on the white figures, upholds the values of the ruling class represented in the novel, which were similar to those of the ruling class of Simms's day. For it he draws with ingenuity on elements from the early eighteenth-century history of the colony. The hero of his story is the Lord Palatine Charles Craven, who throughout much of the novel masquerades as commoner Gabriel Harrison in order to gain the trust of the middle-class pioneers he is charged with leading. More than any of the other numerous commentators on *The Yemassee* have noted, Harrison represents the standards of the early eighteenth-century proprietors: associated with urbane Charleston, he is an aristocrat, a Cavalier, and apparently an Anglican. His fiancée Bess Matthews, whose stern and occasionally foolish father John is a dissenting minister and who lives in a modest cottage

28. Information in the text on colonial Carolina, the Yemassee Indians, and the Yemassee War comes from Crane, *The Southern Frontier,* 162–86; Sirmans, *Colonial South Carolina,* 75–81, 111–17; Wallace, *South Carolina: A Short History,* [86]–92.

29. [Alexander Hewatt], *An Historical Account of the Rise and Progress of the Colonies of South Carolina and Georgia* (1779); rpr. in Vol. I of Carroll (comp.), *Historical Collections of South Carolina.* The quotation in the text is from I, 194.

in the woods, represents both the Puritan component in the colony and its rural middle class. Throughout the novel, Harrison courts Bess within a forest setting that is given appropriate pastoral treatment—the "rich green of the leaves—the deep crimson of the wild flower—the gemmed and floral-knotted long grass that carpeted the path" carry evocations of Eden (I, 169). The marriage of the lovers foreshadowed at the end of the book symbolizes the union of several elements in the eighteenth-century colony—among them aristocracy and middle class, city and forest, Anglicans and dissenters, the proprietors (or their representatives) and the pioneers. It also stands for the victory of the nascent Carolina social and political system over the triple threats of pirates, Indians, and Spain.[30]

In the standard fashion of narratives in nineteenth-century historical fiction, the opponents of Bess and Harrison are constructed to embody precisely these threats. Thus in villain Richard Chorley, Simms blends "the bucanier [*sic*] and Spanish emissary"—for, as he remarks, "in those times and that region, the two characters were not always unlike" (II, 62). Repeatedly throughout the novel, he uses Chorley to signify the Spanish menace, which he otherwise keeps in the background, and to stand for the subordinate but no less real menace that piracy posed as well. Simms emphasizes this point through crucial sequences in his plot: thus late in the novel Chorley, in an action with obvious symbolic value, tries to separate Bess from Harrison and hence to shatter the union of the important elements in the province that the marriage represents. The second villain, Chorley's confederate Ishiagaska, likewise takes out after Bess, trying to stab her during the Indian raid on Pocotaligo. Bess's lover kills Chorley, and her father stops Ishiagaska, but at these points in the book, she is obviously the beleaguered heroine that literary critics traditionally find central to romance.

Throughout his life Simms would be skillful at using his major nar-

30. For detailed comments about what is symbolized by the relationship of Harrison, Chorley, and Bess, see Michael Kreyling, *Figures of the Hero in Southern Narrative* (Baton Rouge, 1987), 42–47. See also Louise K. Barnett, *The Ignoble Savage: American Literary Racism, 1790–1890* (Westport, Conn., 1975), 67, who observes, "By the union of the white American couple at the conclusion, and by the death or defeat of the Indians and foreign whites, the frontier romance conveyed a historical truth which transcended the particulars of specific battles and wars: the ongoing possession of the North American continent by whites who had overcome the native inhabitants, and who had, by also expelling foreign whites, insisted upon a new national identity."

rative structures for effects ranging from melodrama and grotesquerie to satire and humor. His love story in *The Yemassee* is perhaps the first clear example of his ability to achieve these various effects. While emphasizing its melodrama, he also milks considerable humor from it through his portrait of the conflict between Harrison, the high-spirited hero, and Pastor John Matthews, the dour, ascetic Presbyterian minister. Harrison, a typical Cavalier, likes to revel and carouse when he is not fighting battles: he has, according to Simms, a "dashing, free, unrestrainable carriage" that offends his Puritan opponents. Matthews, by contrast, is an extreme nonconformist, "a stern, sour stickler—a good man enough, but not an overwise one," and he cannot endure the jokes and capers that are Harrison's trademarks (I, 62, 61).

Hence Matthews attacks Harrison's speech and manner, charging sharply, "You sing, sir, mirthful songs, and sometimes, though, perhaps, not so often, employ a profane oath." Harrison's rejoinder, both grave and graceful, hints at the flaws Simms sees in Puritan sobriety and incidentally helps to slant the story in favor of patrician social influence in the colony. "I admit the sometime levity—the playfulness and the thoughtlessness," he tells Matthews. "I shall undertake to reform these, when you shall satisfy me that to laugh and sing, and seek and afford amusement, are inconsistent with my duties either to the Creator or the creature. . . . That I shall never be a Puritan, however, you may be assured, if it be only to avoid giving to my face the expression of a pine bur" (II, 66–67).

Simms also mingles social commentary and humor in his portrait of another aspect of the young colony, the relationship of master and slave. Hector, the sturdy servant of Harrison and the first full-drawn black figure in Simms's long fiction, heads a long line of slaves in his novels who energetically devote themselves to their owners' interests. Loyal, affectionate, brave, and saucy, Hector strenuously involves himself with Harrison, scolding him, spying for him, fighting alongside him, caring for his huge dog Dugdale, and saving his life by forcing him to jump from a burning ship. When Harrison tries to give his slave his freedom in gratitude for this last action, the outraged black refuses in a humorous speech that Simms uses to convey his own serious sentiments about the tangible virtues of slavery.

> "I dam to hell, mossa, if I guine to be free!" roared the adhesive black, in a tone of unrestrainable determination. "I can't loss you company, and who

> de debble Dugdale will let feed him like Hector? 'Tis unpossible, mossa, and dere's no use to talk 'bout it. De ting aint right; and enty I know wha' kind of ting freedom is wid black man? Ha! you make Hector free, he come wuss more nor poor buckrah—he tief out of de shop—he get drunk and lie in de ditch—den, if sick come, he roll, he toss in de wet grass of de stable. You come in de morning, Hector dead—and, who know—he no take physic, he no hab parson—who know, I say, mossa, but de debble fine em 'fore anybody else? No, mossa—you and Dugdale berry good company for Hector." (II, 225)

Elsewhere in *The Yemassee,* Simms makes excellent use of yet other colonial social features, often giving them a realistic slant. In a book about the pioneer phase of the low country, he could not portray aristocrats in much detail, but he could depict a frequent feature of South Carolina social alignments, the union of the aristocracy and the middle class during periods of crisis. He shows this bond through portraits of various people who league with Harrison to fight the Yemassee and who are shaped to represent the early eighteenth-century pioneer class. Prominent among them are Dick Grimstead, a blunt, burly blacksmith; Wat Grayson, a scout and woodsman saddled with a sullen brother and a fatuous mother, who leads the pioneers when Harrison is absent; and Mary Granger, the wife of an Indian trader who is in some respects the superior of the pioneer men. Schooled by necessity, she is, as Simms repeatedly stresses, bold and resolute in times of danger. She figures in an arresting sequence in the novel much favored by earlier critics, wherein she keeps an Indian from entering the window of the frontier blockhouse by breaking his arm across the sill. In describing her action, Simms used the kind of graphic realistic details in which he excelled.

> Excited and nerved, she drew the extended arm of the Indian, in spite of all his struggles, directly over the sill, so as to turn the elbow completely down upon it. With her whole weight employed . . . she pressed the arm across the window until her ears heard the distinct, clear, crack of the bone. . . . The jagged splinters of the broken limb were thrust up, lacerating and tearing through flesh and skin, while a howl of the acutest agony attested the severity of that suffering which could extort such an acknowledgment from the American savage. (II, 180–81)

The Indian side, which is in many ways the more affecting side, of the novel is less standardized than is the white side because in it Simms is making a different and more poignant statement, allowing his private sympathies full sway as he indicates the tragic fate in store for the Yemassee tribe. His story of the Indians is consequently somewhat more original in design than is the narrative centering on their white opponents, as he suggested, perhaps, when he praised its "pure invention" (*L*, II, 228). In it he develops the double story of a domestic and a public or tribal tragedy, each involving the Yemassee chieftain Sanutee, the "well-beloved" of his people. The domestic tale emphasizes him, his wife Matiwan, and their son Occonestoga, who, corrupted by the whiskey of the white settlers, has betrayed his tribe and is destined for execution. The public story is, of course, the account of the white defeat of the Yemassee, to which Occonestoga's defection contributes.

Against the explicit wishes of his father, Occonestoga has joined other Indians in selling tribal lands to deputies of the white government in exchange for what Sanutee calls "painted glass" and "poison drink" (I, 94–95). In retaliation, Sanutee and other Yemassee leaders decree that the tribal emblem shall be cut from the offenders' arms, for "without this totem, no other nation could recognise them, their own resolutely refused to do it, and, at their death, the great Manneyto would reject them" from their pastoral heaven (I, 107). Spying for the English, Occonestoga is captured and brought to punishment against a background that shows Simms's command of Gothic settings—"a gloomy amphitheatre in the deep forests," surrounded by "the gnarled and stunted hickory, the ghostly cedar, and . . . the overgrown pine" (I, 208). Despite Occonestoga's pathetic pleas—"Oh! father, chief, Sanutee. . . . Save me,—father"—the ritual of exile begins. "The despair of hell was in the face of the victim"; but Matiwan tomahawks him before the emblem can be cut from his arm, thus insuring him a place in the Indian heaven (I, 216, 219, 222). At a crucial point later in the narrative, the bereaved mother, transferring her affections to Harrison, frees him from Indian captivity and hence ironically enables him to lead the war that results in the virtual extinction of her people.

Despite a fair amount of scholarly commentary, the full implications of this sequence have scarcely, it appears, been explored. Beneath the surface pageantry of the Indian ceremony, which earned Simms considerable praise among contemporary reviewers, there is an action, psychological and even mythical in significance, involving ritual severance from the patriarchal system of Indian society represented respectively by the family, the tribe, and the heavenly society of the good

Manneyto. This ritual, if successful, would have permanently sundered Occonestoga from his family and consigned him to oblivion by thrusting him into the demonic or nightmare realm that forms the dark underside of romance.

Hence in contrast to the patterns in the white narrative, whose triangle of hero, heroine, and villain derives from optimistic, affirmative literary modes, Simms here creates a more basic and more archetypal triangle of father, mother, and son that has, at least at the human level, tragic implications. For just as the action in the white narrative signifies the overcoming of obstacles to the young colony posed by Spain on the one hand and internal political and social strife on the other, so the action in the Indian story, in which Matiwan saves her son for the other world only at the price of tragic rupture in this one, communicates the deep division in that most fundamental of all social units, the family, occasioned by corrupting contacts with whites, including well-meaning whites like Harrison. And because the influences to which Occonestoga is subject infect other chieftains who participate in the land sale, the story of Occonestoga is in part the story of the fall of the Yemassee through their innocent involvement with their white usurpers. The entire episode, originating in family conflict but broadening to include the tribe, its future, and by extension the future of the Indian race, illustrates Hugh Holman's statement that the Indian side of the narrative displays "both the realistic view and the tragic knowledge of Simms." It also illustrates what Northrop Frye means when he says that the romancer creates "stylized figures which expand into psychological archetypes" and that "a suggestion of allegory is constantly creeping in" at the fringes of a romance narrative.[31] The allegorical suggestions of *The Yemassee* appear not only in the traditional outlines of the love story but also, and more movingly, in the narrative of Sanutee, Matiwan, and Occonestoga—through which is prefigured the doom of the Yemassee people.

At the end of the book, Simms portrays the winding down of the historical conflict, which from his perspective admits of no wholly satisfactory resolution. He sketches, rapidly and in the main accurately, the progress of the battle near Pocotaligo, maintaining to the last his sympathy for the "wild warriors of Yemassee, striking the last blow for

31. Holman, Introduction to Simms, *The Yemassee,* xviii; Frye, *Anatomy of Criticism,* 304.

the glory and the existence of their once mighty nation" (II, 239).[32] In a fortunate stroke that results in one of the best conclusions to any of his books, he depicts the end of the battle through Matiwan's eyes, using her and Harrison as representatives of their respective peoples in order to stress both the pathos and the hopelessness of the Indian effort. Sanutee is fatally wounded in the battle—an action that symbolizes the termination of the Yemassee cause. As he dies, Matiwan throws herself upon his body; Harrison approaches; she utters the traditional Yemassee lament; and Simms suggests that the only conceivable compensation for this tragic situation lies beyond the human sphere.

> "Matiwan," said the palatine, stooping to raise her from the body—"Matiwan, it is the chief?"
>
> "Ah-cheray-me, ah-cheray-me, Sanutee—Ah-cheray-me, ah-cheray-me, Yemassee!"
>
> She was unconscious of all things, as they bore her tenderly away, save that the Yemassee was no longer the great nation. She only felt that the "well-beloved," as well of herself as of her people, looked forth, with Occonestoga, wondering that she came not, from the Blessed Valley of the Good Manneyto. (II, 242)

With all its force, *The Yemassee* exhibits flaws in structure that would continue to characterize Simms's fiction. For one thing, the framing action, which centers on the battle at Pocotaligo, is too narrow for his full communication of his theme—as his framing action for the Revolutionary War Romances, centering on the war in South Carolina, would prove to be too narrow for a full picture of the southern phase of the strife. For another, his handling of the several story lines is awkward, and as is often the case in his fiction, there is finally too much narrative material for the novel to carry. Despite his ingenious treatment of romance patterns, readers nourished on realism will probably continue to feel that his Indians, together with his middle-class pioneers, are more appealing than characters such as Chorley, Harrison, and Bess, who are necessarily conceived in accordance with literary convention.

Yet the novel has remained in the public gaze longer than other

32. In view of such comments, which are scattered throughout the book, it is inaccurate to claim, as does Bette S. Weidman in "White Men's Red Man: A Penitential Reading of Four American Novels," *Modern Language Studies,* IV (Fall, 1974), 20, that in *The Yemassee* "there is none of the sense of loss and waste that overpowers white victory in *The Last of the Mohicans.*"

Simms works because it speaks to a situation that continues to trouble the historical consciousness of educated readers. In Holman's words, "The particular events of *The Yemassee* are peculiar to the Carolina coast in 1715; the pattern of these events was to be repeated again and again in the history of the westward expanding nation."[33] The book's two narrative strands, which reflect elements from different literary traditions, also reflect Simms's complex and divided attitude toward his subject. His public confidence and hence his most traditional structures support his white characters and the future they represent for South Carolina while his private sympathy, which gives rise to the originality and vitality of the Indian sequences, imbues his treatment of the Yemassee. In the novel, the verdict of history, the force of the framing action, the statement communicated through the love story, and the weight of established romance conventions all operate on the white side of the narrative. But Simms's underlying sense of the injustice done the Indians and the tragedy inherent in their defeat, as typified by the lives and deaths of Occonestoga and Sanutee, helps to move the reader's emotions toward the Indian side of the story. His compassion for the Indians, his determination to depict them fairly, and his moving portrayal of their plight do much to explain why *The Yemassee,* though it is not his best book, remains perhaps his most enduring one.

33. Holman, Introduction to Simms, *The Yemassee,* xviii.

3

That Unyielding Patriotism: The Early Revolutionary War Romances

By the time *The Yemassee* appeared in April, 1835, Simms was already planning *The Partisan,* and he was also preparing to court the woman who would become, in 1836, his second wife. Chevillette Eliza Roach was the daughter of Nathaniel, or Nash, Roach, a wealthy landowner in Barnfield District, an area that stretches along the southern border of inland South Carolina. The family owned twin plantations, Woodlands and Oak Grove, near Bamberg, South Carolina, in addition to a townhouse in Charleston. The Roaches, who had strong British ties, were a family of some distinction: their relative by marriage, Colonel John Chevillette, had fought under Frederick the Great of Prussia, and other ancestors had battled on the partisan side during the Revolutionary War.[1]

The match with Chevillette was a fortunate one for Simms, as it strengthened his ties to the planter class he would repeatedly portray in fiction and helped solidify the political base he would shortly begin to build. But in fairness to him it should be stressed, as his granddaughter remarked, that at thirty he was something of a catch for Chevillette. Tall and striking, with keen blue-gray eyes and a commanding manner, he could claim some renown in the cosmopolitan literary world to which she was as yet a stranger, and after the sound financial success of his early novels he could look forward, or so it must have then seemed, to prosperity and fame as an author. Nearly twelve years younger and by nature more reserved than he, Chevillette at first regarded him with mingled awe and affection, though she

1. Letter from Mary C. Simms Oliphant to author, June 19, 1976; Salley, "William Gilmore Simms," in *L,* I, lxxvii; [Oliphant, Odell, and Eaves], "The Family Circle," in *L,* I, cxlviii–cxlix; *L,* I, 96*n*49; Trent, *William Gilmore Simms,* [96]–102; annotations to William Gilmore Simms, *The Forayers,* in *The Revolutionary War Novels of William Gilmore Simms,* VI, 587*n*264.30.

would later come to assume considerable status in her own right as well as substantial influence over him. Their marriage was a felicitous union of temperaments, with her calm elegance a happy foil to his uproarious and untrammeled social behavior.[2] None of his letters to her have survived, but his comments about her in his existing correspondence give a winning picture of her personality.

"Sympathize with me, *mon ami*," he wrote Lawson, for instance, after Chevillette had accepted his proposal,

> I have been wooing—I have wooed and—have won. The Lady has smiled, and as much, perhaps, to rid herself of my importunacy as any thing else, has said 'Yes'. She sits at a little distance from me now—a dark eyed, dark haired, sad looking little creature, whose fingers are even now describing a hundred semi-circles in a minute as she whipstitches one of those most mortal frights in the domestic economy, good on winter nights, which ancient huswifes designate a quilt! . . . Sometimes, she looks up at me as I write, as if to ask 'are you talking about me in that letter[']; and now and then she hums the catch of some pleasant love ditty, as if desiring to call my attention from the scrawl before me to the more pleasant contemplation of myself in her. She is the chosen, and she has told me that she loves me, and I have been fond & foolish enough to believe, implicitly and credulously, the sweet assurance. (*L*, I, 83–84)

With the prospect of marriage before him and some debts incurred from the *City Gazette* to pay off, Simms had abundant reasons to move ahead with his Revolutionary War series. It had been gestating since the 1820s, as poems and tales of that decade, particularly "Moonshine," suggest. In the country at large, interest in the Revolution had been running high for at least ten years, fanned by the fiftieth anniversary of the war in 1826 and the flow of historical novels that accompanied it. These works range from James Fenimore Cooper's *The Spy* (1821) and *Lionel Lincoln* (1825) to John Neal's *Seventy-Six* (1826) and John Pendleton Kennedy's *Horse Shoe Robinson* (1835), published the same year as Simms's *Partisan*. When beginning his series, Simms may have hoped to do for the South what Cooper and others had done for the North: some remarks he made at the time he wrote *The Partisan* indicate that he originally planned to treat aspects of the war in several southern states. Such, at any rate, appears to be the import of his comments in the advertisement to the first edition.

2. Conversation of Mary C. Simms Oliphant and author, August 17, 1972; [Oliphant, Odell, and Eaves], "The Family Circle," in *L*, I, cxlviii; conversation of Oliphant and author, August 17, 1972.

> The work was originally contemplated as one of a series, to be devoted to our War of Independence. With this object, I laid the foundation more broadly and deeply than I should have done had I purposed merely the single work. Several of the persons employed were destined to be the property of the series;—that part of it, at least, which belonged to the locality. Three of these works were to have been devoted to South Carolina, and to comprise three distinct periods of the war of the Revolution in that state. One, and the first of these, is the story now submitted to the reader.[3]

But the financial recession of 1837 and Simms's resulting decision to abandon long fiction for nearly a decade affected the development of the Revolutionary War set, causing him to split the books, so to speak, into two groups—*The Partisan, Mellichampe,* and *The Kinsmen* (later retitled *The Scout*), all appearing before 1842; and *Katharine Walton, The Sword and the Distaff* (later retitled *Woodcraft*), *The Forayers,* and *Eutaw,* issued between 1851 and 1856. After the Civil War, he serialized in a northern periodical a final novel about the conflict, *Joscelyn,* which is set for the most part in the South Carolina backcountry during 1775 and bears little resemblance to the other Revolutionary War volumes.[4] The fact that he composed the novels during a period of more than twenty years is reflected in his literary procedures, which mirror some changing fashions in the fiction of the time. His first three volumes exhibit the most orthodox romance patterns in his fiction, while their secondary narratives, which are generally stories of revenge, display the mingled Gothic and grotesque material that is prominent in all his novels of the early phase. By the time he wrote the second set of volumes, however, he was somewhat more flexible in his handling of romance procedures, and he was also heavily influenced by his extensive reading near midcentury in backwoods humor and the novel of manners. Hence although he continued to use

3. "Advertisement," in [William Gilmore Simms], *The Partisan: A Tale of the Revolution* (New York, 1835), I, viii–ix. Unless otherwise indicated, further references to this volume are to this edition, cited by volume and page number within the text (as *P* where necessary for clarity). There is some discrepancy between this statement and the remarks in the introduction Simms wrote for *The Partisan: A Romance of the Revolution* (Rev. ed.; New York, 1854); but such discrepancies are common in a writer of Simms's large ambitions and shifting plans.

4. [William Gilmore Simms], *Joscelyn; A Tale of the Revolution,* with Introduction and Explanatory Notes by Stephen E. Meats, text established by Keen Butterworth (Columbia, S.C., 1975), vol. XVI of John C. Guilds (ed.), *The Writings of William Gilmore Simms: Centennial Edition.* The novel was also issued in the annotated edition of *The Revolutionary War Novels of William Gilmore Simms.* It had been serialized in the *Old Guard* during 1867.

the conventions of romance for the main plots in the second set of volumes, he varied such patterns freely and inventively with satiric portraits of fashionable manners and lively depictions of amusing rural types.

Military action in the Carolina colony from 1780 to 1782 forms the broad framing action for the seven main volumes in the set, enabling Simms to portray most of the important events between the fall of Charleston in May, 1780, and its evacuation by the enemy late in 1782. After the capital city fell, the British, who were centered there, controlled the province through two great rings of forts—an outer one extending from Georgetown through Camden, Ninety-Six, and Augusta, Georgia, and an inner one running through Fort Watson and Fort Motte near Santee and Fort Granby near Columbia to Orangeburg in the south-central part of the state. Nathaniel Greene, who had replaced Horatio Gates in the fall of 1780 as the commander of the southern Continental army, worked to force the British from these bases into Charleston, using Continental troops for major battles and militia to attack the enemy's fringes. In a series of engagements ranging from Cowpens and Guilford Court House to Hobkirk's Hill and Eutaw Springs, Greene and his soldiers relentlessly pursued the troops of Charles Cornwallis or his chief subordinates, Francis, Lord Rawdon and Banastre Tarleton, until the enemy was finally forced to withdraw to the coast and then, as Simms says, into departing vessels (*P*, I, 35).[5]

Simms describes the action at Cowpens and Hobkirk's Hill in lengthy passages of historical commentary, and he centers his books on such battles in South Carolina as Ninety-Six and Eutaw Springs, which represented major phases of Greene's activity in the province. In *The Partisan* (1835), he treats the disastrous patriot losses to the British at Charleston and Camden, while throughout both that novel and *Mellichampe* (1836) he portrays the gradual growth of partisan strength in the coastal region under the leadership of Francis Marion and his militia troops. In *The Kinsmen* (1841), he depicts the war in the upcountry, describing Greene's siege of Ninety-Six and Rawdon's resulting movement of troops toward Orangeburg in what proved to

5. Don Higginbotham, *The War of American Independence: Military Attitudes, Policies, and Practice, 1763–1789* (New York, 1971), Chap. 14; John Richard Alden, *The South in the Revolution, 1763–1789* (Baton Rouge, 1957), Chap. 14, vol. III of Wendell Holmes Stephenson and E. Merton Coulter (eds.), *A History of the South*, 10 vols.; Holman, *The Immoderate Past*, 24–29.

be an early stage of the British withdrawal toward the coast. *Katharine Walton* (1851), set in occupied Charleston and describing the social hostilities of Loyalists and partisans within it, implies that British power in the colony is on the wane; *The Forayers* (1855) and its sequel *Eutaw* (1856) treat events leading up to the clash at Eutaw Springs and the battle itself, which as he observes broke British power in the colony; and *The Sword and the Distaff* (1852), fifth in order of publication but chronologically last in the series, describes the evacuation of the British from Charleston and the slow rebuilding of shattered low-country plantations.

Simms's decision to use the Revolution in South Carolina as the framing action for the series was a natural choice for one as absorbed in the history of the low country as he was, but it involved him in problems that would not have developed had he followed his original plan of depicting the course of the war in several southern states. The nature of the strife in the colony, where Greene's battles were victories of attrition rather than outright triumphs, did not furnish an objective correlative of sufficient magnitude for his frequent celebrations of southern valor.[6] Moreover, his restriction of the action to events in South Carolina prevented him from showing the final American victory at Yorktown and hence from bringing the series to a definite conclusion. But he overcame these drawbacks, at least in part, by stirring and graphic descriptions of the military action and also by the ardor with which he portrayed "that deliberate valour, that unyielding patriotism, which . . . defying danger and above the sense of privation, could keep alive the sacred fires of liberty in the thick swamps and dense and gloomy forests of Carolina—asking nothing, yielding nothing, and only leaving the field the better to re-enter it for the combat" (*P*, I, 17).

The passionate commitment to the Revolutionary cause conveyed through such statements points to some reasons why, of all Simms's novels, the Revolutionary War Romances conform most closely to the conventions of popular romance. In these volumes, his dedication to the war in South Carolina issues in what are perhaps the keenest moral contrasts and the sharpest dialectic of his fiction, and it also issues in

6. George W. Kyte, "Victory in the South: An Appraisal of General Greene's Strategy in the Carolinas," *North Carolina Historical Review*, XXXVII (July, 1960), 321–47; Robert C. Pugh, "The Revolutionary Militia in the Southern Campaign, 1780–1781," *William and Mary Quarterly*, 3rd ser., XIV (April, 1957), [154]–75.

the generic love plots to which the strife imparts a clear symbolic aspect. His tendency to write romance, which was nourished by the Singleton strain in his background, was encouraged by the kind of providential interpretation of history that was common in nineteenth-century America. It was also encouraged by his upbringing in the low country, in his time still redolent of Revolutionary War glory; by his grandmother's tales of the war, which were laced with partisan prejudice; and by his absorption in anecdotes, reminiscences, and other kinds of oral history similarly slanted in favor of the patriots. Simms's personal and cultural inheritance, it can hardly be stressed too strongly, predisposed him, as it were, to construct romances. Cultural traditions resembling romance formulations were the dominant means through which he learned about the past, as they were to underlie the dominant methods by which he would portray it.

*

To a degree that is hard to imagine today, memories of the war pervaded the low-country culture in which Simms grew up: they formed part of the intellectual climate of his youth. Charleston in particular teemed with pride over its role in the conflict—a pride sustained by numerous monuments and battle sites. In its harbor, within his lifetime to witness the firing on Fort Sumter, were places of Revolutionary fame—Fort Johnson on James Island, where according to tradition the patriot William Moultrie had planted the first flag of South Carolina liberty in 1775, and Sullivan's Island, with its fort rechristened in Moultrie's honor after his troops beat back Sir Peter Parker's fleet in 1776. Standing in the city were dwellings of important colonial figures, like the splendid Miles Brewton mansion on King Street that Sir Henry Clinton and Francis, Lord Rawdon had occupied as well as the houses of South Carolina governor John Rutledge and historian David Ramsay on Broad Street. And visible toward the northern part of the city were remains of the fortifications thrown up by soldiers defending the town.

Near Charleston were other sites memorialized in wartime annals—Dorchester with its crumbling Revolutionary fortress, where Simms said he had frequently rambled (*P*, I, [vi]); Biggin (or Biggen) Church, where Francis Marion and Light-Horse Harry Lee ripped into Colonel John Coates's forces; and Quinby Bridge, where Coates's men finally defeated the patriots. Somewhat farther afield but still accessible from Charleston were Camden, where the American general Horatio

Gates was routed and Charles Cornwallis temporarily headquartered; Orangeburg, where Rawdon's army paused on its retreat from the up-country fort at Ninety-Six; and Eutaw Springs, where American and British forces met in the bloody clash that would be the last major battle in the colony. Simms, who throughout his life tried to see for himself the places he described in his writing, toured and studied these and similar localities that loom large in his novels about the Revolution. His early impressions of this first great American conflict were formed by his awareness of such places and the deeds of patriot valor they forcefully recalled.

Among the intimate influences affecting Simms's sympathies were the tales of his grandmother Mrs. Gates, who had lived through the war and was naturally biased in favor of the partisan cause. It was almost surely this spirited old woman, with her flood of recollections and her still-surging patriotism, who first stirred his interest in the Revolutionary period and sparked his own fervent patriotism: as his friend Paul Hamilton Hayne said, she was "loaded to the very muzzle of her mind with anecdotes, narratives, and social gossip, particularly touching the war with England and the various episodes, tragical and humorous, associated with the British invasion of the Carolinas." She had played, remarks Simms in an essay, a minor but exciting role during the conflict. In order to join her husband John Singleton, who was fighting in Charleston, she and her infant daughter had descended the Cooper River in a rowboat, passing at midnight, Simms says, amid "a fearful cannonade, through the thronging barges of the British," and she told Simms this story along with many other thrilling tales of the war. In his letters and other writing, he gave his grandmother abundant credit for inspiring his interest in the conflict. She was, he declares in an autobiographical passage in his fiction, "an old lady who had been a resident of the seat of most frequent war in Carolina during the Revolution. She had fortunately survived the numberless atrocities which she was yet compelled to witness; and, a keen observer, with a strong memory, she had in store a thousand legends of that stirring period, which served to beguile me from sleep many and many a long winter night."[7] Several of these legends described the exploits of

7. Paul Hamilton Hayne, "Ante-Bellum Charleston," *Southern Bivouac,* n.s., I (October, 1885), 261; [William Gilmore Simms], "Ellet's Women of the Revolution," *Southern Quarterly Review,* XVII [n.s., I] (July, 1850), 353 (identified as Simms's in *L,* III, 55*n*169), and *The Wigwam and the Cabin,* 1st ser. (New York, 1845), 2.

Simms's great-grandfather Thomas Singleton, his grandfather John Singleton, and other of his ancestors who played prominent roles in the war.

Helping to reinforce Simms's bias in favor of the patriots were tales by survivors of the war whom, according to his granddaughter, Simms began to seek out and interview when he was about thirteen. In preparation for *The Partisan,* for instance, he talked with men who had served under Francis Marion, and for *Katharine Walton* he took notes from an alleged eyewitness on the story of planter Isaac Hayne's execution.[8] He incorporated humorous oral traditions about the partisan historian David Ramsay into the latter volume, and for the former one he drew, as he said, on local tradition for his description of the Frampton family.[9] Before writing his other novels, he scrutinized the records of individual localities in the conflict, interviewed their inhabitants, contacted friends of Revolutionary soldiers, and carefully surveyed battle sites. Recalling what he knew with some feeling, and speaking of himself in the third person, he said that he had learned

> his lessons at the knees of those who were young spectators in the grand panorama of our Revolution. . . . There was scarcely a personage, British or American, Whig or Loyalist—scarcely an event, mournful or glorious—scarcely a deed, grand or savage—occurring in the history of the low country of South-Carolina, which has not been conned, for his benefit, at the writer's fireside, by venerable friends and loving kinswomen, now voiceless in the dust. . . . [The Revolution] was made life-like to his imagination by personal histories, which appealed to his nearest affections and fondest sympathies.[10]

Buttressing these personal and traditional records of the conflict were the volumes of formal history that Simms used for his fictional treatment of the Revolutionary War. In his library or otherwise available to him were major works about the Revolution by both British and American authors; he knew, according to students of the subject, virtually all of the best authorities then available. His sources can

8. Letters from Mary C. Simms Oliphant to author, February 17, 1973, June 19, 1976, July 4, 1976; Trent, *William Gilmore Simms,* 106; annotations to William Gilmore Simms, *Katharine Walton,* in *The Revolutionary War Novels of William Gilmore Simms,* IV, 521–22*n*469.20.

9. See *KW,* 231, 245–47; *P,* I, ix.

10. [Simms], "Ellet's Women of the Revolution," 351–52.

be reconstructed with certainty from the list he provided at the beginning of his *Life of Francis Marion,* in which he cites works by David Ramsay, Henry Lee, William Moultrie, John Drayton, William Johnson, William Dobein James, and Alexander Garden; he also consulted such British chroniclers of the conflict as Roderick MacKenzie and Banastre Tarleton.[11]

The books of the patriot writers on this list could only have strengthened Simms's inclination to write romances. For almost to a man, these historians with their highly partisan prejudices cast history in the typical patterns of the literary genre. They use a dialectic structure, a providential interpretation, a set of moral antitheses, and a slanted presentation wherein they miss few chances to revile the British or Loyalist foe and glorify patriots. They intermingle sparse praise of the enemy with liberal damnation: Loyalists are "monsters in the human form"; Britons are barbarians who, "without scruple or remorse," in persecuting Whigs abandoned "humanity, honor, justice and every ennobling sentiment." Patriots, predictably, have "ermin" characters that "nothing selfish, nothing mercenary" soils: Nathaniel Greene, for example, is "benign in heart, and happy in manners," "respected for his sincerity, prized for his disinterestedness, and valued for his wisdom."[12] Patriot writers sometimes point to a providential movement in Revolutionary history that resembles the similar movement reflected in romance: Henry Lee, for example, whom Simms frequently quotes, maintains that to "an attentive observer of the events during our war very many strong exemplifications of providential succor occur."[13] These volumes are, in short, so biased in favor of the partisans that after reading them one wonders how Simms managed to be as kind as

11. C. Hugh Holman, "William Gilmore Simms's Picture of the Revolution as a Civil War," in *The Roots of Southern Writing,* 36; W[illiam] Gilmore Simms, *The Life of Francis Marion* (New York, 1844), [vi].

12. William Johnson, *Sketches of the Life and Correspondence of Nathanael [sic] Greene, Major General of the Armies of the United States, In the War of the Revolution* (Charleston, S.C., 1822), extra-illustrated copy, Vol. I, Pt. 2, p. 289; William Moultrie, quoting from the address of the South Carolina House of Representatives, *Memoirs of the American Revolution, So Far as It Related to the States of North and South Carolina, and Georgia* (New York, 1802), II, 317; Henry Lee, *Memoirs of the War in the Southern Department of the United States* (Philadelphia, 1812), I, 164, 245, 227.

13. Lee, *Memoirs of the War,* I, 272. For similar claims, see Moultrie, *Memoirs of the American Revolution,* II, 314, and David Ramsay, *The History of South-Carolina, From Its First Settlement in 1670, To the Year 1808* (Charleston, S.C., 1809), I, 376.

he was to the enemy; in them, as a scholar early in this century said, "all virtue and grand ideals" are on the American side, "all vice, wickedness, effeteness, and degeneration" on that of the British.[14]

Simms's description of the central figures at the historical level of his Revolutionary War volumes repeats the prejudices that he had imbibed from the oral and written history of his era while furnishing the basis for the deliberate pairing of opposites that is so marked a feature of his dialectic scheme.[15] Using the conventions of patriot history, in which Marion, Greene, and other American officers are usually shown as paragons while Cornwallis, Rawdon, and other British leaders are almost universally damned, on page after page he weaves his historical commentary into his literary pattern. Selecting Marion and Greene as the chief patriot leaders in the series, he employs them to represent the best elements in militia and Continental forces respectively. Marion, with his "patriotism, wisdom, and fearlessness," constitutes what is perhaps the loftiest historical ideal in all his fiction—a great hero who is also an unpretentious man of the people bridging the gap between aristocrat and commoner in much the same manner as Gabriel Harrison in *The Yemassee* (*P*, II, 157). Greene, correspondingly, is a "[c]ool, prudent and resolute" leader, "one of the best that could be chosen" for directing the southern campaign. His "fine manly face," Simms says in direct indication of his dialectic base, "wore none of

14. Sydney G. Fisher, "The Legendary and Myth-making Process in Histories of the American Revolution," *Proceedings of the American Philosophical Society*, LI (April–June, 1912), 56.

15. Simms made no effort to disguise his reliance on his sources. In the advertisement to the 1835 *Partisan* he remarked, for instance, that when writing the volume he had "the various and very copious histories of the time" open before him—a statement borne out by the evidence of his borrowings in this and other books (I, ix). For the sections in *The Partisan* (II, Chaps. 19–23) that treat the battle of Camden, he relied on the work of Lee and of Otho Williams (*A Narrative of the Campaign of 1780*, included as Appendix B in Vol. I, Pt. 2, of William Johnson's *Sketches of the Life and Correspondence of Nathanael Greene*), and he also leaned heavily on Johnson's volumes for portions of *The Kinsmen*. He used Moultrie, *Memoirs of the American Revolution*, for important sections of *Woodcraft* (Chap. 7), and he drew liberally on David Ramsay's writing for portions of *Katharine Walton* (Chaps. 24–25). Throughout the entire series, and particularly in *Katharine Walton*, he used episodes from social history that have sources or analogues in Alexander Garden's *Anecdotes of the Revolutionary War in America. . . .* 1st ser. (Charleston, S.C., 1822) or in Elizabeth F. Ellet, *The Women of the American Revolution* (New York, 1848). Simms was, in sum, drenched in the history of the war in South Carolina, as he frequently acknowledged and as page after page of his writing reveals.

that dark disquietude and sullen ferocity . . . which scowled in the whole visage of his able opponent, Rawdon."[16]

In an even more extended contrast, Simms compares patriot Walter Griffin, who appears in *The Partisan* and *Katharine Walton,* with the notorious Loyalist Amos Gaskens. "Griffin was an industrious farmer," he remarks pointedly; "Gaskens the overseer for the Postell estate. Griffin was a sober, quiet man, who had been long married, and found his chief enjoyment in the bosom of his family. Gaskens loved the race-turf and the cockpit, and his soul was full of their associations. It is the instinct of vice to hate the form of virtue," he concludes with allegorizing flourish; "Griffin partook of none of those pleasures which were all-in-all to Gaskens, and the other hated him accordingly" (*P,* II, 131–32).[17]

Established at the historical level, such contrasts are continued in the fictional narratives of the volumes by a system of character pairing branching out from the love plots, whereby Simms makes particularly apposite use of social conditions in the colony. Northrop Frye remarks that characterization in romance "follows its general dialectic structure, which means that subtlety and complexity are not much favored. . . . Hence every typical character in romance tends to have his moral opposite confronting him, like black and white pieces in a chess game." Reflecting the procedures of his genre, Simms uses the convention of horizontal pairing to contrast figures from roughly similar social levels who have different political persuasions—the rival innkeepers Old Prior and Old Humphries in *The Partisan,* for instance, or heroine Flora Middleton and coquette Rose Duncan in *Mellichampe.* He uses the convention of vertical pairing to highlight the friendship of hero or villain with a rustic follower, usually a scout—a pattern found in the association of Ernest Mellichampe with Thumbscrew Witherspoon in *Mellichampe,* of Clarence Conway with Jack Bannister and of Ned Conway with Watson Gray in *The Kinsmen,* and of Robert Singleton

16. [William Gilmore Simms], *The Kinsmen: Or The Black Riders of Congaree. A Tale* (Philadelphia, 1841), I, 14, II, 78. Unless otherwise indicated, all further references to this volume are to this edition, cited within the text (as *K* where necessary for clarity).

17. According to the annotations to William Gilmore Simms, *The Partisan,* in *The Revolutionary War Novels of William Gilmore Simms,* II, 557*n*370.23, Gaskens was known before the war as a thief and trickster. The Postells were ancestors of Simms's first wife, Anna Malcolm Giles (letter from Mary C. Simms Oliphant to author, February 17, 1973).

with Bill Humphries in *The Partisan*. In terms of cultural reference, such groupings represent the union of the aristocracy and the middle class behind the partisan movement or the league of lower-class Loyalists with the British against it. In terms of literary convention, the hero-scout relationship in particular repeats an ancient configuration in the genre of the hero and his trusted companion.[18] However they are finally viewed, these and similar character configurations are a standard component of historical romance that appears in other novels of the period ranging from Cooper's *The Pioneers* and *The Prairie* to Kennedy's *Horse Shoe Robinson*.

If his oral and written sources with their definite bias toward patriotism reinforced Simms's tendency to create romances, they also provided him with the kind of detailed and accurate information about the war in South Carolina that he uses to buttress the realism of the framing action and the fictional narratives in his books. He knew, for example, that the conflict had been won largely through the efforts of militia leaders like Francis Marion and Thomas Sumter, who had helped Nathaniel Greene and other officers of the southern Continental army learn the guerrilla techniques necessary for fighting on southern terrain. He knew also that the struggle in the province was in part a civil war based on social disaffection stemming from the hierarchical class system which was rooted in the geographical conditions of the colony. Rice and indigo planters had settled in the fertile low country, which was suited to the development of large plantations; together with the region's small but substantial middle class comprised of traders and farmers, they tended to support the war. But the Scotch-Irish, Germans, and Swiss who had settled the backcountry resented the authority of the patrician planters and tended to oppose the war as a way of opposing the privileged inhabitants of the low country.[19]

Hence, with South Carolina history validating him, Simms stresses through his main narratives that the war in the low country was spearheaded by aristocrats from Charleston and the plantations, backed by woodsmen and other members of the rural middle class who taught

18. Frye, *Anatomy of Criticism*, 195, 196.

19. Pugh, "The Revolutionary Militia in the Southern Campaign," 174; Stoney, "The Country and the People," in *Plantations of the Carolina Low Country*, 22; Francis Butler Simkins, *A History of the South* (3rd ed.; New York, 1963), Chap. 9; Holman, "Simms's Picture of the Revolution as a Civil War," in *The Roots of Southern Writing*, 45–48.

Greene and his officers in the Continental army valuable combat techniques. At the same time, he acknowledges the civil-war aspect of the struggle by occasionally making the villain who opposes the aristocrats a Loyalist thirsty for land and political power. He uses such a situation in the main plot of *Mellichampe,* wherein the plantation patriots Janet Berkeley and Ernest Mellichampe battle Barsfield, a Tory from the lower class who wants to kill Ernest, marry Janet, and possess the ancestral Berkeley lands. He refines the situation in *The Kinsmen,* a novel set in the South Carolina upcountry, where the strife between Whigs and Tories was particularly strong. In reflection of that fact, in Simms's plot patriot officer Clarence Conway and his sweetheart Flora Middleton fend off Clarence's murderous half-brother Ned, who heads a vicious Loyalist troop. It is worth remarking that such plots, though stylized, have a definite symbolic design. As Moffitt Cecil remarks in his study of *The Kinsmen,* for the fable of the novel Simms employs a complicated series of representative actions "to emphasize the fratricidal aspects of the war and to personalize the historical record."[20]

Simms also uses the central characters in his fictional narratives as vehicles for his detailed knowledge of late colonial social conditions. Distinguishing among these figures by geographical region and ethnic strain, he gives them names that are common to particular South Carolina locales while making their plantation homes convey qualities representing the agriculture and landscape architecture of a given section. Katharine Walton, for instance, is the heiress to a rice plantation on the Ashley River, an area noted for its production of the chief colonial crop. Her lover Robert Singleton comes from an estate in the interior near the High Hills of Santee, a region where (as Simms stresses) corn and similar grains are grown. Ernest Mellichampe and Janet Berkeley, who bear familiar low-country surnames, are from inland estates apparently near the pine belt, as the name of Janet's home, Piney Grove, suggests. In *The Forayers* and *Eutaw,* Willie Sinclair's father (styled "Baron" in reflection of the titles created by the Fundamental Constitutions) owns an indigo plantation in the Santee River area, where the name "Sinclair" and its variant "Sinkler" are common, and Willie's friend Peyre St. Julien, with his proud French patronymic, rep-

20. L. Moffitt Cecil, "The Design of William Gilmore Simms's *The Kinsmen,*" *Mississippi Quarterly,* XXIX (Fall, 1976), 521.

resents the Huguenot strain in Carolina character that gave color to the early history of the province.[21]

Enemy figures in Simms's Revolutionary War fiction likewise point to strands in South Carolina political and social history. The villain Barsfield in *Mellichampe,* for instance, who is modeled on the infamous Loyalist Thomas Browne, stands for the many Tories who craved revenge for mistreatment by the Whigs. Andrew Williamson in *Katharine Walton,* an upcountry farmer who starts out as a patriot, turns Tory, and then apparently turns patriot again, represents the hordes of people who shifted allegiance as royal power waxed and waned. Major John Marjoribanks and Lord Edward Fitzgerald, two British officers in *Eutaw,* symbolize noble strains in enemy character, with Fitzgerald additionally representing the Irishmen who swelled British ranks late in the war. Serving both cultural and literary requirements, such figures, whether on the patriot or the enemy side, indicate the great range of reference in Simms's fiction and reveal his efforts at authenticity in art.

*

The generic features of Simms's literary pattern stand forth prominently in the Revolutionary War novels of the early period, *The Partisan, Mellichampe,* and *The Kinsmen.* The first two of these novels were published within a year of each other, when Simms was eagerly making capital of the fame he had won from his previous books. *The Yemassee* was barely off the press in April, 1835, when he, in May, started on *The Partisan.* He wrote Lawson on May 28 that he had sent five chapters of the work to Harper Brothers; by mid-June he had sent about a dozen; and the book was issued in two volumes during November (*L,* I, 68, 70, 74). Saddled with debts that were holding up his marriage, he followed the fortunes of the novel with an anxious eye, complaining that his income was precarious and insisting, "If the 'Partisan' has failed, it will throw me back greatly, and I seriously meditate, in that event, retiring from the field (*L,* I, 80).[22] Reviews were mixed but generally laudatory (one reviewer called the book a "perfect picture of the early revolutionary times in South Carolina"); the work sold well; and Simms moved on to *Mellichampe.*[23] "I have been busy

21. See the annotations to Simms, *The Forayers,* in *The Revolutionary War Novels of William Gilmore Simms,* VI, 571*n*14.39.

22. Simms makes similar remarks in *P,* I, ix.

23. Review of *The Partisan, Southern Literary Journal,* I (January, 1836), 347.

upon a sequel to 'The Partisan,'" he wrote Lawson in January, 1836; "I have written some hundred pages or more & have forwarded two chapters to the Harpers." The novel was issued in October; Simms was married in November; and he and Chevillette were off to the South Carolina countryside for a honeymoon (*L,* I, 80, 97, 100*n*8).

In *The Partisan,* an energetic, appealing volume, Simms traces the early stages in the British occupation of the colony. Through the framing action he weaves several strands from South Carolina military and social history, including the fall of Charleston to the British in May, 1780, and Horatio Gates's disastrous loss to Cornwallis at Camden in August of that year. The defeat at Camden, which occupies roughly the last quarter of the book, allows Simms, in the service of his romance dialectic, to criticize the vindictiveness of Cornwallis and the ineptitude of Gates while comparing both officers unfavorably with Francis Marion.

Woven through the framing action is another strand from history, involving Richard Walton, the fictional surrogate of Isaac Hayne, a prominent low-country planter who after Charleston's fall took a pledge of neutrality and who, when the parole was revoked, joined the patriots, was captured by the British, and was executed. While Simms uses the Hayne material as an element in his major fictional plot, his real concern, and consequently his chief emphasis in the novel, is the rapid growth of patriot resistance and militia strength after the fall of Charleston. He makes this point in scene after scene of the military action, and he reinforces it through two love stories that reflect, in much the same manner as *The Yemassee,* the alignment of the aristocracy and the middle class in the colony during periods of crisis.

In both of the love narratives in *The Partisan,* Simms stresses the conversion of previously irresolute people to the patriot cause under the sensible tutelage of the hero Robert Singleton, a character bearing the name of Simms's maternal forebears who had fought in the war. The main story, involving plantation aristocrats, centers on Singleton's relationship with his uncle Richard Walton and his cousin Katharine, who are literary descendants of the characters of the same patronymic in "Moonshine." Appropriately for Simms's emphasis on the strong patrician element in the conflict, major scenes in this narrative take place at the Walton plantation the Oaks, which, like other estates in Simms's low-country fiction, is an integral part of the pastoral background from which his major fictional narratives usually spring. It also furnishes an excellent example of the symbolic value he attaches to the plantation, whose role in the continuity of aristocratic standards is made clear through his first description.

> "The Oaks," the dwelling-place of Colonel Walton, was one of those old-time residences of the Carolina planters to which, at this day, there attaches a sort of human interest. A thousand local traditions hang around them—a thousand stories of the olden time, and of its associations of peril and adventure. The estate formed one of the frontier-plantations upon the Ashley, and was the site of a colonial barony. It had stood sieges of the Indians in the wars of the Edistoes and Yemassees; and, from a block-house station at first, it had grown to be an elegant mansion, improved in European style, remarkable for the length and deep shade of its avenues of solemn oak, its general grace of arrangement, and the lofty and considerate hospitality of its proprietors. Such, from its first foundation to the period of which we speak, had been its reputation; and in no respect did the present owner depart from the good tastes and the frank manly character of his ancestors. (I, 121–22)

The estate's chief ornament, Simms remarks a few pages later, is "the extensive grove of solemn oaks . . . thickly placed all around the dwelling" that "stretched away singly or in groups . . . down to the very verge of the river, over which many of them sloped with all their weight of limbs and luxuriance upon them" (I, 133). It is within this gracious, beautiful setting that Singleton convinces Walton to come over to the patriot cause, and it is also here that he pays court to Katharine as they beat back their mutual enemy, John Proctor, the British officer who is the rival suitor for Katharine's hand.

Simms develops his subplot, which shows Singleton moving among rural Whigs and Tories, in an equally appropriate setting—the Ashley River swamps and the little settlement of Dorchester, a Wordsworthian "spot of time" whose colonial history he frequently describes in the novel in order to convey his awareness of the past. Against this background, which like the Oaks is a version of the romance green world, he unfolds a second love story, conceived as partial counterpoint to the main plot in its stress on how the middle class eventually backed the patricians who led the patriot cause. In the subplot, Jack Davis and Bella Humphries—two politically uncommitted members of the lower social orders who are on-again, off-again sweethearts—gradually come around under Singleton's guidance to the partisan point of view, in the process defeating their rival, the swaggering British sergeant Hastings, just as Katharine and Singleton defeat Proctor in the main story. (That Simms means these plots to intersect in a kind of double echo of the framing action is shown by the fact that he concludes them in successive chapters late in the book.)

The central characters in all such romance narratives are meant to be representative and symbolic instead of realistic. Hence in *The Partisan* as in *The Yemassee,* Simms constructs his leading figures to embody the romance qualities of chastity, staunchness, and fidelity at the same time that he shapes them to reflect particular social and cultural features of the time. Robert Singleton and Katharine Walton, the earliest of the patriot-patrician heroes and heroines in his long fiction, are also among the most spirited and attractive ones. Singleton, the complete southern gentleman and the ideal military leader, commands a troop in Francis Marion's brigade; he is committed to the partisan movement and, beyond it, to the preservation of southern civilization. Katharine, one of Simms's most appealing heroines, is intelligent, articulate, brave, and sarcastic; she nearly shoots Proctor when he breaks into the Oaks, and she outfences Singleton during an especially sticky courtship scene (I, 173–74). Her devotion to the patriot effort, coupled with her determination to remain unwed until the war is over, illustrates how chastity may symbolize larger moral or social issues in the romance. Thus in a passage explicitly connecting celibacy and war, she tells Singleton, "Wait the due season: when the war is over; when Carolina shall be free from hostile footsteps; and when the land is cleansed of its pollution;—come to me then" (II, 49).

In partial contrast with these figures are their counterparts in the subplot, Bella Humphries and Jack Davis—the one a coquette whose thoughtless intrigue with Sergeant Hastings involves more danger than she had bargained for, the other a loquacious countryman who reveals Simms's talent for plainspun humor. At the beginning of the novel, Davis is an interested bystander who eventually takes Singleton's part in a fray involving Hastings; later, he captures the impudent Briton and tells him scornfully:

> Bella took a liking to you, and to your coat and buttons—monstrous little else, Sargeant Hastings, now, I tell you, for the gal has sense enough to see that you're not the properest looking chap, nor the finest, nor the best-natured, that comes into these parts. But it was the showy buttons and the

> red clothes—the big feather, and—I don't want to say it, Sargeant Hastings, 'cause, as I said before, you're my prisoner, and it's not genteel to say ugly things to one's prisoner; but my mother always trained me to have an ambition for truth, and a man's not a gentleman if he doesn't speak it; so that's the reason, you see, that makes me tell you that it was partly because you were so flashy, and so impudent, and had such a big way about you, that took in the poor gal at first. (II, 80–81)

Cutting across these story lines is the narrative strand involving Porgy, the fat philosopher and "spoilt child of Simms's imagination" who is the author's most famous comic figure.[24] Simms said that Porgy was compounded of a person he had known and himself in certain moods, and he might also have noted that he worked up his jovial gourmet by the combined methods of comedy and romance, with bits of satire and social commentary thrown in.[25] Porgy is, as a result, an overblown, outrageous, extravagantly humorous person who both blends and contrasts with the prevailing tenor of Simms's Revolutionary War novels. In *The Partisan* and other volumes, Simms uses him for comic effects ranging from wit and elegance to slapstick and buffoonery; yet throughout the series he is concerned to show that Porgy, an exaggerated yet lifelike creation, is a unique character in the Revolutionary War series—an aristocrat from a low-country rice plantation who has been forcibly transplanted by war to the swamp, to which he elaborately transfers his plantation pleasures and where he expounds his curious philosophy of flesh and food.

As Simms rarely tires of remarking, Porgy is a "lively big-bellied man" and sentimental gourmet whose enormous stomach bespeaks his love of fine fare (I, 115–16). He has an odd, fanciful way of speaking influenced by euphuism and laced with proverbs, rhetorical tropes, and biblical quotations; he has an equally odd philosophy that centers upon the interdependence of stomach and brain. Insisting that the body "craves food, indeed, only that the mind may think," he calls dinner "an intellectual repast" and insists, "I am convinced, however

24. Parrington, *The Romantic Revolution in America, 1800–1860,* 131.

25. Trent, *William Gilmore Simms,* 109; C. Hugh Holman, "Simms and the British Dramatists," in *The Roots of Southern Writing,* 73. Among the real-life sources Simms may have had for Porgy was Dr. Alexander Skinner of Henry Lee's Revolutionary legion, a soldier who was extremely fond of food and wine. On this point, see the annotations to William Gilmore Simms, *Woodcraft,* in *The Revolutionary War Novels of William Gilmore Simms,* VIII, 526–27*n*20.26.

people may talk about the brain, that it's a poor business after all, in the way of thinking, in comparison with the belly" (II, 88, 106, 105). Singleton comes upon him lying on his back while attempting to fit a terrapin shell as a shield over his huge stomach; laughing, the commander remarks, "[T]he shield is rather small for the part to be protected." Porgy, unflustered, rejoins: "I am a modest man, sir, and a stale proverb . . . helps me to my answer:—Half a loaf is said to be better than no bread, and half a shelter, in the same spirit, is certainly better than none. . . . Take care of what we can, sir, is a wholesome rule, letting what can take care of the rest" (II, 109).[26] Porgy was immensely popular with Simms's readers, and Simms uses him for many purposes as the Revolutionary War series unfolds. But in *The Partisan* he is chiefly concerned to show how this great gourmet, while preparing princely feasts from forest provisions, functions to connect the plantation and the Ashley River swamps that are the two sides of the romance-based green world.

Through central sequences in *The Partisan* involving Porgy, Simms at first contrasts and then connects him with the officers, the enlisted men, and the swampland surroundings. In the thick woods of the low country, most of the patriots practice the arts used by animals—snake, bird, and beast—to train themselves for guerrilla warfare. Porgy, however, practices such arts in search of food. John Davis finds him in the forest hunting terrapin. To snare them, he decides he will pretend to be a hog and grunt and snort as he inches along a log toward his prey. The physical resemblances between plump Porgy and the animal he is imitating are all too obvious, but the epicure defends his unseemly behavior in typically polished phrases. Pointing to the terrapin, he proclaims: "That's a sight, John Davis, to lift a man from a sick-bed.

26. When Simms revised *The Partisan* for the Redfield Author's Uniform Edition in 1854, he reworked the character of Porgy, expanding his speeches, enlarging his role, and changing authorial commentary about him to make him more of a gentleman and less of a glutton. Originally, for instance, he had introduced his gourmet as "an elderly, drinking sort of person—one of the fat, beefy class, whose worship of the belly-god has given an unhappy distension to that ambitious though most erring member" (I, 115). In his extensive revision of this passage, he made Porgy a lieutenant, called him a "jovial philosopher," and described him as "a good looking fellow" with "a fine fresh manly face, clear complexion, and light blue eye" (Simms, *The Partisan*, rev. ed., 110, 111). For a thorough study of his changes in the character, see Paula Dianne Fix Dean, "Revisions in the Revolutionary War Novels of William Gilmore Simms" (Ph.D. dissertation, Auburn University, 1971), Chap. 5.

That's a sight to make him whole and happy again. . . . There's soup enough in the three for a regiment; and—here, my good fellow, take the rifle, and do the watch, while I circumvent the enemy. You shall see me come upon them like an Indian. I will only throw off this outer and most unnecessary covering, and put on the character of a social grunter. Ah, the hog is a noble animal—what would we do without him?" (II, 86).[27]

After snaring his prey, Porgy again becomes the plantation aristocrat forced to fend for himself in the forest. With the help of his black cook Tom, he creates a fabulous stew; and in rituals reminiscent of the manor yet adapted to the swamp, he serves officers and enlisted men with proceedings "exquisitely true to propriety" (II, 114). Presiding with courtly grace, he sees military and social realms complement each other as commander Robert Singleton pardons a culprit after dining at Porgy's table. Porgy's feast, like many other humorous scenes in Simms's fiction, serves serious functions: it brings something of the plantation into the swamp, yokes the two parts of the green world through a stress on upper-class customs, and confirms the aristocratic element in both halves and in the cause they nourish.

Porgy has a minor role in *Mellichampe,* where (according to his letters) Simms apparently worked him in to please his readers, and *Mellichampe* itself is a relatively minor volume in the series.[28] Conceived as "an episode in the progress of the 'Partisan,'" it is, as Simms notes in his opening pages, a legend of the Santee river region, drawing on oral tradition and designed in part to honor the memory of Francis Marion. The military maneuvers that the novel traces are somewhat less important than those described in *The Partisan,* and perhaps as a consequence, its love stories are rather more prominent in Simms's literary format, in which he works some interesting variations on the sort of linked love plots he had constructed for the earlier book. Throughout *Mellichampe,* he contrasts the staunch devotion of Janet

27. Simms improved the humor of this passage when he revised it for the 1854 *Partisan,* wherein he has Porgy comment: "The Hog . . . has one feature of the good aristocrat. He goes where he pleases, and grumbles as he goes. Still, I am not satisfied that it is proper for the gentleman to put on the hog, unless on occasion such as this. The pleasures of a dinner are not to be lost for a grunt. He must crawl upon his belly who would feel his way to that of a terrapin" (319).

28. In a letter to Lawson, Simms remarked, "[Y]ou have no idea how popular Porgy is with a large majority. He is actually the founder of a sect" (*L,* I, 82).

Berkeley and Ernest Mellichampe with the shallow affection of two people who are mental lightweights—Janet's cousin Rose Duncan, an addlepated girl of no firm political persuasion, and her suitor the British lieutenant Clayton, a dandy abounding in "rose-water compliments" and drawing-room chatter, whose lukewarm politics make him her appropriate mate.[29]

To stress the superiority of patriotism, Simms makes firm points about the strong political commitment and the equally strong affection of his partisan lovers as contrasted with the essential flippancy of their counterparts. He also compares Rose with Janet in standard romance fashion while creating, in the process, some good humorous scenes. Janet, who is overly fond of brooding, mopes about the risks Mellichampe takes to see her; Rose, who likes to rattle on about the inevitable perils of true love, proclaims: "If ever I get a lover, which, Heaven knows, seems but a doubtful prospect at this moment, I vow he should have no quiet—he should be required to do just what you fret that Mellichampe is now doing. He should scale fences and walls, ford creeks when there's a freshet, and regularly come to visit me through the swamp" (I, 121–22).

Simms's description of the Berkeley manor house in *Mellichampe* displays his efforts, which he would continue throughout his fiction, to communicate elements of character through setting. The Oaks in *The Partisan,* whose grandeur he explicitly links to the "frank manly character" of its owner, corroborates the frequently made observation that in literature noble houses usually reveal the traits of the master.[30] No less surely does the Berkeley estate suggest the personal traits of Janet's father, but here the description of house and owner takes a somber turn. Berkeley is a timid, vacillating patriot disposed to humor the British officers who quarter themselves upon him; his house is a big brick edifice with crumbling walls, "yielding frame," and "an insidious and lurking decay." Its general condition, Simms says pointedly, "attested not merely its own, but the decline of its proprietor" (I, 72–73). Established thus in his early novels, this close connection between house

29. [William Gilmore Simms], *Mellichampe. A Legend of the Santee* (New York, 1836), I, [iii], II, 97. Unless otherwise indicated, further references to this volume are to this edition, cited by volume and page number within the text (as *M* where necessary for clarity).

30. See, for instance, Guy A. Cardwell, "The Plantation House: An Analogical Image," *Southern Literary Journal,* II (Fall, 1969), [3].

and master runs through his long fiction to culminate in his final romance, *Voltmeier.*[31]

In his portraits of black characters in *The Partisan* and *Mellichampe,* Simms continues the emphasis begun in *The Yemassee* on the fidelity, intelligence, and courage of South Carolina slaves. He also continues his predominantly patriarchal stance. Perhaps the best-drawn black figure in his early novels is Scipio in *Mellichampe,* a likable, humorous fellow who reveals Simms's typical approach to the characterization of his blacks. Scip, the loyal servant of Janet Berkeley, lets himself be tortured rather than betray Mellichampe; he tricks a British sentinel into letting him pass behind enemy lines in order to help the partisans; and in the book's climactic scene he kills the vicious Tory Barsfield, who is trying to kill Mellichampe. Throughout this last episode, Simms masks gruesome realistic details with lively humor—but it is humor that exploits the antebellum Negro's alleged servility to whites. "[Y]ou say I must knock dis tory?" Scipio asks the scout and woodsman Thumbscrew Witherspoon. "I 'mos' 'fraid—he dah buckrah—I dah nigger." Witherspoon cries, "Strike him!" So Scip buries a pine knot in Barsfield's brain and exults: "Ho! ho! I kill um—I hit um on he head. He's a dirt—he's a dirt—I hab foot on um—I mash he brains. Ho! ho! I kill buckrah. I's a nigger, I kill buckrah! You tink for hang me—you mistake. Mass Wedderspoon say de wud—Mass Arnest no say 'no.' I kill 'em. He dead!" (II, 223–25). The implicit condescension evident in such scenes is one of the least attractive aspects of Simms's fiction for his twentieth-century readers; but his attitudes are those of his social class and age, and his Negro characters, for all their shuffling humor, are among the most appealing figures in his fiction.

In the revenge narratives that he uses to connect *The Partisan* and *Mellichampe,* Simms develops the mingled Gothic and grotesque effects that he favors in his fiction of the 1830s and for which he draws skillfully on South Carolina social classes and locales. One of these narratives is the tale of the maniac Frampton, allied to figures in Brockden Brown's novels, who brutally slaughters Tories in retaliation for their murder of his wife. Another is a long story that originates early in *The Partisan* and concludes near the end of *Mellichampe.* In it, Simms pits

31. For a Freudian view of the connection between Simms's characters and his plantations, see Annette Kolodny, "The Unchanging Landscape: The Pastoral Impulse in Simms's Revolutionary War Romances," *Southern Literary Journal,* V (Fall, 1972), [46]–67.

Bill Humphries, a follower of Robert Singleton from the rural middle class, against two lower-class Tories, Ned, or "Goggle," Blonay and his mother—the one conceived by the methods of southern grotesque and as such a forerunner of figures in Faulkner, Erskine Caldwell, and Flannery O'Connor, the other portrayed in Gothic manner as a witch-woman with two monstrous cats. Goggle, the product of his mother's liaison with an Indian, is a pop-eyed, double-dealing rascal who likes to pick at a large, ugly sore on his arm. Following the standard procedure of southern grotesque, Simms uses Goggle's physical ugliness to suggest his essential depravity, claiming that he is "as warped in morals as he [is] blear in vision" (*P*, I, 186).[32] Goggle and his mother, in the typical fashion, as Simms says, of the lower-class Loyalists in the Revolution, conspire against patriots from the upper class; yet one of these figures becomes the instrument of Goggle's partial redemption. Under the spell of Janet Berkeley in *Mellichampe,* Goggle betrays his Tory master in order to help her and her patriot lover escape the British, at the cost of his own life.

Before this happens, however, Goggle is tracked and almost killed by scout Bill Humphries in a scene that demonstrates Simms's skill at blending a physical setting conceived in the Gothic manner with what twentieth-century critics call "psychological Gothic." Humphries stalks Goggle through the gloomy low-country swamps and finally walls him up in a hollow tree. But as the scout leaves he fancies that he hears the "cries of the Half-Breed in little gusts of wind"—so that, "when he emerged from the wood, a strange chill went through his bones, and he looked back momently, even when the gigantic cypress, which was the sepulchre of his enemy, no longer reared up its solemn spire in his sight" (II, 179). The sentence recalls the Hawthorne of "Roger Malvin's Burial," while the procedure of walling up an enemy and leaving him to die anticipates Poe in "The Cask of Amontillado." It is one of numerous elements in Simms's work that may have influenced Poe, who read and commented copiously during the 1830s and early 1840s on Simms's writing.[33]

32. On Simms's use of the method of grotesque, see the chapter "Mother Blonay's Curse" in William J. Scheick, *The Half-Blood: A Cultural Symbol in 19th-Century American Fiction* ([Lexington], 1979), 29–33.

33. See, for example, Poe's reviews of *The Partisan* in *Southern Literary Messenger,* II (January, 1836), 117–21, which calls the book "no ordinary work" and praises its historical details but criticizes Simms for stylistic infelicities and a too-great fondness for the horrible and revolting; of *The Damsel of Darien* in *Burton's Gentleman's Magazine*

Between *Mellichampe* and the next novel in the series, *The Kinsmen,* there was a lapse of several years during which Simms wrote the Border Romances. When he returned to the Revolution, he shifted his scene to the upcountry, where in 1781 an event of some importance to the progress of the war in the colony had taken place—Nathaniel Greene's siege of the British garrison at Fort Ninety-Six, which was lifted when Lord Rawdon's forces reinforced the garrison but which helped convince the British to evacuate the fort and abandon their effort to control the upcountry. The siege of Ninety-Six, together with the subsequent movement of Rawdon's troops toward Orangeburg, is the major event in the framing action of *The Kinsmen.* Through the framing action, Simms conveys several additional factors significant to the war: the role of the West Indies in it, the conversion of various people to the patriot side as royal power in the province declined, and the bitter civil conflict between Tory and Whig that deluged, as Simms says, the plains of the colony with blood (*K,* I, 17).[34] He designs his fictional narrative to give particular emphasis to the civil strife. His hero Clarence Conway leads a partisan squad in the brigade of Thomas Sumter, the militia leader who historically operated in the upcountry, whereas Clarence's half-brother Ned, the son of the elder Conway's marriage to a woman from the West Indies, heads a vicious Tory band. The prominence in the novel of this group, ominously called the "Black Riders of Congaree," emphasizes the fact that the Loyalists were especially active in the upcountry and that civil strife was thus particularly violent there.

and American Monthly Review, V (November, 1839), 283–85, which says its faults are "few, and seldom radical"; and of *The Wigwam and the Cabin* in *Broadway Journal,* II (October 4, 1845), 190–91, which praises Simms's powers of invention, vigor, and movement. The last review was revised and printed in *Godey's Magazine and Lady's Book,* XXXII (January, 1846), 41–42. Arlin Turner studies the literary relationship of the two men in "Poe and Simms: Friendly Critics, Sometimes Friends," in Richard P. Veler (ed.), *Papers on Poe: Essays in Honor of John Ward Ostrom* (Springfield, Ohio, 1972), [140]–60. On connections between the fiction of the writers, see Guilds, "William Gilmore Simms and the *Southern Literary Gazette,*" 72, and Mary Ann Wimsatt, "Simms's Early Short Stories," *Library Chronicle, University of Pennsylvania,* XLI (Winter, 1977), 166–68. The title of *Godey's Magazine and Lady's Book* varies slightly during the journal's run.

34. In *The Kinsmen,* I, Chap. 1, Simms borrowed information about the war in the upcountry from Johnson, *Sketches of the Life and Correspondence of Nathanael Greene,* Vol. I, Pt. 2, p. 341. He also borrowed from Johnson for his description of the siege of Ninety-Six (see, for example, Johnson, Vol. II, Pt. 1, pp. 138–45; *K,* II, 73–77, 81).

Noteworthy features of *The Kinsmen* are the symmetry of its design and the way that design reveals the general procedures of romance. Visible first at the historical level, where Greene and Rawdon are explicitly contrasted, this symmetry also informs nearly every aspect of the fictional level of the narrative as it is shaped to illustrate military matters. Prominent in it are the paired, contrasted half-brothers Clarence and Ned and their followers, the paired, contrasted scouts "Supple Jack" Bannister and Watson Gray. An important character for the humor of the book is innkeeper Isaac Muggs, who functions as a Loyalist analogue to the staunch patriot Bannister, while dominant in the Black Rider troop are the mutinous Lieutenant Stockton and his henchman Darcy—who grimly parody Ned and Watson Gray even as these characters grimly parody Jack and Clarence.

With so many parallels in the military strand of his narrative, Simms sensibly avoids the creation of comparable parallels in the love plot: in other words, he does not try to make the characters in his two love stories resemble or contrast with each other as closely as he had done in his previous novels about the war. Instead he uses the main love narrative, which as usual unfolds against a plantation background, to convey salient facts about the historical development of the interior region, while he employs the secondary story as a stern warning to his female readers about the dangers of seduction. The first tale centers on the rivalry of Ned and Clarence over Flora Middleton, the heiress of Brier Park, a famous old plantation established by frontiersmen among the Indians along the Congaree River near present-day Columbia. The second tale involves Mary Clarkson, a rustic beauty of the Congaree region whom Jack Bannister had once loved and whom Ned Conway later seduced and betrayed. Mary represents the semiliterate rural classes of interior South Carolina, and in her simple outlook and ruined virtue she also functions repeatedly as foil to the more sophisticated and prudent Flora.

Offsetting the melodrama of both subplot and main plot are the antics of scouts Bannister and Gray, who make particularly vivid the system of romance-based character pairing that buttresses the book and that both the characters and the author are fond of stressing. (Isaac Muggs tells Bannister, for instance, that Gray is "a great scout—the best, after you . . . on the Congaree," and Clarence Conway utters similar statements late in the book [I, 171, II, 237].) Both men are strong, practical, brave, and clever, and both are fiercely loyal to their masters; but Bannister is honorable, whereas Gray is cruel and deceitful, and Bannister is naïvely humorous, whereas Gray is merely sardonic. In the best scene between the two, Gray grabs Bannister's arms from behind; but Bannister hoists the surprised Tory upon his back and canters down a hill, stopping only to bang his adversary against a tree when he grows obstreperous. As Bannister canters down the hill, he taunts Gray in homely metaphors: "I see that you never hearn of the danger of shaking hands with a black bear. The danger is that you can't let go when you want to. A black bear is so civil an animal, that he never likes to give up a good acquaintance, and he'll hold on, paw for paw, with him . . . though it's the roughest tree in the swamp that stands up between him and his friend." Then he makes his point explicit: "I could carry you all day, on [*sic*] a pinch, and never feel the worse for it. . . . I was a little dub'ous, I confess, that you were a better man than myself. I was: but you made a poor fist of this business—a poor pair of fists, I may say" (II, 23–24).

Even better conceived are the scenes between Bannister and Muggs, who are also designed as counterparts—with Muggs, in addition, representing the Tories "converted to the patriot cause, who, at the eleventh hour, displayed the most conspicuous bravery fighting on the popular side" (I, 173). The two have long been friendly adversaries, and Bannister finally decides it is time to bring Muggs around to the American point of view. Through his efforts to convert the innkeeper, Simms explores to the full the qualities that typify many of the partisans in his rural middle class—ingenuousness, heartfelt patriotism, and deeply held religious beliefs. Simms also demonstrates with some flair his gift for slapstick.

Bannister first approaches Muggs by "argyfying," which gives Simms a chance to convey historical information about the progress of the war through humorous passages of dialect. After denouncing royal power, Bannister proclaims to Muggs:

> Well, it so happens that I won't pay George the Third any more taxes. That's the word for all; and it's good reason why I shouldn't pay him, when, for all his trying, he can't make me. Here he's sent his regiments—regiment after regiment—and the Queen sent her regiment, and the Prince of Wales his regiment—I reckon we didn't tear the Prince's regiment all to flinders at Hanging Rock!—Well, then, there was the Royal Scotch and the Royal Irish, and the Dutch Hessians; I suppose they didn't call them royal,

> 'cause they couldn't ax in English for what they wanted:—well, what was the good of it?—all these regiments together couldn't make poor Jack Bannister, a Congaree boatmen [*sic*], drink stamped tea or pay taxes. The regiments, all I've named and a hundred more, are gone like last autumn's dry leaves; and the only fighting that's a-going on now, worth to speak of, is American born 'gainst American born. . . . cutting each other's throats to fill the pockets of one of the ugliest old men . . . that ever I looked on. It spiles the face of a guinea where they put his face. (I, 156–57)

Then, telling Muggs "I've tried to drive reason into your head, but it's no use," he proposes that they "strip to the buff for a fight" and let Providence settle the issue. "If the Lord says I'm right," Bannister declares, "why you'll know it mighty soon by the sprawl I'll give you;—but if I'm wrong, the tumble will be the other way" (I, 157, 158, 161). To offset the fact that Muggs possesses only a single arm, he ties his own right arm behind his back; then, remarks Simms, "he laid his chin on the shoulder of the landlord, grasped him vigorously about the body; and Muggs, having secured a similar grasp, gave him the word, and they both swung round" until a spectator would have doubted "the distinct proprietorship of the several legs which so rapidly chased each other in the air." Bannister eventually deprives Muggs "of grasp and footing at the same moment" and whirls him, "dizzy and staggering, heels up and head to the earth." He offers to repeat the performance, but Muggs, gasping, "No, no, Supple, you're too much for me!" becomes a ready convert to the American cause (I, 165, 166, 168).

The lively humor of *The Kinsmen* is perhaps its most appealing feature, for more than the other Revolutionary War Romances the novel suffers from the melodrama to which Simms was unfortunately prone. Considered carefully, in fact, both it and *Mellichampe* reveal a gradual decline from *The Partisan*. That volume, despite its poor construction, is charming, as Trent remarks, and had Simms proceeded directly to its sequel, *Katharine Walton,* he would have made a good start in his fiction about the war.[35] As matters stood, however, he seemed almost to have lost sight of his original plans for the series, and hence it was not really progressing when he laid it aside in 1841. The historical research he would do in the forties would broaden and deepen his portrayal of the Revolution in his second group of romances about the

35. Trent, *William Gilmore Simms,* 192.

war, while his midcentury reading, particularly in the novel of manners, would add new, vibrant elements to his literary scheme. Before going on to these subjects, however, he temporarily turned aside from both the Revolution and the low country in order to explore the other subject that since adolescence had attracted him, the riotous frontier of the flush times in the Gulf or lower South.

4

The Gulf South, the Frontier Humorists, and "Reverend Devil"

After the low country, Simms's major subject in long fiction was the frontier or backwoods South, represented in his early fiction by the Border Romances. Between the two southern regions, there existed for him a substantial connection forged by culture and reinforced by personal experience. The Gulf plain had been settled by emigrants from the seaboard, and throughout its history it would be heavily influenced by tidewater social traditions. The migration of Simms's father from Charleston to Mississippi epitomized larger patterns in antebellum culture, and Simms, who considered making the same move, later regretted that he had not done so. His several visits to the Gulf states while he was still a young man afforded him the opportunity to see an area of the South that was still in the pioneer stage and inspired him to write, as his biographer Trent remarks, vividly and colorfully about it.[1]

The Gulf South or Old Southwest had been opened to settlement by the final years of the 1790s, but poor roads and primitive conditions discouraged widespread migration there until early in the next century, when the development of the cotton gin and the War of 1812 made expansion financially feasible. Eli Whitney's miraculous invention inspired the production on a large scale of the short-staple cotton that could be grown all over the South, and by 1812 the crop was ready to move into the trans-Appalachian region. The war that began that year helped smooth the way for cotton's conquest by opening trade routes and preparing for Indian removal, while the ruthless policies of removal followed by Presidents Monroe and Jackson encouraged the flow of white settlers into the region. So successful were the government's efforts that by 1819 nearly 200,000 people lived in the Gulf plains, and approximately half of the country's cotton was produced

1. Trent, *William Gilmore Simms,* 15–16.

there. Emigration slackened in the 1820s but swelled again during the flush times of the early 1830s, when squatters, planters, and land speculators poured into the region.[2]

Conditions, as document after document from the era makes clear, were rough and primitive: travelers to the region complained of the infamous "corduroy roads" made of logs placed together and lightly covered with dirt; of having to sleep in inns on sheets that numbers of tourists had used before them; of learning from their hosts that they must catch and cook their own chickens if they wanted dinner; of using, on steamboats, the public comb hung from a string in the ceiling; or of strolling through new settlements where stumps were still in the streets and pigs rooted for garbage there.[3] Yet civilization was slowly improving the area: as a character in Simms's novel *Richard Hurdis* (1838), viewing a new Alabama town, remarks: "Piles of brick and timber crowded the main, indeed, the only street of the place, and denoted the rawness and poverty of the region in all things which could please the eye, and minister to the taste of the traveller. But it had other resources in my sight. The very incompleteness and rude want of finish, indicated the fermenting character of life. The stagnation of the forests was disturbed. The green and sluggish waters of its inactivity were drained off into new channels of enterprise and effort. Life had opened upon it."[4]

The terrain of the Gulf South was perhaps more varied than that of the seaboard, and the tension between civilized elegance and frontier crudeness was sharper. Fertile areas existed near the rivers, particularly the Mississippi, and in the lush Black Belt that curved through

2. Ray Allen Billington with James Blaine Hedges, *Westward Expansion: A History of the American Frontier* (2nd ed.; New York, 1960), 310–28; Frederick Jackson Turner, *The United States, 1830–1850: The Nation and Its Sections* (New York, 1935), [210]–52; Clement Eaton, *The Growth of Southern Civilization, 1790–1860* (New York, 1961), 25–48.

3. These details are taken from travel accounts published in the 1820s and early 1830s near the time of Simms's trips to the Gulf South. See, for example, Basil Hall, *Travels in North America, in the Years 1827 and 1828* (Edinburgh, 1829), III, 113, 264–65, 277; [Thomas Hamilton], *Men and Manners in America* (Edinburgh, 1833), II, 175; [Frances] Trollope, *Domestic Manners of the Americans* (London, 1832), I, 52–53. See also Jane Louise Mesick, *The English Traveller in America, 1785–1835* (New York, 1922), 55–56.

4. [William Gilmore Simms], *Richard Hurdis; or, The Avenger of Blood. A Tale of Alabama* (Philadelphia, 1838), I, 186. Unless otherwise indicated, further references to this volume are to this edition, cited by volume and page number within the text (as *RH* where necessary for clarity).

central Alabama and Mississippi; less fertile were the longleaf pine region near the Gulf Coast and the mountainous area that formed part of the Cumberland Plateau. Rich planters clustered in the floodplains and the Black Belt, where they gradually bought out the small farmers who outnumbered them and who, despite their rough houses and few slaves, aspired to enter the patrician class. Dotting the hill country and the pine barrens were the yeomen, or "one-gallus," farmers; below them on the social scale were the crackers, or sandhillers, who eked out a precarious living on depleted soil.[5] From an early point in its history the region had been terrorized by the infamous Harpes and the Murrell gang that thronged the Natchez Trace, exacting heavy tolls from travelers and settlers. Yet despite these predators, the land remained idyllic in the minds of pioneers, serving, as more than one commentator has noted, as an eternal symbol of the earthly Eden.[6]

Simms visited the Gulf South from 1824 to 1826 in its primitive Indian and pioneer phases; he went there again in 1831, when he witnessed the rush and bustle of the flush times; and he made a final trip to the area in 1842, when he described the great strides made by commerce and business. The lapse of time between his journeys enabled him to judge the progress of settlement in the area and also to voice his comments on the developing relationship between civilization and frontier. The Southwest he had seen in the 1820s had been a raw frontier, a thinly-populated, river-threaded wilderness where settlement was still in the pioneer stage and where swamps, sandhills, creeks, bayous, and the interminable pine forests impeded and irritated him. On his first trip, he made his way through the region by steamboat, stagecoach, and horseback, traveling overland from Charleston to Augusta, Macon, and Montgomery, and down the Alabama River to Mobile. From there he journeyed north on the Tombigbee River to Demopolis, up the Black Warrior River to Tuscaloosa, and then overland again to a site between Georgeville and Hattiesburg, Mississippi, the site of his father's now vanished plantation.[7]

Once there, Simms spent several months with his father and his Uncle James riding horseback through what he said were "some very

5. Billington, *Westward Expansion,* 320–28; Eaton, *The Growth of Southern Civilization,* 35–37.

6. See, for example, Eaton, *The Growth of Southern Civilization,* 33.

7. *L,* V, 398; Hoole, "Alabama and W. Gilmore Simms," *Alabama Review,* 86. Kibler, "*The Album* (1826)," 67, locates the plantation in Georgeville.

wild regions," visiting the Creek and Cherokee nations and sometimes traveling several hundred miles beyond the Mississippi River (*L,* V, 357, I, lxv). He accepted backwoods hospitality when he could find it, slept in the woods when he could not, and stored up memories of his adventures that he later wove into his letters, poetry, and fiction.[8] In mature life he told a correspondent that he had "travelled, in early years, greatly in the South & South West on horseback, seeing the whole region from Carolina to Mississippi personally, and as far back as 1825 when 2/3 was an Indian Country." He continued, "I saw the red men in their own homes; could imitate them in speech; imitate the backwoodsmen, mountaineers, swamp suckers, &c." (*L,* IV, 178).

Autobiographical passages in Simms's Border Romances furnish additional details about his travels in the early 1820s through the wildest and least settled parts of the lower South. His venturesome young heroes, who follow the land routes he himself had taken, may ride "forty or fifty miles per day, very frequently without seeing sign of human habitation."[9] Such habitation as they do find may be a vermin-ridden mud hovel, or a tavern that is merely "a miserable shell of logs," or a shack consisting "of but one apartment into which the whole family, husband, wife, three children and ourselves, were oddly clustered together."[10] They may frolic with sturdy farm girls to "the discordant twang of a half-tuned fiddle," sup with surly half-breeds, or fall in with "New York dandies: men with long coats and steeple crowned hats, great breast-pins, thick gold chains, and a big bunch of seals hanging at their hips" (*HH,* 10; *RH,* I, 189). They may "sleep in a canebrake with the soft ooze of a rank swamp in place of a mattress"; and they may partly walk, partly flounder over roads full of stumps, briars, vines, and broken branches—roads that prompt a backwoods wag in Simms's final Border Romance to exclaim, in verses etched upon a tree: "Here's h-ll, and it / To go through y*it*" (*BB,* II, 101; *HH,* 43).

8. Trent, *William Gilmore Simms,* 15.

9. [William Gilmore Simms], *Border Beagles; A Tale of Mississippi* (Philadelphia, 1840), I, 120. Unless otherwise indicated, further references to this volume are to this edition, cited by volume and page number within the text (as *BB* where necessary for clarity). These passages were identified as autobiographical both by Hoole in "Alabama and W. Gilmore Simms" and by C. Hugh Holman in a conversation with me in August, 1974.

10. W[illiam] Gilmore Simms, *Helen Halsey: or, The Swamp State of Conelachita. A Tale of the Borders* (New York, 1845), 9; *RH,* I, 106. Further references to *Helen Halsey* are to this edition, cited by page number within the text (as *HH* where necessary for clarity).

On his second, better documented journey during 1826, Simms—as James Kibler has shown—sailed from Charleston around the tip of Florida, landing for the first time near New Orleans. After visiting the city briefly, he went by water to Mobile, whence he took a steamboat up the Tombigbee River to Columbus, Mississippi, where he stayed for about a week. Making his way on the Tombigbee again to the Choctaw nation, he proceeded by horseback to the Pearl River in western Mississippi and then probably to his father's plantation.[11]

The important "Letters from the West" that Simms published in the *Album* during 1826 reveal his youthful attitude, which he did not much modify, toward the Old Southwest. The letters show the young southerner, who was not yet twenty, already set in his tidewater ways and scorning the materialistic culture he saw forming in the Gulf South. New Orleans in the 1820s was to him a "vile reservoir of infamy and baseness" where cash was king and gambling hells abounded. Mobile was only slightly better: desolate Indian outcasts from the Choctaw nation, corrupted by their contact with white civilization, lay nearly nude in the streets, and the representatives of that civilization, the lawyers at the Mobile bar, seemed "dull, heavy and unimportant." He left Mobile feeling "perfectly fatigued" with its conditions.[12]

When Simms returned to the Old Southwest in 1831, however, he noted with some surprise the inroads made by civilization during the frenetic era of the flush times. He described his impressions of the early 1830s in another important letter series, which he called (in imitation of the growing body of travel literature) "Notes of a Small Tourist" and which he published in 1831 in his newspaper, the Charleston *City Gazette*.[13] Like the earlier "Letters from the West," "Notes" is colored by Simms's characteristic bias in favor of seaboard culture and also by his fundamental distrust of settlers' craving for land, wealth, and further westward migration. Throughout the series, he remarks with ap-

11. Kibler, "*The Album* (1826)," 66–67.

12. Simms's four "Letters from the West," signed "W. G. S.," appeared in *Album*, II (March 4, 11, April 1, May 20, 1826), 68–69, 76–77, 100–101, 157–58, respectively. James E. Kibler, Jr., discovered the letters in 1983 when he found the long-missing second volume of the *Album*. The quotations in the text are from Kibler, "The First Simms Letters: 'Letters from the West' (1826)," *Southern Literary Journal*, XIX (Spring, 1987), 87, 89. Simms's title may allude to James Kirke Paulding's popular travel account, *Letters from the South, Written During an Excursion in the Summer of 1816* (New York, 1817).

13. These important documents are reprinted in *L*, I, 10–38.

proval the evidence of civic growth and refinement in the Gulf South while recalling the more primitive circumstances he had witnessed in the 1820s. Columbus, Georgia, he remarks for example, then had no existence, but in 1831 it was sizable; New Orleans, that former hotbed of infamy, would, he states, eventually surpass New York in commerce; the "resources of the Mississippi," he claims, "are incomputable . . . and its advantages, over any other single section of territory" are "without any comparison or rivalship" (*L*, I, 26, 35). Yet elsewhere in the Old Southwest, pretension, he implies, outstrips achievement. Augusta boasts "some fine and capacious blocks of buildings," but its theater is "a wretched barn of a place, rather railed than boarded in"; it looks, "for all the world . . . like a temporary stable" (*L*, I, 20–21). Similarly, cotton depots near the Gulf of Mexico possess "very large and sonorous names" but upon inspection dwindle to "a range of log-houses, a tavern . . . and possibly, a meeting-house" (*L*, I, 33).

Cotton depots were, however, thriving metropolises compared to what Simms saw on the last lap of his 1831 travels. The wildest region through which he journeyed was the celebrated Yazoo territory. Only after Mississippi had gained statehood in 1817 had white men ventured into Yazoo land; yet it early had a reputation for enormous riches, and it had sheltered criminals like the Harpes and Masons when the law began to drive them from the Natchez Trace. Made fertile by Mississippi River floods, the territory boasted thick forests, fine soil, and good game; it had just been opened up for settlement at the time Simms went there, and its low-lying, muddy terrain was an annoyance to which he testified.[14] In the last letter of the "Notes of a Small Tourist" series, he told his *City Gazette* readers: "I have just returned from a journey on horseback, of seventeen days into the Yazoo purchase, over and through swamps and creeks and bayous, half the time swimming and wading through mud and water waist deep. We passed through several little townships and country seats, of little note, and not calculated to interest you. Innumerable little villages are springing up in every quarter, averaging in population about three hundred, and stagnating at that" (*L*, I, 37).

What lay in the recently acquired Indian lands beyond the Yazoo

14. See the entries "Mississippi" and "Yazoo River Basin" in David C. Roller and Robert W. Twyman (eds.), *The Encyclopedia of Southern History* (Baton Rouge, 1979), 827, 1366–67.

territory, and what might happen there, interested Simms more. With others he turned his eyes westward, though unlike others he had little hope of finding Eden.

> The great rage at this time in Mississippi, is the possession of the new Indian purchase, the Choctaw lands. Many of the Choctaws have already gone to the Arkansas, and more are upon the go. I cannot but think the possession of so much territory, greatly inimical to the well being of this country. It not only conflicts with, and prevents the formation of society, but it destroys that which is already well established. It makes our borderers mere Ishmaelites, and keeps our frontiers perpetually so. Scarcely have they squatted down in one place, and built up their little "improvements," than they hear of a new purchase, where corn grows without planting, and cotton comes up five bales to the acre, ready picked and packed—they pull up stakes and boom off for the new Canaan, until they hear of some still better, when they commence the same game—death not unfrequently stopping them on the road, before they have had time to hew their burial stone from the quarries which surrounded them. (*L*, I, 37–38)

Pervading this passage is a tension between frontier hopes and civilized doubts that may be construed as a tension between the seaboard and backwoods, or tidewater and frontier, South. It underlies Simms's wryly rendered observations about magic corn and cotton, and it centers upon the greed and gullibility of the settlers who believe that they can actually "boom off for the new Canaan." Such passages suggest the characteristic pessimism of the southern writer about human nature and human hopes, and they foreshadow the similar pessimism that occasionally appears in the Border Romances.[15]

Together with "Letters from the West" and his other writings, then, "Notes of a Small Tourist" suggests that Simms preferred the culture epitomized by the southern seaboard and that he was skeptical about the future, however enticing, of the frontier—which may be why, despite his father's urgings, he did not remain there. Throughout much of his writing about the Gulf South, he paints "the formation of society" and the "security which waits on social order" as desirable states, and the restless wanderings of pioneers as only one step up from barbarism. He reveals his attitude toward these matters in the poem "The Western Emigrants," which he published in the middle 1830s near the

15. On this general point, see C. Hugh Holman, "The Southerner as American Writer," in *The Roots of Southern Writing*, 9–12.

time of his first Border Romances and which, like portions of those books, is patently autobiographical. Its narrator, who is from "old Carolina," sees a group of people also from South Carolina journeying "To the new land of promise, full of dreams / Of western riches, Mississippi-mad!" But like the pioneers in "Notes of a Small Tourist" who "boom off for the new Canaan," these emigrants are deluded, says the narrator, by their hopes of "[g]olden stores" in "Mississippian vales"; and their visions, so attractive to them now, will not be realized.[16] In his speech "The Social Principle" delivered in 1842, Simms further remarks that "every remove into the wilderness, lessens the hold which refinement and society have hitherto held upon the individual man"; and he complains, in phrases that would crop up again in his writing, that "the wandering habit of our people" contributes to the deterioration of society.[17]

Simms in fact shared with other thinkers of his time a theory of social stages that underlies "Letters from the West," "Notes of a Small Tourist," and "The Social Principle" and that helps clarify his attitude toward the transmontane South. It emerges quite clearly in his comments on Kentucky of the 1820s, where society was still in the formative phase.

> Though the savage had for ever departed from its limits, the blessings of a perfect civilization were not yet secured to the new and flourishing regions of Kentucky. Its morals were still in that fermenting condition which invariably distinguishes the settlement of every new country by a various and foreign people. At the distant period of which we write, the population of Kentucky had not yet become sufficiently stationary to have made their domestic goods secure, or to have fixed the proper lines and limits regulating social intercourse and attaching precise standards to human conduct. The habits and passions of the first settlers—those fearless pioneers who had struggled foot to foot with the Indian, and lived in a kindred state of barbarity with him, had not yet ceased to have influence over the numerous race which followed them. That moral amalgam which we call society, and

16. Simms, "Notes of a Small Tourist," *L*, I, 37; *The Social Principle: The True Source of National Permanence. An Oration. . . .* (Tuscaloosa, Ala., 1843), 6; [William Gilmore Simms], *Southern Passages and Pictures* (New York, 1839), 16, 17. "The Western Emigrants" had previously appeared in the *Southern Literary Journal*, II (June, 1836), 270–71. Simms uses its opening lines as the heading for Chap. 9 in both the original and the revised edition of *RH*.

17. Simms, *The Social Principle*, 36, 35. For similar concepts, see *RH*, I, 98, and the letter "Southern Literature" that Simms sent to the *Magnolia* in 1840, reprinted in *L*, I, 195–208 (see particularly 206–207).

> which recognizes a mutual and perfectly equal condition of dependance [*sic*], and a common necessity, as the great cementing principles of the human family, had not yet taken place.[18]

Law, civilized society, and the "security which waits on social order" buttress the "right" side of the dialectic in all Simms's romances about the backwoods or border South.

*

The books that grew out of Simms's experiences in the Gulf region exhibit, he told Rufus Griswold, "great activity of plot, vehement & passionate personality, and pictures & sketches of border character & border scenery . . . equally true & natural" (*L*, II, 225). They are set, as their subtitles indicate, in one or another part of the Old Southwest—*Guy Rivers: A Tale of Georgia* (1834); *Richard Hurdis . . . A Tale of Alabama* (1838); *Border Beagles; A Tale of Mississippi* (1840); and *Helen Halsey . . . A Tale of the Borders* (1845). The term *borders* in the subtitle of *Helen Halsey* connotes, as Simms says, a "neutral ground . . . neither savage nor social" between civilization and wilderness (*HH*, 9). Connected to these volumes in setting or emphasis are works that can only be mentioned in this study—*Confession* (1841), a novel about attempted seduction and murder that is set partly in Alabama and makes reference to frontier Texas; *Beauchampe* (1842) and *Charlemont* (1856), two books based loosely on the famous Kentucky Tragedy of the 1820s that has fascinated southern writers from Poe to Robert Penn Warren; and *The Wigwam and the Cabin*, first and second series (both 1845), two volumes of short fiction later collected as a single volume that treat Indian, pioneer, and Revolutionary War material.

Simms's travels in the Gulf South gave him two strands of material that he wove into the four main Border Romances and that account for their dark and their bright sides accordingly. One of these strands—violent, sensational, and melodramatic—derived from the stories he had heard about border criminals, particularly John A. Murrell, the "Reverend Devil" and "Great Western Land Pirate" who had menaced

18. [William Gilmore Simms], *Beauchampe, or The Kentucky Tragedy. A Tale of Passion* (Philadelphia, 1842), 1, 14–15. Unless otherwise indicated, further references to this volume are to this edition. Vol. I of *Beauchampe* was republished as W[illiam] Gilmore Simms, *Charlemont: Or The Pride of the Village. A Tale of Kentucky* (New York, 1856). Vol. II was republished as W[illiam] Gilmore Simms, *Beauchampe: Or The Kentucky Tragedy. A Sequel to Charlemont* (New York, 1856).

the region in the early 1830s near the time of Simms's third journey there. The other—raucous, comic, raw, and unfettered—arose from his encounters with humorous frontier types on his travels and was encouraged by the lively, unfettered element in his own personality. Each strand furnished fundamental elements for the complicated literary format of the border books. The Murrell material contributed to his emphasis on law and crime, his public or framing action, his dialectic construction, and his central fictional story; southern humor inspired him to create important figures representative of the region who participate in the main narrative while helping to offset its unavoidable melodrama.

Because of these elements, the Border Romances, wild and comic by turns, reflect, sometimes with great precision, the kind of society developing in the Gulf South—a society formed, as Hugh Holman observes, by discontented emigrants from the seaboard who had "joined with the criminal and the displaced to transport a new culture to the region," and who there began to develop customs and construct plantations that recalled the ideal of Cavalier Virginia and of Carolina. Here traditions of honor took shape through a code of violence "elaborate in its fine points and primitively exaggerated in its essential nature," and here, too, the observations of travelers from the seaboard formed a record of "the Tidewater's amused estimate of the raw frontier." This harsh, cruel world, as Holman notes, is reflected by the writing of the antebellum southern humorists and in the twentieth century by the work of William Faulkner.[19] It is also reflected, with vigor and color, by the Border Romances, wherein society, Simms says in a passage corroborating Holman's statement, is formed by such people "as will be found ordinarily to compose the frontier and outskirts of civilization . . . the spendthrift and the indolent, the dreamer and the outlaw . . . some with the view to profit and gain; others, simply from no alternative being left them," and still others "almost purely from a spirit of adventure."[20]

If southern humor formed the leavening for Simms's Border Romances, the Murrell material furnished essential elements in their

19. Holman, *Three Modes*, 28–29. Jay B. Hubbell, in *The South in American Literature, 1607–1900* ([Durham], N.C., 1954), 590, remarks that Simms saw the strain of violence in southern life as plainly as Robert Penn Warren and William Faulkner.

20. [William Gilmore Simms], *Guy Rivers: A Tale of Georgia* (New York, 1834), I, 56–57. Unless otherwise indicated, further references to this novel are to this edition, cited within the text by volume and page number.

structural patterns. Murrell was perhaps the most renowned of the robbers and killers who terrorized the Old Southwest in the general area of the Natchez Trace.[21] Of courteous, genteel manner, the man Mark Twain would later call a "stately old-time criminal" was clever, ingratiating, sensual, hypocritical, and sadistic. When he was in jail for horse theft, Murrell studied the Scriptures and thereafter passed as a Methodist parson, in classic frontier manner fleecing crowds while feigning piety. After murdering several people, he began to steal Negroes—an activity that became the source of most of his wealth and that finally set his captor Virgil Stewart on his trail. As he told Stewart, he would steal a black or persuade him to run away by promising freedom, sell him and get him to escape again, and resell him until the practice became risky because a slave who had made the rounds of several owners might be recognized. Then, said Murrell without any apparent remorse, "I shot him through the head . . . ripped open his belly and tumbled him into the river."[22]

Murrell had ambitious schemes, only partly fulfilled, for crime on a grand scale. According to popular report, he gathered men from all over the Gulf South into a loosely knit band called the "Mystic Confederacy" or "Mystic Brotherhood," which had oaths and signs perhaps derived from Masonry. Its headquarters were in a swamp called the "Garden of Eden," where the two orders of thugs, the grand coun-

21. The most important contemporary accounts of the Murrell saga exist in two versions—the first and shorter by Augustus Q. Walton, *A History of the Detection, Conviction, Life and Designs of John A. Murel, the Great Western Land Pirate. . . .* (Athens, Tenn., 1835); the second by H. R. Howard (comp.), *The History of Virgil A. Stewart, and His Adventure in Capturing and Exposing the Great "Western Land Pirate" and His Gang. . . .* (New York, 1836). During the 1840s there appeared sensational "police biographies" of Murrell—notably *The Life and Adventures of John A. Murrell, the Great Western Land Pirate. . . .* (New York, 1847), also published under the title *Pictorial Life and Adventures of John A. Murrell* (Philadelphia, 184[8?]. The *Union Catalogue* attributes both these volumes to H. R. Howard. Murrell's career is also treated by the following twentieth-century writers: Jonathan Daniels, *The Devil's Backbone: The Story of the Natchez Trace* (New York, 1962), 240–46; Robert M. Coates, *The Outlaw Years: The History of the Land Pirates of the Natchez Trace* (New York, 1930); Ross Phares, *Reverend Devil: A Biography of John A. Murrell* (New Orleans, 1941); Carl W. Breihan, *Badmen of the Frontier Days* (New York, 1957), Chap. 1; Bernard DeVoto, *Mark Twain's America* (Boston, 1932); and James Lal Penick, Jr., *The Great Western Land Pirate: John A. Murrell in Legend and History* (Columbia, Mo., 1981). Penick claims, p. 3, that Stewart was the probable author of the book ascribed to Augustus Q. Walton.

22. Samuel Langhorne Clemens [Mark Twain], *Life on the Mississippi* (Boston, 1883), 312; Howard (comp.), *The History of Virgil A. Stewart*, 66–68.

cil and the strikers, gathered after crimes and where Murrell laid his plans for a massive slave rebellion during which his men would rob the banks and burn the towns of the Old Southwest. Murrell doted on this scheme, boasting to Stewart, "I will have the pleasure and honour of seeing and knowing that by my management I have glutted the earth with more human gore, and destroyed more property, than any other robber who has ever lived in America, or the known world."[23] But thanks to Stewart's efforts, Murrell was captured and the rebellion never took place, although rumors about it raised such a scare in Mississippi that vigilant planters hanged several white men and scores of slaves who had presumably been involved in it.

Intrepid Virgil Stewart was born and reared in Georgia; but he settled on a farm in western Tennessee, where in early 1834 a friend whose Negroes had been stolen set him on the outlaw's trail. Traveling on horseback, Stewart fell in with Murrell, flattered him outrageously, feigned friendliness to crime, won Murrell's confidence, and rode with him to his swamp retreat, where he joined the Mystic Confederacy—secretly scratching the names of its members, so he claimed, "on his boot-legs, saddle-skirts, finger-nails, and portmanteau, with a needle." On a pretext he left the group, set a trap for Murrell, and revealed his true identity only after the rogue was captured. Murrell's fellow criminals then tried to blacken Stewart's character; they also waylaid him, wounded him, and attempted to poison him. While recovering from his injuries, in order to counter the thugs' charges against his character, he procured testimony to his virtues from friends whose depositions are included in published accounts. As a result of Stewart's accusations, Murrell was jailed for ten years on a charge of stealing Negroes; he died shortly after leaving prison. Stewart, according to one version of his tale, felt his life in constant danger and moved to Texas, where he died a natural death shortly after Murrell was released.[24]

Using the notes he had made on the expedition, Stewart told his story to a friend, Augustus Q. Walton, who wrote and published it in 1835. The following year a sensational writer, H. R. Howard, con-

23. DeVoto, *Mark Twain's America,* 18; Walton, *A History of the Detection, Conviction, Life and Designs of John A. Murel,* 41; Howard (comp.), *The History of Virgil A. Stewart,* 59–60.

24. Howard (comp.), *The History of Virgil A. Stewart,* 81; "Uses and Abuses of Lynch Law," *American Whig Review,* XIII (March, 1851), 217.

structed, with Stewart's help, a more detailed narrative that brings up to date the information about Stewart and the Murrell gang. In these sensational accounts with their many implausibilities, fact reads like fiction: as a twentieth-century writer remarks, the tale has a dime-novel quality that does not help its credibility; and therefore, not surprisingly, skeptics have questioned its truthfulness from time to time.[25] Its pertinence for scholarship, however, lies less in its fidelity to fact than in its influence on Simms's fiction. For in selecting the Murrell saga as one strand in the enveloping action of his border volumes, Simms was making, in effect, what was a natural choice for a romancer, for the material, as worked up by Stewart and his friends, shows some familiar properties of romance. It has a journey plan, a forest setting, an emphasis on adventure, and simplified characters sketched in black and white terms. It has also a rigid antithesis of good and evil centered in the opposition of hero and villain, a presentation slanted in favor of the "right" side, and an action that shows, in its broad outlines, a providential movement. At the end of the narrative, justice triumphs, order prevails, and the popular assumption that crime does not pay is vindicated. The accounts of Murrell read, in fact, like inchoate romance; and they resemble police biographies of criminals and other pulp forms that are probably offshoots of the genre.

In a statement raising problems that may never be resolved, Simms, who was in the Gulf South during the early phases of the Murrell crime wave, claimed that he knew "Stuart [*sic*], the captor of Murrell, personally; and had several conferences with him, prior to the publication of his narrative." The crimes portrayed in the Border Romances, Simms continued, "were then actually in progress of commission"; he sketched some of the scenes and several of the characters, he reported, "from personal observation, and after the current reports from the best local authorities." Critics since Trent have accepted Simms's statements at face value: William Stanley Hoole, for instance, conjectures that Simms met Stewart on his journey to the Gulf South during 1831 near the height of the Murrell crimes. But Stewart was not in the area

25. Daniels, *The Devil's Backbone,* 240. J. F. H. Claiborne, *Life and Correspondence of John A. Quitman, Major-General, U.S.A., and Governor of the State of Mississippi* (New York, 1860), I, 138*n,* calls Stewart an impostor and claims: "The whole story was a fabrication. Murrell was simply a thief and counterfeiter, and Stuart [*sic*] was his subordinate, who, having quarreled with him, devised this plan to avenge and enrich himself." Similar claims are advanced in Penick, *The Great Western Land Pirate, passim.*

at the time: as the narratives of Walton and Howard reveal, he did not take Murrell's trail until January, 1834. During much of that year, he was in Tennessee and Mississippi; he went to New Orleans and Cincinnati during 1835. Simms was apparently not in the Old Southwest during those years, nor can it be shown that he returned to the area before 1842, after three of the four Border Romances had been issued. Moreover, his published correspondence affords no proof that he went to Tennessee or Cincinnati to talk with Stewart, as Hampton M. Jarrell, writing near the same time as Hoole, hypothesizes.[26]

But even if Simms's conversations with Stewart cannot be verified, there is little doubt that he was familiar with the printed narratives deriving from Stewart's adventures. Appearing shortly after Walton's and Howard's books and plainly in debt to them was *Richard Hurdis,* which Simms apparently began in 1837. It was finished by April, 1838, when he sent the last two chapters to Carey and Hart; it was so popular that it went through two editions by the end of the year. Simms told Edward Carey to make sure it was circulated in Alabama and Mississippi, where he believed it would be widely read (*L,* VI, 12). Like *Border Beagles* and *Beauchampe,* the novel was issued anonymously because Simms wanted to confound "the small tribe of underling critics" who had sniped at his work. That some of the reviewers in question were taken in by the ruse is indicated by the fact that they praised the anonymous works while contrasting them favorably with Simms's acknowledged writings (*L,* I, 316). Yet in a sense the scheme backfired on Simms, for the anonymous volumes were much less widely noticed in the press than were those bearing the well-known author's name.

Simms in *Richard Hurdis* relies upon the printed narratives of the Murrell saga for his main plot lines and many of his incidental details.[27]

26. Advertisement to W[illiam] Gilmore Simms, *Richard Hurdis: A Tale of Alabama* (Rev. ed.; New York, 1855), 11. On Simms's possible conversations with Stewart, see Trent, *William Gilmore Simms,* 116; William Stanley Hoole, "A Note on Simms's Visits to the Southwest," *American Literature,* VI (November, 1934), 335; and Hampton M. Jarrell, "Simms's Visits to the Southwest," *American Literature,* V (March, 1933), 33. Stewart's activities during 1834 and 1835 are described by Walton, *A History of the Detection, Conviction, Life and Designs of John A. Murel,* 66–68, and Howard (comp.), *The History of Virgil A. Stewart, passim.*

27. In view of the correspondences between the novel and the published accounts of the Murrell saga, Floyd H. Deen's conclusion that Simms follows his authorities in only a general way seems unjustified. See "A Comparison of Simms's *Richard Hurdis* with Its Sources," *Modern Language Notes,* LX (June, 1945), 408.

The title character and hero of the novel is a self-willed, impetuous youth who is restless, rebellious, and inclined to gloom. Influenced in conception by the criminal narrators of such earlier Simms works as *Martin Faber,* he is also shaped to embody "the wandering habit of our people" described in "Notes of a Small Tourist" and "The Western Emigrants." Bent on seeking danger on the frontier of the Gulf South, Hurdis leaves his Alabama farm to seek the Choctaw territory of Mississippi, where he plans to assist his friend William Carrington in buying land. But he is captured by members of the Mystic Brotherhood, a self-styled "parcel of bold fellows, who don't like the laws of the state exactly . . . and who have accordingly associated together, for the purpose of making their own. . . . we get the negroes to run away from their owners, then sell them to others, get them to run away again, and in this way, we probably sell the same negro, half a dozen times. . . . When the affair gets too tangled, and we apprehend detection, we tumble the negro into a river, and thus rid ourselves of a possession that has paid good interest already, and which it might not be any longer safe to keep" (II, 60–61).

Hurdis' vengeful brother John has Carrington killed and then is blackmailed into joining the Mystic Brotherhood. Hurdis, meanwhile, determined to avenge his friend, adopts the dress of a gambler and boards a steamboat, where he falls in with Clement Foster, Simms's fictionalized version of Murrell. Foster is perhaps the most intriguing character in the novel, a complex person who like his real-life counterpart is charming, treacherous, and brutal. Posing as a canting evangelical parson, he cries to Hurdis and some other cardplayers: "My young friends . . . let me beg you not to engage in this wicked amusement. Cards are, as it has been often and well said—cards are the prayer books of the devil" (II, 190). But Hurdis holds fast to his disguise as a crook and flatters Foster outrageously, whereupon the "old reprobate" drops his pose and takes the youth into his confidence (II, 197). He boasts, in passage after passage that Simms borrows from his sources, that he controls fifteen hundred men in the southern states, who practice roguery while professing "religion, law, physic, planting, shopkeeping" (II, 212). Like Murrell, he proclaims that he is "no common robber" and announces, "Societies have been formed, schemes laid, companies raised and juries prompted" to catch him in his crimes, "but all in vain" (II, 214). Finally, he exults to Hurdis, in the manner of Murrell to Stewart: "I have the whole southwest in a string, and have only to pull it to secure a golden draught. You shall be with me at the pulling" (II, 216).

Hurdis follows Foster to his swamp retreat, and Simms draws on his memories of the Gulf South in describing the "low boggy ground" and "turbid yellow water" of the region (II, 234). After learning the secrets of the clan, Hurdis escapes, marshals planters and farmers in the area, and leads the assault on the criminals. Most of the rogues are killed, but Foster gets away by jumping on a bag of cotton and tumbling it into the river. As he floats along, he cries waggishly to Hurdis: "Ah . . . you are a sad dog, and something more of a hypocrite than the parson. . . . We shall meet some day in Arkansas, where I shall build a church in the absence of better business, and perhaps make you a convert" (II, 352–53). Among the many elements from the Murrell saga that Simms makes use of in *Richard Hurdis* are the villain's pose as a preacher, his outlandish boasts, and his comprehensive mastery of crime, together with the hero's disguise as a criminal, his skillful flattery of the villain, and his eventual betrayal of the clan.

When considered alongside the sources Simms used for his Revolutionary War Romances, the Murrell material has some evident limitations as a basis for serious works of fiction. Unlike the patriot histories about the Revolutionary War, it is not lofty and idealistic, but vulgar, sensational, and cheap. It did not evoke in Simms a sense of moral urgency or patriotic pride, nor did it give him the same comprehensive vision of an entire culture at bay that he found in the Revolutionary War material. Its emphasis on villainy, and sadistic villainy at that, encouraged his tendency, already strong, to emphasize crime, while its bombast unhappily stimulated his own appetite for melodrama, so that the merits of his books are sometimes overshadowed by shrill or strident passages. As a consequence, although the soaring backwoods humor of the Border Romances surpasses anything he would do in that vein before the early 1850s, the volumes are in general less firmly conceived than are their Revolutionary War counterparts.[28]

Trent remarked that Simms's journeys to the Gulf South "familiarized him with the life of a peculiar people, and enabled him in after years to describe that life as no other writer has done, or in all probability will do." But Trent also charged that the Border Romances are marred "by a slipshod style, by a repetition of incidents, and by the introduction of an unnecessary amount of the horrible and the revolt-

28. For similar statements, see Trent, *William Gilmore Simms,* 88, 328.

ing." These, however, are also the faults of a body of writing whose authors miss no chance to wallow in the sordid and debased. With its Byzantine complexities, its plots and counterplots, its disguises, deceptions, and intrigues, its poisonings, stabbings, and willful atrocities, the savage story of John A. Murrell, "Reverend Devil," occupies perhaps the lowest rung of the romance ladder, if romance indeed it should be called. The wonder is not therefore, despite Simms's critics, that the books based on that story are extravagant and violent, "purely sensational," "bloody and tearful and barbarously ornate." Given the gore that embellishes the Murrell extravaganza, the wonder, instead, is that they are not worse.[29]

*

Antebellum southern or southwestern humor, the other great influence on the border volumes, was a field in the making at the time Simms began to write. Although it had existed in oral and subliterary versions for decades, its first significant documents in book form appeared at about the same time that he was starting to publish novels in the middle 1830s. Influenced by colonial promotional tracts, by travelers' narratives, by neoclassical satire, and by British and American sporting literature, the field was also affected by such diverse authors as Robert Bolling, William Byrd II, Washington Irving, Parson Weems, Davy Crockett, and James Kirke Paulding, the hero of whose popular drama *The Lion of the West* (1831) was himself derived from Crockett.[30] Although it flourished in all parts of the South, it is particularly associated with the states of Georgia, Alabama, and Mississippi and with the authors Augustus Baldwin Longstreet, William Tappan Thompson, Thomas Bangs Thorpe, Joseph Glover Baldwin, and George Washington Harris—and also, to a lesser extent, with Henry Clay Lewis, William Elliott, and Solomon Franklin Smith.[31]

29. *Ibid.*, 15–16, 88; John Erskine, *Leading American Novelists* (New York, 1910), 158; and Carl Van Doren, *The American Novel, 1789–1939* (Rev. ed.; New York, 1940), 55.

30. General discussions of southern humor may be found in Walter Blair, *Native American Humor* ([San Francisco], 1960), 3–101; Walter Blair and Hamlin Hill, *America's Humor: From Poor Richard to Doonesbury* (New York, 1978), 113–248; Hennig Cohen and William B. Dillingham (eds.), *Humor of the Old Southwest* (2nd ed.; Athens, Ga., 1975), [xiii]–xxviii; and Richard Boyd Hauck, *Crockett: A Bio-Bibliography* (Westport, Conn., 1982), who helps make sense of the bibliographical tangle involving the several books attributed to Crockett.

31. The mode commonly called southwestern humor was in actuality a widespread southern phenomenon. On this point, see, for example, Stephen E. Meats (ed.), "South Carolina Writers in the *Spirit of the Times*," in James L. W. West III (ed.), *Gyascutus:*

For the most part, the creators of this humor were journalists, lawyers, doctors, and other professional men who like Simms had been reared in the seaboard South and had traveled on the frontier. Much of their writing portrays the predictable tensions between tidewater and backwoods customs, with the scale sometimes tipped in favor of frontier freedom from civilized restraints. Giving literary shape to the contrast of region and social level are the figures of gentlemen and backwoodsmen, the former speaking the genteel language associated with the older South and the latter mouthing a broad, colorful dialect characteristic of the backwoods. This pairing of opposites, which of course occurs also in the serious fiction of the time, may be seen as a clash between aristocratic Whigs and rough Jacksonian Democrats or, more broadly, as a conflict between traditional values associated with the East and subversive ones connected with the West.[32] However it is finally described, the contrast serves to indicate the difference between the tidewater South Simms grew up in and the pioneer South that he saw on his travels in the 1820s and the early 1830s.

Because antebellum southern humor was produced by men who in many cases built upon one another's writing, and also because it frequently recycles folk material, it contains recurring subjects and character types that allow its general outlines to be drawn with some distinctness. Its standard figures include boatmen and hunters; braggarts and bullies; crooked politicians and lawyers; whining, canting evangelical preachers; Yankee peddlers and other conmen; fops; inept foreigners; drunkards and gamblers; bodice-bursting rural beauties; and yokels or country bumpkins. Its typical subjects include hoaxes, pranks, and practical jokes; fights or pretended fights; frolics, dances, courtships, and weddings; hunting and fishing; the gander pulling, the shoot for beef, the horse race, and the horse swap; camp meetings and sermons; electioneering and the courtroom.[33] In literary mode it veers,

Studies in Antebellum Southern Humorous and Sporting Writing (Atlantic Highlands, N.J., 1978), [185]–207, and James E. Kibler, Jr.'s edition of a heretofore unpublished antebellum South Carolina backwoods novel, O. B. Mayer's *John Punterick: A Novel of Life on the Old Dutch Fork* (Spartanburg, S.C., 1981).

32. Kenneth S. Lynn discusses some political aspects of the mode in *Mark Twain and Southwestern Humor* (Boston, 1959). Blair and Hill treat comic "reputables" and "subversives" in *America's Humor,* 172–99.

33. For a full list of topics, see Franklin J. Meine (ed.), *Tall Tales of the Southwest: An Anthology of Southern and Southwestern Humor, 1830–1860* (New York, 1930), xxvi; and Cohen and Dillingham (eds.), *Humor of the Old Southwest,* xvii.

Woodlands, Simms's plantation home

Evert A. Duyckinck and George L. Duyckinck (eds.), *Cyclopædia of American Literature* (New York, 1856), II, 427.

Chevillette Eliza Roach Simms

Portrait owned by Mrs. James C. Player.

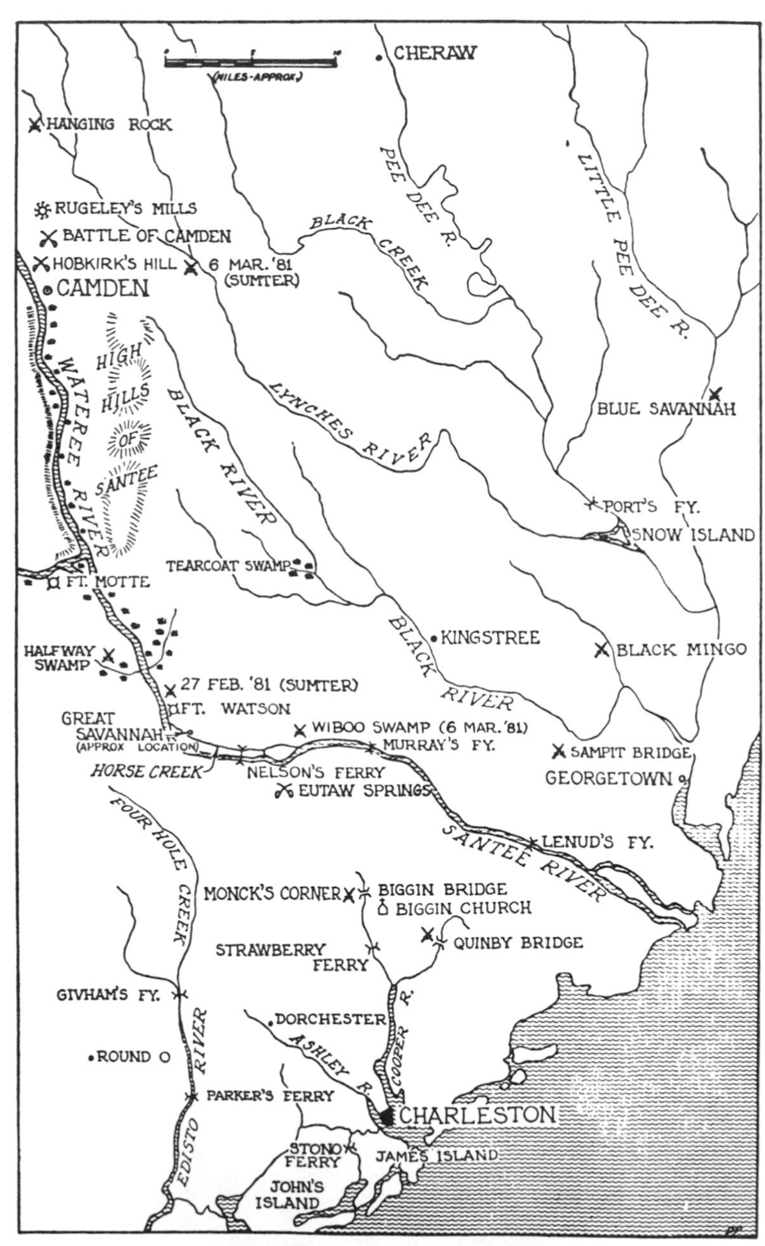

Map of Revolutionary War battles in South Carolina

Mark Mayo Boatner III, *Encyclopedia of the American Revolution* (New York, 1974), copyright ©1974, 1966 by Mark Mayo Boatner III. With permission of the David McKay Co., a Division of Random House, Inc.

James Lawson

Duyckinck Family Papers, Rare Books and Manuscripts Division, The New York Public Library, Astor, Lenox and Tilden Foundations.

General Nathaniel Greene

William Johnson, *Sketches of the Life and Correspondence of Nathanael Greene* (Charleston, S.C., 1822), extra-illustrated copy, Vol. I, Pt. 1, frontispiece. Department of Rare Books, William R. Perkins Library, Duke University.

General Francis Marion

William Johnson, *Sketches of the Life and Correspondence of Nathanael Greene* (Charleston, S.C., 1822), extra-illustrated copy, Vol. II, Pt. 1, facing p. 189. Department of Rare Books, William R. Perkins Library, Duke University.

Drawing of the Mystic Brotherhood attacking Richard Hurdis

W[illiam] Gilmore Simms, *Richard Hurdis: A Tale of Alabama* (Rev. ed.; New York, 1855), facing title page.

Drawing of Ellis Saxon trying to rob Harry Vernon while Tom Horsey sleepwalks

W[illiam] Gilmore Simms, *Border Beagles: A Tale of Mississippi* (New York, 1882), frontispiece.

James Henry Hammond, from a painting by William Scarborough, 1850

Courtesy of the South Caroliniana Library, University of South Carolina.

Evert Augustus Duyckinck

Print Collection, Miriam and Ira D. Wallach Division of Art, Prints & Photographs, The New York Public Library, Astor, Lenox and Tilden Foundations.

Paul Hamilton Hayne

Engraving in *Frank Leslie's Illustrated Newspaper,* February 2, 1861.

John Esten Cooke

Evert Augustus Duyckinck and George Long Duyckinck (eds.), *Cyclopædia of American Literature* (New York, 1856), II, 636.

William Gilmore Simms in casual dress

Evert Augustus Duyckinck and George Long Duyckinck (eds.), *Cyclopædia of American Literature* (New York, 1856), II, 429.

William Porcher Miles

Engraving in *Harper's Weekly,* IV (February 11, 1860), 81.

Drawing of Harry Calvert threatening his wife Zulieme

William Gilmore Simms, *The Cassique of Kiawah: A Colonial Romance* (New York, 1859), facing title page.

Drawing of a man and a panther
William T. Porter (ed.), *The Big Bear of Arkansas* (Philadelphia, 1845), [183].

Drawing of a bear hunt
William T. Porter (ed.), *The Big Bear of Arkansas* (Philadelphia, 1845), [187].

Drawing of Sharp Snaffles accosting Bachelor Grimstead

[William Gilmore Simms], "How Sharp Snaffles Got His Capital and Wife," *Harper's New Monthly Magazine,* XLI (October, 1870), 687.

William Gilmore Simms in late middle age

Engraving in possession of the Manuscript Department, William R. Perkins Library, Duke University.

as Constance Rourke and Edd Winfield Parks have noted, between graphic realism and soaring fantasy, and despite occasional pessimism, it is shot through with a glorious *joie de vivre* that kindled deep responses in Simms's imagination.[34]

As subjects, characters, and episodes in his work reveal, Simms had early been exposed to the broad-based, many-stranded oral and written tradition from which southern humor had evolved. He relished, for example, his father's tales of Mississippi, which included a good bit of comic or semicomic frontier lore; and as the editors of his letters state, he "sometimes amused or outraged friends and acquaintances by acting the role of backwoodsman or of Indian chief" (*L,* VI, 208*n*4). He knew Paulding, and he may have seen *The Lion of the West* on one of his trips to New York or in other cities where the popular drama played. He commented in his letters on Davy Crockett, made Crockett a major figure in his melodrama *Michael Bonham,* and told yarns attributed to that canebrake hero (*L,* III, 375). He probably read Longstreet's *Georgia Scenes* shortly after it was published; he secured the second series of the *Scenes* for the *Magnolia* during the period in which he edited it; and there is little doubt that he recalled such seminal sections of the original work as "The Turf" and "The Gander Pulling" when he wrote about the same subjects in *As Good as a Comedy.* From the 1830s on, he employed character types such as the Yankee and the woodsman that eventually became the humorists' stock-in-trade, and he also employed subjects and settings associated with southern humor, like the fight, the frolic, the country circus, and the shooting match. Finally, he was more adept than scholars yet have granted at contrasting genteel types associated with the tidewater and roughshod characters connected with the frontier—and also at passing judgment upon the backwoods through the aloof, amused language of the tidewater author. His use of southern humor forms one of the most attractive aspects of his writing, and because it has not been studied with any thoroughness, it repays examination in detail.

Simms's interest in this humor near the beginning of his career is revealed by two stories that he published in the 1820s, "Country Comforts" and "The Fisherman—A Fact"—the one a tale of two southern gentlemen inhospitably accommodated in a rural inn, the other a yarn

34. Constance Rourke, *American Humor: A Study of the National Character* (New York, 1931), 67; Edd Winfield Parks, "The Three Streams of Southern Humor," *Georgia Review,* IX (Summer, 1955), 147–59.

of a planter who hopes to make his fortune by fishing for sunken treasure. But the real predecessors of the important contributions he would make to the mode appear in "Letters from the West" and "Notes of a Small Tourist," which detail his travels of the 1820s and 1830s respectively. Two funny little tales he develops in these letter series show him using language and character types associated with southern humor that would shortly become staple elements in his fiction about the lower South.

The anecdote in "Letters from the West" involves that stock figure of early American comedy, the naïve and expostulatory little Frenchman, who is gulled by a native wit into believing that Indian ponies frequently climb hickory trees in order to gather nuts.[35] The tale in "Notes of a Small Tourist" centers on Karl Bernhard, duke of Saxe Weimar, "the princely infant, who," Simms comments playfully, "lately ran through our nation, and made a book thereon." In a generic encounter between patrician and democrat, the Duke becomes embroiled with a sturdy stagecoach driver, whom he threatens to whip. But the driver, "peeling himself for the combat . . . leaped about the vehicle, in the most wild boar style, calling upon the Prince of a five acre patch, to put his threat into execution." The outraged Duke announces he will complain to the governor; but the driver proclaims: "The Governor might go to ———, &c. &c. For his part, he would just as leave *lick* the Governor, as the Duke. He never did like the Governor—didn't vote for him at last 'lections, and wouldn't, if it lay with him, make him a county justice. He'd like no better fun than to give both Duke and Governor a dressing in the same breath—could do it, he had little doubt, &c." And, Simms concludes with a flourish, the driver, "instigating one fist to diverge into the face of the marvelling and panic-stricken nobleman, with the other . . . thrust him down into a seat . . . mounted his box in triumph, and went on his journey" (*L*, I, 23–24).[36]

35. Kibler, "The First Simms Letters," 90. That Simms was fond of the little Frenchman as a comic figure is shown by his reference to the character type in *Woodcraft: Or Hawks About the Dovecote. A Story of the South at the Close of the Revolution* (Rev. ed.; New York, 1854), Chap. 41. Further references to this novel are to this edition, cited by page number within the text (as *W* where necessary for clarity).

36. Karl Bernhard's book was *Travels Through North America, During the Years 1825 and 1826* (Philadelphia, 1828). Frances Trollope read an extract from Simms's account of Bernhard in an antebellum newspaper and observed, "The American people, (speaking of the great mass,) have no more idea of what constitutes the difference between this 'Prince of a five acre patch,' and themselves, than a dray-horse has of estimat-

When set alongside Simms's early fiction, these tales bear witness to the author's interest in the methods and devices of southern humor at a point before that genre had fairly established itself in the public eye, and they further suggest that in employing this mode he was working somewhat in advance of the major antebellum humorists. Clearly he was primed for the sort of backwoods comedy that would animate the pages of his novels about the Gulf South and that, in conjunction with the Murrell material, would form the major influence upon them.

---

ing the points of the elegant victor of the race-course" (*Domestic Manners,* II, 118). Simms, who reviewed Trollope's book sharply in "Mrs. Trollope and the Americans," *American Quarterly Review,* XII (September and December, 1832), 109–33, did not mention her remarks. His review was reprinted as "Domestic Manners of the Americans" in *Views and Reviews in American Literature, History and Fiction,* 2nd ser. (New York, 1845), 1–56.

5

Passing the Alps: The Border Romances

Guy Rivers, *Richard Hurdis*, *Border Beagles*, and *Helen Halsey*, the four main border volumes, are romances with a contemporary setting in which the framing action and the dialectic structure are furnished by the clash between civilization and anarchy, or law and crime, that Simms found in the history of the Gulf South and particularly in the Murrell material. Typically enough, given his tidewater sensibilities, he renders this situation as a clash between the ordered society of the plantation South and the unbridled license of the far frontier. The resolution of the conflict in each book by forces representing the civilized South conveys his view, as articulated in "Letters from the West," "Notes of a Small Tourist," and "The Social Principle," that the institutions developed in the tidewater should serve as models for those of its newer neighbor.

The generic plot Simms constructed for the Border Romances, which embodies these beliefs, shows him combining southern humor and the Murrell stories with details drawn from his personal adventures and imbedding those elements within the ancient literary pattern of the journey—a procedure reinforced by his travels into and out of the Gulf region and also by the narratives of Virgil Stewart, which make use of a journey structure. In each of the Border Romances, a young man who is either from the tidewater region or from the planting society of the Gulf South makes his way to the frontier, where he falls into the hands of a group of criminals modeled on the Murrell thugs. With the aid of farmers, planters, and various comically conceived rural characters, he defeats the criminals, thereby helping to subdue crime in the border areas. At the end of the novel—matured, sobered, and toughened by the crimes he has witnessed—he is ready to return to the responsible life of the agricultural society that embodies, in Simms's view, the fullest potential of antebellum culture.

The major changes Simms makes between the Border Romances and the low-country volumes are the addition of the journey structure and the thematic statement communicated through the framing action. Otherwise, his literary procedures in the two sets of books are much the same. He employs as part of his central narrative a love story that recapitulates elements of his public action and whose central figures represent important aspects of the society of the lower South. His heroes, for instance, stand for the emerging farm-and-plantation life of the Gulf states, which at the time he was writing was more modest than that of its tidewater predecessor, while his heroines, a slightly more varied group than their counterparts in the low-country volumes, come from this same society or from the lawless group that the hero pursues. The villains, who except for Guy Rivers are modeled on John A. Murrell, inevitably represent the criminal element in the region; and just as inevitably, given the dialectic system, they oppose the society that the lovers represent. In the symbolic structure of the volumes, therefore, they are generally suitors for the heroine. They may also be involved in a subplot centering on seduction and betrayal that constitutes the major evidence in these volumes of material deriving from the antebellum sentimental and domestic romance.

Because the public action of the books derives from exceedingly sensational material, it is wild and improbable in places—according well with Hugh Holman's observation that historically the literature of the Gulf South has been characterized by violence and sensationalism. Rough and raucous, the comedy that is a signal feature of these books echoes and balances their melodrama. Northrop Frye remarks that the stiff characters and stylized actions of melodrama constitute a kind of comedy without humor—an observation that helps explain how the rampant violence in the main plot and the boisterous comedy of subordinate narrative lines operate in tandem throughout the border volumes. Repeatedly in them, Simms fits sequences of southern humor into patterns deriving from romance to reinforce the major issues in the central story. In the classic manner of backwoods humor, his procedure suggests that suffering, ugliness, and death do not so much clash with comedy of this sort as they become a part of it.[1]

By the early 1830s there was a tradition of novels about the Ameri-

1. Frye, *Anatomy of Criticism,* 40; Cohen and Dillingham (eds.), *Humor of the Old Southwest,* xxvi.

can frontier, started by Cooper in *The Prairie* (1827) and continued by Paulding in *Westward Ho! A Tale* (1832) and James Hall in *Harpe's Head* (1833). Simms was influenced by these volumes, particularly *Harpe's Head,* but that his third visit to the Old Southwest was the immediate inspiration for the border series is suggested by his comments in his letters about the composition of *Guy Rivers.* He started the novel, he remarks, in 1832, the year after his trip to Mississippi to settle his father's estate; he wrote Lawson in November that "the first volume, in rough, is completed" (*L,* V, 357, I, 45).[2] By January, 1833, he had sent this volume to Harper Brothers, and at his Uncle James's request he was also contemplating a return to Mississippi, which he jovially described as "the stabling place of the Sun" (*L,* I, 49). There is no firm evidence that he made this trip; but at any rate he was at work again upon the book the following November, and it was issued during June or July, 1834 (*L,* I, 53, 59).

Like most Simms volumes of the thirties, *Guy Rivers* was greeted enthusiastically, with only a few voices raised in dissent; it was especially popular in the North, which (as Simms complained) was somewhat quicker than the South to recognize his literary talent. Lewis Gaylord Clark of the *Knickerbocker Magazine,* who would shortly become one of Simms's sharpest critics, said no modern novel could equal its descriptive passages; the critic for the New York *Mirror* commended its "striking originality"; and Henry William Herbert, in a long, glowing essay in the *American Monthly Magazine,* praised the book's "dark and terrible interest" that "chains down our faculties as we read." Comparisons with Cooper, which would haunt the history of Simms criticism, became common: Herbert, for example, maintained that Cooper "could not have written Guy Rivers though he died for it."[3] A few reviewers complained about Simms's prolixity—a complaint that he himself would echo when he told Griswold in 1846 that the style of the novel "betrays the labor and anxiety of a young author,

2. In the index to Vol. V of Simms's letters, the editors say that this work was misidentified in Vol. I as *Martin Faber.* On p. 10 of the Dedicatory Epistle in W[illiam] Gilmore Simms, *Guy Rivers: A Tale of Georgia* (Rev. ed.; New York, 1855), Simms said that the first volume of the novel was written "before I was of age"; but his statements in his letters of 1832 and 1833 are more likely to be accurate than this remark made many years later.

3. See [Lewis Gaylord Clark], "Literary Notices," *Knickerbocker Magazine,* IV (August, 1834), 147; Review of *Guy Rivers* in New York *Mirror,* August 2, 1834; and [Henry William Herbert], Review of *Guy Rivers,* in *American Monthly Magazine,* III (July, 1834), 297, 302.

highly ambitious of his tools but, as yet unpracticed in the use of them" (*L*, II, 224). As *Guy Rivers, The Outlaw*, the novel was issued in London during 1841, and it was translated into German at some point between 1846 and 1854 (*L*, IV, 40*n*103).

Simms wrote Lawson that *Guy Rivers* was "a tale of Georgia—a tale of the miners—of a frontier and wild people, and the events are precisely such as may occur among a people & in a region of that character" (*L*, I, 55). The novel is based upon the gold rush that had taken place in northern Georgia in the early 1830s and upon the activities of the notorious Pony Club. One of "the most abandoned gangs of which the gallows was ever cheated," the Pony Club specialized in terrorizing luckless settlers and stealing their horses; among the features connecting it with Murrell is that branches of the organization existed, so a contemporary writer claimed, in every state then in the Union.[4]

At the time he wrote *Guy Rivers*, Simms had not yet visited northern Georgia; but he may have read about the Pony Club and the gold rush in the New York *American*, which ran articles and editorials upon the subject, or in the *Western Herald*, which was issued from a mining town in the heart of the gold-rush territory.[5] Or he may have heard tales of the miners when he visited the Crowell family west of Macon on his trip to Mississippi in early March, 1831. A son of the Crowells later wrote that Simms "had left Charleston with a view of travelling through Alabama, Mississippi, and Georgia, but especially what was then called the frontier. The wild stories then in circulation of daring adventure and wild lawless life of the frontier had attracted his attention, and he determined to see for himself. It was upon this journey that he obtained materials for *Guy Rivers*."[6]

The activities of the Pony Club, which resembled those of the Murrell thugs, gave Simms ample opportunity to contrast the fragile social and legal structure on Georgia's upcountry frontier with the criminal element engaged in challenging it. Rivers, the vicious leader of the club, represents the wild Georgia upcountry and its criminal forces; Ralph and Edith Colleton, the cousins and sweethearts who are the central romance figures, stand for "old Carolina" and the standards of justice

4. "Intruders upon Indian Lands," New York *American*, October 17, 1833. On the Georgia gold rush, see E. Merton Coulter, *Auraria: The Story of a Georgia Gold-Mining Town* (Athens, Ga., 1956).

5. Coulter, *Auraria*, 55.

6. The letter, published in *Rural Carolinian*, II (October, 1870), 62, is reprinted in Hoole, "A Note on Simms's Visits to the Southwest," 335–36.

associated with it. They are aided in their fight against Rivers by characters who symbolize the good side of frontier life—Lucy Munro, a backwoods girl who falls hopelessly in love with Ralph; Mark Forrester, a friendly woodsman who functions in romance fashion as Ralph's guide and companion; and Jared Bunce, a crafty Yankee peddler who is the chief comic figure of the book.

The violence that characterized the frontier of the Gulf South permeates major sequences of the novel, serving to connect its romance framework with its humorous strands. Rivers, who once loved Edith and therefore hates young Ralph, tries to force him to pay a traveler's tax as he makes his way through Georgia. When the youth refuses, he is shot and wounded; but Mark, who finds him by the wayside, nurses him back to health. Meanwhile, the squatters in the frontier village of Chestatee are threatening to lynch Jared, who has sold them nutmegs made from hickory and clocks that strike thirty-one times. With the help of the crooked lawyer Peter Pippin, the peddler gets away; shortly thereafter, Mark and other squatters savagely assault the Georgia Guard, which has come to remove them from the territory. In the melée that ensues, Rivers kills Mark and frames Ralph for the crime. Ralph is arrested; but aided by Jared and other backwoods friends, he eventually is freed and returns to South Carolina to marry Edith—while Rivers, in jail for Mark's murder, kills himself.

Simms's concern with orderly legal process versus dishonesty, extortion, and violent crime pervades both the main story and the subordinate narrative line, which centers on the luckless peddler Jared. Simms connects the two tales through parallel scenes, thereby mingling the romance material of his novel with sequences of southern humor. Immediately after Ralph falls into Rivers' hands, Simms shows Jared at the mercy of the regulators, a group of wild settlers who share Rivers' scorn for the procedures of civilized life. Jared—who exemplifies the tradition, well established in folklore, of the Yankee on the southern frontier—is, as Mark tells Ralph, a consummate scoundrel: "You can't measure his rascality, 'squire, if you was to try. Why, he can walk through your pockets, and the money will naturally cleave to him as if he were all wax. His very look stands for dollars and cents. . . . He can cheat you out of your eyes, and you won't know about it, till it's all done, and too late to make a fuss" (I, 64).[7]

7. Simms's revision of this passage for the 1855 edition of *Guy Rivers* indicates his interest in enhancing the realism and humor of Mark's description:

Maybe, he ain't a scamp of the biggest wethers. His rascality ain't to be measured.

The initial scene involving Jared reveals Simms's command, already demonstrated in his letter series about the Gulf South, of the subjects and methods of southern humor: classic frontier types like the squatter, the peddler, and the attorney; a gentlemanly voice, whether Ralph's or Simms's, commenting disdainfully from the sidelines; spicy speeches in dialect; and a mixture of danger and humor in which the latter finally predominates. Jared is brought to trial, says Simms in language typical of the tidewater vein in backwoods comedy, by farmers and villagers who "having partaken *ad libitum* of the various liquors distributed freely about the table . . . were sufficiently aroused by their potations to enter readily into any mischief" (I, 67). Chairing the session is pretentious Lawyer Pippin, a small-time crook "excessively expert in making the most of any difficulty among his neighbours" (I, 70). Pippin pompously announces, "I am required to arraign before you this same pedler, Jared Bunce, on sundry charges of misdemeanor, and swindling, and fraud—in short, as I understand it, for endeavouring, without having the fear of God and good breeding in his eyes . . . to pass himself off upon the good people of this county as an honest man" (I, 71).

In language nicely counterpointed to Pippin's stuffy phrases, the settlers charge that Jared, a "white-livered lizard," has sold them manufactured maple seeds, coffee made from rotten rye, and tinware "which went to pieces, the solder melting off at the very sight of the hot water" (I, 72, 75). The peddler slyly defends himself: "The tin wares I sell stand well enough in a northern climate: there may be some difference in yours that I can't account for. . . . Who knows, again, but you boil your water quite too hot?" (I, 75–76). He is shouted down, however, by Colonel Blundell, a rough squatter formed by "the tavern, and the race-course, and the cock-pit," who sneers, "That story of yours about the hot and cold climates may do for the daws to peck at, but you don't think the hawks will swallow it, do ye?" (I, 77–78).

With this, the trial grows violent as the settlers, drunk and enraged, yank Jared's goods from their boxes, tear them to pieces, set fire to the remnants, and, ominously chanting a lynching song, advance upon the hapless peddler. But the double-dealing Pippin—who sees, so he

---

Why, he kin walk through a man's pockets, jest as the devil goes through a crack or a keyhole, and the money will naterally stick to him, jest as ef he was made of gum turpentine. His very face is a sort of kining . . . machine. His look says dollars and cents; and its [*sic*] always your dollars and cents, and he kines them out of your hands into his'n, jest with a roll of his eye, and a mighty leetle turn of his finger. He cheats in everything, and cheats everybody (69).

thinks, a way to make some easy money—lends Jared his horse and arranges to meet him later in order that they may draw up a suit against the settlers. Jared craftily agrees; but with proverbial Yankee cunning he makes off with the horse and thus outwits the two-timing lawyer, whom he taunts in a saucy letter.

> I don't like to be in the reach of them 'ere regulators for some time to come yet, and guess 'twouldn't be altogether the wisest to stop short of a ride of fifteen miles to-night—so, therefore, you see it won't be in my way, no how, to let you have your nag. . . . I'm willing to allow you one hundred dollars for him, though he an't worth so much, no how, and the balance of the money you can send to me, or my brother, in the town of Meriden, in the state of Conneticut [*sic*]. So no more, dear lawyer, at this writing, from
>
> Your very humble sarvant to
> command, &c. &c.
> (Signed) JARED BUNCE. (I, 99–100)

By concluding the scene in this humorous manner, Simms insures that comedy with a strong backwoods flavor finally overmasters the violence with which it has been precariously balanced since the trial began. He also uses it, with some deftness, to offset and counterpoint the melodrama in the main plot, in which the possibility of conflict between the "good" characters led by Ralph and the "bad" ones headed by Rivers poses an ever-present threat to the harmony and stability of frontier life in Georgia.

Simms continues to connect the plot lines involving Ralph and Jared in a manner that emphasizes the contribution humorous backwoods characters make to his romance scheme. The pair leave Chestatee near the same time, and both fall in with a family of settlers traveling westward who evoke the "wandering spirit of our people" that Simms had criticized in "Notes of a Small Tourist" and "The Western Emigrants." Both are shortly thereafter arrested by Rivers' men—Jared for stealing Pippin's horse and Ralph on the trumped-up charge of murdering Mark—and both are taken to the Chestatee jail, where Pippin serves as their common counsel. He drops the charges against Jared, who then travels about the countryside in search of witnesses to help him prove that Ralph is innocent.

But while Jared works actively to secure Ralph's release, Pippin, who anticipates a long line of swindling lawyers in antebellum southern humor, inadvertently operates against young Ralph. At the trial, he so bungles his arguments that the judge reprimands him sharply; he also astounds Ralph's uncle with a wholly imaginary story of the crime. Ralph and Mark, he claims, had planned to leave Chestatee together; but Mark became drunk, and then:

> "Why then he swaggers and swears at every thing, and particularly at your nephew, who, you see, not knowing his condition, swears at him for keeping him waiting—"
>
> "Ralph Colleton never swears, Mr. Pippin," said the colonel, grimly.
>
> "Well—well, if he didn't swear then, he might very well have sworn, and I'll be sworn but he did on that occasion; and it was very pardonable too. Well, he swears at the drunken man, not knowing his condition, and the drunken man rolls and reels like a rowdy, and gives it to him back, and then they get at it. . . . Forrester, being uppermost, sticks his thumb into Master Colleton's eye—the left eye, I think it was—yes, the left eye it was—and the next moment it would have been out, when your nephew, not liking it, whipped out his dirk, and, 'fore Forrester could say Jack Robinson, it was playing about in his ribs. . . ."
>
> "And is none of this truth?"
>
> "God bless your soul, no." (II, 203–204)

At the end of the novel, Jared, telling Ralph, "I guess I must ha' been born by nature in the south, though I did see daylight in Connetticut [*sic*]," follows the Colleton carriage back to South Carolina (II, 307).[8] Pippin, equally provident, migrates to "the valley of the Mississippi," where, Simms remarks, "he got into fine practice—was notorious for his stump speeches," and was finally elected to the state legislature (II, 308–309). Both characters suggest the great social mobility existing on the frontier, while both show Simms, at the beginning of his career as a novelist, making clever use of the methods and materials of southern humor.

8. In a letter he wrote in December, 1846, to Rufus Griswold, Simms called Jared "a good fellow" and added: "By the way, whole pages of Guy Rivers have been stolen by Seatsfield, and have been quoted abroad as superior to what could be done by an American, even describing his own country. My Jared Bunce, is his Jared Bundell,—so close is the plagiarism" (*L*, II, 225–26). "Seatsfield," or, more accurately, "Sealsfield," was the pseudonym of the German writer Anton Postl. The work in question is *The Courtship of Ralph Doughby, Esquire,* first published in 1835 as the second part of *Life in the New World,* which has some scenes involving the peddler Jared Bundle. Karl J. Arndt examines the resemblance between the two peddlers in "Plagiarism: Sealsfield or Simms?" *Modern Language Notes,* LXIX (December, 1954), 577–81. Arndt observes that, because *Ralph Doughby* was published after *Guy Rivers,* Simms could hardly have copied from Sealsfield and concludes, perhaps too simply, that perhaps both authors found the source for Jared in a newspaper sketch (580–81).

Border Beagles, Simms's third novel about the Gulf South and the sequel to *Richard Hurdis,* was, like that work, published anonymously. Simms, who at one point considered calling it "The Yazoo Borderers," apparently began it during 1838 but encountered annoying delays when portions of the manuscript went astray in the mail (*L,* VI, 15–17). The book was finally issued in 1840 and was hailed as "well conceived, perspicuous and stirring," a writer for the *Knickerbocker Magazine* commending its scenes of "unusual power and beauty."[9] One of Simms's liveliest volumes, it is crammed with comic figures—a nosy village rustic, an itinerant actor, a rollicking young woodsman who rivals any character in Simms's fiction for broadly humorous appeal. As in *Guy Rivers,* Simms constructs melodramatic and comic sequences that run parallel to each other and intersect at important points, with the issue of law and crime a common thematic element. His central story picks up where *Richard Hurdis* ends as Clement Foster, the leader of the Mystic Brotherhood, appears in Mississippi. There, under the name Ellis Saxon, he heads a group of thugs known as "border beagles" because they use the beagle's cry as a secret signal. To Mississippi also comes Harry Vernon, a stand-in for Simms who is a young attorney from the older South. At the behest of his friend Ben Carter, Vernon is trying to track down the elderly William Maitland, who has absconded with money for which Carter stands bond. Since Vernon is going into Yazoo territory on his search, the governor of Mississippi commissions him to report on the beagles who are suspected to be in the region.

In his wanderings, Vernon is accompanied by Tom Horsey, a strolling actor whom Saxon has tricked into believing that Vernon is secretly going to join a theatrical troupe playing in the backwoods. Saxon's outlaws lure Horsey into their swamp retreat, announce that he has been killed, and frame Vernon for the murder; but with the help of semihumorous figures representing the "good" side of backwoods life, he gets away. At the end of the book, Vernon and a band of respectable settlers assail the outlaws, see that Saxon is hanged, and help to wipe out crime in Mississippi, as Hurdis and his forces had helped obliterate it in Alabama.

To reinforce his point that the best parts of the backwoods and the plantation South have joined forces in the fight against crime, Simms

9. Review of *Border Beagles, Ladies' Companion,* XIII (October, 1840), 306; [Lewis Gaylord Clark], "Editors' Table," *Knickerbocker Magazine,* XVI (October, 1840), 364.

constructs three sets of character relationships that give figures from several sides of southern life symbolic literary status. Harry Vernon and Virginia Maitland, the well-born couple representing the settled South, battle Ellis Saxon, the outlaw leader who at one point in the novel abducts Virginia and takes her to his swamp retreat. Vernon's friend Wat Rawlins and his fiancée Rachael Morrison, a saucy woodsman and a saintly forest girl, battle Gideon Badger, one of Saxon's henchmen. And Tom Horsey, together with Mary Yarbers, fends off Ned Mabry, an eye-gouging frontier crook who is also a member of the beagle gang. Repeatedly throughout the novel, these patterned romance relationships furnish the matrix from which scenes of rollicking frontier comedy emerge.

Simms's main achievement in *Border Beagles* was to lard the romance plot with an even greater mixture of southern backwoods comedy than he had developed for *Guy Rivers*, using the humor to heighten his emphasis on the subject of law and crime. The first amusing rural figure he employs in the novel is John Horsey, a garrulous old fellow who is a familiar type in the lore of the backwoods—a talkative, inquisitive countryman of the sort sketched by Walter Blair and other scholars.[10] Horsey, father of actor Tom, peppers Vernon with questions at their first encounter: "[M]y name's John Horsey . . . but yours—what's your name? . . . Harry, Harry Vernon! You wasn't christened Harry, I reckon, Mr. Vernon? Must have been Henry, and they call you Harry for short. . . . The old people living, Mr. Vernon? Your health, sir, in the meantime. . . . Did I hear you, Mr. Vernon? the old people, you said they were living[?]" (I, 23–24).

After playing with John Horsey's inquisitiveness, Simms stresses his loquacity to render the broad outlines of pioneer experience in the Gulf South as he himself had witnessed it and also to prepare for Vernon's venture, which in part reflects his own, into Yazoo territory. Like Simms, old Horsey has mingled with the southern Indians, "the Creeks and the Cherokees, the Choctaws and the Chickasaws"; "I used to trade," he tells Vernon, "from Tennessee, through the mountains, into North and South Carolina,—then after that to the Massissippi; and many's the time I've made out to carry a matter of five pack-horses . . . through the very heart of the 'nation,' without so much as losing a thimble, and almost without having a scare" (I, 25). In passages that

10. Walter Blair, "Inquisitive Yankee Descendants in Arkansas," *American Speech,* XIV (February, 1939), [11]–22.

go beyond mere humor to capture the authentic flavor of frontier life, he continues:

> When we'd come to a running water, or a spring, or some such fine place for a camp, why we'd drive stakes, cut bushes, make tents, and fasten our horses. Then we'd feed 'em, git up a fire, and set to preparing our own feed. Well, we'd have to do all this mighty slyly, I tell you, for fear of the Indians. We'd git away from the main track, hide our horses pretty deep in the small woods, and put our fire in a sort of hollow, so that nobody could see the blaze. Then we'd git round it, put down a hoe and a griddle, bake the biscuit and broil the venison. Ah! Vernon, it was mighty sweet eating in that fashion. (I, 33).

Simms links this descriptive sequence to one of the broader concerns of the plot by introducing the issue of law and crime. After further talk, Vernon asks John Horsey how much he may depend upon the protection of the law in Yazoo territory, and Horsey rejoins, in sharp images: "Depend upon a hickory sapling and your own teeth rather. Depend upon steel and bullet, Harry Vernon, when you're on the Yazoo. What the d——l would a man expect to find, out, away on the very skirts, as I may call it, of civilization? Would you have gentlemen and Christians in a part of the world where there's no timber cut, no lands cleared, no houses built, nothing done, but what's done by the squatters and that sort of people?" (I, 39). His remarks, which point the difference between the civilized part of the South from which Vernon has come and the wilder part into which he is going, also suggest the dangers that the young man will encounter on his journey.

Immediately after this scene, Simms introduces Tom Horsey, the bombastic strolling actor who is a major comic figure in the novel. In developing the relationship of Vernon and Horsey, he uses the familiar romance device of paired hero and follower to represent the patrician and the rural aspects of life in the Gulf South, meanwhile shaping the rural figure so as to incorporate elements from southern humor. Staying close to Vernon as he travels toward the Yazoo lands, Horsey functions as a parodic version of the romance counselor figure, who instead of guarding the hero is guarded by him. He also emerges as a backwoods gull, an expert fighter, and a deluded thespian who spouts Shakespeare to uncomprehending rustics in the miry Mississippi swamp called Loosa-Chitta. After he and Vernon are out of civilized territory, he becomes involved in a fight employing "half-horse, half-alligator" braggarts whose outlines had been drawn by travelers, journalists, dramatists like Paulding, and humorists such as Longstreet in "Georgia Theatrics" and "The Fight." Simms constructs the battle in a manner that emphasizes the outlandish capers, extravagant boasts, mixed violence and humor, and elevated authorial commentary that the antebellum humorists had also begun to use.

Like much similar humor in the novel, the fight grows out of one of the romance structures of the book when Horsey, who has been courting the backwoods girl Mary Yarbers, is challenged to a battle by her longtime suitor Ned Mabry. Vernon, with his civilized sensibilities, insists that it should be what is known in frontier parlance as a "fair fight," but Mabry, a nasty fellow who specializes in gouging out opponents' eyes, wants to make it a no-holds-barred rough-and-tumble contest of the most egregious kind. As he approaches Horsey, snarling and prancing, he brandishes his fingers with their hideously long nails in a manner common to such frontier brawlers. Vernon objects, but Horsey interrupts him with a colorful boast: "Don't trouble yourself, Harry, about me,—'egad I'll swallow him, claws and all, though his scales were as rough and large as those of the biggest alligator that ever picked his teeth with a cypress on the banks of Pontchartrain" (I, 156).

Mabry then, in the usual fashion of bullies in literary fight scenes, leaps into the air and circles around Horsey, slapping his hands on his thighs, until "at length, with a whooping shriek, imitated from that of some wild beast of the forest, he threw a summerset, his feet aiming to strike the breast of the actor" (I, 156). To the relief of Vernon and the reader alike, Horsey finally clobbers the obnoxious little "varmint" and then glosses his behavior in a speech that gives the gruesome custom of gouging a humorous slant.

> "[I]t's absolutely necessary now and then to make an example of these fellows. They rely on superior strength to be insolent, and nothing would have pleased this chap so much as carrying home my eyes as a trophy. Years hence he would have a history for Dick Jenkins, and Jim Dobbins, and Peter Pinchback and a dozen others, of the dandy from below that he met at Yarbers' house, and 'how he caught,'"—imitating the patois of the country—"'how he caught the chap mighty soptious with the gal, and how he gin him the cross-buttock, and, before he could say Jack Robinson, had a finger in his shock and a thumb in his eye, and sent him off with the blind-staggers and two holes in his forehead that could make no use of specks, though he was mighty glad to wear them;' and then, to prove the truth of

> what he said, he would bring forth a bottle of eyes preserved in whisky. . . . The eyes of Tom Horsey preserved in whisky! Whew! The thought makes me shudder. . . . Eyes, Harry Vernon, are absolutely necessary to an actor."[11]

For other parts of the novel involving Horsey, Simms draws with some success on his knowledge, both traditional and personal, of the strolling actors who had thronged through the river towns and invaded the villages of the Gulf South. As he indicates in "Letters from the West," such actors, brash and cosmopolitan, regularly encountered naïve rustics whose inability to distinguish between theatrical art and life resulted in hilarious scenes. The classic account of such confusion is furnished by the actor, theatrical manager, and humorist Sol Smith, a traveler in the Gulf South near the time Simms went there, who tells, for instance, how he and his troupe put on a play called *The Mock Duke* in a frontier village. " [W]hen the duke," Smith says, "in answer to a knock at the door, bids his wife to 'see who it is that knocks,' a gentleman who happened to be standing near the stage-door, very composedly opened it, and peeping out, turned to the duke and answered, 'It is nobody but one of the actors; Mr. Tatem, I believe.'"[12]

Anticipating Smith's version of such scenes by about six years, Simms has Saxon's henchmen capture Horsey and beseech him to perform some scenes from a play. Before he can comply, however, a drunken yokel nicknamed Aristophanes Bull rolls forth a speech that for sheer mirth surpasses almost everything else in the novel.

> Tragedy be d——d. . . . tragedy be d——d—that's all in my eye and Betty Martin. . . . Who wants to see a fellow get up and blow out his cheeks, and roll up his eyes, and growl and roar and choke, and shake all over as if he had an agy? None of your tragedy for me. There's no sense in it. 'Tain't raal. I was once down in Mobile, when I saw them making tragedies, and, darken my peepers, but the bloody bitches made me mad enough to swallow 'em, they were so cussed r*e*diculous. . . .
>
> . . . There was a tragedian that came in looking after his enemy. He had his sword out, and he made a show as if he was mighty angry, but, between you and me, he didn't want to find him, no how. The other fellow was hiding behind a tree, and this chap looked for him every where but there. So,

11. *BB,* I, 159–60. In the first edition of the novel, Mary Yarbers is sometimes called Mary Stinson, and the name of the swamp is spelled both "Loosa-Chitta" and "Loosa-Chitto." The name is occasionally left unhyphenated.

12. Sol[omon Franklin] Smith, *The Theatrical Apprenticeship and Anecdotical Recollections of Sol. Smith* (Philadelphia, 1846), 119–20.

> as I wanted to see how they'd fight, I up and told him where to look for him—says I, bung up my peepers, if you don't find him agin that rock, squat, jist hiding behind that tree. . . . Well, instead of thanking me, he dropped his jaws and his sword, looked at me as if he'd seed a ghost, mumbled something in his throat, nobody could tell what, and then there was a spree among the people. (II, 131–32)

Horsey's scenes with Bull and Mabry effectively capture the spirit of life in the Gulf South, but other scrapes in which the actor gets involved are less authentic and amusing. J. V. Ridgely's remark that throughout much of *Border Beagles* Horsey flounders around like a dimwit may be harsh, but it is not inaccurate; and it points to a problem in the book.[13] In portraying Horsey, Simms tends to rely upon a monotonous comic formula that is centered on the actor's obsession with the stage and conveyed through farce and slapstick. A notable example of this formula occurs during Saxon's attempt to search Vernon's bags while Vernon and Horsey sleep. The actor, however, is sleepwalking while declaiming from the fifth act of *Romeo and Juliet.* As Saxon crouches on a ladder, Horsey cuts short his search by leaping on his shoulders and exclaiming, "Wilt thou provoke me?—then have at thee, boy!" (I, 182). One scene of this sort, while preposterous, is not unbearable; but Simms's repetition of the formula with little variation strains the reader's power of belief and sense of amusement alike.

More consistently successful as a comic figure is the strapping woodsman from Alabama, Dick Jamison, who befriends Vernon after Saxon finally captures him. As the hero's guardian, Jamison is conceived in accordance with romance conventions; but with his loud boasts and striking actions, he is fleshed out by the methods of southern humor. He appears in the novel after Vernon has been arrested for the supposed murder of Horsey, in romance manner instantly siding with the hero and threatening his enemies. First challenging Saxon, he shortly thereafter fells a feisty Irishman who has menaced Vernon and who claims to be "Dennis O'Dougherty, of the O'Doughertys of Ballyshannon by the pit of Ballany—a family of the ouldest—there's no telling, indade, when the O'Doughertys were not a family of the ouldest." Jamison tells O'Dougherty, in language streaked with tallish elements, "You're of too old a family, Dennis, to stand up with a young man from Alabama; the stuff's not in you, my lad, and I should

13. J. V. Ridgely, *William Gilmore Simms* (New York, 1962), 81.

swallow you at a mouthful and never ask after the salt" (II, 17, 18). When Saxon's henchmen tie Vernon up, Jamison, announcing "one drive of my six pounder will let more sins out of your carcasses than all the saints could ever put in virtues," cuts his friend loose (II, 84). And when he himself is threatened with arrest for aiding Vernon, he exclaims: "If I'm to be 'rested for cutting loose a free white man, that was tied up wrongfully, say it as soon, and let's see the eend of it at once. P'int your finger now which way you please, and I'm ready, any side. If it's civility, well, I'm all civility—if it's for a close hug, tooth and timber, why there's not a bear in Loosa Chitto, that'll come to the scratch with rougher arms than Dick Jamison" (II, 263–64).

In the conclusion to this last sequence, Jamison helps Vernon escape and then suggests they lynch Saxon's cohorts. Vernon, still bent on replacing backwoods roughness with orderly legal processes, objects, so Jamison contents himself with lashing the offenders instead. "I must write a name on the backs of the critters," he muses, "so that I may know 'em again, when I see 'em. . . . I reckon, if I did'nt lick 'em, my horse would go mighty rough over the road to-night—I know I shouldn't sit well in the saddle, and my spirits would be a cursed sight heavier than a fat parson's after a bad collection-Sunday" (II, 274). Jamison with his colorful language would do credit to the pages of any frontier yarn; and along with Horsey he affords evidence of Simms's ability, already well developed at this relatively early point in his career, at sketching humorous characters like those in the oral and written lore of the backwoods South.

By 1840, therefore, shortly before he temporarily turned away from long fiction, Simms's acquaintance with the traditions of the low country and the Gulf South had issued in two groups of novels that make clear thematic statements about the characteristics of these regions and the relationship in which they stood to one another. The works set in the low country predict a glowing future for southern civilization that is grounded in the continuity between the colonial and antebellum South; the books about the Gulf South assert that the wave of crime sweeping through it had been stemmed by the influence of tidewater institutions. Also apparent in these novels are elements that would vividly emerge in Simms's later fiction. The low-country volumes with their portraits of plantation aristocrats would be followed in the fifties by a second series of historical romances about the region that gives the manners of the upper class a satiric cast; the books about the Gulf South would eventually find their sequel in a group of works set in the Appalachian Mountains that brings Simms's treatment of humorous backwoods subjects to successful culmination. But both sets of volumes, and indeed Simms's entire career as an author, would be seriously affected by the panic of 1837—which inaugurated, in its bitter way, the second stage of his career and which wrought changes in his fortunes of which he never dreamed when he cried to Lawson, after *Guy Rivers* was published, "The Alps may be passed but Rome's beyond them, and I shall not be satisfied short of a fine marble and permanent, not to say classically well-built residence in the Eternal City!" (*L*, I, 59).

6
Begging Times for Authordom

The panic of 1837 was a major economic collapse whose effects, lasting well into the 1840s, damaged the careers of several promising antebellum authors. In conjunction with developments in the publishing industry—the production of cheap paperbound novels and the appearance of inexpensive, mammoth weekly newspapers that pirated the work of popular British authors—the recession made the costly two-volume novels of Cooper, Simms, Bird, and other romancers financially impractical. Simms, already handicapped by his residence in the South and also by his tendency to produce too many works too rapidly, was particularly harmed by the panic. And therefore, after publishing *Beauchampe* in 1842, he wrote no more long fiction until 1850, when he serialized *Katharine Walton* in *Godey's Magazine and Lady's Book*. He turned instead to history, biography, and geography; poems, essays, and orations; "cheap book" novelettes; and tales for magazines. "These are begging times for authordom," he told an aspiring writer, "but it is well to publish—well to keep yourself occasionally & creditably, even if not profitably, before the eye of the public" (*L*, I, 425).

Simms's letters of the late 1830s and the 1840s make evident that it was the sudden loss of income from long fiction attendant upon the panic rather than any covert ambition or fond caprice which drove him into the political activities that consumed a good bit of his time and energy during the 1840s. By 1840 he had begun to correspond with James Henry Hammond, the southern planter and politician who became his closest friend. Hammond, whose plantation Silver Bluff was near Woodlands, shared Simms's interest in agriculture. Simms's first extant letter to him thanks him for the gift of some okra seed, while subsequent letters query him on the "subject of Cotton & Corn Culture and the domestic management of a farmstead about which there are questionings and doubts" (*L*, I, 168, V, 349). Early in their friendship Simms told Hammond, who had served in the United States House of Representatives in the 1830s, "I fancy it would be a great gain in the progress of an honorable ambition should you choose to retire from the service of the nation, to that of the State" (*L*, V, 351). Hammond, who lost the race for state governor in 1840 and won it in 1842, made just such a move; and from 1840 to 1864, Simms served as Hammond's confidential political adviser, so that much of their correspondence has a marked political cast.

It was apparently Hammond who, in the early 1840s, coaxed Simms into politics during the bleak days for authorship of which the southern writer complained. Simms's letters to his friend make it evident, however, that his first allegiance was to literature and that he entered politics chiefly because the prospects for imaginative writing, particularly long fiction, were so dim. "Do not accuse me of caprice," he urged Hammond in December, 1841,

> when I tell you that I am half inclined to comply with your, and the suggestions of other friends, and to take the field as a Candidate for Legislative honour. There are several reasons why I should change my previous determination. Hitherto, the tasks of literary labor have given me sufficient occupation. Now, they do not. Their results are of such moderate importance that they do not require and will hardly justify the entire application of my mind in this direction. In the next place, my mind itself is of that energetic, impatient sort that it must have something to expend itself on more exacting and more compensating than is now the case." (*L*, I, 290)

Somewhat later, and more bluntly, Simms wrote Lawson: "My neighbours have again put me in nomination for the Legislature. I have told them I am no candidate—that I will not canvass for votes, will in no wise electioneer—will neither treat nor speechify—will not in short cross the road for their suffrages. If they elect me, I will do my duty as well as I can; but it will be at considerable personal sacrifices" (*L*, I, 410).[1]

Following Hammond's advice, Simms—who had gained valuable political experience when he worked in his friend's gubernatorial campaigns—ran for the legislature in 1842 but withdrew from the race

1. In view of these and similar statements, it seems unreasonable to assume, as does Jon L. Wakelyn in *The Politics of a Literary Man*, that politics was Simms's primary concern and that once elected "he posed as an indignant writer who was forced to give up precious time" to attend sessions of the legislature (82, 96).

when one of his children died (*L*, I, 304). In 1844 he ran again, however, and was elected. He had campaigned on such issues as the annexation of Texas, the abolition of the protective tariff, and the need for southern unity in the face of what he saw as northern despotism. Such concerns dominate his oration "The Sources of American Independence," delivered at Aiken, South Carolina, in 1844 and designed in part as an instrument of his campaign.

"The Sources of American Independence" begins energetically by attributing the quest for liberty to the Anglo-Saxon spirit and tracing its course from the Battle of Hastings to the American Revolution. During much of the speech Simms addresses himself to national as well as southern interests. The South requires the annexation of Texas, he maintains, in order to retain a just balance of power in Congress; but, he goes on to say, "the great interests of the nation demand it, not less than ourselves. A vast domain, essential to our safety, and, with time, to the natural expansion of the race, is not to be flung from our grasp to satisfy a sectional prejudice, and secure votes for hungry candidates,—creatures, scarcely less blind to their own fortunes—in their excess of selfishness,—than they are indifferent to the great destinies and the superior prospects of the nation."[2] Striking an imperialist stance, Simms also argues that Texas, Cuba, Canada, and the West Indies are all "the natural dependencies of our hemisphere" and must inevitably become "portions of our national domain, and integrals of our spreading empire" (28).

In the address, Simms champions southern unity, declaiming: "Let the South but show itself, moving together, in solid phalanx, as one man, and there will be no conflict worthy of the name. Without this union, we can do nothing. . . . It is only in our divisions that the enemy succeeds" (26). Insisting that the Revolution achieved only independence and did not settle the nature of social institutions, he maintains that the South's moral and social ties to the North have been weakened and almost sundered.

> A few more shocks—one ruder blow—the phrenzy of an audacious, or the malignity of a hostile spirit,—and the noble temple of our confederacy, built by the mighty Architects of the Revolution, is thrown down in irretrievable ruin. When that time shall arrive, my countrymen,—when the sound shall go forth, of fate, and a bitter lamenting throughout the land,—

2. W[illiam] Gilmore Simms, *The Sources of American Independence. An Oration. . . .* (Aiken, S.C., 1844), 29, hereafter cited by page number within the text.

> let it be our boast that our hands have not prepared this overthrow,—that we are not guilty of this ruin. The guilt and the shame of a catastrophe, which shall mock and mortify the whole world's hope of Liberty, must not rest on the fair fame and the conscience of the South. (31)

In 1844 it had been only twelve years since Simms had defended the Union in his capacity as editor of the *City Gazette* and only two years since he had proclaimed himself "an ultra-American" as well as "a born Southron" (*L*, I, 319). His spirited remarks to his audience at Aiken show him catering to his constituency, but they also reveal how far his views had shifted since he had styled himself a Unionist in 1832.

After his election to the state legislature, Simms began to act on the ideas in his oration—offering, for instance, a resolution in the House to invite delegates from several southern states to Asheville to discuss a policy of uniting the South (*L*, II, 10*n*16). The proposal was eventually rejected as premature, but he maintained his concern for the issue; and he would follow with interest the movement for a southern convention later in the decade. Meanwhile, he worked in other ways to enhance the solidarity and independence of his section. An advocate, in both life and fiction, of farming and the pastoral life, in the 1840s he began to investigate southern agricultural conditions in detail. He knew that the emigration from South Carolina he had witnessed in the Gulf South and described in "Notes of a Small Tourist" and "The Western Emigrants" had stemmed in part from the decreased fertility of the soil, and he therefore penned articles on scientific farming and crop diversification. Yet despite his concern for agriculture, he spoke out in favor of the growth of Southern industry as a way of increasing his region's strength and its independence from the North.[3]

Simms lost his campaign for reelection to the legislature in 1846 primarily because he had supported the unpopular Alfred Proctor Aldrich, who headed the opposition to John C. Calhoun. Simms's backers, who were indignant, nominated him for lieutenant governor of the state—a move that many South Carolina newspapers approved. He was defeated in the election, however, by one vote.[4] Although he was disappointed, he told Hammond that the office was "such a

3. See, for example, [William Gilmore Simms], "Editorial Bureau—Agriculture in South-Carolina," *Magnolia*, n.s., II (March, 1843), 200–203, and "Our Agricultural Condition," *Southern and Western*, I (February, 1845), [73]–84, identified as Simms's in *L*, II, 27*n*88.

4. Holman, "A Simms Chronology," in Simms, *The Yemassee*, xxx; Wakelyn, *The Politics of a Literary Man*, 103.

nullity, that one might well feel a sense of shame at being suspected of mortification when defeated in seeking it" (*L,* II, 242). Simms's various comments make it clear that, despite his devoted activities on behalf of state and region, he had never actually craved public office, as some remarks he made to Hammond during his campaign for reelection reveal: "My labours and present engagements are such that I heartily regret having consented to run again, and if you can provide me with a decent reason to withdraw, you will do me a real favor. I feel that there is no serving two mistresses, and the Muses of Politics & Poetry draw badly together in the same harness. Can't you procure me some appointment, which will enable me to back out[?]" (*L,* II, 168).

Of better service to the muse of poetry in the long stretch of Simms's career were his travels during the forties in the Gulf and mountain South. In 1842 he made a three weeks' trip to the Old Southwest, where he received an honorary LL.D. at the University of Alabama in Tuscaloosa and delivered the oration "The Social Principle." He began the talk by contrasting the raw town of the 1820s with the thriving city of the 1840s, in the process revealing just how much civilization had accomplished in the Gulf South since the time of his early visit. "Little did I imagine," he remarked in the flowing oratorical periods of the era, "that the rude and scattered hamlet which I then surveyed,—a fragmentary form, not half made up,—was, in so short a space of time, to become so eminent a city. . . . Then—a decapitated Colossus—the forest tree lay prostrate before her threshold,—the wild vine swung luxuriantly across her pathway,—and, at the close of evening, the long howl of the wolf might be heard, as he hungered upon the edges of the forest for the prey that lay within her tents."[5] While in Tuscaloosa, he also lectured on American history before the Lyceum and was honored with a public dinner. During the ceremonies that followed the speech, he acknowledged his authorship of the Border Romances and said he had collected the material for *Richard Hurdis* when traveling in Alabama twenty years before (*L,* VI, 59–60, 60*n*5).

The festivities in Tuscaloosa indicate the high regard in which Simms was held in the South and his popularity as author and speaker. But more useful for his imaginative writing were his trips to the upcountry of North and South Carolina and Georgia—particularly his journey in 1847 to what were then remote ranges of the Appalachians.

5. Simms, *The Social Principle,* [5]–6.

On September 23 he wrote Lawson from Spartanburg, where he and his family were vacationing: "Tomorrow, I expect to set off on a visit to the mountains of North Carolina. I shall be gone a week or ten days when I begin my slow descent to the low country. My purpose is to visit as much fine scenery, and to see & hear as much as I can. I shall make a book of it" (*L*, II, 350). The tour turned out to be more rugged than Simms's letter suggests. As the notebook that he kept on the expedition reveals, for nearly two weeks he was on the trail with professional mountain hunters, hunting, camping, and telling stories—experiences that would bear fruit much later in his life when he wrote his final group of fictional works, the mountain tales and romances.

At the time, however, Simms seems to have viewed the experience as material for a volume of sketches in the vein of travel writing. To a Philadelphia friend he described the trip in language borrowed from the notebook and already tending toward the literary: "I have been for some weeks the occupant of a camp among the hunters, beyond our remotest bounds of civilization. I have slept with the howling of the wolf & the sudden shriek of the panther in my ears, and have eaten my steaks of venison, fresh from the haunches of the buck, eight hundred feet above the Atlantic levels. I could make you a series of descriptive sketches that might tell much better than most of our foreign travel,—and may do so" (*L*, II, 351). But he did not write directly of this trip until the next decade, and then he employed it in lectures before he realized he could use the experience to advantage in fiction. Worth emphasizing here, however, is that his exposure in midcareer to the sights and sounds of pioneer life furnished a basis in experience for his steadily expanding attention to southern humor, and it encouraged him to use such humor in increased amounts in his fiction written after midcentury.

Simms devoted much time in the middle 1840s to the wars between the Young America and the Knickerbocker literary factions in New York. He had become an influential figure in northern circles, a fact that helped his national reputation; and when he had issued his first novels in the 1830s, Clark and other members of the Knickerbocker group had praised them. By the 1840s, however, Clark was lashing Simms with insults because Simms had joined the Young America group, which was led by Evert Duyckinck and included Cornelius Mathews, Edgar Allan Poe, and Herman Melville. These men, who except for Poe were radical democrats and literary nationalists, hoped to weaken Britain's influence on American letters and establish the romance as the dominant literary form.

By contrast, Clark and his circle, which included Washington Irving and George Pope Morris of the New York *Mirror,* were Whigs, conservatives, and Anglophiles who admired the writing of Lamb and Dickens, disliked the romance, and felt the city should take rank with the wilderness as a subject for American writing. They consequently attacked the Young America program and vilified Simms, who as reviewer and magazine editor had enthusiastically outlined the aims of his group. Hence Clark, who had once praised Simms's "fine descriptive powers," began to censure "his 'lots' of labored romances—upon which Time and the silent indifference of the public . . . are already doing their work." But as Perry Miller comments in *The Raven and the Whale,* Clark made a tactical error when he quarreled with the fiery author of *The Partisan.*[6] Simms retaliated by calling the *Knickerbocker Magazine* an "Augean stable sheet" and referring to Clark in correspondence as a "miserable reptile," a "scoundrel & puppy," a "liar & skunk," and a "dirty crawling creeping creature" (*L,* III, 7, II, 117, 121, 107). He would deliver his last blow in *Paddy McGann,* serialized in 1863; but in the 1840s neither southerner nor northerner could claim full victory. The debacle shows, however, that Simms's literary nationalism remained active even though he was beginning to utter sectionalist political sentiments.[7]

Throughout the 1840s, the financial plight of the publishing industry engaged Simms's attention, and his letters of the period are filled with complaints about the changing complexion of the book market. He deplored the inroads made by inexpensive publications on the work of respectable authors: his Border Romances, he said, "labored under the disadvantage of being issued at old prices, $2, when cheap literature was beginning to make such charges an impertinence. They have therefore never had fair play—have never reached the great body of the people" (*L,* I, 420). *Carl Werner,* he lamented, was "put forth at a most unfortunate season, during the money pressure, and just as the public mind had been made eager & selfish in consequence of the

6. [Lewis Gaylord Clark and Willis Gaylord Clark], "Editors' Table," *Knickerbocker Magazine,* VI (December, 1835), 577; [Lewis Gaylord Clark], "Editor's Table," *Knickerbocker Magazine,* XX (August, 1842), 200; Miller, *The Raven and the Whale,* 105.

7. C. Hugh Holman notes Simms's dual nationalism and sectionalism in "The Status of Simms," 184.

Cheap Literature passion. I made nothing by the venture" (*L*, II, 66). "[M]y income from Literature which in 1835 was $6000 per annum," he mournfully told a friend, "is scarce $1500 now" (*L*, II, 385). "You may form some idea of the wretched wrong done to the native author," he observed to another correspondent, "when I tell you that, prior to the era of cheap publications, I have recieved [*sic*] for one story in an annual, which cost me some three or four sittings, $200" (*L*, II, 54). He gave in 1841 his fullest description of the situation.

> The publishers are very costive—the sales are terribly diminished within the last few years. You will perceive that Irving now writes almost wholly for magazines and Cooper & myself are almost the only persons whose novels are printed—certainly, we are almost the only persons who hope to get anything for them. From England we get nothing. In this country an Edition now instead of 4 or 5,000 copies, is scarce 2,000. My Damsel of Darien was 3,000. My Kinsmen not more than 2,000; and it is seldom now that the demand for novels carries them to a 2d. Edition. . . . Nothing, in short, but the great popularity of an author will secure the publication of a novel now. (*L*, I, 271)

Simms's letters also reveal that the attacks of despair that formed a marked feature of his life after midcentury had their origin, at least in part, in the desperate publishing situation of the forties. By trying to maintain his career as a professional author he was, as he often complained, "drawing water in a sieve" (*L*, III, 36, 131, 211). Under these straitened circumstances, he repeatedly considered moving to the North to secure better conditions for his writing. "My residence in South Carolina," he insisted, "is unfavorable to me as an author. I lose $2000 per annum by it" (*L*, II, 385). "All is well in our little family," he wrote Lawson in 1846; "yet I am struggling against renewed fits of depression, which impair my energies & baffle my successes.—I am again about to make an effort to leave Carolina. This, for the present, must be wholly between ourselves, or must not go farther than your wife." Later that year he observed, using a phrase that echoes through his family annals: "Carolina has been a region of tombs for me, and my worldly prosperity is by no means such as to make me desire to continue here. Mr. Roach's affairs do not prosper, and I seriously deliberate upon the propriety of transferring myself, family or not, to Philadelphia or New York" (*L*, II, 140, 195–96).

Simms was forced to contend with the situation in publishing when in terms of his reputation as a writer he could scarcely afford to do so, and it is not an exaggeration to say that his entire literary career suffered the consequences. The drop in sales for long fiction occurred within a few years after he had begun to write novels, and thus he was pushed out of his major field into varied, occasionally trivial projects that gave the corpus of his writing a distinctly miscellaneous cast. Such ventures may have kept him from the discipline of form and style he needed for his mature work in prose and verse, and they unfortunately deflected attention from the name he had established as a novelist. He would produce better fiction in the 1850s than he had during periods of greater renown, but he would not again enjoy the success or the financial gains that had distinguished the first stage of his career.

Simms's publications between 1842 and 1850 show his efforts to keep up with a market whose shifts he understood and thoroughly deplored. The young author who in 1835 had, in the words of a reviewer, seen "brilliant prospects . . . opening before him" now battled to keep abreast of the literary current.[8] Even an abbreviated roster of his writing in these eight years shows its miscellaneous nature—*The History of South Carolina* (1840; revised edition 1842); *The Geography of South Carolina* (1843); biographies of Francis Marion (1844), Captain John Smith (1846), the Chevalier Bayard (1847), and Nathaniel Greene (1849); and a series of biographical sketches of Sumter, Moultrie, and other South Carolina war heroes that he wrote for Rufus Griswold's *Washington and the Generals of the American Revolution* (1847).[9] He continued to turn out poetry in large quantities, much of it with an increasingly sectional slant: in a three-year period, he produced *Areytos: or, Songs of the South* (1846); *Lays of the Palmetto,* poems praising the South Carolina regiment in the Mexican War (1848); and *The Cassique of Accabee. A Tale of Ashley River* (1849). He also published *Sabbath Lyrics; or, Songs from Scripture* (1849), based on Byron and the Bible and worked up in a manner dear to the readers of magazine verse. In *The Wigwam and the Cabin* (1845), he collected stories of Indians, pioneers, and the Revolutionary War, and in *Views and Reviews in American Literature, History*

8. Review of *The Partisan, Southern Literary Journal,* I (December, 1835), 284.

9. Simms and other nineteenth-century writers spelled Greene's first name "Nathanael." According to Frederick Wagner in "Simms's Editing of *The Life of Nathanael Greene,*" *Southern Literary Journal,* XI (Fall, 1978), [40]–43, Simms did not actually write the biography of Greene. Instead, he simply abridged and paraphrased William Johnson's *Sketches of the Life and Correspondence of Nathanael Greene.*

and Fiction (1845), he brought together important essays in literary criticism that aid in an understanding of his attitude toward "the epochs and events of American history, as suited to the purposes of art in fiction."

In addition to this welter of activities, Simms scribbled for magazines, a task he detested—they "fritter away the mind, exhaust the energies & consume one's most valuable time," he complained (*L,* II, 288). Bowing to the cheap book market, he explored the possibility of reprinting a Border Romance in a mammoth weekly; he also wrote two novelettes, *Castle Dismal* (1844) and *Helen Halsey* (1845), as experiments in inexpensive editions, haggled with several publishers about them, and told a friend, "My object is to get them off of my hands without positively giving them away" (*L,* I, 354, 381–87, 404).[10] During this period, he completed a novel about Spain, *Count Julian* (a sequel to *Pelayo*), which actually belongs to an earlier period in his career, since he had written the first five of its six books during 1836 and 1837.[11] He compiled an edition of the Shakespeare apocrypha; he penned copious letters on business, politics, and literature; he wrote editorials, political orations, and long articles on international copyright; he composed fugitive pieces for magazines and journals that are almost without number and are still insufficiently cataloged. He wrote, in short, nearly everything but novels.

Yet Simms's interest still centered in long fiction, and some of his work in short stories, literary criticism, and history in the late thirties and the forties sheds light on his conception of his major genre. Particularly illuminating are *The Wigwam and the Cabin, Views and Reviews,* and *The History of South Carolina.* In the first of these volumes, generally considered his best collection of short fiction, he gathered tales already furnished to periodicals that reflect, perhaps better than any other source, his many interests up to this point in his career. "Lucas de Ayllon" shows his concern with the early history of South Carolina and with Spanish-American material of the sort he had explored in *The Vision of Cortes.* "The Two Camps," "The Arm-Chair

10. The Border Romance was *Richard Hurdis,* and the weekly was the *Western Continent,* whose editors later asked for permission to reprint all four of the Border Romances (see *L,* II, 132, 132*n*14).

11. The first five sections of *Count Julian* were lost in transit to the publisher (*L,* I, 142*n*13). When they were recovered, Simms completed the work, which was issued in 1845.

of Tustenuggee," "Oakatibbe," "Jocassee," and "Caloya" continue the emphasis on Indian subjects observable in his early poetry and *The Yemassee,* whereas "Grayling" and "The Giant's Coffin," tales set during the Revolutionary era, show the macabre and Gothic effects also evident in his early novels about the war. "The Last Wager, or the Gamester of the Mississippi" resembles the Border Romances in its emphasis on gambling and its setting in the Gulf South; "The Snake of the Cabin," also set in the Gulf South, is a story of seduction that recalls the subplot of *The Kinsmen.* "Sergeant Barnacle; or, the Raftsman of the Edisto" is a comic portrayal of Irish character that looks forward to the similar portrayal in *Paddy McGann.* Several stories, notably "Caloya," "The Snake of the Cabin," and "The Lazy Crow," have well-drawn black figures who resemble the blacks in Simms's long novels. The various stories in *The Wigwam and the Cabin* reveal the many subjects Simms had already developed and would continue to explore in tales, novels, poetry, and lectures during the rest of his life.

The two volumes of literary criticism titled *Views and Reviews* that Simms published midway through the forties deal in part with the relationship between literature and culture and demonstrate his interest in adapting cultural material to literary constructions. For him, though the roles of artist and historian were closely connected, literature was a higher kind of writing than history.[12] Such is the burden of the central essay in the first series of *Views and Reviews,* a long piece in several parts that he called "The Epochs and Events of American History, as Suited to the Purposes of Art in Fiction." This piece, a revision of lectures he had delivered before the Georgia Historical Society and published in the *Southern and Western* during 1845, is an apologia for historical romance, a defense of literature as the proper vehicle for history, and a plea that native materials be used in the creation of imaginative works.[13]

In "Epochs and Events," Simms was trying to combat two un-

12. For connections between Simms's work in history and literature, see Hampton M. Jarrell, "William Gilmore Simms—Almost a Historian," in Robert D. Ochs (ed.), *Proceedings of the South Carolina Historical Association* (Columbia, S.C., 1947), 3–8; John C. Guilds, "Simms's Use of History, Theory and Practice," *Mississippi Quarterly,* XXX (Fall, 1977), [505]–11; and Stephen E. Meats, "Artist or Historian: William Gilmore Simms and the Revolutionary South," in Samuel Proctor (ed.), *Eighteenth-Century Florida and the Revolutionary South* (Gainesville, Fla., 1978), 94–109.

13. According to *L,* VI, 59*n*5, Simms had also delivered the lectures before the Tuscaloosa Lyceum when he visited Alabama in 1842.

friendly points of view—that of the new scientific historians, who insisted that historical writing should be factually accurate instead of imaginatively compelling, and that of the Knickerbocker group, who cried that American authors should not break their ties to British belletristic traditions. When attacking the first of these positions, he makes several related points: that imaginative literature is more comprehensive and humane than scientific writing; that the true value of history lies in "its proper employment for the purposes of art"; and that it is "the artist only who is the true historian." Throughout his essay Simms sees history in terms of its relevance to art, not art as subordinate to history—a fact that helps explain why he chose to become a novelist by profession. A "condition of partial obscurity and doubt in history," he insists, is "that which leaves genius most free to its proper inventions"—for "the poet and romancer are only strong where the historian is weak, and can alone walk boldly" in "dim and insecure avenues of time."[14]

Scarcely less important than Simms's defense of romantic history and the kind of creative writing it resembles is his onslaught on the Knickerbocker school. Much of his essay is a polemic for American writing, a passionate claim that the country has material for great literary works. To make his point, he discusses, as subjects for historical fiction, early Spanish explorers like DeSoto, early French explorers like Coligny, the Indian princess Pocahontas, and the traitor Benedict Arnold. (Simms had used or would eventually use all these subjects in his writing—DeSoto in "The Social Principle" and in *Vasconselos;* Coligny in *The Lily and the Totem;* Pocahontas in poetry and *The Life of Captain John Smith;* and Benedict Arnold in a drama begun in the 1820s and serialized in the 1860s.)[15]

14. William Gilmore Simms, "The Epochs and Events of American History, as Suited to the Purposes of Art in Fiction," in *Views and Reviews,* 1st ser., 34, 36, 76. The first series of *Views and Reviews* was published in New York by Wiley and Putnam in 1846; its companion volume in the second series was issued by the same firm during 1847. Both works, however, bear 1845 as the publication date on their title page (Holman, Introduction, xxviii–xxix). On xxii–xxix, Holman discusses Simms's alliance with the Young America group. On xxxii–xxxiii, he remarks that the two volumes form "a reasonably detailed statement of the purpose, materials, and method of the historical novel as it was practiced in America from Cooper's *The Spy* in 1821 until the hiatus in the publication of book-length fiction in the 1840's."

15. The Arnold drama, which Simms serialized in the *Magnolia Weekly* in May, June, July, and August, 1863, has been studied by Miriam J. Shillingsburg in "Simms's Benedict Arnold: The Hero as Traitor," *Southern Studies,* XVII (Fall, 1978), [273]–89.

Especially pertinent for Simms's fiction is the section of "Epochs and Events" called "The Four Periods of American History," in which the author surveys the English, French, and Spanish attempts to colonize America, the time from the founding of Jamestown to the accession of George III to the English throne, the preliminaries to the Revolutionary War and the war itself, and the progress of discovery and settlement that culminated in the opening of the Middle West and Old Southwest frontiers. After discussing these periods, Simms notes that they contain abundant matter for romance—in the struggle with the wilderness, in "the terrible civil conflicts of whig and tory," and in "the final and complete conversion" of frontier territory to civilization.[16]

Simms was speaking from the heart when he wrote about history, for he was himself a historian of some distinction. He possessed, as his letters reveal, an impressive collection of manuscripts, journals, diaries, and similar materials relating to the Revolutionary War. Stephen Meats estimates that he owned perhaps 1,200 manuscript items bearing on the Laurens family of South Carolina, and in addition he had letters or other records of George Washington, Francis Marion, William Moultrie, John Adams, John Jay, Horatio Gates, Baron Friedrich Wilhelm von Steuben, and the Baron de Kalb.[17] He indicated the value of this archive when he said late in life as he reluctantly prepared to sell some items from it: "I had been making this collection for more than 30 years; it had cost me great painstaking and research, and some money. It was endeared to me by a variety of associations and considerations, and I had been looking forward to a period of repose & quiet when I could address myself to the grave labours of Historian & Biographer, building largely on this material, which had already served me to some extent in fiction" (*L*, V, 44–45).

Simms's *History of South Carolina*, published first in 1840 and revised in 1842 and 1860, serves like *Views and Reviews* to summarize work he had already done and to forecast the kind of writing he would shortly do. As in his fiction set in the low country, he tends in this book to favor the colonial and Revolutionary periods. In the first third of the volume, which treats the era of colonial exploration, he discusses Ponce de Leon, DeSoto, and such French Huguenot explorers as Jean Ribault; he also describes in some detail the founding and settlement

16. Simms, "The Epochs and Events of American History," in *Views and Reviews*, 1st ser., 84.

17. Meats, "Artist or Historian," in *Eighteenth-Century Florida and the Revolutionary South*, 98; *L*, II, 29, IV, 541, 543, V, 258; Meats, "Artist or Historian," in

of the Carolina colony, the Fundamental Constitutions, and the friction of Puritan and Cavalier in the colony that he had already depicted in *The Yemassee.* Perhaps looking back to "Chronicles of Ashley River," he portrays the first British settlement on the river's banks, while, looking forward to *The Cassique of Kiawah,* he spends some time on the menace that pirates posed to the young province. In the remaining two-thirds of the book, which focuses on the Revolution in South Carolina, he discusses battles like those at Hobkirk's Hill and Guilford Court House that the format of his Revolutionary War series prevented him from treating. Generously acknowledging his sources, he cites William Johnson's life of Nathaniel Greene; Hewatt's history of the Carolinas and Georgia; John Archdale, James Glenn, and other colonial writers whose accounts were assembled in his friend B. R. Carroll's *Historical Collections of South Carolina* (1836); and the patriot historians William Moultrie, David Ramsay, and John Drayton.

It is not surprising that, with the patriot historians as authorities, Simms in *The History of South Carolina* exhibits the same prejudices toward Britain and the same proud bias toward South Carolina that he shows in his novels or that, throughout the volume, he tends to cast history in the shape of romance. The sections of the volume that treat the Revolution have a dialectic structure and a pronounced black and white system of characterization. As in his fiction, he attempts to be fair: he commends such Britons as Lieutenant-Governor William Bull and Major John Marjoribanks, and he accords measured praise to Loyalists, particularly of the upper class. But, again as in his fiction, he blames the "overweening arrogance of British officers and agents" in fomenting the war, deplores the "wanton massacre" of patriots by Britons, condemns the "savage murders" and "bitter cruelties" perpetrated by certain Tories, and in general excoriates the "blasphemies, impieties and horrors" of the enemy. Here and in a related work, *The Life of Marion,* he evokes the pastoral world of his Revolutionary War fiction—as when, describing Marion's camp at Snow's Island, he remarks: "The vine and briar guarded his passes. The laurel and the shrub, the vine and sweet scented jessamine, roofed his dwelling, and clambered up between his closed eyelids and the stars."[18]

Eighteenth-Century Florida and the Revolutionary South, 98–99. Simms published some of his manuscript material in an essay-review, "The Baron DeKalb," *Southern Quarterly Review,* XXII [n.s., VI] (July, 1852), 141–203.

18. Simms, *The History of South Carolina,* 136, 167, 206, and *The Life of Francis Marion,* 167.

Of particular interest within the context of Simms's political career are his thinly veiled references to the approaching sectional crisis. At the end of a discussion of the siege of Ninety-Six he claims, for instance, "Surely, when the barbarian drum again sounds to war in Carolina, her children will find themselves all, with one heart, united under the same banner." And in the conclusion of the book he maintains, in phrases that he would echo in *Katharine Walton:* "One lesson, in chief, may be gleaned, among many others, from this imperfect story of the past. It is that which teaches the citizen to cling to the soil of his birth in the day of its difficulty, with the resolution of the son who stands above the grave of a mother and protects it from violation. . . . This rule, preserved in memory and maintained as a principle, would unite a people and make them invincible."[19]

The work Simms did in history and in the biographies of Marion and Greene enhanced his reputation as an interpreter of the southern past and sharpened his skills for the historical novels he was yet to write. Several of his other productions in the 1840s bear even more directly on his later work in fiction. *Confession,* a sentimental domestic romance aimed at the growing body of women readers, portrays a tongue-wagging, tobacco-chewing fellow whose awkward habit of spitting in public annoys the habitués of polite society; *Beauchampe* depicts a bumptious rustic who says of an opponent, "I'd just like to brush up his whiskers with gun-powder" in order to "frizzle them better than ever a speckled hen had her feathers frizzled."[20] *Helen Halsey,* the final (and shortest) Border Romance, has some grim passages of backwoods humor appropriate to its gloomy swampland setting. *Donna Florida* (1843), a comic poem about Ponce de Leon that imitates Byron's *Don Juan,* displays the light satiric mockery of upper-class customs that would occupy Simms in his low-country romances of the 1850s, while both *The Prima Donna* (1844) and *Flirtation at the Moultrie House* (1850) show his growing talent for brisk descriptions of city life. But the major influences on his work written after midcentury spring directly from the reading and book reviewing that he did during his several stints as magazine editor in the 1840s.

The state of periodical publication in the South had occupied Simms at intervals since his first experience with editing in the 1820s. Throughout much of his life, in an effort to give his region an outlet for imagi-

19. Simms, *The History of South Carolina,* 233, 319; see *KW,* 126.
20. [Simms], *Beauchampe,* I, 299.

native productions and an organ for its growing sectionalism, he would tirelessly support southern journals, causing one of his critics to complain that he deflected his attention from fiction and frittered away his magnificent energies in the venture.[21] His letters of the 1840s and early 1850s indicate, however, that he turned to editing less from choice than in an effort to shore up his flagging income from literature. Between 1842 and 1855, he occupied with some distinction what he called the "editorial *fauteuil*" of three important southern journals—the *Magnolia*, the *Southern and Western*, and the *Southern Quarterly Review*. For these journals, he developed substantial critical departments of the sort he had created for the *Southern Literary Gazette* in the twenties, and he personally reviewed many of the books discussed in their pages.[22] As reviewer, he read widely in two types of writing that would influence his fiction after midcentury, southern backwoods comedy and the British and American novel of manners.

Southern humor as a literary genre was well under way by the end of the 1830s with works by Longstreet and Crockett and the burgeoning of comic sketches in almanacs, newspapers, and jest books. During the 1840s, it commanded a national literary audience as it appeared more and more in book form and helped fill the gap left by the decline in the publication of long fiction. Among important volumes appearing in the forties were William Tappan Thompson's *Major Jones' Courtship* (1843), Johnson Jones Hooper's *Some Adventures of Captain Simon Suggs* (1845), Sol Smith's *Theatrical Apprenticeship* (1846), and two landmark anthologies—*The Big Bear of Arkansas* (1845) and *A Quarter Race in Kentucky* (1846), which the Philadelphia publishing firm Carey and Hart, long a sponsor of native writing, had asked William T. Porter, editor of the New York–based sporting and humorous weekly newspaper the *Spirit of the Times*, to compile. Simms, who would remain interested in southern humor throughout

21. Parrington, *The Romantic Revolution in America, 1800–1860*, 127.

22. Simms's remarks in letters and periodicals make it reasonably certain that he wrote most of the critical notices published in the journals during the time he edited them. Even before he took over the *Magnolia*, he told Carey and Hart that its editorial bureau was "entirely yielded" to his control, and as editor he stated that his responsibility "extends to every thing published as original in the Editorial Bureau," whose contents, he continued, are with a few exceptions "written by one hand" (*L*, I, 308; *Magnolia*, n.s., II [May, 1843], 336). Similarly, when editing the *Southern Quarterly Review*, he spoke of the extensive "Critical Notices" section as though it were entirely his. See, for example, *L*, III, 120, in which he says, "I have been dishing up my Critical Notices for July."

his life, reviewed these and similar volumes of the 1850s in the pages of his magazines, there or in other publications commenting enthusiastically on Longstreet's *Georgia Scenes,* Hooper's *The Widow Rugby's Husband* (1851), Joseph Glover Baldwin's *The Flush Times of Alabama and Mississippi* (1853), and another landmark collection of humorous sketches, *Polly Peablossom's Wedding* (1851).

Simms's numerous descriptions of antebellum humor reveal that he recognized the diverse strains in the genre, liked the sporting lore that bulked large in it, and preferred comedy that was genteel, realistic, and believable to that which was extravagant, exaggerated, or grotesque. The latter preference helps explain his comments about Henry Clay Lewis and William Tappan Thompson, the two southern humorists he particularly disliked. He denounced the ludicrous humor of Lewis' *Odd Leaves from the Life of a Louisiana Swamp Doctor* (1850), and, somewhat more surprisingly, what he saw as the "extravagancies" of *Major Jones' Courtship.*

> This is some of our Georgia humors,—a series of charcoal sketches in low life, abounding in extravagancies, which will doubtless gratify numerous readers, and persuade to broad grin and vociferous cachinnation, on the part of some,—to the heart's content of the author. We cannot say in what degree the "scenes, incidents and adventures," here detailed, in "a series of letters" by Major Jones himself, are true to the life in the region, and among the people, to whom they are made to relate. It has never been our lot to perceive much approximation to the actual and the true in this sort of writing. We regard it, even in its modern master, Mr. Dickens, as one great, gross caricature. . . . In justice to Major Jones, however, we must acknowledge that some of his incidents are full of life and spirit. Take, for example, his coon hunt, which is very fresh and full of fire.[23]

Simms praised the work of other southern humorists highly, however: he found Baldwin's *Flush Times of Alabama and Mississippi* re-

23. Simms's comments about Lewis appear in "Critical Notices," *Southern Quarterly Review,* XVII [n.s., I] (July, 1850), 537. His remarks about Thompson appear in the "Editorial Bureau," *Magnolia,* n.s., II (June, 1843), 399. His personal reaction to Thompson is described by O. B. Mayer, an acquaintance of the two men who had invited them to dinner. Simms, says Mayer, held Thompson in contempt: "This was shown by his mobility of of [*sic*] eyebrow (elevation—in this instance) and a curling of his upper lip. When Major Jones attempted a story, and failed miserably, Simms annihilated him by telling a *snake story* such as I never heard before" (O. B. Mayer to [Paul Hamilton] Hayne, February 4, 1886, in Paul Hamilton Hayne Papers, Manuscript Department, William R. Perkins Library, Duke University, Durham, N.C.).

plete with fun and spirit, "a lively picture of the salient and racy, in a rough unsophisticated society"; Hooper's *Widow Rugby's Husband* a "series of very lively stories, roughly and adroitly told"; Longstreet's *Georgia Scenes* "the best specimens in this field that the American genius has produced"; and *Polly Peablossom's Wedding* a "collection of broad-grin, Southern and Western exaggeration—comicalities of the woods and wayside; such as will compel laughter if not reflection. Just the sort of volume to snatch up in railway and steamboat, and put out of sight in all other places."[24] With his interest in salty dialect, Simms of course liked the language of southern humor—"its queer allusions, sudden repartee"—and he liked its buoyant, unconventional spirit, which chimed with a streak in his own personality.[25] His reading and reviewing of the humorists during his enforced occupation of the "editorial *fauteuil*" reinforced his interest in the kind of backwoods comedy he was already adept at creating and convinced him that such comedy formed a profitable strain for him to employ extensively in his fiction of the next decade.

Slightly more complicated were Simms's feelings about the satiric social realism in the novel-of-manners vein that Cooper, Edward Bulwer-Lytton, Benjamin Disraeli, and Thackeray, among others, were producing. Simms treated Cooper's novels at length in an essay collected in *Views and Reviews*, discussed Lytton's fiction in an important *Magnolia* article called "Bulwer's Genius and Writings," commented copiously on Disraeli in an even more important essay in the *Southern Quarterly Review* titled "Spirit of the Age," and reviewed Thackeray's many publications in a host of squibs and notices in the same periodical and somewhat later in the Charleston *Mercury*. He denounced Cooper's imitation in *Precaution* of "a very inferior school

24. [Simms], "Critical Notices," *Southern Quarterly Review*, XXV [n.s., IX] (April, 1854), 555, "The Humourous in American and British Literature," in *Views and Reviews in American Literature, History and Fiction*, 2nd ser. (New York, 1845), 178, and "Critical Notices," *Southern Quarterly Review*, XX [n.s., IV] (July, 1851), 272.

25. Simms, "The Humourous in American and British Literature," in *Views and Reviews*, 2nd ser., 179. Simms makes similar comments about southern humor in the manuscript "Wit and Humour of the Professions," 32, where he says, "The Georgia Scenes of Judge Longstreet are unquestionably among the most admirably humourous and truly American, of all books of the kind" and adds that the Old Southwest, "perhaps, affords samples of the freshest and most original forms of Humour." Mary C. Simms Oliphant kindly granted me permission to use this manuscript, which is in the Charles Carroll Simms Collection at the South Caroliniana Library, University of South Carolina.

of writings, known as the social life novel," wherein "a large gathering of the set, at ball or dinner, affords incident of which the novelist is required to make the highest use," and he also denounced Lytton's presentation of his personal ideal in seducers, fops, and gamblers, along with his refusal to condemn the excesses of the fashionable society he portrayed.[26] In similar manner, he criticized Thackeray's fondness for savage portraits of humanity, his "wholesale suspicion of its fraudulence, its folly, its vice and brutality" without recognition of its compensatory virtues.[27] And he registered the predictable discontent of a romancer with the concentration of such writers on the familiar and the commonplace; to them, he said, the "ordinary events of the household, or of the snug family circle, suggest the only materials." But he nevertheless praised their pictures of the coldness and selfishness of the nobility, "the absurdities, the frivolities and the vices of fashionable life." He particularly admired Thackeray's talent for domestic humor, his meticulous renditions of social details, and his "satirical delineation of human life in its ordinary conditions." Thackeray, he felt, "is not to be humbugged by the *simulacra* of society; no social masks deceive him; he is a stern antagonist of the fraudulent and pretentious, and will tear away cloak and cassock from the pretender, with as little scruple as he would the mask from the fashionable woman, or the bandit of society."[28]

The fiction Simms would shortly produce about the South Carolina low country shows him using, with increasing skill, the methods of these writers when he ventures into the elegant world of the city. His midcentury editing and reviewing had exposed him to strains in the literature of his time on which he would draw for the rest of his life. They changed the texture of his fiction, gave it additional spice and

26. Simms, "The Writings of James Fenimore Cooper," in *Views and Reviews,* 1st ser., 259; [Simms], "Bulwer's Genius and Writings," *Magnolia,* n.s., I (December, 1842), 333.

27. [Simms], "Critical Notices," *Southern Quarterly Review,* XXIV [n.s., VIII] (July, 1853), 266. During the period when he was editing the *Southern Quarterly Review,* Simms published an anonymous article on Thackeray, "The Genius and Writings of Thackeray," in XIX [n.s., III] (January, 1851), 74–100.

28. Simms, "The Writings of James Fenimore Cooper," in *Views and Reviews,* 1st ser., 259; [Simms], "Bulwer's Genius and Writings," 333; [Simms], "Critical Notices," *Southern Quarterly Review,* XXIII [n.s., VII] (April, 1853), 521; [Simms], "From our Literary Correspondent," Charleston *Mercury,* February 27, 1856; [Simms], "Critical Notices," *Southern Quarterly Review,* XIX [n.s., III] (April, 1851), 559; [Simms], "Thackeray's Virginians," Charleston *Mercury,* January 5, 1860.

verve, and brought it into line with prevailing tendencies in the literature of his region. Hence, although the labor he was forced to do in editing, history, and criticism during the "begging times for authordom" of the 1840s was not entirely to his liking, it would stimulate his imagination when he returned to the production of major fiction in the 1850s.

7
Simms at Midcentury: The Comedy of Plantation Manners

The 1850s opened auspiciously for Simms, whose literary and political influence continued to grow and whose reputation reached heights it had not attained since the 1830s. As the decade wore on, he formed important new friendships and consolidated old ones; he continued to figure prominently in New York circles; and he passionately involved himself in the politics of secession. He discussed these politics with fiery old Beverley Tucker of Virginia, the author of *George Balcombe* (1836) and *The Partisan Leader* (1836), the latter a futuristic novel purporting to describe the formation of a southern confederacy in 1849. The popular image of Simms as a southern firebrand is one his comments to Tucker do little to dispel: he charges, for example, that abolition is an implacable madness, that the Union would dissolve by 1855, and that if he were to trust his feelings he would tell South Carolina to "secede at once" (*L,* III, 76). Partly because of his protracted correspondence with Tucker, Simms's proslavery rhetoric grew shriller in the fifties: he told John Pendleton Kennedy, for instance, that "Negro Slavery is one of the greatest of moral goods & blessings, and . . . slavery in all ages has been found the greatest and most admirable agent of Civilization" (*L,* III, 174). As William R. Taylor remarks, Simms had become "the historical consciousness of the South"; and he functioned as a persuasive spokesman for the intellectual and literary concerns of his section.[1]

Despite his involvement in politics, however, during the fifties Simms threw himself wholeheartedly into his writing, which remained his pri-

1. Taylor, *Cavalier and Yankee,* 269. For lucid comments on Simms's role as an antebellum "man of mind," see Drew Gilpin Faust, *A Sacred Circle: The Dilemma of the Intellectual in the Old South, 1840–1860* (Baltimore, 1977). See also Faust's comments on Simms in *James Henry Hammond and the Old South: A Design for Mastery* (Baton Rouge, 1982), *passim.*

mary concern. He continued his trips to New York to superintend the publication of his novels and maintain his ties with northern men of letters, in the process strengthening important existing relationships. The friendship he had formed with Evert Duyckinck during the Young America-Knickerbocker wars grew stronger as Duyckinck aided him with his publishing projects and he helped Duyckinck plan the *Cyclopædia of American Literature* (1855), an enormous compilation of biographical and publishing data about men of letters throughout the country. Meanwhile, from Charleston and Woodlands, he dispensed advice and aid to authors ranging from Kennedy and Thomas Holley Chivers to William Elliott and John Esten Cooke. Late in the decade, he became active in the group of scholars and literary men who congregated in Russell's Bookstore on Charleston's busy King Street, and his exertions on behalf of *Russell's Magazine* cemented his friendship with its editor, Paul Hamilton Hayne, who along with Cooke became perhaps his most adoring young admirer.

Simms's literary influence by 1859 was so great, in fact, that it involved him in more tasks than he could comfortably handle. He was, he wrote Hammond ruefully, constantly on call for budding historians and fledgling literati: "Every body that needs information about the South; about our History; every young author who wishes to be delivered; every beginner that desires to know how to begin; all apply to me; and it would be thought very churlish should I refuse. So every Editor, or Publisher that begins a Cyclopædia or a Magazine, or a Collection of any sort, writes me for succour." He continued: "What am I to do. I frequently send a batch of 10 to 20 letters to the P.O. It is breaking me down" (*L*, IV, 173).

Yet notwithstanding such tasks Simms was able to continue his own literary endeavors. By 1850, the book trade had partly recovered from the damage done by the panic of 1837, and the publication of novels was again a profitable enterprise, though less so than it had been when he began to write. He therefore returned to the production of long fiction and brought out his last four Revolutionary War Romances—*Katharine Walton* (1851), *The Sword and the Distaff* (1852; retitled *Woodcraft*, 1854), *The Forayers* (1855), and *Eutaw* (1856). After the saga was finished, he dropped back to the early colonial phase of Carolina for *The Cassique of Kiawah* (1859), a companion piece to *The Yemassee* and his last treatment of the low country in long fiction. He also began to revise his fiction and some of his verse for the Author's Uniform Edition of his writing brought out by Justus Starr Redfield of New York, which eventually ran to twenty volumes and included the Revolutionary War Romances, the Border Romances, poetry, and drama. The many changes he made in volumes reissued in the Redfield edition show that he was much more concerned with revising than most of his critics have realized: he sharpened figurative language, for instance, expanded passages of dialect speech, and in general increased the element of realism in his books.[2]

The ostensibly encouraging developments in Simms's literary career, however, belie the harsh financial realities of American authorship at midcentury. The profession of letters in the antebellum period had been seriously affected by the continuing instability of the book market. The vicissitudes of the late 1830s and the 1840s had damaged the trade and colored Simms's attitude toward professional authorship: as he wrote a correspondent, "Literature in the South is hardly worse than ditching, I grant you, but it is hardly better" (*L,* VI, 144). With the writing of novels still a somewhat hazardous financial venture, he continued to produce miscellaneous work as he had trained himself to do in the 1840s. He brought out *The Lily and the Totem* (1850), a volume of lightly fictionalized historical sketches of the Huguenots in Florida, and he wrote two plays with contemporary settings, *Norman Maurice* (1851) and *Michael Bonham* (1852). He also produced two lively short novels, *As Good as a Comedy* and *The Golden Christmas* (both 1852), as well as his final Spanish-American romance, *Vasconselos* (1853). Most important, perhaps, he collected his verse in the impressive two-volume *Poems Descriptive, Dramatic, Legendary and Contemplative,* published both by Redfield and by John Russell of Charleston during 1854.[3] In addition, he issued the pamphlet *South-Carolina in the Revolutionary War* (1853), assembled his short fiction in *Southward Ho!* (1854), and contributed, with Hammond, William Harper, and Thomas Dew, to the influential volume *The Pro-Slavery Argument* (1852). Finally, he may have begun an

2. Dean, "Revisions in the Revolutionary War Novels of William Gilmore Simms," *passim;* Miriam J. Shillingsburg, "The Influence of Sectionalism on the Revisions in Simms's Revolutionary Romances," *Mississippi Quarterly,* XXIX (Fall, 1976), [526]–38; Thomas Darwin Lane, "Two Versions of Simms's *Guy Rivers:* A Record of Artistic Development in Changing Times" (Ph.D. dissertation, Texas Christian University, 1972).

3. Kibler, *Poetry of Simms,* 96, remarks that though the volumes bear an 1853 publishing date they were actually issued early in 1854.

energetic novel set in rural South Carolina, *Paddy McGann,* which came out in serial form during 1863 (*L,* IV, 421).

Given the fluctuating conditions of the market, it was natural for Simms to draw upon his reading of the 1840s in manners fiction and backwoods humor as a way of enhancing the appeal of his midcentury writing. With his characteristic interest in assimilating diverse literary elements, he often incorporates both traditions within a single work, but frequently one or the other dominates. In *The Forayers, Eutaw,* and *Woodcraft,* for instance, he stresses the comic foibles of plantation aristocrats, while in *The Golden Christmas, Katharine Walton,* and *The Cassique of Kiawah* he emphasizes satiric descriptions of errant city socialites. In *As Good as a Comedy* and *Paddy McGann,* on the other hand, he uses large amounts of southern backwoods humor; portions of *Southward Ho!, Woodcraft, The Forayers,* and *Eutaw* also show the influence of that mode. Simms's fiction in the highly productive 1850s, then, falls into three groups—the first centering on portraits of plantation manners; the second stressing high-toned city life; the third emphasizing depictions of rural characters developed by the techniques of antebellum southern humor.

The comedy of manners that is the dominant mode of the first two groups begins as an amused and genial survey of the foibles of the planting aristocracy and then gradually sharpens into satire as Simms trains his sights upon the Charleston social scene. He had some precedent in his own writing for his decision to concentrate on the manners of the gentry, since his customary plantation setting with its emphasis on ceremony and the formal display of wealth invited the description of patrician behavior. Up to this point in his fiction about the Revolutionary War, however, his commitment to the patriot cause conveyed through his serious romance plots with their Gothic appendages had prevented him from treating his planters humorously; instead, he had been concerned to show the uncertain loyalties and vacillating political commitments of such characters as Mr. Berkeley. By the 1850s, however, he had replaced the Gothic element in his fiction with the kind of comic portrayals of high society in which his magazine reading and reviewing had schooled him, and perhaps because of his growing interest in criticizing the southern upper class he made a point of depicting certain of its representatives in a mildly unflattering light.

Simms's concern for southern agriculture during the forties had led him to portray in "Maize in Milk" (serialized 1847) a lovable but foolish planter, Colonel Openheart, whose imprudent generosity to orphans and field hands nearly beggars his own family. But his first real success with comically heedless old aristocrats is his portrait of Colonel Sinclair, a gouty veteran of the Cherokee War who is a central actor in *The Forayers* and *Eutaw*. The first humorous and one of the few sympathetic upper-class Loyalists in Simms's fiction, the Colonel is an irritable, explosive, and charming patrician in whose attitudes political and social prejudices blend. Proud of his aristocratic lineage, disdainful of Huguenots, and intensely loyal to the British king, he is tormented by the actions of his son Willie, a major in Marion's brigade who loves Bertha Travis, a girl whose family is below him and whose father his own father detests. Willie's sister Carrie is also a partisan, and she loves a patriot officer, Peyre St. Julien—who, as his name suggests, is a Frenchman and hence distasteful to the ardent old Anglophile. Colonel Sinclair's prejudices give Willie, functioning as Simms's spokesman, the chance to dilate upon the theme of natural aristocracy that is a prominent topic in the book. As he tells Carrie early in *The Forayers:* "There are persons to whom refinement is *native*—who are *born* nobles—delicate and just in sentiment, magnanimous in soul, generous in courage, endowed with noble talents, and devoted to noble purposes. It is the duty of an aristocracy to acknowledge all such persons, as soon as found, and take them lovingly into their embrace, and seek to do them honor" (86–87). Two such persons, in Willie's view, are Bertha Travis and Peyre St. Julien; but it takes almost the entire course of the two novels for him to persuade his opinionated father to think so.

In portraying Colonel Sinclair, Simms blends comedy and realism to exploit the natural inconsistencies of human personality, thereby creating a believable and wonderfully amusing figure. He exaggerates the Colonel's bluster, his adherence to entrenched beliefs, his rage when thwarted, and the peculiarities of his speech, especially his tendency to repeat himself when annoyed. His speech, which is full of explosive asides and humorous digressions, is perhaps his funniest feature. The Colonel often solves a problem or alleviates an embarrassing situation with one of his outbreaks. When Carrie praises the "liberty party," for instance, he sputters: "Liberty devils! Rebels, Miss Sinclair! Heartless, soulless, insensible, savage, ridiculous rebels!" and he later denounces the patriots as "dirty blackguards, who carry rifles and shot-guns, and pretend to be military, and impudently dream of such a thing as liberty."[4] When Willie and Peyre St. Julien visit the Sinclair barony, the Colonel's Loyalist sentiments continually involve him in minor disagreements with the two partisan officers, until he cries in exasperation to St. Julien: "Sir, will you not agree with me to damn this war? I say, sir—damn this war! This most abominable, unnatural war, which will not suffer a gentleman to declare his honest natural sentiments. Sir—Mr. Julien, be pleased to say damn this war" (*F*, 219). And when he is unable to aid some British troops quartered at his estate, he moans in despair that quickly turns to irritation as his thoughts lead him in several directions: "I am a poor, old, worthless, miserable, invalided cripple, and feeling as I do, I begin to doubt if I were ever in the Cherokee war at all—if I ever crossed the mountains with Grant and Middleton—d——n Middleton—he too is a rebel—all the Middletons are rebels—and more shame to them, too, when they could send into the field, a fellow, with the ability to lead a regiment in the Cherokee war" (*E*, 204).

In the course of the two novels, however, Colonel Sinclair's encounters with Britons, Loyalists, and partisans lead him to modify his pronouncements and gradually discard his prejudices. The chief ruffian of the two novels, Hell-Fire Dick, makes plain to him that outlaws are in the king's service; Lord Rawdon convinces him that British power over South Carolina is waning; and Bertha Travis' gentleness, along with Peyre St. Julien's gallantry, encourages him to drop his prejudices about nationality and social class. Thus when Bertha, prudently adopting the pseudonym "Annie Smith," nurses the Colonel during a severe attack of gout, he grows extremely fond of the thoughtful girl, and he admits to Carrie that his views about marriage as well as politics have been wrong. "I have been harsh to Willie! . . . True, he had joined the rebel cause! But the world changes. Laws change. Nations change. . . . Let Willie choose his own master . . . marry whom he pleases!" (*E*, 414–15). "I should not quarrel with him, *now*," the Colonel muses, "were he even to declare for this gentle little creature, with the plebeian name of Smith. . . . How the devil, child, did such a creature become the proprietor of such a name?" (*E*, 415).

4. W[illiam] Gilmore Simms, *Eutaw: A Sequel to The Forayers, or The Raid of the Dog-Days. A Tale of the Revolution* (New York, 1856), 293, 294. Further references to this novel are to this edition, cited within the text by page number (as *E* where necessary for clarity).

When Bertha is kidnapped and the Colonel learns her true identity, he sobs brokenly to his son, humorous even in the midst of grief: "Oh, Willie, have you not heard—do you not know? That girl—that sweet, loving, dear creature—Annie Smith—no, not Annie Smith (d——n the Smiths!)—but *your* girl, your affianced—yes, Bertha—she!—O my God, preserve my brain!" (*E*, 474). But Bertha is recovered and eventually marries Willie. The Colonel—who winces when Carrie weds St. Julien—thereafter frequently mocks his own former prejudices, calling Bertha to his side "by her *nom de guerre* of Annie Smith" (*E*, 580).

Colonel Sinclair might stand forth as Simms's best comic patrician figure were it not for the superior claims of Lieutenant (later Captain) Porgy. After his appearance in *The Partisan,* Porgy had virtually faded from the Revolutionary War series for a time—he appears very briefly in *Mellichampe* and not at all in *The Kinsmen*—but Simms brought him back triumphantly in *Katharine Walton,* and thereafter found an important role for him in each of the other late Revolutionary War novels. The manner in which Simms sketches Porgy demonstrates the character's intimate connection with the history of the low country and with southern literary traditions of aristocratic social comedy. More fully conceived than the typical romance figure and, though lovable and admirable, emphatically not idealized, he shows both the virtues and the flaws of his plantation upbringing with its emphasis on manly honor and leisurely living. Life on the plantation accounts for his integrity, compassion, and courage on the one hand, and, on the other, for his sensuality, his improvidence, and his love of ease and pleasure. With his vast bulk, his peculiar manner of speaking, and his readiness to engage in facetious and even farcical action to achieve his aims, he is easily the most noteworthy character in Simms's fiction.

In the last four Revolutionary War novels, Simms spins a minor but significant story about Porgy's progressive adaptation to the army. Throughout *The Partisan,* this "native epicurean" had mainly been preoccupied with getting and preparing food, but as the series progresses, fighting comes to rival eating as one of his principal concerns (*KW*, 167). In the late novels, to a greater extent than in their predecessors, the fat captain engages in a number of wild exploits developed in the main by slapstick, which Simms uses to highlight Porgy's great natural dignity that derives from his plantation heritage. Whether fighting or eating, Porgy keeps and cherishes the grace, wit, and refined tastes native to his upbringing. He exhibits these qualities as he clowns around with his fellow militiamen, dwarfing his dilemmas by gilding them with words and reveling in undignified antics that contrast with his stately speech. To explain Porgy's behavior, Simms constructs a psychological theory of humor that forms a major addition to the revised version of *The Partisan,* issued during 1854 as one of the first volumes in the Redfield Author's Uniform Edition.

Porgy, Simms insists in two long passages midway through the novel, is an actor who deliberately magnifies his tastes, whims, speech, and actions for comedy that masks his private self and shields him against the barbs of those who do not understand him. For him, the humor of self-mockery, caprice, and deceptively pompous behavior is a mental suit of armor, a method of protecting himself against the criticism of people lower than he on the social scale who sometimes comment unkindly on his postures. Porgy has, Simms stresses, "a certain artificial nature" and "certain affectations" at which he is "quite content that the world should laugh, believing what it pleased." Born to wealth and given a gentleman's education, in his capers he "might *play* the buffoon," Simms continues, but he is not a buffoon. Instead he is "a sort of laughing philosopher, who, as if in anticipation of the free speech of others, dealt with himself as little mercifully as his nearest friends might have done. . . . He jested with his own tastes, his own bulk of body, his own poverty, and thus baffled the more serious jests of the ill-tempered by anticipating them."[5]

Porgy openly demonstrates these qualities in *Katharine Walton,* in which he appears as the partisan social leader who is close to the troops and thoroughly accustomed to the forest. Frolicking in camp, he butchers and eats a deer, instigates a coon hunt, portions out Jamaica rum, and participates in a card game without losing his magisterial air. When a militiaman suggests, for instance, that he join the coon hunt, he expostulates: "Out upon thee, you young varmint! Do you mean me? With such a person as mine—a figure made for state occasions and great ceremonials only? Do you mean *me?* . . . Why, this is flat treason! It's a design against my life, as well as my dignity. *I* hunt coons! *I* splash and plunge among these hammocks,

5. Simms, *The Partisan,* rev. ed., 348, 358–59.

bestraddle fallen cypresses, rope myself with vines, burrow in bogs, and bruise nose and shin against snags and branches! Come closer, my son, that I may knock thee upon the head with this lightwood knot" (168).[6]

Later in the novel Porgy is shown in battle using both weight and appetite to advantage. During a clash between Marion's men and a British troop, the supercilious Briton Lieutenant Meadows damages Porgy's sword and slices off the tip of his ear. Enraged, Porgy rushes upon the officer and, "in a totally unexpected form of attack," throws his "gigantic bulk" upon him, announcing, "It's no use, my fine fellow; your faith may remove mountains, but your surrender only shall remove me." When Meadows gasps, "Will nobody relieve me from this elephant?" the insulted Porgy, preparing to pummel him into submission, roars: "Elephant! . . . By the powers, but you shall feel my grinders!" Singleton intervenes, however, and Porgy sputters: "It is well for him, Colonel Singleton, that you made your appearance. I had otherwise beaten him to a mummy. Would you believe it?—he called me an elephant! Me! Me an elephant!" Singleton soothes him; but when Porgy discovers that his ear is injured, his wrath rises again, and he invokes his patrician background as he challenges Meadows to a duel, remarking, "To have one's ears or nose slit, sir . . . is, I have always been taught, the greatest indignity that could be inflicted upon a gentleman" (181–83).

After the dispute is settled, Singleton sends Porgy and the young trooper Lance Frampton to tell Mrs. Griffin, mother of Lance's fiancée, that her husband has been killed in battle. There ensues an amusing sequence through which Simms prepares for the courtship plot in *Woodcraft.* Musing on Lance's approaching wedding, Porgy announces, "I begin to think that marriage is a good thing," and turns his thoughts to Mrs. Griffin (*KW,* 368). After telling her of her husband's death, he attempts to console her; but he and Lance are forced into the woods by the approach of British troops. Surprised by an enemy dragoon while cooking in the forest, Porgy blends his chief concerns by using food to fight. He flings boiling hominy into the soldier's face, knocks

6. Porgy's manner of speaking in this and other passages resembles that of Dr. Alexander Skinner as quoted by Alexander Garden in *Anecdotes of the Revolutionary War in America,* 139. See, for example, Skinner's comments when asked whether he would ford a river: "By no means . . . I am not fond of romantic enterprise, and will not seek for the perilous achievements where the elements, more than the enemy, are to be dreaded. The river too is deep, and my spirits are not buoyant; I should sink to a certainty and meet a watery grave. Death by water drinking! I shudder at the thought of it!"

him in the head with the iron hominy kettle, and hurries farther into the forest with the rest of his dinner—only to lose it in another brawl.[7]

In other parts of the late Revolutionary War Romances, Simms is at some pains to highlight Porgy's aristocratic upbringing in order to use him, as in *The Partisan,* to form a human link between manor and swamp. In *The Forayers,* for instance, Porgy hosts a magnificent feast for Continental and militia officers that reveals how adept he has become at transplanting plantation customs to a forest environment. He employs young troopers accustomed to his habits to construct tables from long green poles placed on notched sticks, and drapes the poles with "a verdant tablecloth" of "great oak-leaves" (533). He greets his guests, who range from Marion and Sumter to Nathaniel Greene and Henry Lee, with "the easy good nature, the frank politeness, the smiling grace" of a plantation owner. And, Simms remarks, never was a gentleman "more perfectly at ease in crowded assembly, yet more solicitous of the claims of all about him, than our corpulent captain" (540).

For the dinner, Porgy and his cook Tom have transformed the frog and alligator of the swamp into pungent, mysterious dishes called "alerta" and "lagarta," which satisfy the most fastidious palate. As the punch flows into fresh goblets, the merriment grows high; but the social realm remains clearly linked to the military one as throughout the revelry the stress on war remains: Porgy toasts the "cause of Liberty," and Singleton toasts "South Carolina—almost freed from the footstep of the foreign tyrant" (547, 548). Meanwhile, through a striking detail, Simms shapes patterns in the forest to suggest the estate. In other novels of the series, a stately colonnade of trees lines the approach to a typical plantation. The forest site Porgy chooses for his aristocratic banquet has a comparably grand entrance—"a great natural avenue of lofty green pines" to which Porgy, with his memories of the manor, is attracted (541).

In *Eutaw* Porgy temporarily forgoes his customary preoccupation with food to expatiate on military errors committed in battles ranging

7. *KW,* 382–89. Simms's treatment of this scene shows his attentiveness to detail when revising his work. *Katharine Walton* originally appeared as a serial in *Godey's Magazine and Lady's Book* during 1850; but while preparing it for publication, Simms apparently had to condense portions of what he had written, for in the magazine version this scene involving Porgy is hastily, flatly summarized. Simms restored the passage for the 1851 edition of *Katharine Walton,* published in Philadelphia by Abraham Hart, and kept it in its entirety for the Redfield edition.

from Camden to Eutaw Springs, in the process revealing how acclimated he has become to the army. Wounded, hungry, and splenetic, he defends the honor of the partisans while making charges against Lee and Greene that more restrained officers such as Willie Sinclair, though disgruntled, will not make. Porgy's claims, which are clearly Simms's own, reflect the author's keen sympathy for the South Carolina Revolutionary patriots, which had increased rather than abated during his nearly thirty years of writing about the Revolution, while Porgy's consistent praise of South Carolina militiamen reflects Simms's active promotion of his state in the years before the Civil War.

Insisting that his portly captain is "no mean authority in such matters," Simms has Porgy dissect errors at Eutaw Springs, elevate patriots over Continentals, and criticize Continental leaders of the southern army, "from . . . Bob Howe, who was half-witted," to Benjamin Lincoln, "who might have been a good army nurse, or chaplain, but should never have been suffered to enter the camp in any other capacity" (354, 360). Porgy belabors Gates, who like other leaders used state troops "*to draw the enemy's fire, in order to lessen the dangers to the regulars when the bayonet is required to be used!*" He claims the militia fought well enough at Eutaw Springs to make the Continentals stare, and maintains that veteran militia should be handled like Continentals and intermingled with them in battle (534, 529). Finally, he blames Greene along with Gates for tactical errors in battle and implies that Marion would not have made them (530–34). Only near the end of *Eutaw* does he turn from his tirade to eat: the leisurely epicure of the 1835 *Partisan,* preoccupied with feasting, has evolved into an eloquent and persuasive military critic to whom food is only one of several concerns.

In what is perhaps his best Revolutionary War novel, *Woodcraft,* Simms shows Porgy trying to keep alive his memories of war while slowly adjusting to the claims of peacetime. A story of "soldier's pay" set immediately after the Revolution, the novel depicts Porgy's return to his ravaged plantation Glen-Eberley and his use of military maneuvers to defend it.[8] One strand of the book, evoking his carefree bachelor life, portrays him gradually gathering his army comrades at the plantation: Tom, his body servant and saucy black cook; Dr. Oakenburg, a ragged fop who prances through the forest prating of his need for per-

8. Both Donald Davidson in the Introduction to *L,* I, xlv, and Ridgely, *William Gilmore Simms,* 99, use the phrase "soldier's pay" in describing the novel.

fect security; Geordie Dennison, a poet and musician; Lance Frampton, a farm boy and natural noble; and Sergeant Millhouse, "a man of altogether inferior appearance, tall, rawboned, and awkward, with features harsh and irregular" (50). Another strand, developed from *Katharine Walton,* shows Porgy indolently courting both Mrs. Griffin, the widow of his former army comrade, and wealthy Mrs. Eveleigh, whose slaves he has saved from theft.

Central to the comedy of plantation manners that is the dominant mode of *Woodcraft* are the exchanges of Porgy with two of his social inferiors, Tom and Millhouse. Of these scenes, the ones with Tom, which echo similar sequences in the earlier Revolutionary War novels, are more sheerly comic in tone. Throughout the series, in keeping with his humorous presentation of Porgy, Simms stresses the amusing aspects of the tie between the fat partisan officer and his servant—an effort in which he is aided by the several resemblances he develops between slave and master. Both Tom and Porgy love pleasure and covet ease; both crave fine fare and are skillful in preparing it; and both are vociferous and overbearing. When Porgy commends the merits of Tom's "broils" to Millhouse, for instance, the sergeant replies, "Tom's jest as good, I'm a-thinking, at a fry as at a brile, cappin." But Tom is offended.

> "An' why you no say *bile,* too, Mass Millh'us'?" demanded Tom, apparently not satisfied that there should be any implied demerits in his case.
>
> "En [and] so I mout [might]," answered the sergeant. "This here hominy now, to my thinking, is *biled* to a monstrous softness."
>
> "An' de bake—de bread—wha' you say for him?" was the next exaction of Tom's vanity. (182)[9]

Like other loving but authoritarian plantation masters in antebellum fiction, Porgy genially berates his servant for real or imagined offenses, in *Woodcraft* as in other volumes in the series. Tom is more domineering toward the other slaves at Glen-Eberley, however, than Porgy usually is toward him. To a young house servant who calls him "uncle Tom," for instance, he snaps, "Don't you uncle me, you chucklehead!"—a remark that may glance at Harriet Beecher Stowe's antislavery novel *Uncle Tom's Cabin,* published in 1852 (179).[10] In *Woodcraft* Simms uses Tom, as he uses Hector in *The Yemassee,* to further

9. Here and elsewhere in the passages quoted from Tom's remarks to Porgy, the bracketed words represent Simms's glosses of Gullah dialect for his readers.

10. Ridgely, *William Gilmore Simms,* 103.

his determined sectionalist propaganda. Thus when Porgy tries to free Tom at the end of the novel, Tom upholds the master-slave relationship while demonstrating his possessive attitude toward Porgy: "'No! no! maussa,' he cried, with a sly shake of the head, 'I kain't t'ink ob letting you off dis way. Ef *I* doesn't b'long to *you, you* b'longs to *me!* You hab for keep dis nigger long as he lib; and him for keep you. . . . Free nigger no hab any body for fin' 'em he bittle [victuals]. . . . I no guine to be free no way you kin fix it; so, maussa, don't you bodder me wid dis nonsense t'ing 'bout free paper any more'" (509).

Serving a more serious purpose in the novel than Porgy's exchanges with Tom are his verbal battles with his loquacious overseer, Millhouse. Their repeated arguments about plantation management constitute Simms's major means of comparing two social and economic orders to suggest the problems the South had faced after the Revolution and would face again after the Civil War—money-grubbing pragmatism on the one hand and humane aesthetic values on the other. Porgy, who as Trent says is in many ways a representative southerner, brave, sententious, prodigal, signifies the profligate youth of the South and its painful postwar maturation. Hence, recalling his boyhood, he muses, "[T]he curse of my generation was that our fathers lived too well, were too rapidly prosperous, and though they did not neglect the exercise of a proper industry in themselves, they either did not know how to teach it to their children, or presumed on the absence of any necessity that they should learn." As a result, he tells Millhouse, he had learned no prudent economic lessons: "Pray believe that I was a very foolish, profligate person, who, in ceasing to be young, did not cease to be foolish, and continued his absurd vanities and excesses to the last" (206). In such passages Porgy, as William R. Taylor notes, plainly symbolizes the Cavalier South and the problems faced by a society harmed by the imprudence of its leading representatives.[11]

In opposition to Porgy stands the egregious Millhouse, a utilitarian and an opportunist whose only standard of value is financial gain. Because the sergeant is more practical than his master, from time to time he has attracted defenders who argue that he overmasters Porgy in his arguments about agricultural economy.[12] Careful attention to the

11. Trent, *William Gilmore Simms,* 109; Taylor, *Cavalier and Yankee,* 288.

12. See, for example, Taylor, *Cavalier and Yankee,* 290, 291, and Wakelyn, *The Politics of a Literary Man,* 174. Moffitt Cecil, however, rightly observes that Simms rejects Millhouse's "miserly economy" and "calculating utilitarianism"; see "Simms's Porgy as National Hero," *American Literature,* XXXVI (January, 1965), 482.

tenor of dialogue and commentary in the novel, however, reveals Porgy's, and Simms's, disdain for what Millhouse at his worst represents. Porgy denounces him to Mrs. Eveleigh as "a grub, a human grub," and throughout the narrative Simms stresses that, whereas Porgy is eloquent and charitable, Millhouse is crass, bumptious, and inhumane (352). Millhouse decries the indigent Oakenburg, whom Porgy in generosity plans to support, and complains that Dennison "warn't a reasonable, useful man. He couldn't cook a steak, or bake a loaf, or, sew his own breeches, or do nothing" (281). Human beings, in Millhouse's view, to be useful must be productive and acquisitive. The chief end of man, he blithely informs Porgy, is

> to go on gitting, and gitting, and gitting, to the end of the season, ontill Death gits him. As he gits, he kin increase his comforts—git better bread, more meat . . . ef he likes it, git wine . . . git better clothing. . . . Then he's for gitting as good bargains as he kin—then he's for gitting to be a ruler ef he kin—gitting to be a colonel or a gineral in the militia; gitting to be a representative and a senator in the legislatur; gitting to be a justus of the peace; gitting to be a sawt of king over the people." (293)

Determined to make Glen-Eberley solvent, Millhouse decides that Porgy should marry the rich widow Eveleigh; and recalling his army training, he recommends that the courtship be conducted by military methods. "You must go it with a rush," he tells his master, "sword in hand, looking mighty fierce, and ready to smite and tear everything to splinters." He continues, "With a woman of ixperence, storming's the way;—and a fort, you know, that's been once stormed knows all about it, and kin be easily stormed again" (298, 299). During dinner at the widow's home, he continues his army talk as, winking and leering, he tells his amused hostess, "thar's but leetle cha*i*nce for happiness, to any grown woman, onless she has a nateral guardeen, and that guardeen ought to be a good husband; and ef I was the woman, Madam Eb'leigh, to choose, I'd be for taking my husband out of the army" (358). Furious, Porgy finally turns Millhouse's army talk against him, shouting "Silence in the ranks, sir!" (358–59). Later, at Glen-Eberley, he squelches the presumptuous overseer.

> If you were suddenly to find yourself among bears and buffaloes, you might reasonably undertake to show them how to find their food or prey; if among snakes, I have no doubt you could teach them superior modes of beguiling young frogs into their jaws . . . but I doubt if these capacities of yours should entitle you to think yourself appointed to teach young oysters

> how to swim, or young angels how to fly; and I am even doubtful how far they should justify you in an endeavor to set yourself up as a teacher of love and courtship. Of one thing let me assure you, before I stop, that if ever you undertake to make love to any woman on my account, again, and in my presence, by the Lord that liveth, sergeant, I will fling you from the windows, though the house were as high as the tower of Babel. (365–66)

Porgy himself, however, cannot wholly forget the army; and he uses his military training to good purpose in a sequence near the end of *Woodcraft* that brings Simms's comedy of plantation manners to a hilarious conclusion. In two well-conceived scenes, the captain and his friends defend Glen-Eberley from the sheriff and deputy who come to serve the papers of the villain M'Kewn, holder of a mortgage on Porgy's estate. The sheriff, himself a former army man, attends a military mad tea party—a dinner with guests in full battle garb, a saber laid across the table, and a plate of guns as one of the dishes. When he hints at his mission, Porgy seizes the pistols from the plate and points them at him; Millhouse swings his saber over the man's head; and Lance, grabbing a sword, grasps him by a shock of hair (423–36).

During an equally outlandish sequence, the offensive deputy Absalom Crooks, a "mean copper-headed son of a skunk," is first shorn of his beard and then forced to chew and swallow the documents he has brought as Millhouse shouts "Feed or suffocate" in his ear (446, 451).[13] Finally Porgy—fully in control of the proceedings—instigates a deliberately farcical action in which he and his friends, flourishing pistols and swords, repulse the sheriff's forces and defend the estate (481–89). Throughout the closing pages of *Woodcraft,* Porgy's use of humor as both weapon and shield against his foes has served him well.

Even more plainly than these military demonstrations, the love plot in *Woodcraft* shows the straits to which Porgy's army habits grafted upon his plantation upbringing have brought him. The two women

13. Trent, *William Gilmore Simms,* 203, says this scene is "taken bodily from an Elizabethan play," which no critics, to my knowledge, have heretofore identified. It appears to be Robert Greene's *Sir George a Greene,* in which Sir Nicholas Mannering demands provisions for the rebel troops from the citizens of Wakefield, and George a Greene stoutly refuses. When Mannering angrily waves his commission, Greene tears it and forces him at dagger's point to eat its two great seals. See *A Pleasant Conceited Comedy of George a Greene, The Pinner of Wakefield,* in Felix E. Schelling (ed.), *Typical Elizabethan Plays* (New York, 1926), I, ii. In the annotations to *Woodcraft* in *The Revolutionary War Novels of William Gilmore Simms,* VIII, 545*n*443.24–452.39, it is claimed that the scene may derive from an episode in the life of Colonal Hezekiah Maham, an American officer in the Revolutionary War.

whom he courts objectify, in a sense, the two dimensions of his background. His natural mate would seem to be the portly Widow Eveleigh, owner of a well-run plantation and as well-educated and gently bred as Porgy, whom she entertains with good food and cultivated talk. But she is wholly a product of plantation culture while he, with his military experience, no longer is: as he tells her, "The camp makes sad havoc in the tastes of a gentleman" (354). The loose manner he had acquired there, his habit of smoking and swearing, offends Mrs. Eveleigh, who strikes at something very much a part of him when she warns him that "the *brusquerie* of his army habits" will not "altogether answer" in her parlor (373).

Porgy therefore also seeks the company of Mrs. Griffin, who is lower on the social scale than Mrs. Eveleigh but also prettier and more adaptable. As a poor soldier's wife, she has known, like the captain, the hardships of war in a way that Mrs. Eveleigh has not; and since her "social experiences were more adapted to his own later habits," she accepts him as an army man: she lights the pipe he cannot smoke around Mrs. Eveleigh and looks up "with great reverence to the captain of partisans" (373). At her humble cottage he recalls the life he has lost, for more than Mrs. Eveleigh's trim, tailored fields, Mrs. Griffin's home with its trees and "seductive recesses" reminds him of the woodland world with its "green fields and forest shelter" (372).

But Porgy is no longer an inhabitant of that world, and as a result he finds fault with Mrs. Griffin. In the army, he had thought only "of the excellent management of the housekeeper," at which she is incomparable. Now, however, he is back on his estate, where he has resumed his old tastes and former refinements. Mrs. Griffin, who has little education, cannot read his books with him; she lacks sensible conversation to charm his idle hours, and she is finally "as difficult a case as Eveleigh" (400). Porgy eventually proposes to Widow Eveleigh, but his heart is not in the gesture, and she has the prudence to refuse him; he then tries to propose to Mrs. Griffin, but the Eveleigh overseer has preempted him. Thus Porgy is brought to a standstill from humorous yet distressing problems that recapitulate all he has become in the sweep of the Revolutionary War series. Life in the swamp has spoiled him for the one widow; life on the plantation ruins him for the other.[14]

14. In an unpublished paper on *Woodcraft* delivered in May, 1976, at a conference in Charleston entitled "William Gilmore Simms and the Revolution in South Carolina," Rayburn S. Moore discussed Porgy as a military man, examined the legal aspects of his

Porgy is finally saved from bankruptcy when M'Kewn is unmasked as a villain and put in jail, where he commits suicide. At the end of the novel, the captain and his followers have overcome the threats to Glen-Eberley: the sheriff has been soothed with apologies, and Crooks has been silenced "with good words and hush-money" (509). The broad and zestful comedy that from *The Partisan* onwards has been Simms's dominant method of portraying Porgy prevails: the captain resumes his customary role as a feudal baron, and Glen-Eberley becomes "a sort of centre for the parish civilization . . . which drew the gentry, all around, within the sphere of its genial, yet provocative influences" (508). As Lewis Simpson remarks, however, *Woodcraft* concludes with the puzzling spectacle of "an all-male community, white and black—a world without issue doomed to come to an end with its present generation, that of the American Revolution."[15] Nor would Simms's fascination with the fat captain and his exploits produce further literary progeny. Although he fondly meditated a final volume about his engaging epicure called the "Humour of Glen Eberley," he never completed it: there would, in short, be no more Captain Porgys.[16]

---

situation, and noted that *Woodcraft* is, among other things, a novel of manners. On the legal element in the novel, see also L. Lynn Hogue, "The Presentation of Post-Revolutionary Law in *Woodcraft:* Another Perspective on the 'Truth' of Simms's Fiction," *Mississippi Quarterly,* XXXI (Spring, 1978), [201]–10.

15. Lewis P. Simpson, *The Dispossessed Garden: Pastoral and History in Southern Literature* (Athens, Ga., 1975), 60.

16. In 1859 Simms wrote John Esten Cooke: "I am anxious to write the 'Humour of Glen Eberley', but I am not yet *matured* enough for it. It will require three years more of life in solitude & in the growth of my own soul, to make the work what I design. For Porgy, in that work, is to become a Legislator, and he will probably close his career in its denouement. I must prepare him & myself together to drape our sunsets with dignity" (*L,* IV, 168). Simms also refers to the projected work in *Woodcraft,* 509.

8
Simms at Midcentury: Charleston Social Stabbing

Alongside Porgy there developed in Simms's fiction of the 1850s a new strain, heralded by a character in *The Golden Christmas* who says antebellum Charleston society is marked by "[l]oose morals, vulgar fashions, bad manners, and gross, coarse, nameless people." Her comments point to Simms's growing concern with satiric portrayals of the fashionable city world, worked up by the methods of the novel and comedy of manners. In depicting this world, he combined his personal experience in Charleston with the knowledge of "social life" fiction he had gained by his reading and reviewing in the 1840s; and as a result he produced several noteworthy books in which polite "social stabbing," as he termed the charade, is his principal concern.[1]

His attacks in the 1850s upon fashionable folly had their origins, as he acknowledged, in the conflict between his ambitious nature and the "proud, wealthy & insulated" community into which he was born. He wrote Lawson that as a young man he had been overbearing, impatient, and highly sensitive, ever suspicious that the city would be hostile to his talent (*L*, I, 164). Compounding such problems was his choice of a career: like much of the antebellum South, Charleston tended to neglect belles-lettres and their devotees, an attitude for which Simms never forgave her. In the 1830s he had lamented to Lawson "the general dearth of letters prevailing among us" and observed in extravagant fashion, "I have said elsewhere & repeat again, that in Charleston, a literary man is obnoxious—he is decidedly a nuisance, & were it not for the outrageous indecency of the thing they would

1. [William Gilmore Simms], *The Golden Christmas: A Chronicle of St. John's, Berkeley* (Charleston, S.C., 1852), 26, hereafter cited by page number within the text. The novel had been issued in three semiweekly supplements to the *Southern Literary Gazette*, n.s., I, during 1852 (*L*, III, 160*n*39). "Social Stabbing" is the title of Chap. 2 of *Katharine Walton*.

legislate upon him as such" (*L*, I, 8, 5). As the antebellum period wore on and his own career faltered, his grievances against the city multiplied. Despite the fact that Charleston newspapers regularly reviewed and praised his books, he insisted that he and "that city . . . do not agree and have never agreed. I am one of those sons who never found favor in her eyes" (*L*, III, 299). And near the end of the 1850s, with several of his children dead and his literary production declining, he vented his despair in an impassioned tirade as he recalled his father's advice in the middle 1820s that he should settle in Mississippi.

> Thirty odd years have passed, and I can now mournfully say the old man was right. All that I have [done] has been poured to waste in Charleston, which has never smiled on any of my labors, which has steadily ignored my claims, which has disparaged me to the last, has been the last place to give me its adhesion, to which I owe no favor, having never received an office, or a compliment, or a dollar at her hands; and, with the exception of some dozen of her citizens, who have been kind to me, and some scores of her young men, who have honored me with a loving sympathy and something like reverence, which has always treated me rather as a public enemy, to be sneered at, than as a dutiful son doing her honor. *And I, too, know it as a place of tombs.* I have buried six dear children within its soil! Great God! what is the sort of slavery which brings me hither![2]

Simms's growing unhappiness with Charleston spilled over into his publications near midcentury, so that his private and his public statements frequently correspond. To Hammond he charged, for example, during 1848: "This community takes little interest in anything which requires thought. It is essentially feeble—approximating the Italian & Spanish nobility—satisfied to pass the time indolently if not pleasantly . . . full of assumption, conciet [*sic*] and ignorance, and, in majority of cases, scarcely capable of recieving [*sic*] the truth" (*L*, II, 434). In the same year, he issued a long satiric poem, *Charleston, and Her Satirists,* in which he mounts a concerted attack on

> The mourning lounge, where fashion sports her plume,
> The evening ride—at night, the crowded room;
> The call, where soft inanity, grown starr'd,
> Just stirs the knocker once, and leaves the card;
> The glittering rout, where, till the supper woos,
> The drowsy spirit slumbers with the blues;

2. Trent, *William Gilmore Simms,* 238–39, quoting from Simms's personal memoranda. The brackets in the passage are Trent's.

And that dull pageant which the Battery sees,
Its stream of butterflies as thick as bees,—
A long procession, buggy, coach and cart,
Where poor pretension still must play its part,
Pleased to be seen and seeking nought beside,
But just to say, "Behold we too can ride."

And in *Father Abbot,* a series of imaginary conversations that he published in the Charleston *Mercury* during 1849 and collected in book form the same year, he laments the loss of vitality in Charleston, insisting that life there has become "a mere drowse in the lap of vanity" (*L,* II, 565*n*206).[3]

But there was another side to Simms's relationship with Charleston, one that has been obscured by decades of scholarly commentary on his acrimonious feelings about his birthplace. For even as he voiced his bitterness toward the city, he also loved and admired it, as both his own remarks and those of his friends reveal. In the essay "Charleston, the Palmetto City" that he published in *Harper's New Monthly Magazine* during 1857, he commends Charleston's proud past, her role in national history, "the refinements of her society," and "the polish of her people." When the ordinance of secession was passed in Charleston, he wrote a friend in Congress whom he was schooling in secessionism: "Do not be rash, but, do not let this old city forget her *prestige.* Charleston is worth all New England" (*L,* IV, 315). And after the war, when South Carolina lay in ruins and his own career was shattered, a northern visitor in the South heard him proclaim in ringing phrases: "Charleston, sir . . . was the finest city in the world; not a large city, but the finest. South Carolina, sir, was the flower of modern civilization. Our people were the most hospitable, the most accomplished, having the highest degree of culture and the highest sense of honor, of any people, I will not say of America, sir, but of any country on the globe."[4]

Simms's mixed and complicated attitude toward Charleston lies behind his portraits of city life in his fiction of the 1850s, lending spice

3. [William Gilmore Simms], *Charleston, and Her Satirists; A Scribblement* (Charleston, S.C., 1848), [5], lines 9–20, and W[illiam] Gilmore Simms, *Father Abbot, or, The Home Tourist; A Medley* (Charleston, S.C., 1849), 145.

4. William Gilmore Simms, "Charleston, the Palmetto City," *Harper's New Monthly Magazine,* XV (June, 1857), 1; John Townsend Trowbridge, *My Own Story with Recollections of Noted Persons* (Boston, 1903), 310.

and sauciness to his depictions. In the novels in which the city figures as a major setting—*The Golden Christmas, Katharine Walton,* and *The Cassique of Kiawah*—he uses the conventions of romance and romantic comedy to work out his structural patterns. Within these patterns, he increasingly employs the methods of the novel of manners, a move that is natural enough since, historically, the low country or tidewater society he grew up in has been a particularly congenial setting for this mode. Almost alone among antebellum societies, it offered the spectacle of a genuine aristocracy whose rigid social codes and civilized diversions would nourish generations of southern novelists, from Simms and his friend John Pendleton Kennedy to Ellen Glasgow and James Branch Cabell. With its emphasis on correct and elegant social behavior, this relatively stable, class-ridden culture was, in Hugh Holman's apt phrases, "perhaps as fruitful an area for the novel of manners as America has ever produced."[5]

Among Simms's first extended ventures in the manners vein is *The Golden Christmas,* a graceful short novel that affords a useful preview of how he accommodates "social life" fiction to his usual literary framework. His portraits of upper-class behavior in the novel relate it to the comedy of manners, whereas its love narratives and the values expressed through its woods and plantation episodes relate it to his long romances. For the love story he adopts the classic structure found from New Comedy onwards, in which a young man courting a young woman is hindered by parents or other relatives from marrying her but who finally marries her anyway after an unexpected twist in the plot. In such comedy, with its tendency toward paired or doubled characters, both the heroine and hero may have an oppressive or a stubborn parent; and there may also be a second set of lovers whose situation parallels that in the main narrative line. The new society formed when the lovers finally get together is typically symbolized by a party or some other kind of celebration.[6]

That romance elements and satiric studies of manners are so closely linked in *The Golden Christmas* is in large measure due to Simms's

5. Holman, *Three Modes,* 13. Cooper's move toward the novel of manners with *Satanstoe* (1845) may have encouraged Simms's comparable move in his midcentury fiction, and Kennedy's revised edition of *Swallow Barn* (1851), the subject of an article in the *Southern Quarterly Review* while Simms was editor—in XXI [n.s., V] (January, 1852), 71–86—probably influenced Simms's graceful pictures of plantation culture in *The Golden Christmas.*

6. Frye, *Anatomy of Criticism,* 163, 181.

deft management of comic structure, from the lovers and their relatives to the final pageant. His narrative, which abounds in paired figures, centers on two young men who court young women and on overbearing relatives who repeatedly try to block the matches. Dick Cooper, the narrator, loves Beatrice Mazyck, and his friend Ned Bulmer loves Paula Bonneau. But Ned's marriage is opposed by Paula's grandmother, a snooty old Frenchwoman who hates the English, and by Ned's father, an ardent Anglophile who hates the French and schemes for Ned to marry Dick's girl, Beatrice. Like other such characters in comedy, Madame Agnes-Therese Girardin and Major Bulmer are dominated by humors, or ruling passions—Madame by pride in her social standing, the Major by his fondness for old English customs that, he says, are "sacred as the practice of my ancestors" (35).[7] With considerable flourish, Simms dramatizes the follies of these old aristocrats against the city and plantation backgrounds that suggest the derivation of his story from both social comedy and romance.

The first part of *The Golden Christmas* takes place in Charleston, where fashionable behavior is displayed in the kind of sophisticated urban milieu that had been a common setting in British manners comedy and fiction from Congreve and Sheridan to Bulwer-Lytton and Thackeray. In this lighthearted novelette Simms is not disposed to criticize his native city harshly; thus his satire on upper-class conduct is mild rather than severe. Likable, sensible Dick Cooper, whose family "represents an English cross upon a Huguenot stock," and who therefore occupies a neutral position between the two warring factions, persistently recommends moderation and good sense (17). In the service of this aim, he accompanies Madame Girardin on a shopping tour of King Street, thronged with elegant ladies and crowded with carriages, where he narrowly observes her behavior. She functions, he says slyly, as "a sort of social barometer, exactly telling by her manner, what sort of blood flowed in the veins of each to whom she bowed or spoke. To some few she unbent readily, with a spontaneous and unreserved and placid sweetness"; but to others, "her look was vinegar and vitriolic acid" (20). Thus she bows to a sniggering, doddering old gentleman who Dick says had "wasted his means like a fool" because *she* says his family is "in the highest circles" (23, 22). Yet she snubs as

7. The Major's fondness for English customs recalls that of Simms's father-in-law, Nash Roach, as described in [Oliphant, Odell, and Eaves], "The Family Circle," in *L*, I, cxlviii–cxlix.

a parvenu one of Dick's particular friends, a "fine-looking, cheery lady" whose grandfather had the misfortune to sell shoes, by sneering "A vulgar creature! . . . what a coarse voice,—what a fat vulgar face she has" (21). She spurns Dick's suggestion, which reflects Simms's view, that families with wealth and talent will eventually develop aristocratic graces; and she likewise spurns Major Bulmer's claims to gentility by insisting, "[Y]ou can never make a gentleman of an Englishman" (78). (The Major, for his part, snorts, "None of your French kickshows for me" [34].) With their emphasis upon the delusions and pretensions of aristocrats within an intricate social framework, the Charleston episodes in *The Golden Christmas* relate Simms's work to the novel of manners, to which he was even then devoting a good deal of attention in his midcentury essays and reviews. And they also reveal his desire to rebuke, if ever so gently, the shallow pride and ingrained prejudices of his native city.

Simms's ridicule of patrician manners and prejudices continues in the rural section of the story, though here it shares the stage with the plantation-pastoral background, the intertwined love narratives, and the defense of the southern agricultural system that is part of his romance-imbued procedure. To show this system at its finest, he portrays all the trappings of a golden Christmas, South Carolina style—stately visits, family feasts, a hunt for a magnificent buck, a hunt to furnish the boar's head for Christmas dinner, and a visit of "Father Chrystmasse" to the slaves.[8] Since Madame and the Major have ties to the plantation, as Simms sees it their values are essentially sound, though their social snobbery obviously requires rebuke. Therefore, through a series of clever twists in comic structure, he makes these two old people see the folly of their prejudices, reconciles them to each other, and also reconciles them to the lovers. Hence Ned and Paula, Dick and Beatrice, finally come together against the background of a lavish Christmas pageant, which supports the truism that in comedy the new society formed by the lovers is generally announced by a festive rite.[9] "The golden period had come round again as so long promised," Dick sighs happily, and the double climax of love story and plantation pleasures serves to reinforce Simms's propaganda for the

8. Simms describes the southern tradition of Father Christmas to a northern friend in *L*, III, 486.

9. In light of the book's strong ties to comedy, it is interesting that a former manager of the Charleston Theatre wanted to have *The Golden Christmas* dramatized; see *L*, III, 161.

planting system and the southern aristocracy in a decade when both were under increasingly sharp attack (146). With its intermeshed plots, its happy ending, its patrician-pastoral values, and its merging of realistic and satiric episodes with romance patterns, *The Golden Christmas* illuminates the methods Simms uses during the decade in his full-length studies of manners, *Katharine Walton* and *The Cassique of Kiawah.*

In these volumes Simms continues to employ the traditions of his major genre for his structural features while using them to shape and control his social comedy, which therefore tends to function in the service of romance rhetorical demands. Such a procedure lets him keep the format he had already established for his long fiction while giving it a different emphasis that reflects his growing awareness of the power of the novel of manners in the marketplace. He says as much in the introduction to the Redfield edition of *Katharine Walton*—where, stressing his preoccupation with new concerns, he remarks that "a large proportion of the work, and much of its interest, will be found to consist in the delineation of the social world of Charleston, during the Revolutionary period. . . . The descriptions of life, manners, customs, movements, the social aspects in general, have all been drawn from sources as unquestionable as abundant. The social reunions, in many instances, as described in the story, were real occurrences. The anecdotes, the very repartees, though never before in print, are gathered from tradition and authority" (3–4).

A belated sequel to *The Partisan, Katharine Walton* is set in and around the British-occupied Charleston of 1780 and 1781, controlled by Francis, Lord Rawdon and his subordinate Nesbitt (or Nesbit) Balfour, who were headquartered in one of the most elegant mansions of the city. Perhaps more than in his earlier volumes, the circumstances of war-torn South Carolina aided Simms in blending social comedy and romance. Earlier in the war, the upcountry had been the seat of Loyalist strength; but after Charleston's fall, enemy power had shifted to the coastal region. The Loyalists, who controlled government, churches, and clubs, continued the city's tradition of glittering amusements—a fact that made it ripe for treatment in the novel of manners vein.[10] For the first time in the Revolutionary War series, accordingly, Simms makes social hostilities rather than military maneuvers the

10. George Smith McCowen, Jr., *The British Occupation of Charleston, 1780–82* (Columbia, S.C., 1972), 116.

backbone of a book. He depicts, as in the episodes involving Porgy, some skirmishes between the British and Marion's men outside the city; but his real interest lies in the "social stabbing" between Loyalists and partisans within it. To portray these hostilities, he blends his customary plantation and forest setting with the kind of urban social milieu that he uses in *The Golden Christmas,* moving his leading figures as necessary between city and estate.

In the opening pages of the book, Simms anchors his narrative in the pastoral world, which he uses to establish the central values of the book and provide a standard by which the trivialities of Loyalist social life may be judged. His major characters, familiar from *The Partisan,* are Robert Singleton, his fiancée Katharine Walton, and Katharine's father. As in *The Partisan,* the Walton plantation the Oaks functions as a gracious and lovely background for the main story while also indicating the fierce patriotism of Colonel Walton, who fires the rice stacks rather than let the British batten on them. It is also at the Oaks that Simms shows Katharine and Singleton outwitting Balfour, even as their royalist friends and romance counterparts in the city, John Proctor and Ella Monckton, will eventually outwit Balfour's mean assistant, Major Vaughn.

In the sections of the book set in the city, the attitude of characters toward manners—broadly defined by the context of the novel as "fashionable social behavior"—points to Simms's dialectic base. His Loyalists court fashion, his patriots reject it; and thus in Charleston the action of *Katharine Walton* develops on two different planes, which reflect different literary traditions that are handled for the most part in different ways. The one, centering on royalists and using the tradition of the novel of manners, is shown humorously and satirically; the other, centering on the partisans and using the tradition of the romance, is idealized in accordance with the conventions of Simms's leading literary genre.

Throughout the city sequences, Simms contrasts Loyalist and partisan values by an extended contrast of social groups established through commentary and dramatized through portraits of rival widows and rival fashionable belles. Putting characters from the novel of manners to romance uses, he molds rich, witty Mrs. Rivington, "the leader of *ton*" in Loyalist Charleston, as the social counterpart and moral opposite of rich, witty Mrs. Brewton, a central figure in the partisan movement (211). Both are socially prominent widows who espouse their late husbands' politics; both are relatively young, attractive, and susceptible of courtship in the haut monde; and, most pertinently for Simms's social comedy, both delight in repartee. Their important differences lie in the ends to which their energies are addressed. Mrs. Rivington, a sunshine Tory, uses politics chiefly to promote fashion: at her glittering levees, she snubs partisans, courts Loyalists, dictates conduct, and punctures pretentiousness. Thus she saucily rejects the portly majors of foot who flatter her, and in a nicely pointed sequence she outwits a snob who denounces the mixture of social classes in her salon.

> "La, you there?" she said to Penfield, who wrote gent. after his name, and had once been a lawyer in hope to be attorney-general of the province. He had turned up his aristocratic nose at some of the *oi poloi* of the saloon [*sic*].
>
> "La, you there, counsellor, and be merciful to yourself if not to me. Were we to admit the quality only, we should die of atrophy, or commit suicide, or some other less-dignified sin. . . . Shall I make the Smiths known to you? They are really very clever people—good company enough for the summer."
>
> "I thank you. But how is the name spelled? With an *i* or *y*?"
>
> "What difference does that make?" inquired Mrs. Rivington.
>
> "All the difference in the world, madam. The Smythes and not the Sm*i*ths are to be known in society. It is the former only which you will find among the noble families of England. Indeed, the Smiths have all snub noses, which, as my venerable grandmother always assured me, is a sign of low birth and doubtful origin. Excuse me; but as they are crossing here, I'd rather find my way to the opposite end of the room. These steel mirrors of yours exhibit the outline admirably. They are just at the proper hang. Ah, my dear Mrs. Rivington, could we only choose properly our guests!" (216–17)

From Mrs. Jeremiah Smith, the mother of the clan, Mrs. Rivington learns, however, that Penfield's supposedly aristocratic grandfather was actually a silversmith whose mark is on all of the Smiths' plate. Encouraging fat Mrs. Smith to set Penfield "right in his genealogy," the mischievous widow watches the Smiths, "in a drove," follow "in the wake of the mother as she waddled across the room, in full chase of Penfield, the gentleman" (217–18).

Yet Mrs. Rivington, for all her sprightliness, is chiefly concerned with the establishment of social tyranny through her "lively and thoughtless mornings" (227). "[W]itty if not wise," Simms remarks, she cuts "most others with little hesitation," but her shafts are aimed at social rather than political offenses (211). By contrast, her partisan counterpart Mrs. Brewton uses manners to promote patriot politics, thus aiding her country's cause in both its military and its social dimensions. A "profound policy," Simms says slyly, prompts her wish to acquire "the reputation of a mere lover of pleasure," and fashionable Loyalist assemblies conveniently conceal her true purposes (278). At social gatherings in Charleston, she collects enemy secrets for Americans in the countryside, routs bold British suitors, and scolds royalist upstarts. When Balfour foolishly dares, for instance, to criticize her references to the classics, she utters a killing rejoinder: "My metaphor lacks nothing. My allusion was to the case of the Roman augur, Accius Nævius. Your Livy will tell you all the rest" (240). And she snaps to a wild enemy officer, "Let me tell you that there is no extraordinary renown in being considered the madman, *par excellence,* of a very silly garrison of foot and horse" (283). Mrs. Rivington, in short, expands Simms's emphasis on Loyalist frivolity, while Mrs. Brewton enhances his portrait of partisan merit. The latter succeeds so well in bringing her charms to the "succour of patriotism" that Balfour finally expels her from the city.[11]

Furnishing even better evidence of how the conventions of Simms's major genre shape his procedures in the Charleston sequences is his pointed contrast of the heroine Katharine Walton with the villainess Moll Harvey, romance characters whom he puts to the uses of social comedy. Chaste, serious Katharine, "an heiress . . . a beauty, and consequently a *belle,*" is "little disposed to endure" the attentions of her British suitors (190, 191). But her Loyalist counterpart Moll, who cares only for the soiree and the fashionable lover, was reputedly the mistress of the English prince William, and later of Balfour before he met Katharine. As a romance moral opposite should, Moll hates Katharine, whom she calls (with some justice) an "icicle" (392). But she hates Balfour more; and therefore, near the end of the novel, she steps in to save Katharine from the forced marriage to him that he demands as the price of her father's life. Loyalist socialites love to compare the belles, and British verse maker Harry Barry writes a poem

11. Simms uses the quoted phrase in his essay-review "Ellet's Women of the Revolution," 327, where he is describing a generic partisan woman who resembles Mrs. Brewton.

about them. Its trim couplets keep, however facetiously, Simms's images of Moll as earthly beauty and Katharine as heavenly ideal before us.[12]

At the center of *Katharine Walton* (Chapter 26) is an episode, faintly allegorical, that summarizes the main elements of Simms's procedure in the novel. Here he unfolds a fable of patriot fortunes and enemy pretensions as old Tom Singleton, an eccentric partisan humorist who sees the links between social and military folly, parades his collection of beasts before a bemused Proctor. A "lesson against pomp and vanity," Singleton's fine menagerie is a replica, in miniature, of occupied Charleston as well as a pageant that dramatizes its plight. With its strutting, swaggering monkey garbed as a British general officer called, sotto voce, "Colonel Balfour," its venomous but fangless snakes suggesting "envy" and "malice," its cats, like "fashionable married people" quarreling "even when in clover," and its "spiritless eagles"—caged, like American patriots, but soon to be free—it is a comic charade grounded in the serious grievances that Singleton and his countrymen endure (255). But it is also a construction that stresses Simms's manners sequences and romance dialectic while showing, through well-wrought comedy, how they come together.[13]

After 1855, Simms's personal circumstances took a sharp downward turn, and the tenor of his writing, in both correspondence and fiction, changed accordingly. The decade that had opened happily for him with the publication of some of his best work closed in tragedy, with the failure of a highly publicized lecture tour, family deaths, and plantation losses. The first of these things was also the least predictable, for Simms, with his Celtic fluency and his southern flair for story telling, had long been a popular speaker in the South. During the difficult 1840s, he had supplemented his income by lecturing in the region.

12. When bounteous Fate decreed our Harvey's birth,
We felt that heaven might yet be found on earth;
But when the Walton to our eyes was given,
We knew that man might yet be raised to heaven.
Indulgent Fates, one blessing more bestow—
Give me with Harvey long to dwell below;
And when, and last, ye summon me above,
Then let the Walton be my heavenly love!
(*KW*, 224)

13. Old Tom Singleton is a fictionalized portrait of Simms's great-grandfather, Thomas Singleton, who actually kept a menagerie like the one described in the novel.

Still in need of money, in the middle fifties he asked Duyckinck to arrange a speaking tour for him to several northern cities, and in November, 1856, he formally accepted an invitation issued by a committee composed of Duyckinck, William Cullen Bryant, George Bancroft, and others to lecture in New York State and New England. With "Marion, the Carolina Partisan," "The Apalachians [*sic*]," and "South Carolina in the Revolution" as his topics, he set out enthusiastically for the North.

But public relations between the sections had declined considerably between the time Simms proposed the tour and the time he began it, in part because of a celebrated incident in Congress in which Preston Brooks of South Carolina had caned Charles Sumner for cruel verbal attacks during his "Crime against Kansas" speech on Brooks's uncle, Senator Andrew Pickens Butler.[14] Northern animosity toward the South was running high, and Simms's lectures, particularly "South Carolina in the Revolution," increased it. He so offended crowds by derogatory allusions to Sumner and strident praise of South Carolina that the more extreme northern papers attacked his presentation as "an ill-digested, bitter and . . . offensive defence of South Carolina politicians of the Brooks school" (*L*, III, 457*n*122). Surprised and hurt, he canceled the rest of the tour, gave the money he had earned to public charities, and returned to Woodlands.[15] His bitterness about the experience may have left its mark on his late fiction, particularly on some highly sardonic portions of his final novel about the low country, *The Cassique of Kiawah*. At the very least, it was a factor in his growing despair during the final years of the decade.

The disappointments of the lecture tour were soon to be eclipsed, however, by more severe afflictions. In early 1858 his father-in-law Nash Roach died after a long illness, and upon Simms devolved the

14. David Donald, *Charles Sumner and the Coming of the Civil War* (New York, 1960), [278]–311.

15. "South Carolina in the Revolution" is reprinted as an appendix to *L*, III, 521–49. Simms based much of the speech on his two long essay-reviews of memoirs and histories of the war, "South Carolina in the Revolution" and "The Siege of Charleston in the American Revolution," *Southern Quarterly Review*, XIV (July, October, 1848), 37–77, [261]–337, respectively. He expanded these essays for his volume *South-Carolina in the Revolutionary War* (Charleston, S.C., 1853). His northern lecture tour has been studied by John Hope Franklin, *A Southern Odyssey: Travelers in the Antebellum North* (Baton Rouge, 1976), 234–43, and Miriam J. Shillingsburg, "The Southron as American: William Gilmore Simms," in Joel Myerson (ed.), *Studies in the American Renaissance 1980* (Boston, 1980), 409–23.

task of managing Woodlands—which, as he had already told Lawson, for twenty years had barely paid its expenses (*L,* III, 453). With his zeal, he was able to revive the estate if not make it prosperous; the last years of the decade found him "clearing lands, making compost, cutting ditches, making fences, building houses, giving physic, killing hogs, rearing cabbages, speculating on fertilizers, trying experiments in lime, salt, guano, &c!" (*L,* IV, 112). But such work was not fundamentally congenial to a person of his temperament, and as he frequently complained, it took him away from his desk.

Among the saddest events for Simms in these years were the frequent deaths in his family—not only that of Roach, who had lived a reasonably long life, but also those of his own offspring. By 1851, he and Chevillette had lost four of eight children; by 1856, they had only six of eleven living; and by 1859, he had buried seven of his descendants (*L,* IV, 113). The death of each child grieved him deeply, but all his previous losses paled before the dreadful ones of 1858. In that year, during a period of particularly burdensome and uncongenial plantation labors, he endured the worst blow, save one, that fate would ever deal him—the deaths of two favorite little sons from yellow fever on the same day. More than a century later, the pain he felt still throbs through his letters, like the pathetic one to Hammond beginning: "Oh! dear Hammond, weep for me! I am crushed to earth. I have buried in one grave, within twelve hours of each other, my two brave beautiful boys, Sydney, & your little namesake, Beverley Hammond, two as noble little fellows as ever lived. . . . It is a terrible stroke of fate, leaving us almost desolate. I feel heart broken, hope crushed, and altogether wretched" (*L,* IV, 93).

It was during this period of increasing responsibility and personal misfortune that Simms composed *The Cassique of Kiawah,* his last piece of long fiction set in the low country and his most unsparing indictment in fiction of the Charleston social scene. Like other of his late works, it had been slow to mature: he had apparently started it in the middle 1820s and returned to it briefly in the 1840s; but he did not tackle it in earnest until those disastrous days of 1858—when, mourning for his two small sons, he wrote Lawson's daughter Mary: "I have a book nearly finished now, & which I hope to finish soon, which has been lingering & languishing in my hands for more than a year. My griefs & miseries of the last year made me almost oblivious of what I have written, & in resuming my task I had to summon fancy against her will, & sometimes felt the necessity of writing sportively, with a head aching, a heart full almost to bursting, & eyes dropping great tears upon the paper even as I wrote" (*L*, IV, 128). Despite such sorrows, he finished the novel in the spring of 1859, and Redfield seems to have issued it during May of that year. Although it was widely and favorably reviewed, it was not republished during his lifetime or in the editions of his works reprinted from the Redfield plates—and therefore, although it is probably his best book, it has remained obscure.[16]

The Cassique of Kiawah has the main elements of Simms's other long fiction set in the South Carolina coastal region; it constitutes, in fact, a kind of finale to his novels about the area. It has Indians, semihumorous woodsmen, and lively passages of dialect speech; it has also the elements of manners comedy as he had refined them by this point in his career—although here, to a greater extent than in his earlier books, he gives that comedy a satiric slant. For the framing action of the novel, he employs the clash, well documented in seventeenth-century history, between England and Spain over their New World possessions. Earlier in the era, Charles II of England had commissioned privateers like Simms's hero Harry Berkeley to prey on Spanish ships. The treaty of Madrid, however, had brought peace and had guaranteed to England the safety of her American holdings; royal decree therefore branded privateers as pirates and outlaws. Simms's use of piracy as a subject allows him to exploit the charm and danger of a picturesque occupation, to hint at crime, and yet to stress that his hero is at bottom far more virtuous than the government that condemns him.

Simms's leading characters in the novel embody features of his framing action—piracy, English-Spanish relationships, the proprietary government of the colony, and its class configurations. They reflect also his point, made in chapter after chapter of the novel, that his potentially ideal romance world has been marred by meddling social-

16. On the composition of the novel and its publishing history, see *L*, I, 285*n*111; II, 81*n*245; IV, 128, 152*n*137, 269, 575*n*139. Comments in Simms's letters indicate that the novel was published by someone other than Redfield. There were apparently only two printings of *The Cassique of Kiawah:* one in 1859 under the Redfield imprint and one in 1884 by Dodd, Mead, which had evidently bought the Redfield plates. See A. I. Appleton *et al.*, (comps.), *The American Catalogue, 1884–1890* (New York, 1941), 472. Keen Butterworth in a letter to me of July 1, 1977, suggests that Dodd, Mead's purchase of the plates explains why the novel was not included in editions reprinted from the Redfield plates.

ites—a development that the involutions of the love story dramatize. There Simms tells the connected tales of two ill-matched pairs, the conventional dark and blonde couples of popular romance: the privateer Harry Berkeley, now called Harry Calvert; his wife, the black-haired Spanish-Moorish beauty Zulieme; his older brother Edward, the philanthropic cassique of Kiawah; and Edward's fair-haired, melancholy wife Olive, who was once engaged to Harry. All four of these figures spring directly from the realm of romance; but their fortunes have been harmed by a creature from the realm of social satire—Olive's caste-conscious, money-hungry mother, Mrs. Masterton, who has forced her daughter to wed Edward, whereupon Harry, in despair, weds Zulieme. Making this bad situation worse are the antics of figures from the Charleston social sphere who try to spoil romance fortunes further—notably Mrs. Perkins Anderson, a nouveau-riche lady who wants to seduce Harry and, when he will not have her, persuades her friend the fop Keppel Craven to try to seduce Zulieme, who will not have him.

This complicated story develops against two sharply contrasted backgrounds, the city and the forest or plantation, which of course reflect the domains of social comedy and romance respectively. The shifts Simms makes in portraying these domains suggest how much more cynical his view of human life had become since the completion of his Revolutionary War saga and particularly since *Katharine Walton*. In that novel, the values of romance dominate the city sequences, and patriot standards finally prevail in Charleston while the trivialities of Loyalists are repeatedly criticized. In *The Cassique of Kiawah*, however, which has a different tenor and a different kind of dialectic, the division between the two settings is plainer and literary values are polarized accordingly. The city is consistently represented as materialistic, showy, and corrupt, whereas the plantation, even more than in Simms's earlier fiction, forms—initially, at any rate—an innocent retreat, a place remote from city concerns where Edward dreams of "sweet content in the primitive forest."[17] It is a dream that will be ruined, as the unfolding of the narrative reveals. In the novel Simms depicts a world in which his romance lovers are sorely tried and in

17. William Gilmore Simms, *The Cassique of Kiawah: A Colonial Romance* (New York, 1859), 236. All further references to this novel are to this edition, cited by page number within the text (as *C* where necessary for clarity).

which the plantation ceases to function as a sheltering matrix, becoming finally the home of death and grief.

Despite his elaborate presentation of a setting associated with romance, to a greater extent than in his earlier books Simms allows his social comedy to dictate his handling of fictional elements. Perhaps reflecting the bitterness toward Charleston that he had accumulated during a lifetime of real or imagined slights, it is class conflict rather than international rivalry at the historical level that determines his dialectic base. Or, translated into literary terms, it is the opposition of the social and the romance worlds, connected through narrative construction but contrasted in values, that provides the major source of conflict in the novel. Throughout the novel, Simms stresses that the Carolina colony from its beginning harbored two kinds of people—the landgraves, cassiques, and barons created by the Fundamental Constitutions, who are associated with the emerging plantation system; and the "fashionables" or "wealthy parvenues" of the town, who have "no *entrée,*" he says, "at the baronial seats" (134, 137). Predictably enough, given the heritage of his fiction, he depicts the aristocrats according to the idealizing methods of romance. He characterizes their sophisticated rivals, however, by the methods of satiric social realism as he had refined it by this point in his career.

A chief tool of that realism is Simms's narrative persona, which has no exact counterpart in his earlier novels, though certain passages of commentary in *Eutaw* look forward to it. In *The Cassique of Kiawah,* Simms—a mature author still at odds with the city of his birth—strikes the pose of a slightly jaded observer of the values and pursuits of Charleston (which he often slyly calls "Oyster Point") since its founding in the seventeenth century. For this pose he draws on Thackeray, whom he had met in Charleston shortly before he completed the novel and whose writing he had regularly reviewed.[18] Thackeray in some of this writing, most notably perhaps in *Vanity Fair,* had created a narrator who makes cutting comments from a satirist's perspective on the fashionable follies of the day—mingling in the social circles he portrays, gossiping about their members, and using fanciful descrip-

18. For Simms's relationship with Thackeray, see James Grant Wilson, *Thackeray in the United States, 1852–3, 1855–6* (New York, 1904), I, 274, who says Simms was "frequently to be seen at his brother novelist's lectures, and was included among those with whom Thackeray became acquainted, and often met in Charleston" when he lectured there in the 1850s.

tive names that recall the names in Restoration comedies. He says, for example: "I remember one night being in the Fair myself, at an evening party. I observed old Miss Toady there also present, single out for her special attentions and flattery little Mrs. Briefless, the barrister's wife. . . . What, I asked in my own mind, can cause this obsequiousness on the part of Miss Toady?" He soon learns that Mrs. Briefless' father is about to become a baronet: "And Toady asked Briefless and his wife to dinner the very next week."[19]

Especially when Simms is describing the vanities of socialite Charleston, his method is close to Thackeray's, and like Thackeray he shows considerable distaste for the society he is portraying. Heightening his distaste are his feelings about the similar society of his day, which he felt had snubbed him and his literary productions. Hence he criticizes the pretensions of colonial Charleston—and, by extension, those of contemporary Charleston—through a spokesman who mingles in city circles past and present, uses fanciful descriptive names, and makes caustic comments on fashionable folly. He says, for instance:

> And so, already, Charleston (then Charles town) had its castes and classes, its cliques and aristocracies; in which, people, insisting upon their rights of rank, grew rank in doing so. . . . There were people who were "in society" then as now; who turned up their noses so high, that their eyes failed to recognise the existence of their nearest neighbors. And there were very excellent people, who, in spite of virtues and talents, were dismissed from all regard, even the human, for the simple but sufficient reason that they were *not* "in society." . . .
>
> And so, Charleston had its Lady Loftyhead and Lady Highheels, Lady Flirtabout and Lady Fluster, and no small number of a class besides, whom these good ladies universally voted to be no ladies at all. (108–109)

Mixing with his characters and addressing them in Thackeray's manner, Simms's narrator observes: "You are to-day, Mrs. Frill, but a development of Mrs. Perkins Anderson. The tail is longer and broader, and there is something more of fullness about the pin-feathers; but you are birds of the same feather. I do not see that Mrs. Loftyhead, of 1684, differs in much from Mrs. Furbelow, whom I met last week nightly in all the four fashionable sets of the present city" (429).

19. William Makepeace Thackeray, *Vanity Fair: A Novel without a Hero* (London, 1848), 134.

Largely through such passages of satiric commentary, Simms shows how deeply human corruption has penetrated his romance world. England and Spain are officially at peace, yet privately at war; King Charles encourages piracy and then for political reasons bans it; the greedy governor of the colony, Robert Quarry, is sworn to hang Harry Calvert but secretly cherishes him and his Spanish gold; and wealthy city socialites like "Ladies Loftyhead, Highheels, Flirtabout, and Fluster" are "all satisfied to enjoy the gallantries of the rover without asking to see too closely the color of his hands" (109). Meanwhile, Mrs. Perkins Anderson, the most lubricious of these socialites, is stalking Harry. This lady, rich, pretty, and calculating, epitomizes the vices Simms sees in colonial Charleston. The essence of a false aristocrat, the quintessence of a sophisticated hypocrite, she is able, he says, "to disguise a passion of very doubtful quality so dextrously, that it passes current as a virtue among half of the fashionable circle in which she moves and has her being" (316).

Through heavily ironic praise Simms condemns Mrs. Anderson's procedures: it is "beautiful to see . . . the meekness" with which she bears the yearly ten months' absence of the husband she despises; "admirable to see how happily" she contrives "to console herself under her privation" by chasing Harry (137–38). When she loses him, in revenge she tries to ruin Zulieme by pushing her into the arms of Keppel Craven. That gentleman, a mixture of the Restoration stage fop and the seventeenth-century English cavalier, boasts ruffled smallclothes, an elegant lisp, and long, perfumed hair. Zulieme, who persists in calling him a "funny little fellow," unequivocally rejects him; and so both Mrs. Anderson's bedtime stratagems come to naught (435). In an action that reveals the victory of ideals in a world beset by lust and greed, Simms's leading romance figures therefore triumph over his leading manners socialites.

The other part of Simms's blended satire-and-romance scenario, his characterization and the structure of his love plot, moves in the direction of dark romance and, through its techniques, toward a sober, realistic utterance. To appreciate how these elements operate, it will help to probe more narrowly his character types and the outlines of his main narrative against the background of some well-established conventions in the fiction of his time, including his own earlier work. Except perhaps for Leonard Voltmeier in his last novel, the hero of *The Cassique of Kiawah,* dark-haired Harry Calvert, is the major example in his fiction of what may be called, in a paraphrase of Leslie Fiedler on Scott's Di Vernon, the "good-bad" guy—a compound of the conventional "straight," pure-hearted hero of romance and the equally conventional dark, wild, temperamental, or violent figure who in certain of his phases earns the appellation "Byronic" or "Satanic."[20] An essentially noble person, Harry—made miserable by the loss of Olive—sulks, broods, rages at the ship's crew, and nearly strikes Zulieme when she interrupts his work. His saucy Spanish bride is also a compound, though of a different sort: a combination of the Victorian child-wife figure and the romance dark lady whose essential chastity is never seriously in question, she torments and defies Harry, flirts with his lieutenant, dances with the ship's crew, and deftly eludes Keppel Craven.[21] She also ministers to Olive, who is dying from grief and madness brought on by her loss of Harry and the machinations of her mother.

Simms's treatment of these characters, it can hardly be said too plainly, shows some major innovations in the romance formulas of his time. These are especially significant in light of the fact that, for the most part—in Scott, in Cooper, in Hawthorne, and in Melville—it is the dark or unconventional figures who are vanquished and the pure or straight ones who triumph and live to enjoy the typical happy or providential ending. In *The Cassique of Kiawah,* however, it is the mismatched Harry and Zulieme who finally find a muted happiness that is the closest thing to a providential movement in the narrative, while it is the likable, unlucky Edward and Olive who, at least in terms of the marriage story, fail.

Strange as it may seem, this reworking of romance formulas is also Simms's major gesture toward realism in the novel, the glitter of his social sequences notwithstanding. For through the love plots, with their romance trappings, he acknowledges the force of the ruinous social world that has defeated Edward and Olive and has done its best to defeat Harry and Zulieme. He acknowledges, in other words, that an

20. Leslie A. Fiedler, *Love and Death in the American Novel* (Rev. ed.; New York, 1966), 178.

21. Zulieme is a type of the dark yet innocent heroine whose foreign blood, as Simms stresses, explains and excuses her unconventional behavior. On this type, see Ralph P. Boas, "The Romantic Lady," in George Boas (ed.), *Romanticism in America* (1940; rpr. New York, 1961), 67. On Zulieme, see also Thomas L. McHaney, "William Gilmore Simms," in Matthew J. Bruccoli (ed.), *The Chief Glory of Every People: Essays on Classic American Writers* (Carbondale, Ill., 1973), 184–85.

ideal once lost may never be recovered and that human beings, in this case his four lovers, must cope or try to cope with the conditions that result from its loss. Mrs. Anderson, Mrs. Masterton, Keppel Craven, and the other creatures from the tradition of social satire who loom so large in this late work are cleverly drawn representatives of a snobbish, slanderous society that has made considerable inroads into Simms's standard romance milieu. It is a relief to note, then, that at the end of the novel, Harry and Zulieme—reconciled, expecting a child, and reasonably happy—sail away from the vain city of Charleston to work out their destiny in an orthodox romance realm, the free-flowing, halcyon sea.

Since *The Cassique of Kiawah* is Simms's last long novel set in the low country, it may be well to pause here and review the development of his treatment of that region in fiction. During more than thirty years, increasingly embittered by harsh and even harrowing experiences, he moved steadily away from the happy and confident world of the early Revolutionary War Romances to the landscape of shattered dreams that is the dominant landscape of *The Cassique of Kiawah*. He began his fictional survey of the South Carolina low country with novels in the orthodox romance mold; he concluded it with an admission, which is his personal concession to realism, that "lusts, and vanities, and human passions" have their place in his literary scheme (*C*, 94). Reflecting his youthful convictions, the world of his first Revolutionary War novels, if not wholly happy, yet promises to become so: the Revolution remained for him, as for many of his fellow southerners, a golden era; and his beliefs are reflected in the shape of his series about the war, with its movement from despair to hope and its implicit prediction that the South would again provide great heroes in the approaching civil strife.[22] But the other side of this picture is the "cooling, hardening, and selfishly-exacting" realm of the city that distinguishes his fiction from *The Golden Christmas* onward, shown in darkening hues until it assumes the mordant and sinister aspect that it wears in *The Cassique of Kiawah* (*E*, 492). Simms's oft-expressed resentment toward Charleston, which grew worse as he grew older, led him persistently to claim that the city, in his case, "has but too commonly taken the service, but rejected the doer of it"; and his attitude, pro-

22. See Ridgely, *William Gilmore Simms*, 118: "The grand movement from *The Partisan* through *Eutaw* had been from despair to hope, from military defeat to a South triumphant in arms."

jected backward onto the past, is shown at its harshest in the passages of social commentary that constitute the most arresting feature of the novel (*L,* V, 424). It is difficult not to be affected by his statements; but although his picture of Charleston social vices is compelling, there is finally little evidence that the city neglected and abused him as much as he liked to maintain.

What is always important in Simms's fiction is the literary shape that historical, political, and social matters assume. In his low-country novels the central shape of these elements is that of romance, though they also nourish the pronounced realistic and satiric strains in his mature writing. Surveying the circumstances of low-country culture, one can hardly imagine that an author of Simms's background and temperament would not have constructed romances about it. More than other American regions, perhaps, the low country had a strong sense of history and, by the time he began to write, a long and colorful past that furnished abundant examples of conflict—social, economic, political, religious, with Indians, with pirates, with Spaniards, and finally with the English—on which historical romance, like much other romance, depends.

From its ties to the British Isles and the West Indies, from its formation as a proprietary colony, and from its early if abortive nobility, the low country had also a strong patrician bias that enabled Simms to adapt the upper-class values long associated with romance to his picture of conditions in the coastal region. It had an agrarian economic system that supported these standards while making possible the elaboration of the plantation or pastoral realm that, in conjunction with the forest, functions as the green domain in his fiction and that is, from *The Yemassee* and *The Partisan* to *The Golden Christmas* and *The Cassique of Kiawah,* its most significant setting. Finally, it had the city, the center of the low-country universe, which embraced and enhanced patrician values at the same time that it attracted snobs and social climbers, encouraging him to study manners within a framework of values established by romance. Inveigh against it as he might, deplore its snobbery, complain that it neglected his talent and damaged his art, Simms could hardly have written the kind of fiction he wrote had it not been for the material that his native state, and particularly his native section, supplied him. If, during his fairly long lifetime, it did nothing else for him—and it did, of course, a considerable amount—in literature, beyond any doubt, low-country South Carolina served him well.

9
Midcentury and After: Catching the Popular Smile

The decade of the fifties that saw Simms's increased attention to the sophisticated society of the low country also witnessed his expanding interest in the customs and behavior of people in the rural South. To some extent this interest was prompted by his growing southern sectionalism and his resulting desire to portray his region as fully as possible in fiction; it was also inspired by his concern with what he called "home travel" as relationships between the South and North grew worse. From the 1820s on, he himself had traveled extensively in the South; now he began to urge his fellow southerners to do so. He voiced this concern in a number of pieces published near midcentury that have some bearing on his extended interest in rural life—*Father Abbot, Southward Ho!,* "Summer Travel in the South," and the lectures on the Appalachians that he had planned to deliver on his abortive lecture tour in 1856.[1] Connecting these otherwise diverse pieces is his emphasis on the attractions of southern scenery, the historical associations of southern landmarks, and the general advantages of travel in the region.

Enhancing Simms's interest in rural living was the increasing prominence of southern humor, which repeatedly attracted his attention.[2] Throughout the 1850s, publishers continued to pour forth comic

1. W[illiam] Gilmore Simms, *Southward Ho!* was published in the Redfield edition during 1854; "Summer Travel in the South" appeared in the *Southern Quarterly Review,* XVIII [n.s., II] (September, 1850), 24–65; the two Appalachian lectures remained in manuscript until they were transcribed by Miriam J. Shillingsburg in "An Edition of William Gilmore Simms's *The Cub of the Panther*" (Ph.D. dissertation, University of South Carolina, 1969), Appendix B. Shillingsburg later edited and published the first lecture in two parts as "The Idylls of the Apalachian," *Appalachian Journal,* I (Autumn, 1972, Spring, 1973), 2–11, 147–60, respectively. The spelling "Apalachian" is Simms's.

2. Arlin Turner, "Seeds of Literary Revolt in the Humor of the Old Southwest," *Louisiana Historical Quarterly,* XXXIX (April, 1956), [143]–45.

works, among them Thomas Bangs Thorpe's *The Hive of "The Bee-Hunter"* (1854), S.P. Avery's *The Harp of a Thousand Strings* (1858), and Thomas Chandler Haliburton's influential collections, *Traits of American Humor* (1852) and *Americans at Home* (1854). The popularity of the mode together with Simms's growing interest in the rural South apparently encouraged him to incorporate backwoods humor in the Revolutionary War Romances he published during the fifties and also to try his hand at two short novels that are solidly in the humor tradition. For as he had already openly acknowledged, "to a scribbler of all work, like myself . . . it is all important to catch the popular smile & to provoke its desires" (*L*, I, 190).

Simms's uses of southern humor in his writing of the 1850s reveal some changes from his practice during earlier decades. In the Border Romances, he had employed patterns stemming from romance to shape his comic episodes and character types; now, however, with his greater knowledge of the humorists' work, he was ready to impose their standard devices like the frame narrative and the tall tale upon his romance format. Interestingly enough, his new approach appears first in the short novels, in which he apparently felt freer of romance structures and constraints than he did in his long fiction. Both of these novels, *As Good as a Comedy* and *Paddy McGann*, are set in rural areas of the South, and both show the intermingling of genteel and rustic types. Both also use the methods and devices of southern humor while combining them with other literary elements. *As Good as a Comedy* deals with town and village life in the interior of Georgia, while *Paddy McGann* portrays the mixture of plantation and rural characters in the interior of South Carolina.

Simms was no stranger to Georgia: he had traveled and lectured in the state, and his first novel, *Guy Rivers*, had been set there.[3] From his letters it appears likely that the success of *Border Beagles*, with its numerous comic backwoods figures, encouraged him to plan a volume that was primarily humorous; at any rate, he consistently speaks of *As Good as a Comedy* as representing a different vein for him. In 1839, shortly after finishing the anonymously issued *Border Beagles*, he told its publisher, Edward Carey of the firm of Carey and Hart, "It may be that in a month or two, I will require you to break ground for another, new, anonymous author, in an entirely new field" (*L*, VI, 17). Circum-

3. Simms's last Revolutionary War Romance, *Joscelyn*, is also set in Georgia.

stances, however, delayed his work on the book; and his correspondence contains no further mention of it until 1845, when—inspired, perhaps, by the cheap-book craze of the decade—he offered a different publisher "a story with the title 'A Dead Shot, or as Good as a Comedy'—a thing of 150 pages to be written" (*L,* II, 84).

In the following years Simms continued to dicker with publishers about the project, telling Carey and Hart, for instance, that he had made little progress on the volume and stipulating that it be issued anonymously, "as it enters a field which I had but partially before attempted" (*L,* II, 349, III, 105). Abraham Hart, the successor to Carey and Hart, finally brought out the book in the Library of Humorous American Works, the popular series in which important volumes of antebellum sporting and humorous lore appeared. Simms, who had wanted the volume to be issued in a standard format, indicated some dissatisfaction with it once it was published (*L,* III, 105); but reviews were favorable, a writer in *Godey's Magazine and Lady's Book* calling its humor comparable to that of Dickens at his best and one in the *Literary World* maintaining, "The publishers have given us many amusing books in their humorous library, but the last is worth all the others."[4] The book apparently sold well, and it was due to be reissued in the 1860s, when, as Simms said, "The advent of Sherman was fatal to its publication" (*L,* IV, 518).

As Good as a Comedy is set in middle Georgia, which had been the prime territory of Longstreet's *Georgia Scenes* and Thompson's *Major Jones' Courtship.* The book shows the impact these and kindred volumes had made on Simms's imagination, and it also shows his persistent interest in the intermingled cultural traditions of the genteel and the rural South. It opens with a framing story and then shifts to a main tale in which characters from the upper class consort with sensible plain people, brassy social upstarts, and lower-class, double-dealing backwoods types. The frame in particular constitutes important evidence that Simms was consciously employing the narrative techniques of the southern humorists. Set in a stagecoach that follows a route he himself had traveled from Madison, Georgia, to Montgomery, Alabama, it is introduced by his fictional surrogate, a genteel figure who emphasizes the regional diversity of the other passengers in a way that

4. Review of *As Good as a Comedy, Godey's Magazine and Lady's Book,* XLIV (June, 1852), 515; Review of *As Good as a Comedy, Literary World: A Journal of Science, Literature, and Art,* X (March 27, 1852), 222.

had been standard in southern humor at least since "The Big Bear of Arkansas," in which Thorpe had deliberately created an array of national types. Among Simms's passengers are a New Yorker, a Pennsylvanian, a machinist from Maine, a Mississippian who yells in frontier fashion, "Go ahead, old horse," and "a broth of a boy in the shape of a huge Tennesseean" who sports "great fat haunches" and a "mutton fist."[5] This last figure, broader drawn, sloppier, and funnier than the backwoodsmen of Simms's earlier writing, gradually comes to dominate the frame; and as he does so he engages in exchanges with the gentlemanly narrator that reflect what Simms had learned in the 1840s from the humorists about the comic contrast of polite and rustic speech.

> "Stranger," says he to me, "ef so be you will only *skrooge* yourself up so as to let me have this arm of mine parfectly free for a swing, as I find it necessary, I'll let out a little upon you in relation to sartain sarcumstances that come pretty much to my own knowledge, a year or two ago, in Florida."
>
> To *skrooge* myself up, in the expressive idiom of my neighbor, into a yet narrower compass than I had been compelled to keep before, was a thing wholly out of the question. But a change of position might be effected, to the relief of both parties, and this was all that he really wanted. I contrived, after a desperate effort, to satisfy him, and, in some degree, myself. (11)

Although the Tennessean is the most appealing character in the frame, Simms was not yet ready to let a backwoods narrator tell the entire story, and so he has the genteel speaker tell it for him. While this move is the opposite of what the humorists usually did, it enables Simms to elaborate the romance elements in the volume, and it also lets him blend his raucous backwoods scenes with satiric social comedy of the sort found in his midcentury fiction about the low country. In the main narrative, he employs the kind of love triangle familiar in his long novels while shaping his characters to represent various elements of middle Georgia society. His ideal figures—the hero Randall Hammond and his widowed mother—embody the polite standards of

5. [William Gilmore Simms], *As Good as a Comedy: or, The Tennesseean's Story*, with Introduction and Explanatory Notes by Robert Bush, text established by James B. Meriwether (Columbia, S.C., 1972), 14, 8, 11, vol. III of John C. Guilds (ed.), *The Writings of William Gilmore Simms: Centennial Edition*. Further references to this novel are to this edition, cited by page number within the text. In the Introduction, xiv–xv, Bush briefly discusses Simms's use of southern humor in the novel.

the interior South, a region that lacked the wealth and polish of the coastal section but that nonetheless boasted considerable gentility of its own. Sprightly Geraldine Foster, the girl Randall loves, is essentially of the same level as the Hammonds, but she has been tainted by the values of her crass stepmother Mrs. Foster, "an ill-bred, pretentious woman"; and she consequently needs the elevating influence of the Hammonds in order to assume her rightful social position (54). Geraldine's second suitor, Miles Henderson, is a stripped-down version of Randall Hammond, well-bred but lacking Randall's personal gifts; her third one, Jones Barry, is a nouveau-riche social climber who like Mrs. Foster is intent on aping the aristocracy.

The pretensions of both Barry and Mrs. Foster make them fair game for the tricks and deceptions of Tom Nettles, a bright-eyed, laughter-loving wag from the middle social level who embodies the common sense and love of practical jokes of the rustic. The aptly named Nettles, whose particular mission is to sting and goad the foolish Barry, guides the dandy through mishap after mishap designed to mortify his vanity, bring him to his senses, and (not entirely incidentally) keep him away from Geraldine. Nettles functions as Simms's chief link between the romance and comic strands of the book and the instrument by which its happy denouement is brought about. In an irresponsible moment, Geraldine tells her three suitors that whoever wins a horse race may claim her hand—a proposal that introduces the folk-based "race for a wife" motif into Simms's romance plot.[6] Shocked by Geraldine's proposal, Randall and Miles privately agree to race and then to retire from the field, leaving Geraldine to wed clumsy little Barry. But Nettles, who knows that this is not the way things should work out, intervenes; and by means of a series of well-timed maneuvers, he insures that Randall finally marries Geraldine and that Barry weds the vulgar Mrs. Foster. Thus *As Good as a Comedy*, like the long romances to which it is partially kin, ends with couples appropriately paired.

Intertwined with the love narrative are episodes revealing Simms's familiarity with customs and pursuits in the rural South together with his knowledge, gleaned from his midcentury reading, about the char-

6. *The Spirit of the Times*, I (April 7, 1832), carried on its front page an item called "Race for a Wife." The custom is also listed in standard folklore indexes; see, for example, Stith Thompson, *Motif-Index of Folk-Literature* (Rev. ed.; Bloomington, Ind., 1955–58), III, H331.5.

acteristic subjects and procedures of the humorists. More obviously than in his previous books, he writes with one eye on the work of such predecessors as Longstreet and Thompson. The result is that his romance plot in *As Good as a Comedy* unfolds against a series of scenes that are directly in the tradition of southern humor—a horse race in which "sharps" prey on "flats," a gander pulling in which Barry proves himself a greater goose than the bird, and a country circus in which a prankish clown takes the fop on a dangerous ride around the huge circus ring. Simms enlivens these sequences with vivid dialect, spices them up with slapstick, and centers them on the pratfalls of Barry, who for sheer dim-witted ineptitude outdoes the other fools and gulls in his fiction, including Tom Horsey.

In depicting the horse race, Simms had his own knowledge of the sport to draw on, and he had, in addition, written precedents ranging from Longstreet's "The Turf" to Thomas Kirkman's "A Quarter Race in Kentucky," the first story in William T. Porter's volume of the same title and perhaps the best-known comic antebellum portrayal of the track. Looked at one way, Simms's race-course sequences blend the social criticism of Longstreet's presentation with the emphasis on chicanery in Kirkman: like Longstreet, Simms scores the pretentiousness of the upper classes, while like Kirkman he revels in the wild language and wilder behavior of the lower ones. In the process, he reveals his own great ability for rendering the images and the cadences of rural speech. One countryman shouts to another, "Thar you ar', Daddy Nathan, as bright as a bead of brandy, always bringing something for a tharsty sinner!" Daddy Nathan answers: "And what would you hev', you great jugbelly with a double muzzle? Ain't I here for the saving of such miserable sinners as you[?]" (37). Meanwhile, two sharps—ragged Ned Ramsey and an elegant stranger—work the crowd, judging horses and shrewdly manipulating bets. Ramsey and a character called Lazy Jake Owens converse in metaphors so thick it takes a specialist in southern dialect to understand them.

> "Halloo, there, monkey! ain't you afeard of that tail of your'n getting in the wolf-trap?"
>
> "No, Jake; for I know you hain't got the teeth to raise the skin of that varmint."
>
> "Hain't I, then? Just you try it, then, with another sort of look in your face, and see if I ain't a peeler."
>
> "Will you peel?"

"Won't I, then?"

"Jake, my boy, I've come here to-day to strip the skin off you altogether."

"You! Tain't in your skin to do it, Ned."

"Yes, or there's no snakes. I'm here with the best nag at a heat that ever was seed in Hillabee." (43)

Ramsey then approaches Jones Barry, who, says one of the onlookers, is "rich enough to make any sort of fool of himself, and nobody see the harm of it" (47). Ramsey tricks Barry, who carries a big bankroll, into laying down a good deal of cash on two horses that cannot win, and as part of his game he even lets the fop chastise him. "Now, if you're a man," says Barry, "I banter you to empty your pockets on the match; every fip down; and I cover it, fip for fip, and eagle for eagle." The clever Ramsey, acting crestfallen, mutters: "Thar, squire, you've pushed me to the edge of the water, and now I'll go my death on the drink. Thar! Count! Ef my figuring ain't out of the way, thar's one hundred and five dollars in that heap!" (50–51). Later, however, after Barry's horses have lost, Ramsey happily collects some "cool hundreds" from the chastened fop (99).[7]

After losing at the horse race, Barry swallows plenty of liquor and makes his way to the gander pulling, where he proceeds to disgrace himself by grabbing "not the goose, but the rope by which it was suspended" (95). Undaunted, he moves on to the circus, which had been a topic in antebellum humor at least since Thompson's "Great Attraction," a long story appended to the 1843 edition of *Major Jones' Courtship*. Barry, who has never been to a circus, believes that a performer there can jump through the eye of a needle; and he even believes Nettles' story about how the clown "uncorks a bottle with his eye, sets fire to a wheelrocket with his whiskers, and afterwards swallows his own head" (89). The gullible dandy is ripe for the machinations of the clown, who offers him a brandy cocktail and then, after tossing some streamers in his face, quaffs the drink himself, proclaiming, "Perhaps you'll wait till you can get it!" Barry, enraged, assaults the clown and inadvertently tears away "what seemed to be the entire head and neck of the unfortunate jester" (103). The clown, however,

7. *Fip* is an abbreviation for "fippenny bit" (Bush, Explanatory Notes to *As Good as a Comedy,* 515, 50.34). An eagle is a United States ten-dollar gold coin. After the novel was published, Hammond lectured Simms on errors he had made in describing the horse race. His remarks are quoted in *L,* III, 178*n*109.

hoists Barry upon his shoulders, carries him around the ring, and pitches him headlong

> into the arms of a great fat negro wench, one of the most enormous in the assembly, who sat trickling with oleaginous sweat, on the third tier. . . .
>
> "Here's an abolitionist for you, mother Possum-fat!" cried the clown, as he plumped poor Barry into her embrace.
>
> "I no want 'em!" cried the woman, shuffling herself free from the burden. (104)

The entire sequence, including the conclusion with its derogatory portrayal of blacks, reflects the spirit of southern humor; and in fact Simms borrowed some key elements in it from Thompson's story "Great Attraction!"—in which, as in this novel, a dandified physician named Jones gets into a scuffle with a circus performer who rides him around the ring on his shoulders and then pitches him into a crowd of Negroes, who squall "in concert with the general shout."[8] Simms's explicit details about "oleaginous sweat" and "mother Possum-fat" make his scene more graphic than Thompson's; but the similarities between the two episodes suggest that the Carolinian, despite his criticism in the *Magnolia* of Thompson's "extravagancies," used him with profit for a funny chapter in his own book.

With its romance-related main story and its substantial humorous undercurrent, *As Good as a Comedy* is an energetic but occasionally awkward combination of two literary modes—as Simms probably realized when he asked a publisher in 1854, "Are you willing to try an edition of 'As Good as a Comedy', the introduction omitted, and the title changed to 'Tom Nettles, or a Race for a Wife.'—or 'The Fair Geraldine, a Story of the Backwoods [?]'" (*L*, III, 293). His novel suffers from his careless splicing of frame and central story, and also from the repetitive slapstick that he uses in depicting Barry's dilemmas, which are matters that tend to detract from his skillful handling of the circus and the horse race. The backwoods scenes in the novel suggest unmistakably, however, that his reading of the humorists in the 1840s had sharpened his ability to construct dialect, broadened his knowledge of comic backwoods subjects, and impressed upon him that a

8. See [William Tappan Thompson], "Great Attraction! or The Doctor 'Most Oudaciously Tuck In.' A Sketch From Real Life," in *Major Jones' Courtship* . . . (Madison, Ga., 1843), 74.

framing narrative followed by an inner story was an effective means of constructing a tale.

After *As Good as a Comedy,* Simms published several works in which he continued to employ funny rustic figures, tall talk, or frame stories. Hell-Fire Dick of *The Forayers* and *Eutaw,* the most comic of his ruffians in the Revolutionary War Romances, bounds into the former novel shouting to another scoundrel: "Hello, in thar, Pete Blodgit! Up with you, my yaller chicken, and let's see ef you've got over the pip yit! Open to the sky-scrapers, and the bouncing wild cats; and hear 'em scream to beat all nater! Whoo! whoo! whoo! whoo! . . . We are the beautiful sinners of salvation, and don't care for the man that prays. Let's in, Pete!" (52). Poor whites in the same volumes, who cringe and whine before Dick and his crew, are in Constance Rourke's phrases "[s]calawags, gamblers, ne'er-do-wells, small rapscallions . . . drawn . . . against a background of pine barrens, sandy wastes, half-plowed fields, huts with leaky roofs."[9] But the Simms volume of the middle 1850s that reveals the most striking use of antebellum humor is *Southward Ho!,* a group of stories strung along a frame narrative about a number of people traveling by steamboat from New York to Charleston, a trip that Simms himself had frequently made.

As he does in *As Good as a Comedy,* Simms designs the characters in the frame to represent various national types while sprucing up both frame and stories with elements from the backwoods. Like many tales from that region, "Legend of the One-Legged Lady" treats physical disability humorously in its depiction of a woman with a wooden leg who marries a cobbler with "no leg at all," whereas "Oyster Wars," another lighthearted story, reveals Simms's knowledge of tall fish yarns in its picture of a hero who "enjoyed a hand-to-hand combat with a shark, of sixteen feet, in five-fathom water."[10] But perhaps the best examples of backwoods humor in *Southward Ho!* appear in the framing narrative, where an eccentric orator from Alabama gulls a feisty lub-

9. Rourke, *American Humor,* 69.

10. W[illiam] Gilmore Simms, *Southward Ho! A Spell of Sunshine* (New York, 1854), 136, 24. Further references to this volume are to this edition, cited by page number within the text. For the frame story of the book, Simms used a revised version of "Spells of Sunshine; or, a Summer in the South," a narrative supporting "home travel" that he had published in the Charleston *Evening News* during June and July, 1849 (*L,* III, 314*n*144). "Oyster Wars" and "Legend of the One-Legged Lady" are titles given by J. Allen Morris, an early student of Simms's short fiction, to untitled tales. See "The Stories of William Gilmore Simms," *American Literature,* XIV (March, 1942), 26.

berlander from North Carolina by spinning tales about the Old North State. He tells a yarn that Simms cleverly adapts from the Arkansas Traveler story, in which, in a standard confrontation between civilization and backwoods, a poker-faced denizen of Arkansas tricks a traveler by telling him outrageous lies about the region's poverty to avoid giving him any provisions.[11] As Simms's Alabamian recounts the story, once he and some friends were forced to dock at a lazy town called Smithville, where

> A few of us got to shore, counting on an oyster supper. We met a fellow seven feet high, with his back against a bank of sand that kept off the wind, while the fragment of an old cutter's deck, hanging over the bank, covered him from the rain. . . . We questioned him about oysters.
>
> "Reckon it's hard to find 'em now."
>
> "Why?"
>
> "Why, you see, we've done cleaned off all a 'top, and them down low in the water's mighty hard to come at. Don't get much oysters at Smithville now. Reckon there mought have been a right smart chance of 'em long time ago—'bout the Revolution."
>
> "Well, do you think we can get any broiled chickens anywhere?"
>
> "Chickens don't do so well at Smithville. I'm thinking they drink too much of the salt water, and the gravel's too coarse for 'em, but they die off mighty soon, and there's no cure for it."
>
> "Eggs?"
>
> "Well now, as for eggs, somehow the hens don't lay as they used to. Folks say that there's a sort of happidemic among the poultry of all kinds. They don't thrive no more in Smithville."
>
> "And what *have* you got in Smithville?"
>
> "I reckon there's pretty much all the Smiths here that was here at the beginning. Old granny Pressman Smith lives thar in that rether old house that looks a'most as if it was guine to fall. 'Lijah Smith keeps opposite. . . . Rice Smith owns that 'ere flat, you sees thar' with its side stove; and the old windmill yander with the fans gone b'longs to Jackson W. Smith, the lawyer. . . . I'm a Smith myself—my name's Fergus Smith, but I'm the poorest of the family. I don't own nothing, no how, and never did." (315–16)

The best example of Simms's backwoods humor during this period, however, is *Paddy McGann; or, the Demon of the Stump,* a frame narrative set in rural South Carolina that was serialized in a Richmond

11. For a scholarly discussion of the famous yarn, see Gene Bluestein, "'The Arkansas Traveler' and the Strategy of American Humor," *Western Folklore,* XXI (July, 1962), 153–60.

weekly paper, the *Southern Illustrated News*, during 1863. With its emphasis upon the relationship of rustic characters and the gentry, it forms a bridge between Simms's works that emphasize the low country and those that center on the backwoods South. A nostalgic recreation of his camaraderie with planter friends in the vicinity of Woodlands, it was intended in part as a cross section of southern social classes. This fact is suggested by the way Simms designs his principal figures—the title character, a liquor-loving Irish backwoodsman who boasts that he was "nursed on whiskey, weaned on whiskey, and vaccinated with whiskey"; the planter Wharncliffe, who alternately urges Paddy to industry and lectures him about his drinking; the frame narrator, Stylus, a writer who is probably a fictionalized version of Simms; and D. F. Jamison, a South Carolina politician who had served as president of the state secession convention.[12] In their easy interchanges, Paddy and the gentlemanly characters make palpable the strong sense of community among social classes that existed in the antebellum South.[13] The aristocrats, particularly Wharncliffe, stand in a "mixed patriarchal and feudal relation" with the woodsman, who brings them fish and game in exchange for produce and loans of cash (240).

Perhaps more obviously than characters in Simms's earlier fiction, the patrician figures in this story serialized midway through the Civil War demonstrate his conviction that the genteel element in southern culture had produced a civilization of great refinement, cultivation, and intelligence; and they also serve, somewhat obtrusively at times, as mouthpieces for his fervent sectionalism. In the first chapter of the book, for instance, Stylus refers to the war—"The cry is havoc; the war-dogs are again unleashed!"—and then predicts eventual victory for the South. A little later, Wharncliffe echoes his sentiments in what is from the vantage point of history an ironic passage: "It is not all over—our happy life, my friend! We shall enjoy the old sports of our sweet little river once more, in communion with our noble-hearted companions. It cannot be that God will deliver us into the hands of these atrocious heathens" (220, 221).

12. [William Gilmore Simms], *Paddy McGann; or, The Demon of the Stump*, with Introduction and Explanatory Notes by Robert Bush, text established by James B. Meriwether (Columbia, S.C., 1972), 254, vol. III of John C. Guilds (ed.), *The Writings of William Gilmore Simms: Centennial Edition*. Further references to this volume are to this edition, cited by page number within the text.

13. On this general point, see Louis D. Rubin, Jr., *The Writer in the South: Studies in a Literary Community* (Athens, Ga., 1972).

But though it is to some extent a sectionalist screed, *Paddy McGann* is also a narrative conceived from first to last in the spirit of southern humor. A triumph of Simms's comic imagination and the first protracted example of his fine ability in the tall tale, it is that rare thing in antebellum backwoods comedy—a short novel, as opposed to a story, told almost entirely in dialect by the title character. The figure of Paddy indicates Simms's interest, doubtless partly autobiographical, in the idiosyncracies of the Celtic character, and it also reflects his knowledge of three stock figures—the raftsman, the Irishman, and the backwoodsman—as they had developed in fiction and drama during the antebellum period. Strong, earthy, and imaginative, Paddy, with his appetite for liquor and his fondness for country brawls, could have stepped from the pages of a tall tale. He speaks a rich dialect, a mixture of Irish brogue and backwoods slang that is laced with the striking images for which southern humor is famous. When describing a frightening experience, he says, for instance, that his hair stood up from the roots "as stiff as young corn growing in a clay field"; of a nearly empty bottle of whiskey, he remarks, "I'm jubous there's not enough to clear the eyesight of a sand-fly"; and a would-be city belle, he says, looked at him "with a softness and a fire mixed together that would have melted the bowels of an alligator" (269, 287, 419).

In Paddy's story, Simms mingles two strains in southern humor, what Constance Rourke calls the "true tall tale with its stress upon the supernatural" and the more prosaic but equally effective comedy of the plain folk.[14] The first strain predominates in the early sections of the narrative, which take place in the woods near the Edisto River and on a raft in the Atlantic Ocean; the second colors its closing chapters, set in New York City and rural South Carolina. Together the strains make *Paddy McGann* unique in Simms's fiction: an original, ingenious devil story, an excellent example of the tall tale, and an affecting exposition of backwoods religious experience. It differs from most southern humor in its combination of radically diverse elements and also in the fact that instead of trying to hoax his hearers Paddy is determined to convince them that the strange events he narrates are true.

Throughout the long initial section of the novel, Simms combines standard material from printed humor like the fight and the shoot for beef with elements derived from oral tradition, such as a bewitched

14. Rourke, *American Humor*, 67.

gun and a deer that cannot be killed. Some years back, Paddy tells his planter friends, he found that one of his guns was apparently under a spell and that he was no longer able to kill any game—a dilemma that he blames on the devil, who he thinks is haunting the woods. At the urging of his friend Sam Hartley, he takes his guns to a witch doctor, who spits on them and smokes them with "yairbs," but they shoot as badly as before. Sam then persuades Paddy to take part in a shoot for beef—the first of several sequences drawn from the tradition of southern humor and one that probably glances at Crockett's and Longstreet's well-known sketches of the rural sport. During the match, Paddy is heckled by Isaac Clymes, a loud-mouthed, drunken bully of the rough-and-tumble school. When Paddy prays before the contest begins, Clymes sneers, "[D]o you calkilate that praying will take the witch pison off your rifle?" and he also mutters, "I wonder if in getting religion, he's left off whiskey!" After praying, Paddy calmly fires at the target, an ace of hearts nailed on a pine tree. But he misses the tree altogether, he says, "jest as if there had been no bullet in the gun!" (274–76).

When Paddy fails, there is "a most infarnal yelling, and whooping, and shouting, and hallobalooing, from all the fellows that run up to look for the shot." In a rage, he smashes his rifle; Clymes bedevils him; Paddy calls the bully "a d——d dirty beast . . . something of a cross between a polecat and a skunk"; and the two men square off for a fight. Paddy pitches Clymes over an ugly stump and breaks his leg; but "it was all the Devil's doings, gentlemen," he tells his hearers; "he caused me to miss the tree; he put the ugly stump in the way that broke Clymes' thigh bone, and 'twas him that worked me up to smash the poor we'pon that had sarved me, like a most faithful sarvant, now going on twenty years. It was the Devil that had the strong gripe of me through all that season!" (277–80).

In subsequent scenes, Paddy hears annoying whispers, laughter, and shouting in the woods; he encounters signs of a supernatural presence as he hunts under leaden skies in a strangely silent forest; he sees a dark shape rush by, discovers his coat torn and his shoes scattered, and finds "all the signs of fighting . . . the brush scattered; the airth tore up; but no signs of dog or beast!" (297). Finally an enormous buck comes thundering down upon him in a sequence that shows Simms drawing on folk material about invincible supernatural animals that was widespread in literature of the time. Foremost among such literature is Melville's *Moby-Dick;* but perhaps more directly pertinent for *Paddy McGann* is Thomas Bangs Thorpe's account of the Big Bear of Arkansas, "*an unhuntable bar*" that "*died when his time come.*"[15] At one point in Thorpe's story, narrator Jim Doggett thinks the bear may be an incarnation of the devil, and Paddy likewise assumes that the devil has come to taunt him in "the innocent figger of the buck." He shoots both barrels of his gun at the deer; but the creature seems to feel nothing, and it torments Paddy and his friend Sam, neither of whom can bring it down. As if to trick and annoy them, it doubles back and forth, swipes a hunting dog with its antlers, and leads Paddy across a railroad track directly in front of a speeding steam engine. The next day Paddy and Sam start out after the buck with more than fifteen dogs, but Paddy remarks that the dogs "might jest as well been at home in the kennel, for the good they waur in the chase of that devil buck." He concludes that even Sam began "to feel shy of keeping company with a man so onfortynit as me . . . and I didn't blame him; for who could blame a man who wanted to eat his hominy in peace, without the human sartinty of finding the Devil, all the time, dipping his spoon into the dish!" (289–92).[16]

The apparent meaning of these episodes emerges after Paddy has killed a string of partridges feeding on the ground and the devil has rebuked him for his unsportsmanlike behavior: "Murder, I calls it . . . to take 'em in a line upon the ground! To give 'em not the shadow of a chaince! . . . But I'll punish you for your murdering acts, you dirty villain. I'll see that you get no more meat!" There ensues the most comical sequence in this section of the book as Paddy sees the devil in the shape of a "big red eye" looking from a "big, ugly, black stump." En-

15. William T. Porter (ed.), *The Big Bear of Arkansas, and Other Sketches, Illustrative of Characters and Incidents in the South and South-West* (Philadelphia, 1845), 31.

16. Contemporary works Simms probably knew that use the folk motifs of magic animals or bewitched guns include [James Kirke Paulding], *Westward Ho! A Tale* (New York, 1832), I, 136–38; [Washington Irving], *A Tour on the Prairies* (Philadelphia, 1835), 213–14; and William Elliott, *Carolina Sports, by Land and Water; Including Incidents of Devil-Fishing, &c.* (Charleston, S.C., 1846), 124–38. Charles Fenno Hoffman's *Wild Scenes in the Forest and Prairie* (1839; rpr. Upper Saddle River, N.J., 1970), I, 186–90, contains a brief narrative of a spirit that inhabits a stump. James Hall's "Pete Featherton," in *The Wilderness and the War Path* (New York, 1846), 152–68, constitutes a possible direct influence on *Paddy McGann.* Hall's story has a southern woodsman as a major character and centers on a devil, an enchanted gun, a witch doctor, and deer that cannot be killed. Simms dedicated *Beauchampe* to Hall and mentioned the stories in *The Wilderness and the War Path* in a manner that suggests he had read them (*L,* II, 165).

raged, he shoots his gun "pint-blank" at the eye, and the devil shouts, "You've burned my eyebrow, you buzzard!" Paddy shoots again, and the devil cries, "[Y]ou've . . . shet up my front window, you blackguard!" (315–17). The contest concludes when Paddy grabs the stump, uproots it, and rolls with it down a hill: before he can destroy it, however, it turns into a great bird and flaps away. The devil is obviously punishing Paddy for his heedless destruction of forest game, and through the sequence Simms voices a concern about the proper treatment of the wilderness that has preoccupied later southern writers such as William Faulkner.[17]

In the next major section of the novel, Paddy passes from the woods to the raft, and Simms moves into an elaborate, colorful description of primitive spirituality; though there is comedy in his account, its chief emphasis is on visionary religious experience. In the third section, in which Paddy is shipwrecked, picked up by a brigantine, and taken to New York, Simms employs the device—widespread in antebellum humor—of the greenhorn in the city as a vehicle for topical satire on abolitionism, Fourierism, city literati, and emancipated women. Particularly notable here is his attack upon his old enemy, Lewis Gaylord Clark of the *Knickerbocker Magazine:* he introduces Clark by name into the narrative as the editor of the "New York Niggerbitcher" and has him shamelessly swindle poor Paddy. After pumping the woodsman about his adventures, Clark takes him to a fancy restaurant for oysters and beefsteak; then, having indulged in mush, milk, brandy, and cigars, he ducks out, leaving Paddy to pay the bill. The waiters tell the woodsman that his presumed friend is a "cunning Yankee sponge" who "squeezes his supper out of a green horn, sucks it dry, and then makes himself skearce." ("Dernation," says Paddy, "I ought to ha' known that a fellow who takes a platter of mush and milk a'ter a dozen oysters and a steak, must be a skunk" [384–88].)

But it is the final section of the novel, in which Simms grafts vivid pictures of the southern poor white upon the conventions of the frontier courtship yarn, that displays his most successful use of the modes and traditions of southern humor. Courtship and marriage had been prominent subjects of that humor from *Georgia Scenes* and *Major Jones' Courtship* through "Polly Peablossom's Wedding"; in a typical story, a rustic suitor woos and wins a toothsome country girl, often

17. For a similar point, see Bush, Introduction to *Paddy McGann,* xxiii.

after a series of ridiculous mishaps. Susan Heffernan Pogson, Paddy's intended bride, is—like Thompson's Mary Stallings and George Washington Harris' Sicily Burns—a tempting morsel, "a smooth-faced young thing, with round, rosy cheeks" and a "plump round figger" (449). Paddy courts her in familiar rural surroundings, the parlor and the meeting house, and though he dislikes her slovenly family, he marries her. The marriage ceremony is distinguished by the sort of slapstick that Harris' Sut Lovingood would shortly exploit. At the wedding, a pet monkey escapes from the pocket of Paddy's ripsnorting friend Jim Meredith and jumps up onto the shoulder of Sally Hartley, Sam's sanctimonious wife. The ensuing chaos unmasks the cosmetic deceptions of Sally. In Paddy's words, the monkey put his fingers in Sally's headdress, and in "her red hair, which warn't so fine, and it was all hanging about her ears in a minute. Lord, how she screamed."

> "Take it off! Take it off! The dreadful beast!"
>
> Oh! she was roaring mad; and it made her furious to see iverybody laughing fit to split! . . .
>
> At last, Col. Jim got in a passion, and knocked the beast over his nose, and gin him a pull, and with that the leetle wretch give one spring, and jumped away; and made all worse than ever, for he pulled off the whole head-dress. But that warn't the worst of it; for, to the supprise of everybody, the hair come along with it—the whole shock.—Nobody—not even Sam Hartley himself—iver know'd, till that minute, that his wife wore a wig!—for who would think of a woman gitting a wig of red hair?—her scalp was as bald as a pumpkin! (486–87)

Interwoven with such scenes are descriptions of the Pogson family, as loathsome a group of poor whites as can be found, perhaps, in antebellum literature. Like their spiritual kindred, Simms's Blonays before them and Faulkner's Snopeses afterwards, the Pogsons are worthless scoundrels bent on causing mischief. The father, says Paddy, is "a tall, lank-sided varmint . . . sharp-faced as an Ingin's hatchet" with skin "draw'd so tight over his cheekbone, that it was beginning to show cracks all over it, or with big creases as to look like cracks. He spoke with a long, saft voice, like a hungry hawk in the air over a field of brown straw, looking out for rabbits, of a warm spring a'ternoon" (475). The mother, who has "a very sharp *reddishy* nose," is "one of those persons who thinks it a binding duty to be talking all the time," and the daughters, except for Susan, "have the daddy's face and the mammy's tongue" (472, 475). Their farm bespeaks the family's slovenliness and indigence. As Paddy says, the "fences waur hardly more than knee high; the houses waur going to ruin . . . and iverything show'd, what iverybody said, that Pogson was a poor crather, that either didn't know his business, or didn't attend to it" (473).

After Susan marries Paddy, she drops her pretty poses and reveals herself to be as wasteful and spendthrift as her family, running up debts for gaudy clothes while dressing her mother and sisters at Paddy's expense. Her father and brother similarly make free with Paddy's meat, whiskey, and tobacco, steal his buckshot, and rifle his money drawer. Paddy ousts them from his home; but then, after quarreling with Susan, he abandons her and joins the Confederate army. The devil, meanwhile, has taken leave of him, declaring that in marrying, "[Y]ou'll find, ould fellow, you're in worse hands than mine iver waur!" (490).

Despite their compelling humor, *As Good as a Comedy* and *Paddy McGann* are not wholly satisfactory as narratives; they are too uneven in texture and too various in content for complete success. In designing them, however, Simms had moved much closer to the humorists than in his previous fiction: he had started to employ their structural techniques, and he had also, in *Paddy McGann,* made gestures toward the kind of tall tale in which he would excel in the last decade of his life. With these two books behind him, during the 1860s—in tales set in the Appalachian Mountains that he had visited in midcareer—he would compose his most impressive works in the comic tradition of the southern frontier.

10
The Furnaces of Affliction: The Mountain South and Voltmeier

In the 1860s, the misfortunes that had plagued Simms since the middle of the previous decade continued to mount, and the chronicle of his activities during this period entails a sometimes painful discussion of his various woes. During the last dozen years of his life, he faced trials, as Hayne says, of no common severity: the loss of two young children in 1861 and, in 1863, of his wife; the deaths of his close friends Hammond and Jamison during the Civil War; the sale of cherished volumes from his library to meet plantation expenses; the burning of Woodlands by accident in 1862 and by Sherman's forces in 1865, with the consequent destruction of the rest of his library; and, throughout the decade, the multiple afflictions of poverty, illness, depression, and war.[1] His letters of the period, with their descriptions of his privations, contrast strongly with the lively and hopeful correspondence of his youth, when he was confidently hoping to capture the national literary marketplace. He had indeed, as he observed to Lawson in 1868, been tried "in all the furnaces of affliction"; and he would face graver tests of his character and endurance before the 1860s closed (*L*, V, 174).

Heading Simms's problems early in the decade was his poverty. Woodlands continued to drain his financial resources; he wrote William Porcher Miles, one of his Charleston friends, that "a rascally overseer ruined my crop, got drunk, neglected the plantation, let the grass run away with my fields & instead of 125 bales of Cotton, I made but 50" (*L*, IV, 193). To combat his losses, he wrote John Esten Cooke, he had been forced to sell

> some rare old books out of my Library, and some thousand or two of current ones! . . . I could & should weep here, if the eyes did not refuse

1. Hayne, "Ante-Bellum Charleston," 258.

> me. . . . I have been collecting my books for quite 30 years. I have imported rare books at rare prices; caught them up wherever I could; and what I had thus amassed has been the sole accumulation left me from my Literary labours during all this time. I had about 12000 volumes. Briefly, for my situation—a day & night laborer, it was too much capital to invest in such unprofitable wares! This year, dreadfully unfortunate in my crop & overseer, I have been driven to the necessity of selling Milton for a bushel of corn, Shakspeare [*sic*] for a bunch of onions, Chaucer for a string of fish, and Bacon for a barrel of beans, &c!! (*L*, IV, 215–16)

Such misfortunes, coupled with recurrent physical illness, contributed to Simms's profound and nearly incapacitating depressions. With his volatile Celtic temperament, he had been a prey to despondency at intervals throughout his life; but in the 1860s, with family and plantation problems pressing in upon him, despair was a frequent companion. "I am getting old and weak," he wrote Miles in 1860, "and the defeat of reasonable expectations, the mortification of justly founded hopes, the failure of all proper results from patient industry, the denial of proper meed for patriotic performances involving much self sacrifice, the gnawing anxieties belonging to a complication of worldly & domestic necessities—these have conspired to unhinge me, and make me cast myself down in a momentary paroxysm of despair" (*L*, IV, 193). These moods prevented him from accepting the kind of public honors he once had craved; hence despite his earlier political ambitions, he rejected his friends' suggestion that he be nominated for the United States Senate because, he claimed, "I have lost my impulse to exertion" (*L*, IV, 60). "I am speaking honestly, my dear Hammond," he explained; "for whatever my political ambition might have been, it is very fairly burnt out; & whatever my vanity may be, I am still satisfied to feed it, in my own obscure fashion, as a simple bookworm . . . satisfied that the notion of success would be idle, and burdened as I am with so large a family, & so many home cares, I am resigned to this Fate which would seem to have denied a field to all my more youthful aspirations" (*L*, IV, 54).

For similar reasons, he refused the editorship of the Charleston *Mercury*, declined to be a candidate for the state secession convention, and, with great reluctance, rejected the signal honor of delivering the oration at the unveiling of a statue of George Washington in the nation's capital. "How eagerly would I have leapt at such an office in other days!" he mourned to Miles. "But . . . I am in trouble! . . the very money which would carry me to Washington, & bring me back, I cannot spare! I should feel, while speaking, that people would see that I wear an old threadbare coat; that there would be those in the crowd to say, 'better pay your shoe bill, your tailor, than be splurging here with your grand nonsense!'" Then, in a passage that reveals just how far his vision of personal achievement had slipped since the 1830s, he lamented, "I have been overworked; I have been unsuccessful all my life; my books fail to pay me; I am myself a failure!" (*L*, IV, 185–86).

Increasing the sorrows of this severely tested man during these years were the persistent shafts directed by "the insatiate archer Fate" against his family (*L*, IV, 402). Simms had scarcely finished grieving for the two little sons he had lost in 1858 when he was called upon to bear new afflictions. His son Sydney Hammond and his small daughter Harriet Myddleton, called Hattie, died in 1861. He felt Hattie's death, which occurred on Christmas Day, especially keenly; as he wrote her godfather Miles, "I am under these successive shocks, growing feebler, rapidly aging, and shudder with a continued sense of winter at my hearth" (*L*, IV, 393). Less than two years later, he sustained the greatest loss he would ever have to bear when his beloved Chevillette died suddenly of what was apparently acute appendicitis (*L*, IV, 437*n*61). They had enjoyed a deeply satisfying marriage; and though she was not, as he acknowledged, a literary person, she had been in many ways his closest companion. The letter he wrote Paul Hamilton Hayne after her death displays in full his despair.

> I have been ill, my friend, I may say dangerously ill, from the moment when I was struck down by the heaviest bolt of all that ever shattered my roof-tree. I was, I think, insane. I neither slept nor ate for four days and nights. Fever seized me, and I should have gone mad but for the administration of timely opiates. I am once more on my legs, but very weak. Today, is the first that I have given to the desk, and this I could do only in snatches of brief period. I move about the house & try to see to things. But every thing seems blank, & waste, & very cheerless. I am alone! Alone! For near 30 years, I had one companion in whose perfect fidelity, I felt sure. To her I could go, and say, 'I suffer!'—or 'I am glad,' always satisfied that she would partake the feeling with me, whatever its character. Your eulogy is not mere varnish & gilding. She was all that you describe,—a dutiful wife, a devoted mother, and the most guileless of women. Ah! God! And I am lone! (*L*, IV, 437–38)

Helping Simms through these periods of grave personal crisis was his active involvement in the secession movement. During the 1830s and most of the 1840s he had been both "an ultra-American" and "a born Southron" (*L*, I, 319). By the 1850s, however, as Jon L. Wakelyn remarks in *The Politics of a Literary Man*, he had become a respected adviser to secessionist politicians; and in the 1860s, the heated public and private letters he wrote in defense of southern separatism form a vital part of the intellectual history of the period. Vernon L. Parrington's description of antebellum southern politicians "blown up like a pig's bladder after butchering" is unfortunately corroborated by Simms's correspondence.[2] He wrote Lawson, for instance, that northerners had become despots: "Nothing but secession could open their eyes, and nothing but the evils accruing from it will ever coach them, and it will be quite too late for their own good, when they are made to see. They have committed the greatest political & social suicide that History has ever shown. Never was such blind ignorance so insolent, never good fortune so blind, never presumption so riant and imbecile at the same moment" (*L*, IV, 339). In similar vein, he wrote his northern friend John Jacob Bockee, "The Union had survived its uses, had got to be a mere shop . . . of faction, fraud, and peculation, was no longer a guardian of the feeble, was a bold, impudent aggressor upon the rights of others, an usurper, waxing fat and kicking in its lustihood, and needed to be taken down and driven to short commons" (*L*, IV, 270). And an essay in the Charleston *Mercury* attributed to him commends the work of the secession convention: "Inscribed among the calends of the world—memorable in time to come—the 20th day of December, in the year of our Lord 1860, has become an epoch in the history of the human race. . . . South Carolina has resumed her entire sovereign powers, and, unshackled, has become one of the nations of the earth."[3]

The war absorbed Simms's interest, energy, and emotion; it also increased his despondency and the strain on his constitution, hampered his ability to write, and harmed the sale of his books. Although too old to fight—"I chafe, and roar & rage, but can do nothing"—he threw himself wholeheartedly behind the Confederate cause (*L*, IV, 315). His letters from 1861 and 1862 are filled with plans, sometimes accompanied by diagrams, for firing on the forts in the Charleston harbor,

2. See Wakelyn, *The Politics of a Literary Man*, Chaps. 5–6; Parrington, *The Romantic Revolution in America, 1800–1860*, 136.

3. "The 20th Day of December, in the Year of Our Lord, 1860," Charleston *Mercury*, December 21, 1860. The ascription to Simms is not certain. Wakelyn, *The Politics of a Literary Man*, 241 and 252*n*69, attributes the item to him.

reinforcing defenses with iron, constructing water batteries, and seizing Union vessels in the bay.[4] His son Gilmore fought in the conflict, the progress of which Simms followed with increasing alarm. Hearing at Woodlands the booming of the cannon in Charleston harbor, seventy miles away, he wrote a friend: "[M]y anguish & anxiety are very great, for our poor old city, & our gallant boys—the best blood of the country confronting the vilest scum of Europe & the North. My eldest son, the only one grown, is on the coast, in the cavalry & has been two years; and with every shot that I hear I tremble, and think of him" (*L,* IV, 434).

Given these conditions, it is not surprising that as the war developed Simms's inclination to write declined. During the early years of the conflict, he published poems and strove to republish tales and novelettes "for reading in camp and along the highways"; but accustomed to a broader canvas, he viewed these things as trifling activities (*L,* IV, 420). "I have done little or nothing in literature for two years," he wrote John Reuben Thompson early in 1863, and later that year he remarked to Hayne, "[M]y heart is too full of anxiety to suffer me to write, and though I have a contract for some $200 worth of prose, I find myself unable to divert my thoughts from the crisis in which the country trembles in suspense" (*L,* IV, 421, 436).

Further hindering Simms's ability to write were the problems among his publishers and the loss of his books and manuscripts by fire. In the fall of 1860, J. S. Redfield had failed and the business had been taken over by W. J. Widdleton in conjunction with Duyckinck's brother-in-law Henry Panton. At the time of his failure, Redfield owed Simms about six hundred dollars; but Simms had trouble procuring the money from Widdleton, and much of his correspondence in the final months of the year is taken up with his efforts to secure the copyrights of the novels brought out by Redfield in the Author's Uniform Edition. The war apparently interrupted these negotiations, and in 1862 Simms wrote a friend in Charleston that his copyrights and plates had all been "confiscated and lost—some $25,000—the whole earnings of my life, save my library" (*L,* IV, 399).

The library itself, however, would become the chief casualty of the ordeals by fire Simms would shortly undergo. In 1861 some of his books in Widdleton's possession had been burned, and at the time he

4. See, for example, *L,* IV, 319, 322, 344, 356–60.

had remarked half jestingly: "It seems to be my luck to be always in danger of fire. My plates destroyed by fire in Harper's vaults; my House destroyed by fire; my books in Widdleton's hands by fire; my books (Areytos) in Redfield's hands destroyed by fire. . . . It is certainly very strange that I should be peculiarly subject to these fiery fortunes!" (*L,* IV, 350).[5] Only a year later, he experienced the destructiveness of fire on a larger scale. Early in the morning of March 29, 1862, Woodlands, to which he had been making extensive additions, caught fire and burned, Simms escaping by ladder from an upper window while the floors above were falling in. He estimated his loss in money at about $10,000, and said half of his furniture had been destroyed outright (*L,* IV, 400, 401, 403). As at many points in the past, he felt himself pursued by an angry Fate. But "if the Fate smites, the God strengthens," he declared; and within a few days some of his friends had raised a sum of $3,600 to help him start rebuilding his estate (*L,* IV, 403, 409).

Simms was not to be free of persecution from "fiery fortunes," however, for in 1865 Woodlands burned again, this time because it lay in the path of General Sherman on his march toward Columbia. Simms had accurately predicted Sherman's course through the South, and as northern forces approached he had moved his family to the capital city. He had hoped to return to Woodlands to remove his books and manuscripts, but before he could reach the plantation some stragglers from Sherman's troops had fired the main part of the house and his magnificent library of more than ten thousand volumes was destroyed. "My books! My books!" he lamented. "My heart is ready to break when I think of them" (*L,* IV, 501).[6]

Simms was in Columbia when Sherman's forces swept through it, and with great fury he described the devastation in a series of essays for the Columbia *Phoenix* that he subsequently revised and brought out as a book, *Sack and Destruction of the City of Columbia, S.C.* (1865). He also described the destruction of the city and surrounding area in vivid letters to the wartime governor Andrew Magrath and to Benjamin Franklin Perry, later to be provisional governor during

5. Simms is here referring to the burning of his house in Charleston in 1860. The fire at Harper's had occurred in 1853 (see *L,* IV, 219*n*99, 350*n*86).

6. The discrepancies in Simms's estimates of the number of books in his library probably occurred because he had been forced to sell about a thousand volumes from his collection before it burned.

Reconstruction. For Magrath he chronicled Sherman's progress through the state and the path of destruction left in his wake.[7] Vehicles, dwellings, and clothing were wantonly destroyed, he observed; "[e]very [mou]thful of provisions, of every sort, was stolen or destroyed. [The] people have been living since, [u]pon the offal left by [the men] in their camps, or by their horses where they fed. For [wee]ks after their departure the wretched inhabitants thus [plu]ndered might be seen daily—old men & women & children—[pa]infully gleaning from the closely-scraped earth, the mis[erable] refuse of gr[a]in in which the improvidence of the robbers had [let] waste upon the g[round]" (*L*, IV, 495–96). Even more searing are his observations to Perry. "The incendiary & Robber have done their work," he remarked. "Half of the population, male & female, have been robbed of all the clothes they had, save those they wore, and of these many have had overcoat, hat & shoes taken from them. Watches & purses were appropriated at every corner; and the amount of treasure & wealth, in cloth, gold, silver & other booty borne away by the Huns & Vandals of the Century, is incomputable" (*L*, IV, 485–86).

In the famine that followed the war, Simms later wrote from Charleston to a friend, thousands of people were having to sell family heirlooms to procure food. And thousands, he continued, with large dependent families were "going from house to house incessantly seeking any & every sort of employment, simply to secure food, and the terrors of famine threaten a vast multitude" (*L*, V, 18). Conditions in the countryside were no better; "[i]n a precinct of fifty miles in this district," he informed the Charleston *Mercury* from Barnwell, "there is not more than one planter in fifty who has corn enough to last him a single month; not more than one in two hundred who has enough for two months; none that have any that can last three months; and of these there is hardly more than five in the hundred who will be able to supply themselves with provisions of any sort" (*L*, V, 50–51). Despite his own privations, Simms generously did what he could to ease the trials of his countrymen. He procured money and work for Henry Timrod, who he said was "dying by inches" in Columbia, distributed funds collected by New Yorkers for the people of the South, gathered other funds for the same purpose from his brother Masons in New

7. Magrath had requested this report from Simms. Brackets in the passage quoted in the text are supplied by the editors of Simms's letters, who remark that the manuscript of this document is torn and defaced.

York, and tried his best to help the correspondents who begged him to aid in publishing their books.[8]

Simms himself was left nearly destitute by the war, "wrecked," as he said, "upon a lea shore" (*L,* V, 180). He wrote Lawson that Sherman's army had destroyed his dwelling, stables, and barns at Woodlands, that his mules, horses, and cattle had been driven off or taken away, and that he had not even enough money to telegraph his northern friends about his plight (*L,* IV, 498–99). "Of all that I had," he wrote Duyckinck, "slaves, stocks, furniture, books, pictures, horses, mules, carriages &c.—a property which was worth $150,000 in gold—I have nothing left me but my Lands" (*L,* IV, 577). His family was scattered, sleeping in garrets about Columbia. In Charleston, he himself slept "in a chamber which has been shattered by shells, with orifices in the walls through which the winds stream & the rains beat"; he used a picture sent by a friend to help cover the bombshell holes still in the walls (*L,* IV, 529, V, 32). "Verily," he remarked to Duyckinck, "that I can write or think at all, is wonderful" (*L,* IV, 515).

Although as the editors of his letters observe, Simms was "broken in health and sick at heart" at the end of the war, he gamely began to wrest what livelihood he could from literature.[9] From New York, where he was seeking work, he wrote his children, "Your father will divide himself among you, & so long as his poor brains can be turned to profit, he will use them for your good" (*L,* IV, 601). His need for money forced him to sell his collection of Revolutionary War manuscripts, which he had been collecting for thirty years and had saved in 1865 when the rest of his library burned. It also forced him, though briefly, into editorial work for two South Carolina newspapers, the Columbia *Phoenix* and the Charleston *Daily South Carolinian,* and spurred him to grind out miscellaneous pieces for southern periodicals, which, as in the past, after seeking his contributions often failed to pay him.[10] He engaged in various other literary chores, editing *War*

8. *L,* V, 32, 40, IV, 522, 524; Trent, *William Gilmore Simms,* 294.

9. Oliphant and Eaves (eds.), Introduction to *L,* VI, xxix.

10. For Simms's work on the former paper, see James E. Kibler, Jr., "Simms' Editorship of the Columbia *Phoenix* of 1865," in James B. Meriwether (ed.), *South Carolina Journals and Journalists* (Spartanburg, S.C., 1975), 61–75. The editors of Simms's letters say he was associate editor, with Henry Timrod, of the *Daily South Carolinian* (*L,* IV, 527*n*147). On the pieces for periodicals, see *L,* V, 109–11, 113–14, 153, VI, 258–63. The periodicals were *Southern Society, Southern Opinion,* and the *Southern Home Journal* (*L,* V, 153*n*158).

Poetry of the South (1866) and serializing *Joscelyn* in the *Old Guard* during 1867. Meanwhile he continued to strive to recoup his fortunes, at least in part, by writing tales and romances. "[W]orks of fiction, alone, in the present desultory & superficial condition of the public mind . . . are the only books likely to be bought & to interest," he observed; and at various points in the decade he planned volumes on Cadillac, on Texas and Mexico, and on "the Old French Wars, including Washington's early career & Braddocks [*sic*] defeat" (*L,* V, 141, 43, 205, 171). Perhaps recalling his success with the subject of piracy in *The Cassique of Kiawah,* he wrote over 170 pages of a pirate romance still in manuscript, "The Brothers of the Coast," and as late as 1868 he was still trying to reprint some refurbished short stories that he said he had furnished "to annuals & periodicals some 20 to 30 years ago."[11]

As before, he looked to northern publishing centers for succor. He considered—as he had in what must have seemed, by contrast, the halcyon 1840s—a remove to New York, "where in some obscure chamber," he believed, "I can live at moderate cost, & have the press at my command" (*L,* IV, 537). Although he did not make this move, he went north each summer between 1865 and 1870 to renew literary associations, collect on publishing debts, and seek new contracts. In New York, while visiting close friends like Lawson, he wrangled with Widdleton over back payments due him and over the ownership of his stereotype plates; and he tried to make arrangements for work at Woodlands during the winters (*L,* V, 93–94, IV, 577). Although he complained he was not good at serial writing, he acknowledged that it compensated better than any other kind (*L,* V, 191). Therefore, "[i]n the extremity of . . . need," he "took contracts in N.Y. in the autumn of 1868 for no less than three romances, all to be worked, at the same time" (*L,* V, 282).[12] And with this overwhelming load of work, his final tribulations—and also his final use of the South as a major subject in his fiction—began.

For two of the romances, *The Cub of the Panther* and *Voltmeier,* and also for two fine tall tales, "How Sharp Snaffles Got His Capital

11. *L,* IV, 539, V, 157. "The Brothers of the Coast" is in the Charles Carroll Simms Collection at the Caroliniana Library, University of South Carolina.

12. The three romances for which Simms received contracts were *The Cub of the Panther, Voltmeier,* and a volume planned but never completed on the Old French Wars and Braddock's defeat (*L,* V, 171*n*194).

and Wife" and "Bald-Head Bill Bauldy," Simms turned to the Appalachian mountain region, the third great area of the South and the only one that he had not yet treated extensively in imaginative writing, for material. In so doing, he drew on notes and memories of his several visits to western North and South Carolina in the 1840s, when, forced away from long fiction, he was consciously searching for experiences from which to make "a book descriptive of Carolina—its history, manners of its people, scenery &c" (*L,* II, 330). In 1842, near the time he made his last journey to the Old Southwest, he had taken a five weeks' tour on horseback of North Carolina in the vicinity of Flat Rock, where he had gone for his wife's health. In the summer of 1849, he had revisited this region on the way to Warm Springs, Georgia, and the mountains of that state, outlining the trip in a letter to Beverley Tucker and also in the *Southern Quarterly Review* essay "Summer Travel in the South," where he mentions the route he had taken from Asheville to Warm Springs and describes the French Broad River, which with its "curling, flashing, white billows" would also work its way into *Voltmeier.*[13] In the summer of 1855, he had made a fairly elaborate expedition into the South Carolina mountain region, where he delivered lectures and visited a Revolutionary War battle site (*L,* III, 390–403). Each of these journeys had increased his knowledge of mountain people and scenery, but the trip that mattered most for his imaginative writing was his tour of western North Carolina in the early fall of 1847 with friends and professional hunters.[14]

The most important records of this trip survive in the notes Simms made in a journal that he later used as the basis for a substantial body of writing—the essay on summer travel, the tall tales and romances written after the Civil War, and the two lectures on the Appalachian Mountains that he had intended to deliver on the 1856 speaking tour. Supplementing the information in these pieces are letters he wrote near the time of the trip that describe its two stages—the first, with Chevillette and children, to Spartanburg, South Carolina, and the nearby

13. *L,* II, 544–45; [Simms], "Summer Travel in the South," 47.

14. Trent, *William Gilmore Simms,* 306, alleges that Simms made yet another trip to the mountains in the early fall of 1867; but from the details he describes it seems likely that he was confused about the date and had been reading either the manuscript of the journal Simms kept on the 1847 trip or some undated correspondence deriving from the trip. (He says, for instance, that Simms is found "among his favorite North Carolina mountains, shooting deer, listening to hunters' yarns, making notes on the proper construction of bear-traps.")

fashionable watering place of Glenn Springs; the second a tour of about two weeks' duration in what was, Simms wrote Lawson, "the very realm of wolf & panther" (*L*, II, 356). After leaving his family in Spartanburg, he visited his wife's relative Columbus Mills, who lived near Mount Tryon, sketched the mountain (in drawings still extant) from Mills's west porch, and on Sunday, September 26, ascended it, describing his view of "the several successive tiers distinguished as the Glassy, the Hogback, Rocky Spur, Brushy, Muldrow or Hogback, and Table Mountain."[15] Two days later, he, Mills, and a group of about six persons left for the Balsam mountain range in North Carolina. "Our point of destination," he remarked in his journal, "was about 60 or 70 miles, through a country comparative destitute—a country of wilderness, in which save at two or three isolated points, we could hope to find no settlements" (111). By the third day, the party was in camp at the foot of the Balsams.

Twentieth-century studies of the mountain region show that the area, at the time Simms saw it, formed a retarded inner frontier that in its way was almost as wild and primitive as the turbulent frontier of the Old Southwest. The region had been settled by diverse peoples, the Germans, Scots, and Scotch-Irish, who in the eighteenth century had poured south from Pennsylvania through the Valley of Virginia to establish themselves in the Appalachians, where they built rude cabins and scratched out small farms, and where the harsh terrain forced fundamental economic, social, and psychological adjustments. Its rocky soil, its heavily wooded slopes, and its steep cliffs could not support the large plantations of the coastal area or the sturdy, sizable farms of the Piedmont. It fostered instead a many-faceted economy based on smaller, less prosperous farms, on livestock grazing and herding, and in the most isolated reaches on hunting, that most basic frontier occupation. In the mountains, perhaps even more than in the Gulf South of the pioneer era, social life was rowdy but sporadic; religion emotional, evangelical, expressive; existence in general precarious and rough. The rugged land and the seemingly endless forests forced people to live far apart or in small settlements widely separated by the woods. As a result, "mountain isolation," states a prominent student of the region, became "mental and cultural isolation," seen at its sharpest, perhaps, in the lives of mountain hunters—individuals or

15. Quoted from the transcript of the 1847 journal by Shillingsburg, "An Edition of *Cub of the Panther*," 109, hereafter cited by page number within the text.

groups of families banding together in the ritual of the hunt that was the chief form of community available to them. It was in just such a ritual that Simms participated during his two weeks' visit to the region. For once fairly deep into the mountains, he and his companions joined several noted hunters who serve as models for characters in Simms's late fiction—Jim Fisher, prototype of the "Big Lie" in "Sharp Snaffles" and "Bill Bauldy"; the "strange hunter, Green" (or Greene), whose exploits form the basis for several scenes in *The Cub of the Panther;* Bill and Nathan Langford of that novel; and other figures.[16]

Pictures of the hunting life abound in Simms's journal, where he describes in detail the hunters, dogs, and hunting stories, the killing, butchering, and cooking of game, and the marvelous mountain scenery. The notebook constitutes vital evidence for the biographical material that lies behind Simms's late works, and it therefore warrants some examination; with its hurried entries and its uneven grammar and spelling it shows, more directly than the published works based on it, his absorption in the rude mountain life and his varied responses to the scenes he had witnessed. He notes, for example, "Camping—how practised—the sluggishness of hunters except when on the scent—their temperance the result of their lives—the loneliness of their lives—the effect of the solitude of these mounains [*sic*] upon the moral nature of the man" (112). He remarks "the prettiness of the younger women—the muscular activity of the men," comments on the generally low status of pioneer women, and in fairly long entries describes the hunt, the kill, and the process of curing and cooking meat (112, 117). He shows the hunters as they "dart upon the deer," slash his throat, disembowel him "on the spot where he is slain," and throw his entrails to the greedy dogs that stand waiting to devour them (115). In passages that he later incorporated nearly verbatim into "Sharp Snaffles," he observes that the deer "once slain is soon upon the fire. . . . Great collops hiss in the frying pan, and redden richly upon the coals. Other portions are stewed, and make a delightful dish. The

16. Vance, *Human Geography of the South,* Chaps. 1–4; Rupert B. Vance, "Social Change in the Southern Appalachians," Joseph H. Fichter and George L. Maddox, "Religion in the South, Old and New," and Edgar T. Thompson, "The South in Old and New Contexts," in John C. McKinney and Edgar T. Thompson (eds.), *The South in Continuity and Change* (Durham, N.C., 1965), [404]–17, [359]–83, [451]–80, respectively; Holman, *Three Modes,* Chap. 4; Shillingsburg, "An Edition of *Cub of the Panther,*" 111, 6–7. The quotation about mountain isolation is from Vance, "Social Change in the Southern Appalachians," 410.

head including the brains, is put upon a flat rock in place of gridiron & then baked befor [*sic*] the fire. . . . This part of the deer is greatly esteemed by the hunters" (116).[17] He commends the self-sufficiency of the mountaineers in repairing shoes, rifles, and breeches and praises their ingenuity in curing and tanning hides: "The skin of the young fawn wraps up the rasor [*sic*] or things of equal delicacy, or forms a fitting present for the forest damsel, with the velvet like fur left upon it" (116). And, in a short entry that shows his contact with the kinds of backwoods boasting he already knew about from southern humor, he notes, "Hunter's [*sic*] bragging, about horse, dog & rifle—what they have done, what they will do & what nobody else has done or can do" (112).

Other sections of the journal reveal Simms recording anecdotes, often with a comic slant, that he hoped to weave into his fiction. Of Jim Fisher, a famous hunter nearly seventy years old, he remarks: "Rem'ber Fisher's Indian story—the scare of the Indian—his own scare at the visit of T—their dialogue—they conduct him to their retreat on Hogback—on the Canebrake Fork of Toxaway. They offer him a pipe, by the Squaw. He declines it saying that he does not smoke. Then she cooks venison. Fisher changes of opinion as to Indian cleanliness" (123). Another entry recounts Fisher's conversation with an Indian and Simms's amused observation:

> "Oh, Sio Sinola"—["]Good morning, Sir."
>
> ---
>
> "And I see you too. D——m you!" was the answer of Fisher, to whom Cherokee was only a living language while it seemed to resemble his own. (122–23)

Further entries reflect Simms's interest, always active, in dialect and humor. He muses, for example: "Do not forget the encounter of JFi. with a Bear, when his daughter accompanied him & was sent back to bring assistance. The girl but 12 years old, showed no alarm, but followed Fisher where he shot the beast remarking—'Why daddy, he

17. See [William Gilmore Simms], "How Sharp Snaffles Got His Capital and Wife," in *Stories and Tales*, ed. John C. Guilds, with Introductions and Explanatory Notes by John C. Guilds, texts established by John C. Guilds (Columbia, S.C., 1974), 422–23, vol. V of Guilds (ed.), *The Writings of William Gilmore Simms: Centennial Edition*. Further references to this work are to this edition, cited by page number within the text. This story had originally appeared in *Harper's New Monthly Magazine*, XLI (October, 1870), 667–87.

climbs tree jest like a frog'" (124). He observes that one of the hunters "traded in the meat that yet ran in the woods," making contracts for venison hams and hides that still belonged to living animals. And hunter Bill Langford, he notes, "was accompanied by a little Spanish cur which it would be easy to mistake for a dwarf raccoon. I verily bilieve [*sic*] that most of the other dogs regarded him as such, in very imperfect disguise of a dog. Nothing but the presence of his master . . . secured their tolerance of his pretensions" (114).

Still other entries indicate Simms's interest in minute aspects of the trip that contributed to the copious details of his late fiction based on it. There are notes, for example, on "[t]he habits of the Bear, the deer & the panther, Bees, Hornets, Ants, Honey &c. How the bear gathers chesnuts [*sic*]. How he tramples the ground, tearing up decayed trees & the loose debris of the rocks—His fights, with the panther, with man,—&c" (113). A brief note describing the superstitions concerning a "spirit deer" may have reinforced the folk material about the indestructible buck that went into *Paddy McGann* (112). Longer entries show the interest of Simms-as-author in narrated material—in the way a tale is told, in the character and speech of the teller, and in the potential usefulness of this material to the professional writer. Scattered throughout the journal are Simms's notes to himself to remember certain episodes for later use: "remember anecdote" of Fisher's rifle; "[r]emember his stories of the sagacity and courage of Wonder," his hunting dog (122, 119). Such references recall Simms's claim to Lawson at the outset of his trip that he would "make a book of it" and his humorous observation, in lines that he paraphrased from Robert Burns's poem "On the Late Captain Grose's Peregrinations Thro' Scotland," "A chiel's among '*em* taking notes, / & i' faith, he'll prent 'em!" (*L*, II, 350).

With its hastily formed sentences and its miscellaneous assortment of notes and sketches, the mountain journal reflects a happy, carefree time in Simms's life on which, in sadder times, he would draw for his writing. It shows his instinctive response to the kind of life that he saw as well as his method of collecting and recording material; together with the works based on it, the notebook sheds light on his creative processes by suggesting how his observations cooperated with his awareness of literary elements, particularly in southern humor, to nourish his art. It reveals a fuller biographical record and a more complete correspondence between his life and work than the border and

Revolutionary War books, and in this and other ways it is therefore an extremely useful document for a study of the connections between the literary and the cultural elements in his writing.

At the same time, however, the journal's fairly narrow range and its brevity suggest the limitations of Simms's trip to the southern Appalachian region as a basis for fiction of wide scope or reference beyond the level of individual experience. The events it records, though new for him, were not as rich or diverse as those involved in the lifetime of work he had put into his collection of manuscript material about the Revolution, which reflected his continuing immersion in low-country South Carolina culture. Nor did they touch his life so centrally as did his trips to the Old Southwest, where he had developed both personal and social ties that enriched his response to the region. His early experiences in the low country and the Gulf South had connected important aspects of his personal knowledge to larger areas of southern culture that were part of major historical processes—the Revolution to the South's establishment of its independence within the greater framework of American independence, the trips to the Old Southwest to the settlement patterns of the region, involving the issue of the frontier and westward expansion that is central to America's historical development. Although his trip to the mountains also exposed him to an important part of southern culture, it was one that had ultimately less pertinence for southern social development than did his earlier pursuits. It was an experience, moreover, that was relatively circumscribed and short in duration when compared to his persistent interest in the Revolution and the Old Southwest.

In several ways, these facts affect the nature of Simms's late fiction and influence its direction and emphases. The lack of strong cultural imperatives behind his work may explain in part why he did not think of this fiction in terms of a single genre but instead cast it in a variety of literary forms. It may also explain why, in the absence of social elements that contributed to romance, he experimented fairly freely in his late work with realism and with the humor of the plain folk that is associated with that mode. More important, perhaps, the material from the journey suggests why *The Cub of the Panther* and *Voltmeier,* the two works that have the clearest affinities with Simms's earlier literary productions, are not romances of his usual sort. The material the journey gave him did not give rise to romance as he conceived it: the material furnished no real dialectic, no example of a central, important conflict that reflected a culture's projection of notions about good and evil onto events whose outcome had affected its development. There is thus little need in his mountain fiction for an explicit historical dimension or for a framing action that gives large social issues a literary shape.

But if Simms's experience in the mountains was not rooted in the polite southern culture whose official literary instrument was the romance, it was rooted in an important part of southern life that revived his interest in American pioneer experience. And if it did not connect with romance in the manner of his journeys to the Gulf South, it did connect, in a direct, immediate way, with the kind of material that was even then inspiring southern backwoods humor. During the period of his Appalachian travels, his exposure to current literature and his real-life observation coincided. At the very time that he was reading and reviewing the humorists for southern magazines, his trip brought him into contact with the sort of people and happenings they wrote about: men ignorant of polished society, engaged in daily struggles with nature for their livelihood that involved fundamental backwoods routines—the hunting, slaughtering, cooking, camping, and story telling that constitute a ritual of community extremely important to southern culture in all its phases, but especially, perhaps, to the life of the nineteenth-century frontier South. Although these experiences are recorded in formal southern literature, they have little to do with its structure or moral slant; but they do affect that significant branch of antebellum writing that draws on yet diverges from the polite tradition—the sporting and hunting yarns and the humorous backwoods stories that flourished in the hands of the humorists and eventually enriched the writing of Twain and Faulkner. Such yarns accord with the strain in Simms's character inherited from his father—a strain hearty, earthy, masculine, and perhaps a little crude, a strain that indicates a man who relished male society and who was, in Trent's euphemistic phrases, "fond of the story that is told to men only."[18] Itself part of southern character, this element in Simms's nature had impelled him toward southern humor at a time when that humor was firmly establishing itself in the popular favor he would always crave for his writing. As a result, such humor bulks larger in the fiction of his final phase than in any other group of his works.

18. Trent, *William Gilmore Simms*, 326; see also C. Hugh Holman, Review of *The Letters of William Gilmore Simms*, in *Journal of Southern History*, XIX (February, 1953), 86.

Simms began the first of his works based on his Appalachian travels, *Voltmeier, or The Mountain Men,* in January, 1868, as a serial for the *Southern Home Journal,* whose editors had agreed to pay him six hundred dollars for it (*L,* V, 106). He labored on it during the spring and early summer, only to have the publishers void the contract when he asked for pay; and in July he told Duyckinck he was nearly penniless (*L,* V, 153). Fortunately, however, he was able to place the serial in a new periodical, the *Illuminated Western World,* a New York weekly run by a reliable businessman, Orville James Victor. Simms worked diligently on *Voltmeier* during the fall and winter of 1868, writing a friend in December: "Here for six weeks have I been toiling religiously day by day, and in that time have written nearly a thousand pages MS. such as this, not including a vast deal of correspondence, &c. I have left the plantation, but once during the six weeks that I have been at home" (*L,* V, 177). The first installment of the serial appeared in Victor's journal on March 6, 1869; the last, in the issue for August 28.[19]

Meanwhile, Simms may have begun to compose "Sharp Snaffles" and "Bill Bauldy," the two tall tales deriving from his mountain trip, and he was also hard at work on *The Cub of the Panther* for the *Old Guard,* the magazine that had serialized *Joscelyn* in 1867.[20] Although the enormous load of writing contributed to his growing physical distress, *The Cub of the Panther* on the whole seems to have given him less trouble than the lengthier and more ambitious *Voltmeier.* By late December, 1868, while finishing the longer work he had also written "103 MS. pages," comprising four chapters, of the shorter one, whose first installment appeared in the *Old Guard* in January, 1869 (its last one was published in December of that year [*L,* V, 188]). Simms apparently hoped to finish *The Cub of the Panther* during February; but in a grim forecast of things to come, he told his oldest daughter Augusta that "incessant *mental* labour at the desk, resulted at last in my

19. "Textual Apparatus," in [William Gilmore Simms], *Voltmeier, or The Mountain Men,* with Introduction and Explanatory Notes by Donald Davidson and Mary C. Simms Oliphant, text established by James B. Meriwether (Columbia, S.C., 1969), 446, vol. I of John C. Guilds (ed.), *The Writings of William Gilmore Simms: Centennial Edition.* Quotations from the body of the novel are hereafter cited by page number within the text. The editors of the book conjecture that Simms coined the name Voltmeier by combining a German suffix with the name of an Italian physicist, Alessandro Volta (xxi). Simms may also have recalled the name of the character Wolfert Valtmayer in Charles Fenno Hoffman's novel *Greyslaer: A Romance of the Mohawk* (New York, 1840), a book to which he alludes in *L,* I, 229.

20. Guilds, in [Simms], *Stories and Tales,* 799–80, 807–10, suggests several possible dates of composition between 1865 and 1870 for the two stories.

temporary overthrow," and in March he informed Hayne he was still at work upon the novelette (*L,* V, 211, 214). He sent off 150 pages of manuscript in April, however, and by mid-May had finished the work (*L,* V, 217, 221). But his efforts to "keep pace with & in advance of the Printers" had sad results (*L,* V, 185). In December, 1869, he wrote Hayne, "For . . . the last six months, I have been literally *hors de combat,* from overwork of the brain—brain sweat . . . and no body sweat—no physical exercise." Then, after explaining his contracts for simultaneous work on three novels, he continued:

> I got advances of money on each of these books, and the sense of obligation pressing upon me, I went rigidly to work, concentrating myself at the desk from 20th. Oct. 1868 to the 1st. July 1869.—nearly 9 months, without walking a mile in a week, riding but twice and absent from work but half a day on each of these occasions. The consequence was that I finished two of the books & broke down on the third, having written during that period some 3000 pages of the measure of these which I now write to you. . . . I have been forbidden the studio, & do little beyond my correspondence which, at all times has been very exacting. (*L,* V, 282)

Simms's mountain fiction hence was written in the hardest period of his life, and the diverse material that characterizes *The Cub of the Panther* and *Voltmeier,* their scrappiness of structure, and their general unevenness of texture suggest, if indirectly, the multiple strains under which he labored. Yet, as in the case of his earliest fiction, this same unevenness shows with special clarity the various elements, biographical and cultural, that lie behind his writing. Notable in the works are vivid descriptions of mountain scenery and sprightly episodes of backwoods humor. In *Voltmeier,* the only full-length novel of the lot, he subordinates the love story of his usual long fiction to the tale of a tormented criminal pursued by a ruffian who is both frontier swindler and naïve yokel; in *The Cub of the Panther,* he enlivens the mountain legend that forms the basis of his central story with the tirades of a humorous rural woman; and in "Sharp Snaffles" and "Bill Bauldy," he displays his fully matured talent for backwoods comedy through two tall tales in which he grafts his experiences with the mountaineers on forms and structures that had by that time become standard elements of southern humor.

Voltmeier, the most conventional of the several narratives, reveals, in addition, Simms's lifelong interest in German literature and culture and his fascination with the psychology of crime. For the title figure, as the editors of the novel remark, he finally develops the heroic and tragic dimensions of the man with an advanced intellectual education who lacks a correspondingly thorough moral education. This type had interested Simms from his earliest novels, as characters like Guy Rivers and Clement Foster reveal; but such figures had heretofore served as the villains of his works, whereas Voltmeier despite his crimes is ultimately a sympathetic, charming person. Simms could probably not have effected such a transformation in this character type had it not been for the influence of German literature, which had attracted him from the 1820s on. He had learned some German at the College of Charleston and had been a prominent figure in the group of Charleston friends who had studied German language and literature with Augustus Sachtleben, a native of Germany and a professor at the University of South Carolina.[21] In the *Southern Literary Gazette* during the period of his editorship, Simms had printed an essay on German literature that discusses Albrecht von Haller, Friedrich Klopstock, and Gotthold Ephraim Lessing, and he had commended Goethe's work in pieces for the *Southern and Western* and the *Southern Quarterly Review*.[22] He had also, in such youthful stories as "Sweet William" and "The Spirit Bridegroom," accentuated the bizarre and irrational effects that he like his countrymen associated with Germany.[23] Among his earlier works that are particularly relevant for *Voltmeier* is the tale "Carl Werner," in which an essentially good character is subjected to evil influences through demonic visions of a dead friend.

The German influence on *Voltmeier* appears in scenes where Fergus Wallace and Mignon Voltmeier, the young hero and heroine of the novel, study the language or read Schiller together; in the friendship of

21. Davidson and Oliphant, Introduction to Simms, *Voltmeier,* xv, xxii; *L,* V, 326, III, 148*n*211.

22. [William Gilmore Simms], "German Literature," *Southern Literary Gazette,* n.s., I (September 15, 1829), 197–201; [Simms], "Editorial Bureau—Correspondence Between Schiller and Goethe," *Southern and Western,* I (June, 1845), 432–33; [Simms], "Editorial Bureau—Review of *Goethe's Essays on Art,*" in *Southern and Western,* II (December, 1845), 423–25; [Simms], Review of rev. ed. of *Wilhelm Meister,* in *Southern Quarterly Review,* XX [n.s., IV] (July, 1851), 248. J. Wesley Thomas, in "The German Sources of William Gilmore Simms," in Philip Allison Shelley (ed.), with Arthur O. Lewis, Jr., and William W. Betts, Jr., *Anglo-German and American-German Crosscurrents* (Chapel Hill, 1957), I, 150*n*7, attributes the first essay to Simms.

23. Thomas, "The German Sources of William Gilmore Simms," in *Anglo-German and American-German Crosscurrents,* I, 129. The stories, which had appeared in other versions in periodicals during the 1830s, were published in the 1837 *Martin Faber* and *The Book of My Lady,* respectively.

Leonard Voltmeier with Goethe; in the lyrics, generally from *Faust*, that Voltmeier quotes or paraphrases; and in the idealized German landscape to which he hopes to escape.[24] But it is evident most of all in his passionate, imaginative nature; and it is even responsible, in a curious way, for some of the melodrama of the volume. For in depicting Voltmeier at his most deranged, Simms imitates the "Teutonic extravagance" of German literature that he had noted in the advertisement to the "Tales and Sketches" section of the 1837 *Martin Faber*. His procedure issues in passages like the following, where Voltmeier howls to the shadowy forms of the Fates or Furies that he thinks surround him: "Gather around me as ye will, ye scowling aspects of the grave; I defy ye! Ye mock, and I howl back your mockeries with scorn! . . . Back to your chaotic empire, and know that, even though I may hold your prophecy to be true, ye shake no sinew of this body; ye enfeeble no power in this soul!" (341–42).

For other aspects of the novel, Simms draws upon specific details of his 1847 trip. The principal story line of the book derives, at some distance, from the activities of Allen Twitty, a member of an important western North Carolina family who about 1805, along with some of his henchmen, had been arrested for counterfeiting. Tales of Twitty, the editors of *Voltmeier* conjecture, formed a frequent topic among Simms's hunting companions; but though this may be so, he did not bother to record such stories at much length in his journal.[25] He notes merely: "Friday mg. Off for Hickory Nut Gap—Pass Green River and Broad river—residence of Allen Twitty, the famous counterfieter [*sic*]—his farm—his cave—& anecdotes of his career—his character—his *virtues*" (128–29). The influence of Simms's 1847 trip shows up also in the movement of young Fergus Wallace, like Simms before him, from Spartanburg into the mountains and in Simms's often eloquent descriptions of mountain scenery.

In an action unusual in Simms's long fiction, the hero-villain Leonard Voltmeier displaces the hero Fergus as the major center of interest and the means by which much of the action is shown. The son of a German immigrant, Voltmeier had once loved Fergus' mother; but after losing her to his half-brother, Fergus' father, he had kept them from property that was rightly theirs and thus in effect had caused their lifelong pov-

24. Davidson and Oliphant, Introduction to Simms, *Voltmeier*, xxi.
25. *Ibid.*, xx.

erty. When she is dying, Fergus' mother writes Voltmeier a letter that she gives to her son. Armed with it, Fergus seeks his uncle in the mountains—where the wealthy, respected planter, under the alias "Bierstadt," runs a secret counterfeiting operation with the help of half-criminal rustics like Mother Moggs, Brown Peters, Swipes, and Richard Gorham, who do not know his real identity. Swipes wounds Fergus; but when Voltmeier learns his identity, with the aid of friends he nurses his nephew back to health, establishes him as a lawyer, and eventually marries him to his cousin Mignon, thus uniting the severed branches of the family and partially atoning for the wrongs to Fergus' parents.

The villain Gorham, however, seeking to defeat Voltmeier, implicates Fergus in the counterfeiting operations, which have become a community scandal. Fergus is arrested, but Voltmeier secures his release and sends him with Mignon to Germany, where he hopes to join them. Racked by guilt for his crimes and in physical pain, he takes doses of opium that derange him. In an unsettled state, he flees to the mountains, where Gorham tracks him and where, after a wild fight, they plunge to their deaths in the thrashing, foaming French Broad River that forms a memorable part of the novel's setting.

With his customary enthusiasm for his newly completed projects, Simms called *Voltmeier* "one of the most remarkable books I have ever written" and described it as "an art-romance—a something which passes above the sensational, into the psychological & largely imaginative; subordinating and using the passions without suffering their domination" (*L,* V, 181, 197). His comments point to the combination of literary elements that is one of the striking features of the book. He merges the romance with the psychological novel, which in his hands had usually centered on characters with tormented consciences who had committed great crimes; and as a result he is able to make transformations in the romance mode that connect it with fiction of a different type.

For the most part these transformations arise from Simms's handling of his dialectic base. In his novels about the low country and his Border Romances, the conflict that serves as the source of the dialectic arises from external circumstances and filters down to the personal level from the historical or public sphere. In *Voltmeier,* however, the source of the conflict is internal and psychological, springing from the main character's dual nature, which generates both the chief good and the major evil in the book. "[E]levated by education, by fine tastes, the love of art, a naturally brave and beautiful intellect," Voltmeier is yet, as Simms says, "morally and mentally corrupt"; and his divided character is reflected in his two lives, the two plots that flow from them, and the two domains he inhabits (414). As Voltmeier, he is youthful, lithe, and handsomely dressed, the embodiment of "a brave soul and a perfect manhood" and the chief source of humane action in the novel (355). As Bierstadt, however, he is old, toothless, and roughly dressed, the leader of the counterfeiting gang and the principal source of criminal activity in the mountains. In the first of several passages connecting character to setting, Simms suggests that the split in Voltmeier's character is traceable to the mountain environment and the secret passions it encourages:

> Far away, along the line of the great hills, from Virginia to Georgia, stretch fastnesses as wild, savage and unknown as when, two hundred years ago, the feet of the Cherokee trod them; and, to-day, amid those retreats, dwell men as wild and rude as if the signs and sounds of civilization were forever banished. In some sequestered spot one bold spirit would settle, and, in time, become a kind of baron among the rough people, who dispensed his bounty freely, and in return received such homage as at once assured his safety and his prosperity; or, if he were disposed to act the part of leader or chief of the bad characters whose haunts were among the hills, he could maintain his two-fold character of planter and outlaw, unmolested and unwatched. (25)

As in all Simms's major romances, the natural setting functions to link different sections of the narrative; but in this last work of long fiction it does so in a particularly noteworthy way. Throughout the novel, the main settings, Voltmeier's home Keovala and his mountain lairs, connect the two sides of his nature in a paradigm that indicates the psychic origins of his conflict. Keovala is a mountain paradise, a "domain of wealth and peace and beauty" and a sunlit world of reason, order, and dignity that deliberately suggests the public, respectable side of Voltmeier's personality (259). His Appalachian hideouts, however, just as clearly suggest the other side, the concealed urges and lawless strivings of the master criminal. The stone hovel called the Wolf-Den, where witchlike Mother Moggs keeps house for the other thugs, nestles in "a deep hollow of the hills, hidden from the sun" and seems "only fit for the habitation of that ugly beast from which it took its name" (44). And the cave where the counterfeit money is made is approached by "the thick darkness of the deep gorges" and located directly above the waters that reflect Voltmeier's tumultuous passions—"the great French Broad River . . . which tears open the vast mountains . . . splits wide the unwedgable rock, and, in grand upheavals and terrible convulsions, forces its way, under perpetual struggle . . . roaring and moaning as it goes" (99).

The relationship between wild nature and cultivated estate that Simms sets up in his earlier fiction takes, in *Voltmeier,* a sinister turn that suggests the conjunction of the leading character's two personalities. For just as the dual aspects of his existence merge in the character of Fergus Wallace, wounded by Bierstadt's outlaws and nursed to health by Voltmeier's friends, so elements in the natural setting link Keovala to the cave, thus further and more subtly connecting his two lives. The dualities of his physical and psychic environments are yoked by dark fissures in the mountain approach to Keovala, which momentarily obscure it from view and recall the surroundings of the cave; by the unpleasant valley called the "Shades of Death" that lies behind the estate and leads to the mountains; and finally by the two branches of the French Broad River, which epitomize the bright and the dark of his temperament: "the one beautiful, the other grand and terrible; the one wandering through a fertile, though undulating country" like that near Keovala, "the other tearing its way through the rocks; a river of perpetual strifes and rapids" that courses beneath the counterfeiters' cave (242). Thus the different settings echo and link, if they do not entirely reconcile, the polarities of Voltmeier's nature—his reason and passion, his superego and id, his rational, humane behavior and the intensities of his guilt and rage.

A similar division in character appears in the villain Gorham, the agent of Voltmeier's punishment and the object of his revenge, who is locked with him in a spiraling course of crime. As Simms develops him, Gorham has origins in two different but related character types—the standard villain of romantic melodrama and the ruthless swindler of southern backwoods humor. Simms emphasizes the two sides of Gorham's nature as the needs of his plot require. Gorham as villain is given appropriate attributes—black hair, long black beard, cold, gleaming eyes, and menacing manner; he speaks acceptable English, with few traces of dialect beyond an occasional "I reckon." But Gorham as confidence man is another matter altogether. In this role he assumes two aspects, that of a shuffling, grinning bumpkin apparently too idiotic for his own good, and that of a canny rogue of the Simon Suggs derivation. Trailing his enemy, he breaks into Keovala, finds the wig and false teeth that transform Bierstadt into Voltmeier, and taunts his master with his discovery in a rambling speech couched in deliberately heavy dialect.

> You see . . . I know'd, for a'most two years, an old gentleman named Bierstadt; and I sarved under him in doing a mighty smart chance of business. I was cute enough, and know'd a thing or two, but he know'd a mighty deal more, and he taught me more. Well, when I first know'd him, and for a'most two years after as I told you, he was quite old, and walked old with a great stoop in the back, and his head was bald a'most all over the top, only on the sides he had a little shock of white hairs. And I do believe he hadn't a tooth in his head. . . . Well, one day, or rather one night, I happened to slip into a grand gentleman's grand bedroom . . . and Lord love you, what do you think I found on the table, by the glass—the prettiest set of teeth you ever did see, as much like them you carries in your mouth, now, as one eye is like another; and then, there was the finest head of hair, as much like that you're a-wearing now, as if 'twas the brother twin to it. . . . and I let my "shady-glim" shine for a minute over his face, and what do you think! Why, there was the grand young gentleman, changed all at ons't into the old one; the youngish Col. Voltmeier was the identical "Old Grizzly," as we called him, that I used to know as Mr. Bierstadt! (347–49)

Later in the narrative, Simms draws on humorous tales of horse swaps, particularly one in which Simon Suggs cheats his old father out of a pony, when he has Gorham tell a mountain attorney:

> I was always cute, Lawyer. Fayther did say I should be a lawyer. He said I was a lawyer by natur. He was sharp himself, and he taught us boys the lesson every day. He had a sort of song, that said—
>
> "Jist git what you kin and keep what you git,
> And Dicky you'll be a rich man yit."
>
> And one day—I was only fifteen then—I traded off his own nag, blind of one eye, and mighty weak in t'other, for a pony, and twelve dollars to boot, and borrowed the money from him with my own consent only. Then he said to me:
>
> "You must go, Dicky, go down to New York. Two sharps kain't live well together! Go down among the flats, and carry on business for yourself." So I went, but I had a key of my own for the stable-door, and when the old man got up in the morning, he found I was gone, and the pony too! He wrote me two years after, when he haird whar I was, telling me all about it.

> But, he wan't much vexed . . . for he said, at the eending of his letter—"Go on, Dicky; I see you'll do!"—and hevn't I done? and I ain't done yit! (371–72)

Gorham, the last confidence man in Simms's long fiction, forms an instructive contrast with Jared Bunce, his first one. Jared is a "shadow-skinning" peddler who eventually proves to have the Yankee's proverbially generous nature: he uses his talent for lying and deception in the service of hero Ralph Colleton and thereby helps defeat Guy Rivers in his attempt to have Ralph hanged.[26] Gorham, who like Jared is "jest as cunning a Yankee sarpent as ever skinned his own shadow to git something for the Sunday market," is unlike him a sinister, cruel fellow: using his talent, which is greater than Jared's, for prevarication and deceit, he penetrates the Bierstadt-Voltmeier disguise and finally brings the flawed but noble hero down (92).[27] The characters in *Voltmeier* and the structure of the action in which they are involved reveal the same kind of pessimism about human nature that characterizes *The Cassique of Kiawah*—a pessimism increased by the furnaces of affliction that threatened to consume the unfortunate Simms in the final years of his life.

26. *GR*, II, 100. On the Yankee folk character, see Blair, *Native American Humor*, 17–62.

27. On this element in the Yankee folk character, see Richard M. Dorson, *Jonathan Draws the Long Bow* (Cambridge, Mass., 1946), 78–79.

11
The Final Mountain Fiction

By the time Simms finished *Voltmeier,* he was physically exhausted, but he was also determined to fulfill his publishing contracts; and he swiftly completed the last pieces of major fiction he would produce. The three works he composed after *Voltmeier* are all indebted to his 1847 journey, and all evince his persistent interest in realistic and humorous portrayals of plain mountain people. *The Cub of the Panther* and "Sharp Snaffles," in particular, are based on folk material and oral legend, with the former turning his writing toward the dark side and the latter toward the bright side of folk tradition.[1] *The Cub of the Panther,* though not the most successful of the three works, is in certain ways the most ambitious; and since it shows Simms working, as he insisted, "out of the beaten track," it forms a useful introduction to his final work (*L,* V, 279).

As he indicated in his letters, Simms had drafted the first portion of *The Cub of the Panther* at the same time that he was completing *Voltmeier.* He told Cooke in late December, 1868, "I have sent off to the Old Guard the first Book of a *Romancelet,* to be comprised in half a dozen issues of the magazine"; and as late as the first week in March, 1869, he still believed that the novelette would be completed in seven or eight numbers of the journal (*L,* V, 190, 214). But the narrative as it finally appeared occupied a full twelve issues, running from January through December, 1869.[2] After it was completed, he tried to arrange for its publication in book form, telling Duyckinck it made "a 12 mo.

1. See Richard Dorson, "The Identification of Folklore in American Literature," in "Folklore in Literature: A Symposium," *Journal of American Folklore,* LXX (January–March, 1957), 5.

2. W[illiam] Gilmore Simms, *The Cub of the Panther; A Mountain Legend,* was published in *Old Guard,* VII (January–December, 1869), 11–26, 91–102, 183–200, 255–68, 331–45, 411–23, 491–504, 571–83, 651–65, 731–48, 811–26, 891–99. Page references in the text are to this, the only printed version of the novel.

of about 400 pp., and is, I persuade, quite a readable romance" (*L*, V, 279). The piece, however, has never been reprinted, although editorial apparatus for a textual edition and two chapters excised from the serial version appear in Miriam J. Shillingsburg's dissertation, "An Edition of William Gilmore Simms's *The Cub of the Panther.*"

For the main narrative line of the novel, Simms elaborates upon two folk tales that he had heard on his 1847 travels—a tale of a pregnant girl conveyed through a song called "The Ballad of the Big Belly" and a hair-raising little story about the male panther's craving for women in pregnancy. The ballad, which Simms says in *The Cub of the Panther* is "still sung along the mountains," treats the situation of illicit love and its results (581*n*).

As I walkd [*sic*] out one morning in May
As pretty a little girl as ever I did see,
Came trudging alone by the side of me—
Crying O Lawd! my Big belly!
What will my mammy say to me,
When I go home with a big belly.
    Bis.—Olaw! my big belly!

When my blly [*sic*] lay so low,
The boys they came through rain & snow;
But now my belly is up to my chin
They all pass by & ne'er come in.
    Olaw! my big belly.

I wish my sweet little babe was born,
A-setting on its fathers [*sic*] knee
And I poor girl was dead & gone,
And the green grass growing over me.
    Olaw! my big belly &c.[3]

Simms uses the ballad as one basis in the novel of his story of Rose Carter, a capricious mountain beauty beloved by hunter Mike Baynam. Rose, who rejects him, is tricked by the upcountry aristocrat Edward Fairleigh into a marriage that later turns out to be fraudulent. Following the tradition of his hunting companions, Simms attributes the ballad to Rose, who was said to have sung it during a spell of delirium when she fled from Fairleigh Lodge in the snow; and he quotes a bowdlerized version of the final stanza (581*n*). The germ of the pan-

3. Shillingsburg, "An Edition of *Cub of the Panther,*" 125.

ther story likewise appears in a journal entry in which Simms records "Fisher's story of the Panther, with himself & Green—Green's wife's story of the male panther—The appetite of the beast for women in pregnancy &c—Horrid story of his eating one in this situation & of the discovery of her remains by her husband" (112). In *The Cub of the Panther* he employs this legend as the foundation of the tale of how a panther stalked Rose through the snow and how, as she was dying, she gave birth to a child with a panther-shaped mark upon his forehead that earned him the sobriquet "The Cub of the Panther." This child, whom the mountain people regard with superstitious awe, grows up to be a great hunter. Near the end of the book, in self-defense he kills the unpleasant Edward Fairleigh without realizing that the man is his own father.

It was apparently Simms's idea to join the "Big Belly" ballad and the panther legend, which are not explicitly connected in his journal, in order to fashion the backbone of his plot. It was also his idea to embellish this story deriving from his 1847 trip with pointed criticisms of local aristocrats and hearty portraits of homespun mountain people that look to southern humor and, beyond it, to trends in the local-color writing that was just beginning to appear. His treatment of these characters reveals, as Trent remarks, a new direction in his writing.[4] For the first time in his long fiction, he makes plain people rather than aristocrats the principal actors in the plot and uses them to convey his standards of value. In so doing, he relies heavily on the tradition of horse sense, or mother wit, that had invigorated native writing, particularly with a humorous slant, from Seba Smith and Davy Crockett to William Tappan Thompson.[5] His uneducated, outspoken mountaineers—Mike Baynam, his sister Mattie Fuller, her husband Sam, and Rose's aunt, Betsy (or Betsey) Moore—have sounder values and better judgment than his aristocrats, as indicated early in the novel by Mattie's stern warning to Mike to stay away from the fickle Rose Carter, who, as she says, is "jest as light as air, and as full of change as the clouds" (14).

Mattie fires a fairly effective shot when she tells Rose Carter and her haughty mother Jane that Mike "never yit could meet with a woman

4. Trent, *William Gilmore Simms,* 315, says *The Cub of the Panther* shows Simms had realized the day of the romancer was over and that of the realist dawning.

5. On this tradition in native humor, see Walter Blair, *Horse Sense in American Humor: From Benjamin Franklin to Ogden Nash* (Chicago, 1942), and Merrill Maguire Skaggs, *The Folk of Southern Fiction* (Athens, Ga., 1972), 67–72.

who had the right sense to be company for a raal genooine man!" (189). But it is Betsy Moore, the angular, sensible, tongue-wagging sister of Jane, who is the chief purveyor of homely mother wit in the book. In portraying Betsy, Simms elaborates upon traditions that had long been staples in native humor. For alongside the wilder yarns of hunting and cavorting, that humor had developed a broad domestic streak, as evidenced by the letters of Jack Downing and Major Jones with their emphasis on corn huskings and hearthside rituals. Moreover, there was emerging a convention of talkative women characters heralded, perhaps, by Old Betty Blab in *The Farmer's Almanac* and epitomized near the time of *The Cub of the Panther* by two appealing ladies whose loquacity was part of their charm, Frances Whitcher's Widow Bedott and B. P. Shillaber's Mrs. Partington.[6] Aunt Betsy resembles these figures in her incessant conversation, her shrewd common sense, and her domestic preoccupations. Scolding, gossiping, jogging around the countryside on horseback, she is flavored with the hearth: she is "the housekeeper, who looked to the kitchen, the house cleaning, the meat curing, the sausage making; in brief, to all the drudgery of farm and cottage" (188). She also serves as the foil to her pretentious sister Jane, a fancy, silly woman who deplores Betsy's pungent vernacular: "Earnest is not *airnest,* sister Elizabeth; nor is person *pusson;* nor is just *jist.* You know better, Elizabeth, and should speak properly." When Betsy says, "Oh, git out, sister Carter, with your fine words!" Jane retorts, "*Git* out! How very vulgar" (21).

Simms uses the contrast between the two sisters to furnish comic relief for the melancholy main story and also to stress the superiority of humble Betsy to her supposed betters. Betsy, who calls Edward Fairleigh "that cussed topheavy Cocksparrow," does her best to advance Mike Baynam's courtship of Rose—a suit that if successful might have saved the girl from her unfortunate fate.[7] When Jane berates her sister's

6. Blair, *Native American Humor,* 201, 49; Frances M. Whitcher, *The Widow Bedott Papers* (New York, [1856?]); B[enjamin] P[enhallow] Shillaber, *Life and Sayings of Mrs. Partington, and Others of the Family* (New York, 1854). According to John Q. Reed, *Benjamin Penhallow Shillaber* (New York, 1972), 53, Samuel P. Avery capitalized on Mrs. Partington's popularity by publishing *Mrs. Partington's Carpet-Bag of Fun* (New York, 1854), which contains several Shillaber pieces. Simms reviewed the volume in "Critical Notices," *Southern Quarterly Review,* XXVI [n.s., X] (July, 1854), 262.

7. The quoted passage occurs in one of the two chapters of the novel omitted from the serial version but transcribed in Shillingsburg, "An Edition of *Cub of the Panther,*" [27]–47 (the quotation in the text is from 44). I follow Shillingsburg, p. 56, in regularizing the spelling of Betsey's name to "Betsy."

speech in a particularly unkind manner, Betsy rushes stammering "towards her refined and accomplished sister," with "one fist doubled" and "the other grasping a wet mop, as if it were a spear" (419). Perhaps her best scene, however—and Simms's most earnest evocation of the destiny awaiting her niece—occurs when she employs her solid horse sense in a vain attempt to discourage the follies of her relatives. After Rose has accepted rich gifts from the Widow Fairleigh, Betsy berates Jane:

> I do think, Jane Carter, that you air about the biggest ninny of a woman I ever did see or hear in all my born-days! You're a raal Jackass-woman, with no more sense in your head than a raccoon carries in his tail! . . . And you to think of sich a fool action as to git Rose married to this old woman's gentleman son, as ef she dreams of sich a thing! as ef he dreams of it, and yet that's the game you're a'ter, with your highty-tighty-flighty fool idees! Lawd! Lawd! hev marcy upon us, and the poor woman, and I may say the poor child too! Oh! Rose, my child, I hed my misgivings about you when I seed you bring home them presents. It misliked me mightily to see 'em, and I said to myself, "now," says I, "I hed rether a thousand times she hed boxed the child's ears than put them topazy bobs in 'em, and I hed rether she'd a tried to choke her with her claws, than to put that shiny topazy nickalace about her neck; and I'd rether them topazy brasseylits hed been made of iron than of gold and shiny stones!" . . . Lawd! Lawd! hev' marcy on the pair of fools, and put in and save them if you kin; for they haint, neither on 'em, got the right sense to save themselves! Unless you helps, Lawd o' marcy! salt kain't save 'em! (342–43)

Simms handles with equal dexterity the sections of *The Cub of the Panther* in which he elaborates upon the mountain scenery and hunting episodes recorded in the 1847 journal. The cabin Mike Baynam shares with Mattie and Sam Fuller, which occupies "a peak of the grand Apalachian chain," seems "literally to swing in air." Simms observes that the mountains "constitute the Helvetia of all this region." From them, "you gaze, as it were, over a vast sea. . . . Great gorges and valleys, massed together with deep thickets of laurel, separate the heights, adown whose sides the frequent cataract dashes headlong, like some sheeted ghost, eager to escape the dazzling glances of the sun" (11). Following these passages are unvarnished descriptions of Mike and Sam, the hearty mountain hunters who resemble figures in Simms's journal. Also resembling these figures is the Cub, whose prowess on the trail enables Simms to expand upon the hunting sequences, particularly the bear hunts for which he had stored up abundant information and which he had already worked over for the essay "Summer Travel in the South" and the Appalachian lectures.[8] Late in the novel, Sam Fuller imprudently rushes upon a wounded female bear that suddenly rises up and grabs him; in the fracas, Sam drops his knife and calls the Cub to get it. But the boy, who does not seem to hear him, "clapped the muzzle of his rifle to the very ears of the bear . . . and, steady as if all his nerves were made of steel . . . blew the bullet through the head of the beast." Then, "never stopping to witness the effects of the shot, he threw down the gun, and dropping on his knees, crawled between the legs of the two combatants, grasped the knife which had fallen from Sam's hands, and instead of giving it to the latter, as he desired, drove it himself into the belly of the bear . . . slashing into the very body of the beast, so deeply . . . that [her] bowels rolled out upon him" (735).[9] Shortly after this adventure, the Cub, hunting alone, meets a bear on a narrow ridge, rises up "with shout and shriek, and yell," and forces it over a cliff (740).

The appropriate climax to the Cub's adventures and the conclusion to which the story has been tending occur when the hunters run afoul of Fairleigh and his friends in the woods. Fairleigh, who has become steadily more debauched since Rose's death, drunkenly wounds a buck; the Cub, who does not know of the shot, kills the animal; Fairleigh strikes the Cub with a whip; and the boy stabs him in retaliation. As the others stand amazed, Sam Fuller delivers the opinion of the folk: "The boy is the son of Rose Carter, that perished in the snow, this day seventeen years ago! Ef it ain't a God's judgment, my friend, then I don't believe in any judgments at all!" The final picture of the Cub is of an amoral child of nature, a "wild-eyed and strangely-branded boy" who stands before his dying father and gazes upon him indifferently (898).

Through his depiction in *The Cub of the Panther* of heroic mountaineers and his detailed descriptions of regional scenery, Simms

8. See, for example, [Simms], "Summer Travel in the South," 44, and the second Appalachian lecture in Shillingsburg, "An Edition of *Cub of the Panther,*" 213. See also Shillingsburg's full discussions of Simms's use and reuse of journal material in "From Notes to Novel: Simms's Creative Method," *Southern Literary Journal,* V (Fall, 1972), [89]–107, and "Simms's Last Novel, *The Cub of the Panther,*" *Southern Literary Journal,* XVII (Spring, 1985), [108]–19.

9. The text in the *Old Guard* reads "his bowels," but since the bear is female, "her" is obviously the correct reading. On this point, see the table of textual emendations in Shillingsburg, "An Edition of *Cub of the Panther,*" 86, 735.b.25.

emerges as a pioneer of the local-color movement. Like other local colorists, he elaborates upon the conflict of social groups that is one hallmark of this branch of regional fiction as he demonstrates how the wily mountain people outwit the corrupt and wealthy socialites. And for the heart of his plot he employs a particularly popular subject of the mode, a rural girl's love for a rich outsider who brings her only infamy and suffering. As Charles S. Watson sensibly observes, "At the end of his long career as the dominant literary force in the antebellum South, Simms helped to initiate the first literary movement of the postbellum South, a movement which was to enlist the talents of Mary Noailles Murfree, George Washington Cable, Mark Twain, and Joel Chandler Harris."[10] *The Cub of the Panther* constitutes firm evidence of Simms's talents as a local colorist, and it is, in addition, a vigorous and an interesting document deriving from his travels in the mountain South.

Simms's final use of the Appalachian material occurs in "Sharp Snaffles" and "Bill Bauldy," two fine tall tales that are linked by characters, subjects, and setting. It is impossible to say precisely when he composed these tales, though they apparently date from the last five years of his life. "Sharp Snaffles" was published posthumously in *Harper's New Monthly Magazine* in October, 1870; "Bill Bauldy," its companion piece, remained in manuscript until it was published in the Centennial Simms textual edition in 1974. Together the stories crown his achievement as a backwoods humorist and make him eligible to be studied alongside other masters of the mode.

Several elements in the tales show that by this point in his career Simms felt comfortable enough with the material of southern humor to manipulate freely its stock elements—a campfire setting, a group of yarn-spinning hunters, a frame or box structure, a cultivated "outside" narrator, and a dialect-speaking "inside" narrator who tells the main tale. Particularly noteworthy in both stories is Simms's carefree combination of two major strains in backwoods humor—the homely realism of the domestic strand and the wilder flights of the tall tale. He achieves this blend in "Sharp Snaffles" by yoking the frontier courtship

10. Charles S. Watson, "Simms and the Beginnings of Local Color," *Mississippi Quarterly*, XXXV (Winter, 1981–82), [25]–39; Miriam J. Shillingsburg, "William Gilmore Simms and the Myth of Appalachia," *Appalachian Journal*, VI (Winter, 1979), 111–19; Carvel Emerson Collins, "Nineteenth Century Fiction of the Southern Appalachians," *Bulletin of Bibliography*, XVII (September–December, 1942), 186; Watson, "Simms and the Beginnings of Local Color," 26.

story to the narrative of a fabulous hunt; he creates it in "Bill Bauldy" by grafting an anecdote of the second Seminole war upon a tale of a magical underwater realm peopled by half-human alligators.

The frame of "Sharp Snaffles," the first and better known of the tales, is partly a reconstruction and partly an imaginative expansion of some details from Simms's Appalachian trip. As the story opens, both the amateur and the professional hunters are in camp in the Balsam Mountains after a week on the trail during which they bagged some bucks and a doe; and they are engaged in butchering and cooking the deer by methods outlined in the journal—"[t]he deer, once slain, is, as soon after as possible, clapped upon the fire" (422).[11] Other passages, describing scenery, similarly draw on the notebook.

> [journal] The Balsam range of mountains. The ascent covered with huckleberries in October & very good ones too. The prospect from the summit, looking into Tennessee, Virginia, South Carolin [*sic*] & Georgia & over North Carolina. We have crossed the Blue Ridge. The waters now take a westerly direction. (113)

> ["Sharp Snaffles"] It was early winter, October, and the long ascent to the top of the mountains was through vast fields of green, the bushes still hanging heavy with their huckleberries.
>
> From the summits we had looked over into Tennessee, Virginia, Georgia, North and South Carolina. In brief, to use the language of Natty Bumppo, we beheld "Creation." We had crossed the "Blue Ridge;" and the descending water-courses, no longer seeking the Atlantic, were now gushing headlong down the western slopes, and hurrying to lose themselves in the Gulf Stream and the Mississippi. (422)

The characters in the frame of "Sharp Snaffles" are the mixture of frontiersmen and cultured professional people that permeates southern humor and bodies forth the two domains of frontier and civilization. They also represent actual parties on Simms's trip, some of whom are identified by name—Jim Fisher, Columbus Mills, Major Henry—and one by a title, the "Jedge," presumably Simms himself. Gently mocking his own "venerable aspect" and dignified bearing, like other such frame narrators the "Jedge" lards his narrative with foreign phrases and literary allusions (425). As a newcomer to the camp, he has not yet heard Sharp's oft-told tale, and hence Sharp, who is also

11. See the corresponding passage in the mountain notebook, transcribed in Shillingsburg, "An Edition of *Cub of the Panther*," 116.

dubbed "Yaou" (which means "yes" in the Cherokee language), addresses it directly to him.

The occasion for Sharp's story is the Saturday Night Lying Camp, a weekly ritual among the hunters over which Jim Fisher, as the "Big Lie" adorned with buckskin and antlers, presides. By common consent of the storytellers, truth at the Lying Camp is prohibited, exaggeration encouraged. As Simms says: "The hunter who actually inclines to exaggeration is, at such a period, privileged to deal in all the extravagances of invention; nay, he is *required* to do so! To be literal, or confine himself to the bald and naked truth, is not only discreditable, but a *finable* offense! He is, in such a case, made to swallow a long, strong, and difficult potation!" These rules lie behind Jim Fisher's tart injunctions to Sharp when he grows too factual: "Look you, Yaou. . . . you're gitting too close upon the etarnal stupid truth! . . . Jest crook your trail!" (423, 426).

Even by Fisher's standards, the yarn that Sharp eventually spins is tall—a story of an ordinary courtship that succeeds through an extraordinary hunt. At the beginning of the tale he is courting a conventionally luscious mountain beauty, Merry Ann Hopson, "the very yaller flower of the forest"; and in the spirit of southern humor he indulges in a fair amount of sexual byplay ("I'll marry you this very night, Merry Ann," says I, "though you hedn't a stitch of clothing at all!" [426, 453]).[12] Her father, however, who is a mercenary farmer, wants her to marry John Grimstead, a rich, repulsive bachelor; and hence he humiliates Sharp, impugning his manhood by impugning his ability to accumulate capital. Marching him before an ornate mirror, Squire Hopson makes the poor hunter "obsarve" his face and figure and then announces, "You may think, in your vanity, that you air a man; but you ain't, and never will be, onless you kin find a way to git *capital*" (433).

Sharp goes home to brood, but he is consoled in a dream by a beautiful woman who tells him he will get the capital. At this point, the story takes its first turn from the realistic to the magical realm, or from the world of farming and money and marriage to a place where natural laws are suspended and miracles occur. The next day Sharp rides to a region with an aura of the supernatural, "a hollow of the hills that I

12. The sexual element in the story is discussed by James B. Meriwether, "Simms's 'Sharp Snaffles' and 'Bald-Head Bill Bauldy': Two Views of Men—and of Women," *South Carolina Review*, XVI (Spring, 1984), 68–69.

hed never seed before," with a lake "like so much purple glass" where "[t]har wa'n't a breath of wind stirring" (437). There is even a hint of enchanted sleep as he slumbers on the margin of the lake and wakes to find "tens and twenties and fifties and hundreds" of wild geese settling upon the water (437).

Having ventured into the marvelous, the story instantly returns to the ordinary. Once he is home, at the urging of the dream lady, Sharp goes to town, buys twine, cord, plowlines, and fishhooks, makes a snare for the geese, and catches them; but in his haste he wraps the ends of the net around his own leg instead of a tree. In the first of the comic perils of the story, the geese carry him into the air and then back to the ground as the net becomes entangled in a hollow tree into which he plunges, falling up to his neck in honey. But after praying to the "blessed angels" in the stars, he gets out by hanging on to the hindquarters of a bear that had backed into the tree and is frightened out (444). Once out, he pushes the bear off the tree, breaking its neck, and calculates that he has three sources of capital—bear, geese, and honey.

The reappearance of mundane details signifies the end of the marvelous portion of the story, as Sharp assesses his new-found wealth: "From the b'ar only I made a matter of full one hundred dollars. First, thar waur the hide, $20; then 450 pounds of meat, at 10 cents, was $45; then the grease, 14 pounds, $14; and the tallow, some $6 more; and the biled marrow, $11" (449). He also, he says, "wrung the necks of all the geese that waur thar . . . and counted some twenty-seven hundred," but in one of the funnier passages of the story his listeners, who except for the "Jedge" have heard the tale before, interrupt: "'Twenty-seven hundred!' cried the 'Big Lie' and all the hunters at a breath. 'Twenty-seven hundred! Why, Yaou, whenever you telled of this thing before you always counted them at 3150!'" (448). To silence them, Sharp explains that he gave the other geese away and adds that he made $1,400 on the honey.

Then, in a series of scenes in which Simms carefully reverses the opening sections of the story, Sharp settles his score with Squire Hopson. After buying the mortgage on the Hopson farm and taunting the Squire with the prospect of foreclosure, he marches the mercenary old man to the mirror and says, "[A]x yourself ef you're the sawt of looking man that hes any right to be a feyther-in-law to a fine, young, handsome-looking fellow like me, what's got the 'capital?'" (461). He marries Merry Ann; and to the delight of the hunters and the incredulity of the "Jedge," he insists that he and she have since had thirty-six children: "First we had *three* gal children, you see. Very well! Put down three. Then we had *six* boys, one every year for four years; and then, the fifth year, Merry Ann throwed deuce. Now put down the six boys a'ter the three gals, and ef that don't make thirty-six, thar's no snakes in all Flurriday!" He concludes the story with a flourish: "We're doing right well; but I hes, every now and then, to put my thumb and forefinger on the Squaire's collar, and show him his face in the big glass, and call on him for an *obzarvation*—for he's might fond *of going shar's* in my 'capital'" (465).[13]

Sharp's rollicking account of geese, bear, honey, and capital has connections with several literary modes that enrich its range of implication. Its resemblance to Simms's earliest dream-visions and fairy tales is seen in the magical world Sharp enters at the lake, the possibility of enchanted sleep, and the vision of the beautiful woman. Its derivation from comedy appears through its use of the type of structure already noted in *The Golden Christmas:* a young man wants a young girl; an oppressive parent prevents him from getting her; but he gets her anyway through a twist—in Sharp's case through several twists—in the plot. Its association with romance, in a parodic or displaced manner, is evident in other aspects of its structure: the triangle of Merry Ann, Sharp, and Grimstead, the separation of the lovers, the testing of the hero, the perils overcome, and the exuberantly happy ending. Its ties to local color arise, as Charles S. Watson observes, from Simms's use of a mountain hunter as protagonist and from his vivid descriptions of mountain scenery.[14] And its connection with oral folk material, as James Kibler notes, appears in the three separate narrative strands that Simms carefully weaves together: the wonderful hunt, the man borne into the air by geese, and the man pulled from a hollow tree by a bear.[15]

That these three motifs constitute authentic folk material is established by the fact that they possess "independent traditional life" out-

13. For Simms's emphasis throughout the story on capital, see Ian Marshall, "The American Dreams of Sam Snaffles," *Southern Literary Journal,* XVIII (Spring, 1986), [96]–107.

14. For a detailed consideration of local-color elements in "Sharp Snaffles," see Watson, "Simms and the Beginnings of Local Color," 36–38.

15. James E. Kibler, Jr., "Simms' Indebtedness to Folk Tradition in 'Sharp Snaffles,'" *Southern Literary Journal,* IV (Spring, 1972), 56.

side Simms's story, existing in both printed and oral versions.[16] The wonderful hunt, which to some extent embraces the other two motifs, had been a literary staple at least since Baron Munchausen, and indeed he has been cited as the principal source for Simms's story by older critics more aware of European than of frontier influences.[17] Somewhat closer to "Sharp Snaffles," however, are several American versions of the fable, like the one James K. Paulding apparently plucked from an almanac and inserted into the pages of *Westward Ho! A Tale* (1832), a book Simms probably knew, in which the backwoodsman Amos Bushfield cries:

> I saw a deer and its fawn across a creek the other side of the mountain, and I wasn't altogether slow in letting fly, I tell you. The ball ranged them both. I had to wade through the creek, *and* I found the ball had entered in a hollow tree, after going right clean through the two deer, where there was a hive of honey, *and* the honey was running away like all natur; so I stooped down to pick up something to stop it, when I put my hand on a rabbit hid under a great toadstool. But somehow or other, coming across the creek, my trousers had got so full of fish, that one of the buttons burst clean off, *and* I will agree to be eternally derned if it didn't hit a wild turkey right in the left eye. Whoop! *ain't* I a horse?[18]

Another version of the yarn, published nearer the time of "Sharp Snaffles," had appeared in a collection of humorous stories that Simms probably knew, T. C. Haliburton's *Traits of American Humor* (1852). The sketch, called "Colonel Crockett, the Bear and the Swallows," uses like Simms's story the theme of a man in a hollow tree extricated by a bear, though in this case he falls up to his neck in swallow dung instead of honey. Even closer parallels to Simms's story are provided by a yarn called "Old Long John—the Bear Hunter," which made the rounds of several midcentury newspapers and which Simms clipped and pasted in a scrapbook. James Kibler, who has carefully studied several versions of the wonderful hunt story, concludes that though "Old Long John—the Bear Hunter" contains only one of Simms's dominant motifs, that of the man, the bear, and the hollow tree, it also

16. *Ibid.*, [55].

17. See, for instance, Alexander E. Jones, "A Source for William Gilmore Simms's 'Sharp Snaffles,'" *Journal of American Folklore,* LXX (January–March, 1957), [66]–69.

18. [Paulding], *Westward Ho!*, I, 172–73. Simms mentions the novel in *L*, I, 169, and II, 225.

shares with "Sharp Snaffles" the structure of a frame story told by an educated speaker who introduces a dialect narrator. The strongest resemblances of all, however, Kibler continues, exist in an oral version of the wonderful hunt that was extant in Simms's century though not set down in print until ours. Told in the Beech Mountain area of North Carolina near where Simms hunted, it uses all three of the strands he later employed in "Sharp Snaffles," and there is hence a strong possibility that he heard his companions in 1847 tell a version of the same tall story.[19]

One of the most impressive aspects of the yarn as Simms develops it is its tightly knit organization: the frame and tall tale are neatly spliced, the episodes are closely linked, and the beginning and end are symmetrical. Also noteworthy is the combination of realistic and fantastic episodes. The tale consists of two outer rings of highly detailed, realistic narrative, the frame story and the marriage plot, which surround an inner ring of fantasy, the wonderful hunt. Broadly speaking, the "search for capital," or the marriage plot, its mundane details deliberately made humorous, places the story among the important number of courtship yarns that constitute a distinctive strain in southern humor. The wonderful hunt, on the other hand, with its hints of the supernatural, forms an authentic tall tale with roots in folklore. Particularly striking in "Sharp Snaffles" is the manner in which Simms subordinates the tall tale to the marriage plot. Many tall yarns suggest an ideal of a masculine society, a community of hunters deliberately shielded from the feminine world of domestic concerns and assimilated into the wild realm of the forest. In Simms's story, by contrast, Sharp hunts alone, and he enters the magical forest world chiefly in order to insure his ultimate residence in the domestic realm with comely Merry Ann.

The companion tale to "Sharp Snaffles" and the offering at the second week of the Lying Camp is a lively narrative that Simms titled "'Bald-Head Bill Bauldy,' and How He Went Through the Flurriday Campaign!—A Legend of the Hunter's Camp." Fittingly enough for one of the last tales he ever wrote, the piece shows him bringing together material from several areas of his writing. As John Guilds and Stephen Meats indicate, it combines the tradition of the tall tale with a parody of the Indian captivity narrative and also of the epic, as Bill

19. Kibler, "Simms' Indebtedness to Folk Tradition in 'Sharp Snaffles,'" 60–68.

tells of his capture by redskins, his descent to an underwater realm, his enslavement by an alligator queen, and his visit to the land of the dead.[20] Additionally, in its emphasis upon the sea it looks back to such poems as "Apostrophe to Ocean" and *Atalantis,* and it may even glance at the story "The Maroon" (1847), which depicts a shipwrecked foreigner enthralled by an enticing but destructive native beauty. Its use of the second Seminole war evokes the ending of *As Good as a Comedy,* also set in that period, and its stress on Bill's great flair for cooking terrapin and his prowess in felling a redskin with a frying pan inspire recollections of Porgy's exploits with a hominy kettle. The tale, in sum, is a potpourri of elements from Simms's earlier writing and a fine culmination to his career as backwoods humorist.

Unlike the fairly ordinary Sharp Snaffles, Bill Bauldy is a fantastic figure, with "a head as clean of hair as the palm of a damsel's hand."[21] To disguise his baldness he wears a ridiculous wig, "a great shaggy mass of reddish brown hair"; and it is "only as a favour to the amateurs of the party" that he shows his naked skull (467). "I wan't much of a sodger," he admits, "and hed no more idee of fighting than I had of flying to Heaven on the wings of the wind, as is writ in Holy Scripters" (473). The chief cook of a regiment in the second Seminole war, at first he lives an easy, enviable life, beating a little scullion to make him do the work of the camp while stealing into the woods to drink the officers' liquor, smoke their cigars, and dream of "Susannah Sykes, the prettiest gal in all Lexington District!" (477). His idyll ends, however, when he is captured by Indians, tortured, nearly killed, and finally forced to tote a "cussed leetle dirty wretch of a red skin papoose, from daylight to dark" (488). He escapes from the Indians by riding an alligator to the bottom of a lake, where, in an obvious glance at the epic tradition, he is made captive by a woman he calls "the Calypso of Flurriday; a Type Unknown to Ulysses" (497).

The vision that ensues is a blend of paradise and Tartarus, with elements looking back to the book of Revelation and forward to the Wizard of Oz. Bill enters a beautiful realm where "the pathway was wide and spread with white sand"; he sees hills "stuck full of shiny shells";

20. Guilds, in [Simms], *Stories and Tales,* 804–805; Stephen E. Meats, "Bald-Head Bill Bauldy: Simms's Unredeemed Captive," paper delivered at the annual meeting of the Modern Language Association, 1977.

21. [William Gilmore Simms], "'Bald-Head Bill Bauldy,' and How He Went Through the Flurriday Campaign!—A Legend of the Hunter's Camp," in *Stories and Tales,* 467, hereafter cited by page number in the text.

and he finds himself "in a most tremendous big hall, all kivered over with shells and chrystals" where alligator courtiers are coming and going (498). The queen of the fabulous domain, who is half Indian and half alligator, has floating black hair, eyes like lightning, and teeth "sharp as a dog's grinder" (502). When she grows amorous toward Bill, she flings out from her body some twenty feet of tail, catches him around the waist, pulls him into her lap, and kisses him until the blood comes. He finally realizes that he is being fattened for the kill—for, he says, when kissing him, "The infarnal critter was a-tasting me all the time, and calculating the meal she was to make of me!" (508). After he sees "a whole pile of skillytons, more than a hundred," he knows that the queen has killed and eaten a host of men before him (507).

Bill eventually gets away from the alligator queen, who is a darkly comic version of the woman in Keats's poem "La Belle Dame sans Merci." But he falls into the hands of his regiment, whose members charge him with desertion and threaten him with court-martial. When he confronts the "Gineral," he says in a particularly vivid passage, "I fell all over in a heap, wilting up, and running together, and quaking, like a great platter of seablubber, jist brought ashore by the rollers" (513). But the General forgives him, for reasons that the men approve: "Who kin fry a trout, a pairch, or a bream, with Bill Bauldy? Who kin bile a bluecat, to make it eat hafe so sweet? . . . A great sodger, Gentlemens, is *one* thing . . . but a great cook is a greater;—he's a sort of life-presarver, and comforter, and saviour of the body, which, you know, is next to being the saviour of the soul!" (519). In the conclusion of the narrative, the members of Bill's troop declare that he has been away from camp for only one day, and the General insists that his tale is a drunken dream that derives from a bottle of Jamaica rum. Their remarks recall the ending of one of Simms's earliest dream-vision stories, likewise concerned with the ocean, in which an awkward, fumbling narrator awakens from a nightmare about shipwreck to find himself floundering in the pew of a church and concludes, "So much for taking late dinners with a friend, drinking my two bottles of Madeira, and going to a night meeting, when I should have gone to bed."[22]

22. [William Gilmore Simms], "A Story of the Sea," in *The Book of My Lady. A Melange* (Boston, 1833), 121. The tale had previously been published in other versions with other titles in newspapers and magazines; Simms republished it at least three times after it appeared in *The Book of My Lady*. See Betty Jo Strickland, "The Short Fiction of William Gilmore Simms: A Checklist," 597.

"Sharp Snaffles" and "Bill Bauldy" represent Simms's final use of the Appalachian material and also the impressive climax of his experiments with backwoods humor. In their colorful language, their soaring fantasy, and their extravagant inventiveness, they rival the best efforts of his fellow humorists, and they also serve to recapitulate many of his earlier efforts in the mode. Discerning critics from Edd Winfield Parks and Donald Davidson to John Guilds have recognized the merits of the narratives: Parks maintains that "Sharp Snaffles" is "one of the finest tall tales ever written by a Southern humorist"; Davidson insists that it "stands almost without a peer, surely," among American tall stories; and Guilds calls "Bill Bauldy" an example of "Simms's excellence in the genre of Southern and Southwestern humor." Taken together, the stories warrant the praise Vernon L. Parrington bestowed on Simms's longer fiction; they evince his vigorous, spontaneous nature, his "abundant sea of salty speech." Above all, they demonstrate that the aging author, even during the worst struggles of his life, was still able to create the kind of comedy that his contemporaries praised and that exemplified what Paul Hamilton Hayne called his "bold, bluff, and masculine" personality.[23]

23. Parks, *Simms As Literary Critic,* 9; Davidson, Introduction, *L,* I, lii; Guilds, in [Simms], *Stories and Tales,* 804; Parrington, *The Romantic Revolution in America, 1800–1860,* 127; Hayne, "Ante-Bellum Charleston," 258.

12
Last Things

Poverty and affliction, Simms's familiar companions, kept pace with him as he composed his final works. The tumult of war and Reconstruction, the strain of his virtually constant writing, increasing physical infirmities, and "Care . . . a gaunt spectre" dogging his footsteps combined to age him prematurely (*L,* V, 125). Paul Hamilton Hayne, seeing him in 1866 for the first time in five years, felt the war had done the work of half a lifetime: his hair was white, Hayne reported, his beard grizzled, "his fine forehead scored with wrinkles, and over the once fiery eyes a film rested as of unshed tears!"[1] Simms himself mused sadly to a correspondent, "Time rolls up a cycle in a single season, and we grow aged before we well know that we have lived" (*L,* V, 190). And he told Duyckinck that age and illness were pressing in upon him more rapidly than he had anticipated. "They shall not lessen my courage & resolve," he maintained, "though they may lessen my vigour and capacity; nor shall I complain though it be decreed me, evidently as I see, to die in the harness" (*L,* V, 222).

"[D]rearily drudging at the desk," Simms felt more and more out of step with the world of letters in which he had once occupied a high place (*L,* V, 201). Even before he had written *The Cub of the Panther* and *Voltmeier,* he had told a friend he sometimes felt like folding his robes about him, "solicitous only, to die decently" (*L,* V, 17). His repeated misfortunes, he remarked to correspondents, made him timorous and apprehensive in approaching them; he construed their silence as neglect and admitted he had little to write that would interest

1. Hayne, "Ante-Bellum Charleston," 267. Hayne, who had moved away from Charleston, finally settled near Augusta, Georgia, in 1866. See Rayburn S. Moore (ed.), *A Man of Letters in the Nineteenth-Century South: Selected Letters of Paul Hamilton Hayne* (Baton Rouge, 1982), 5–6, and also Moore, *Paul Hamilton Hayne* (New York, 1972), 21.

them (*L*, V, 179, 207). But he needed their frequent reassurances, and as he labored away in his study he yearned for New York news. "Write me soon & often," he begged Duyckinck, "if you would suffer me to keep in unison with the living literary world" (*L*, V, 171). Although he had continued to visit New York after the war, he refused to go to Washington, for he said he would no longer find there the "array of sterling friends & noble gentlemen whom once I knew" (*L*, V, 180). And glancing back at his former ambitions, the man who once had been "a luminary of first magnitude" in the "literary heavens" told Hayne that he lived obscurely, both at home and abroad.[2] "[Y]ou will seldom see my name hacknied in the papers," he observed. "I do not now write for fame or notoriety or the love of it, but simply to procure the wherewithal of life for my children" (*L*, V, 213).

Yet Simms retained to the last his conception of literature as an art requiring serious imaginative commitment; and even as death began to stalk him, he never lost the will or the desire to create. The serial writing for magazines into which he had been forced by the war annoyed him; he detested, so he said, the necessity of toning down his mind "to the miserable requisitions of stupid publishers, and low toned readers" (*L*, V, 190). To such labor he opposed his own firmly held and dearly purchased convictions that the muse of poetry in her highest manifestations was the only mistress worth serving. Although he complained of his obscurity, would-be writers still sought his help; and he continued to perform numerous gratuitous tasks—helping old maids, widows, and orphans, for instance, to write and publish books (*L*, V, 125). Adding to his burdens was his self-imposed role as counselor to younger writers such as Cooke, whom he told to stress the elements of character, action, and variety in his novels (*L*, V, 193). And though after his serial writing was concluded he complained that he was doing little work, he wrote columns for the Charleston *Courier*, the *Mercury*, and the *Daily News* and produced a series of articles on southern artists and writers for the *XIX Century*, a monthly magazine published in Charleston (*L*, V, 152–53, 252*n*175, 253*n*182). Through his endeavors he continued, in effect, as the dean of southern letters, and he was also a respected figure in the city: he told William Cullen Bryant, with obvious satisfaction, "My people honour me, and the young men gather around me with proofs of love and reverence" (*L*, V, 308).

2. *Ceremonies at the Unveiling of the Bronze Bust of William Gilmore Simms at White Point Garden, Charleston, S.C., June 11th, 1879* (Charleston, S.C., 1879), 20.

Simms's attachment to his children continued undiminished; in his numerous letters to them near the end of his life, he coaxed them to industry, scolded them for imprudence, and lectured them on topics ranging from farming to education and travel. For a while after the war he lived with his eldest daughter, Augusta, and her husband, Edward Roach, on Society Street in Charleston; but poor food and crowded conditions prompted his remove to Woodlands, which he had set about once more to rebuild (*L,* VI, 266–67). He had planned to reconstruct one wing of the dwelling but ran out of money before he could complete it, so that his "little flock," as he liked to term his family, was eventually forced to occupy crowded quarters. Gradually he let his children assume the direction of the plantation, telling Duyckinck that like King Lear he now sat as a guest at their table (*L,* V, 178). Friends from the North sent him gifts "of affection & sympathy—books, paper, a knife, a pipe, and . . . some good wine" (*L,* VI, 269). But his family, which consisted of his oldest son, Gilmore; his married daughter Chevillette and her husband; his unmarried daughter, Mary Lawson; and his two young sons Govan and Carroll, subsisted almost entirely on the productions of farm, wood, and stream—fish in abundance, "English & acorn ducks, doves, partridges . . . with an occasional variation with buck & wild turkey" (*L,* V, 191). Despite privations, he wrote Cooke in one of the flourishes of optimism that form a striking element in his late letters, "we have great cause of gratitude to the Good God that he hath left us so much, with Hope still at the bottom of our Pandora's casket" (*L,* V, 191).

Well before beginning *Voltmeier,* Simms had started to complain to friends and relatives of various physical afflictions. His descriptions in his letters take various forms: at one or another point during the last three years of his life, he referred to headaches, indigestion, vertigo, liver problems, and frequent abdominal unrest accompanied by nausea, vomiting, and dysentery. He also, as the 1860s drew to a close, began to suffer from what he called "paroxysms" of acute chills and fever that resembled mild cases of malaria. Observing that at sixty-three he had had to begin life anew and work harder than he had ever had to do in his youth, he wrote Duyckinck in the spring of 1869 that after his protracted work on *The Cub of the Panther* and *Voltmeier* he had endured several successive attacks of fever, had lost flesh, and had feared a renewal of the illness (*L,* VI, 275, V, 221). He was still capable of writing playfully—he called Lawson, who had criticized one of his speeches, "You venerable Donkey! You inveterate, Fadladeen! You would-be Aristarchus!" (*L*, V, 280).[3] But increasingly his letters were shadowed by references to what was to him as yet a mysterious array of illnesses.

In July, 1869, Simms made his customary visit to the North. He saw several of his old companions; but preoccupied with various problems, he complained that money was tight and books did not sell. He discussed with Widdleton a new edition of his books, to commence with *The Cassique of Kiawah,* which he rightly termed one of his best romances. (The edition, however, was not issued until after his death, and *The Cassique of Kiawah* was not in it [*L*, V, 241*n*147].) In August he went to New England; but once there he endured a bad attack of dyspepsia, "and have been suffering ever since," he wrote Lawson, "starving myself & taking physic" (*L*, V, 244). Back in Brooklyn, he complained of almost unrelieved discomfort. "I have been able to do no business thus far this season," he informed his New York friend William Hawkins Ferris; "have done no work, earned no money, and shall probably have barely enow to pay my travelling expenses to Woodlands. Depression of spirits, with pain & infirmity of body are aging me fast, and prompting a degree of despondency, which . . . now threatens to become chronic" (*L*, V, 248). Telling Duyckinck, "May God save my friends from such harassing experiences, as have preyed upon me during the last eight years," early in October he borrowed money and sailed for Charleston (*L*, V, 251).

For the first time, apparently, Simms suspected that his malady—which was probably cancer—might be fatal.[4] In November he wrote Lawson that while in New York he had detected certain symptoms that had determined his premature departure. He had a kidney infection, he continued, and was feeble; he felt that his pain might be alleviated but believed that the case itself was incurable (*L*, V, 260). But he was still energetic; and with a flash of wry self-mockery he wrote Duyckinck: "Were you here with me, and I talking with you, while stretched at length upon my sofa, you certainly would be slow to conjecture that I was suffering pain the while. There is a wild Arabian tale of a living head that delivered oracles while joined to a dead or petri-

3. Aristarchus (ca. 220–150 B.C.) was a Greek grammarian; Fadladeen is the chamberlain in Thomas Moore's poem "Lalla Rookh."

4. Holman, Review of *The Letters of William Gilmore Simms,* in *Journal of Southern History,* XXIII (November, 1957), 545.

fied body. I sometimes think of that story, while I am talking here to some one or other of my circles" (*L,* V, 270). The fact of his naturally strong constitution, he observed, made such misery difficult to bear. "My brain still seethes with thought," he commented to Duyckinck in another letter, "and my designs fill my dreams. . . . It is possible that the world will see them yet" (*L,* V, 262).

Such hopes, however, were not destined to be realized. The year 1870 opened ominously for Simms, who told Hayne that he could write only in fits and starts and could scarcely work for half an hour at his desk. "I am rapidly passing from a stage," he observed, "where you young men are to succeed me, doing what you can. God grant that you be more successful than I have been" (*L,* V, 289, 290). He spent much of the spring in Charleston, where Augusta and her family ministered to him and where he was attended by his friend and physician Eli Geddings. In the city, on May 3, he delivered his last public address, "The Sense of the Beautiful," to what he termed "a large & brilliant audience" at the Horticultural Society. "I was quite feeble, & exhausted from delivery," he wrote Lawson, "but contrived, by sheer will, to hold out & hold forth to the last" (*L,* V, 313). He advised his friend, who himself was rapidly aging, to enjoy home and quiet occupations, and in a pathetic passage he contrasted Lawson's situation and his own. "With health good, appetite good, good sleep, a happy homestead, you have no need to repine at any thing," he wrote his friend. "For myself, how different. Poor, suffering, distressed, nothing made secure for my children, my own resources dried up, my health such that I can no longer labour, except at intervals of pain . . . I congratulate myself that I am not impatient with God" (*L,* V, 315).

In early May Simms went to Woodlands for the last time. Since his marriage, it had served as his haven, his retreat, and his particular pastoral domain: he had cataloged its beauties, luxuriated in its "calm repose," and declared that in its groves his heart recovered its "*ancient freshness*" (*L,* V, 256, III, 61). Now, seeing it in spring, he declared: "It is all very beautiful here. Woods, forests, fields, the grand old trees, a delicious atmosphere, and the whole of God's world wearing a happy smile" (*L,* V, 316). But in mid-May he began to suffer renewed abdominal attacks, and shortly afterwards he returned to Charleston. From it, on May 27, he wrote Ferris that he had had one of his "atrocious paroxysms" and was still quite feeble. He concluded the letter by stating, "I write simply to tell you that I still live" (*L,* VI, 279).

This was perhaps the last letter Simms would ever write, for the end, when it finally arrived, came swiftly (*L*, VI, xxv, 279*n*1).[5] On June 11, 1870, at five o'clock in the afternoon, he died at his daughter's home in Charleston.[6] His friend R. S. Bruns cabled the news to James Lawson; other friends and relatives gathered sorrowfully to prepare his body for burial. His valiant struggles were concluded; and on June 13, in Magnolia Cemetery north of Charleston, William Gilmore Simms was laid to rest.

The city that throughout his life Simms had both defended and berated did not neglect the memory of her gifted son. In 1872 a committee composed of Geddings, Augustus Sachtleben, and other prominent Charlestonians was formed to plan the construction of a memorial to Simms. The group contacted William Cullen Bryant, who secured the prominent sculptor J. Q. A. Ward of New York to design a bust. Ward grew so interested in the project that he reduced his customary fee; friends of Simms inspected and approved the plaster model; and on June 11, 1879, the ninth anniversary of his death, the bronze monument was unveiled at White Point Garden on the tip of the Charleston peninsula, the site of the settlement at Oyster Point that he had described in "Chronicles of Ashley River" and *The Cassique of Kiawah*. The inaugural speaker, William D. Porter, who had served as lieutenant governor of South Carolina in the middle 1860s, gave a comprehensive description of Simms's career, praised the amount, variety, and

5. Trent, *William Gilmore Simms*, 318, mentions a letter Simms wrote on June 2 to Hayne, but apparently the letter has been lost, as it does not appear in the published volumes of Simms's correspondence.

6. Simms's Charleston relatives and friends described his death to Hayne in affecting letters. Augusta wrote Hayne that, on June 9, Dr. Eli Geddings saw her father at midday and reported that he could not live much longer. At four o'clock that afternoon, she said, he "got up from the bed & walked down stairs . . . he was death struck then—the cold sweats of death rolls [*sic*] in strains from his face." She added, "I never could imagine such wonderful force of will that kept him up much longer than he would otherwise have lasted." According to his close friend Sallie F. Chapin, who helped nurse him during his last illness, to the end he was concerned about his children. His final words were "Where is Gilmore[?] It will not be long." When she helped prepare Simms's body for burial, Mrs. Chapin told Hayne: "I made garlands of Laurel, and Bay" and wove "a cross of white Imortelles [*sic*], which I placed in his poor emaciated hands, the fingers of which refused to take any other position than their natural one, *drawn up as if to write*" (Augusta Simms Roach to [Paul Hamilton] Hayne, June 6, 1871, Sallie F. Chapin to [Paul Hamilton Hayne], June 15, 1870, in Hayne Papers). This letter is misquoted slightly in Hayne, "Ante-Bellum Charleston," 268, and in Davidson and Oliphant, Introduction to *Voltmeier*, xxix.

quality of his writing, and emphasized the fact that never before had the city erected a public monument to a man who was "*an author* by profession." And citizens of Charleston dedicated "the living tablet to him whose words inspired the patriotic pride, the high resolve, the sensitiveness to wrong, and sublime courage which make heroism."[7]

Written tributes poured in from friends and other contemporaries of Simms who were unable to attend the ceremony. General James Chesnut, husband of the later-to-be-famous Mary Boykin Chesnut, observed of Simms, "I knew him well, I loved him well." William Porcher Miles recalled that in "the *abandon* of his own home, in the easy chair of his Library, or at the head of his simple but hospitable table, how would his large, generous nature expand and glow, throwing out brilliant repartees, jokes, stories, puns, in endless profusion." And Alfred Proctor Aldrich, in an affecting summary of his old friend's career, declared, "Reviewing all his history, from the hour when I saw him, unarmed, and, hero-like, fronting and defying the hissing crowd of young politicians who surrounded his office of the '*City Gazette*'—when the nullification excitement ran so high—to the last days of his toilsome life, after his 'laurel-laden brow' was bent with age and sorrow; it seems to me that South Carolina gave no son to the world more worthy to be loved, revered, honored and cherished, than William Gilmore Simms."[8]

Speakers and correspondents alike acknowledged Simms's devotion to the South; as Porter said, it was "his chosen field, because he knew it, and loved it well."[9] From that love had issued a steady flow of poems, novels, essays, orations, and other works. The South had indeed served as the generating force behind his writing, and the record of his achievement in letters is closely bound up with the record of his attachment to his section. With the ardor of his Celtic temperament as augmented by his southern pride, he had immersed himself in a culture whose strong self-consciousness and patriotic assessment of its past had vivified his fiction and encouraged him to create in it a picture of a distinctive, sophisticated civilization. At the same time, the intensity of his attachment had encouraged his employment of the romance mode, with its affinity for stirring action, bold drama, and weighted presentations.

7. *Ceremonies*, 14, 13.
8. *Ibid.*, 53, 57, [33].
9. *Ibid.*, 22.

To this mode the historical diversity of southern civilization as reflected in oral and written traditions had made vital and sweeping contributions. The essential South for Simms throughout his life was the low country, which with its history of conflict, its agrarian values, and its patrician heritage provided fundamental elements of his literary scheme and furnished the perspective from which he would view the emergence of newer southern regions. To the structural framework forged by the convergence of cultural traditions and literary form the Gulf South or Old Southwest contributed important comic elements, and it also introduced him to the crime that has been an almost constant accompaniment of America's rampaging frontier. The Appalachian Mountain South, which completed the process begun in the Old Southwest, honed his skill at the tall tale while spurring him to describe the lives of plain, honorable mountain people in a manner that combines the realism of the local-color movement with the extravagance and fantasy of frontier humor. Because Trent and his successors have stressed, perhaps unduly, the imitative aspects of Simms's work in letters, it is worth remarking here once more that in local color, backwoods comedy, and satiric portraits of manners, he was an originator as well as an adapter of native literary traditions.

In his fiction and other writing, Simms exhibits many of the traits traditionally associated with major authors: commitment to the literary vocation, zeal and talent in pursuing it, fluency, creativity, stability in genre, continuity in subject matter, and the gift of treating similar topics and themes from a variety of angles. What he lacked was a sensitivity to certain formal properties of literature, particularly those of style and structure that are important to twentieth-century readers. His weaknesses in these areas are obvious and pronounced, and they have been the subject of much adverse criticism, beginning in his own time and continuing with increasing emphasis into the present. His problems with structure ultimately reflect his great spontaneity and personal disorganization: as he said in one of several perceptive statements about himself, "I . . . write usually as I talk; and as the world goes, am accounted a somewhat rude, blunt man" (*L,* VI, 27). Perhaps partly because of these aspects of his nature, he tended, as Hayne observes, to diffuse instead of concentrate his powers. During the 1830s, the period of his career when favorable publishing circumstances afforded him the greatest opportunity to polish his writing and solidify his reputation by mining deeply one or two veins of literature, he instead shifted rapidly among Spanish, border, and Revolutionary War romances in addition to poetry, essays, and short fiction—choosing, as Hayne remarks, to treat "a thousand topics imperfectly, instead of treating one great topic, or series of kindred topics, fully, exhaustively, with the entire consecration of thought, will, inventive faculty, and imagination."[10]

Simms's disorganization also affected his approach to literary tradition and particularly to his major literary genre, whose conventions themselves pose certain problems in the formal construction of prose narratives. Historically the romance form has tended to portray large, seemingly disparate areas of human experience. To do so, it developed the convention of loosely connecting several apparently diverse story lines in order to show the underlying links among them. Described another way, romance, in Henry James's apt if tart phrases, is a loose, baggy form capable of rendering many different types and levels of experience through literary patterns that give shape to human aspirations, fears, desires, hopes, and dreams. When written by a man whose personality was itself somewhat loose and baggy—"I wear my character pretty much out of door, & possibly somewhat out at the elbows"—it will be more amorphous and less compactly organized still (*L*, III, 191).

Equally troublesome to Simms's twentieth-century readers have been the problems observable in his style. At its worst, that style, as too many of his critics have claimed, is florid, melodramatic, sentimental, and bombastic. Readers would like his writing better today if he had pruned his sometimes tangled sentences, eliminated certain of his highly charged outbursts, and observed the rules of syntax and usage more precisely. Again, however, some of the awkwardnesses in his writing may be traced to the literary traditions in which he worked as they were influenced by his personal circumstances. During the wide, undisciplined reading of his youth and adolescence, he had absorbed the conventionalized manner of expression that had developed in nineteenth-century British and American fiction and that had become a hallmark of historical romance, a major branch of early nineteenth-century popular writing. As Scott and Cooper had shaped it, the authorial commentary of historical fiction aims for stateliness; but too often it is merely ponderous and pretentious, weighty and dull. His-

10. Hayne, "William Gilmore Simms," 138. Hayne is speaking of Simms's poetry, but his description also characterizes the author's practice in other genres.

torical fiction, moreover, like other forms of nineteenth-century popular romance, is a fundamentally middle-class form of narrative expression. Sentimentality and melodrama characterize it as relentlessly as they do many such middle-class art forms, which are products of what the twentieth century has learned to call mass culture.

But in addition to sententiousness and sentimentality, nineteenth-century historical fiction had developed a variety of styles appropriate to the several social levels that it, like much other romance, has often been intent on portraying. And Simms, who had greater talent for felicitous expression than he has usually been credited with possessing, is at his best firm, direct, bold, and moving. His sly social satire and saucy dialect humor show his ability for pointed style and pungent statement. They also convey the vigor, realism, and unmediated response to life that delighted his contemporaries and communicated the exuberance native to his personality.

Simms's weaknesses in style and structure, which are the weaknesses of his nature, genre, and age, do not wholly account, however, for the obscurity into which his work has fallen. It is appropriate to consider some other important factors affecting his reputation that have never been fully described and need to be examined. To these factors a writer in his time and one in ours point the way. Edgar Allan Poe, like Simms a veteran and victim of the antebellum literary marketplace, remarked that had Simms been a northerner his fame would have been immediately assured. And Donald Davidson, in the introduction to Simms's collected letters, maintains, "There is clearly something wrong if American scholarship can bring itself to publish a definitive edition of Melville—all of him, good, bad, and indifferent—and still not allow Simms, out of his eighty-two books, good, bad, and indifferent, a decent dozen, or even a slim half-dozen, of his best."[11] Simms himself declared that his residence in the South harmed the sale of his books; and assessing the midcentury situation in letters, he insisted that "English & Yankee authorities" have "done more than any thing besides to play the devil with all that is manly & original in our literature" (*L*, II, 90). The statements of all three writers point to a situation that is even now only partially redressed and that needs to be viewed more narrowly in regard to Simms.

Simms's reputation has declined not because, as Trent and Parring-

11. Poe, Review of *The Wigwam and the Cabin,* in *Godey's Magazine and Lady's Book,* XXXII (January, 1846), 42; Davidson, Introduction, *L*, I, xxxiii.

ton would have it, he was bound to a slave-holding civilization or because, in Parrington's dubious assertion, he was ostracized by its patrician class, whose attitudes he had enthusiastically endorsed. Nor are his shortcomings as a writer entirely responsible for the gradual eclipse of his fame: the fiction of Melville and Thomas Wolfe, two writers whom in scope and vigor he resembles, displays some of the same structural and stylistic weaknesses that his work does—which in their case readers have consistently managed to excuse or overlook. He has suffered, in large measure, because of the way literary reputations have been made and marketed in America since the early antebellum period. He did not live in the urban centers of the North, where writers less creative and ultimately less forceful than he—Irving, Bryant, and (he would have insisted) Longfellow—were able to guard and promote their reputations and watch over the publication of their books. Although he visited New York almost annually and to the end of his life was in touch with its leading men of letters, he was forced to conduct a great deal of his publishing business through Lawson, a well-meaning but sluggish man of modest talents, and Duyckinck, who was influential in the literary circles of the city but who lacked Simms's vigor in business dealings. Simms had no publisher who closely tended his interests as James T. Fields did Hawthorne's, no one who told him, as Carey and Lea told Cooper, what he should and should not write.[12] After the middle 1840s, the record of his transactions with publishers—the well-meaning but inept Redfield, and Widdleton, an opportunist—presents an irritating spectacle of protracted haggling over minor matters, unconscionable delays in publication, inattentiveness to his wishes about the format of editions or single volumes, and failure to look after his financial interests.

Ever since literary publishing established itself in the late eighteenth century, there has been a tendency in the country, encouraged by the emergence of New York as its publishing capital, to view northern traditions as the dominant American traditions and to assign to the South before the twentieth century an inferior role in literary history. This well-entrenched consensus of criticism has recently come under attack, yet authors of standard studies of American romance continue to con-

12. Charvat, *Literary Publishing in America,* 56–60; see also William Charvat, "James T. Fields and the Beginnings of Book Promotion, 1840–1855," in Matthew J. Bruccoli (ed.), *The Profession of Authorship in America, 1800–1870: The Papers of William Charvat* ([Columbus], Ohio, 1968), [168]–89.

centrate on Cooper, Hawthorne, Melville, and Brockden Brown while treating in detail no southern writers save Poe. Some scholars dutifully acknowledge Simms's statements in the preface to *The Yemassee,* which preceded Hawthorne's similar formulations in *The House of the Seven Gables* by more than a decade; but as Jay B. Hubbell remarked long ago, writers for the most part seem more versed in Trent or Parrington than they are in Simms—or in any other antebellum southern writer except the durable author of "The Raven."[13]

To some extent such scholars, wittingly or not, are the heirs of the literary battles of Simms's era, in which the South fought fiercely but northern opinion finally prevailed. Throughout much of the 1840s, Simms was Lewis Gaylord Clark's chief target, and Clark was a powerful arbiter of taste in literary New York. In his volley of attacks on Simms he did not focus solely on the writer's southernism, but he missed few chances to point out his regional attachments. Sectional politics and Simms's immersion in them, which drew the battle lines more firmly, increased his critics' sense of his regional affinities; and after the war, with his homeland prostrate and his own ambitions crushed, he fell victim to the condescension of the North and, what has almost been worse, to that of the New South. A chief exemplar of this condescension was Trent, who missed few chances to score hits at Simms's expense. Except for Hubbell, Holman, and Parrington—and such devoted Simmsians as Guilds, Shillingsburg, and Kibler—leading scholars of the twentieth century have taken their cue from Trent, and therefore Simms has suffered almost as much as if he had been left to languish in dignified neglect.

The result of this unfortunate situation has been the creation, and then the acceptance, of a body of opinion that has become increasingly negative about Simms's work. Although writers who have read widely in that work, like Parrington and Hubbell, have known that there is more merit in it than prevalent critical opinion allows, apparently no one has been able to do the enormous amount of reading that discriminating assessment of Simms's oeuvre demands. This is perhaps the major reason that so few scholars have been willing to address the issue of his ultimate literary status. On that issue I see no point in

13. Hubbell, *The South in American Literature,* 596–97. Here and elsewhere in his discussion of Simms, Hubbell makes points similar to those in this chapter about the ways in which Simms's work resembles that of other antebellum authors.

equivocating: the most perceptive of his contemporaries acknowledged that he did not occupy the first rank of American authors, and with that assessment there is little cause to quarrel.

I would, however, place Simms higher in the second tier than many critics have placed him and would argue that an unfortunate combination of circumstances has operated to obscure the substantial merits of his fiction. Among these circumstances are the vicissitudes of the marketplace and consequently of his literary reputation, the nearly overwhelming volume of his writing and its flaws, misconceptions about it current since Trent, the preference of readers for realistic fiction, and a lingering prejudice against older southern literature and popular novels. I would also point out that the aesthetic principles of historical fiction, that complex, diverse, protean form—together with the fact that there is as yet no comprehensive study of the evolution of that fiction in Britain and America—have kept scholars from a full understanding of his literary practice.

Hammond said while Simms was still reasonably young that he was "condemned to drudge" when he was "qualified to soar," and Hayne, who was by no means a sparing critic of his old friend, insisted Simms's genius "*never had fair play!* Circumstances hampered him!" (*L,* II, 547*n*161). Simms himself voiced the same sentiments when he said, in the epitaph composed though not used for his tombstone, that despite unceasing labors he had left all his better work undone. The merits of his existing work when it is seen in relationship to the circumstances of its composition indicate the element of truth in this distressing statement. Had he not fallen victim to political and economic crises, had he not been so tragically burdened by business pressures and crushing personal misfortunes, he might have been able to focus and develop the talent he obviously possessed. Had he emigrated to the Gulf South, as his father suggested, he might have expanded his extraordinary ability for rendering the characters and speech of backwoods areas. And had he, as Hubbell comments, received any real encouragement to write novels about contemporary southern life, he might have refined his ability for social satire while exploring what was for his era a virtually unexplored field.[14]

But to wish these things is to wish away the intricate combination of

14. Hayne to Francis Peyre Porcher, July 9, 1870, quoted in Trent, *William Gilmore Simms,* 322; Hubbell, *The South in American Literature,* 593.

personal, cultural, and literary forces that issued in the impressive series of books Simms did produce through which he gave artistic shape to the southern civilization he knew and loved. We owe it to ourselves, as students of American and southern literature, to see that these books are not neglected in the future. Simms is central to the historical development of literature in the South, and to ignore this fact or pretend that it does not exist is to strip our literary heritage of one of its most vigorous and compelling figures. The simple, final truth is that we as scholars have yet to grapple with Simms's complexity as man and author, to scrutinize his work in other fields besides his fiction, to describe the bibliographical complications of his many publications, or to study thoroughly the manifold connections between his personal life and work. When we do so, we may well be able to appreciate the charm and buoyancy, the energy and vitality, the enthusiasm for existence in many aspects that characterize his writing and that constitute the final, fitting legacy to us of the man.

Bibliography

Primary Sources

BOOKS AND ARTICLES

Archdale, John. *A New Description of That Fertile and Pleasant Province of Carolina. . . .* 1707; rpr. in B. R. Carroll, comp. *Historical Collections of South Carolina. . . .* 2 vols. New York: Harper and Brothers, 1836.

Avery, S[amuel] P., comp. *Mrs. Partington's Carpet-Bag of Fun.* New York: Garrett and Co., 1854.

Baldwin, Joseph G[lover]. *The Flush Times of Alabama and Mississippi. A Series of Sketches.* New York: D. Appleton and Co., 1853.

Bernhard, [Karl]. *Travels Through North America, During the Years 1825 and 1826.* 2 vols. Philadelphia: Carey, Lea and Carey, 1828.

Burke, T. A., ed. *Polly Peablossom's Wedding; and Other Tales.* Philadelphia: T. B. Peterson and Brothers, 1851.

Clemens, Samuel Langhorne [Mark Twain]. *Life on the Mississippi.* Boston: James R. Osgood, 1883.

Crockett, David. *A Narrative of the Life of David Crockett of the State of Tennessee.* Edited by James A. Shackford and Stanley J. Folmsbee. Knoxville: University of Tennessee Press, 1973.

Elliott, William. *Carolina Sports, by Land and Water; Including Incidents of Devil-Fishing, &c.* Charleston, S.C.: Burges and James, 1846.

[French, James Strange]. *Elkswatawa; or, The Prophet of the West. A Tale of the Frontier.* 2 vols. New York: Harper and Brothers, 1836.

Greene, Robert. *A Pleasant Conceited Comedy of George a Greene, The Pinner of Wakefield.* In *Typical Elizabethan Plays,* edited by Felix E. Schelling. 2 vols. New York: Harper and Brothers, 1926.

[Haliburton, T. C.]. *Traits of American Humor, By Native Authors.* 3 vols. London: Colburn and Co., 1852.

Hall, Basil. *Travels in North America, in the Years 1827 and 1828.* 3 vols. Edinburgh: Cadell and Co., 1829.

Hall, James. *The Harpe's Head; A Legend of Kentucky.* Philadelphia: Key and Biddle, 1833.

———. *The Wilderness and the War Path.* New York: Wiley and Putnam, 1846.

[Hamilton, Thomas]. *Men and Manners in America.* 2 vols. Edinburgh: William Blackwood, 1833.

Harris, George W[ashington]. *Sut Lovingood. Yarns Spun By a "Nat'ral Born Durn'd Fool.[") Warped and Wove for Public Wear.* New York: Dick and Fitzgerald, 1867.

———. *High Times and Hard Times: Sketches and Tales of George Washington Harris.* Edited by M. Thomas Inge. [Nashville]: Vanderbilt University Press, 1967.

[Hoffman, Charles Fenno]. *Greyslaer: A Romance of the Mohawk.* 2 vols. New York: Harper and Brothers, 1840.

———. *Wild Scenes in the Forest and Prairie.* 2 vols. 1839; rpr. Upper Saddle River, N.J.: Gregg Press, 1970.

[Hooper, Johnson Jones]. *Some Adventures of Captain Simon Suggs, Late of the Tallapoosa Volunteers; Together With "Taking the Census," and Other Alabama Sketches.* Philadelphia: Carey and Hart, 1845.

———. *The Widow Rugby's Husband, A Night at the Ugly Man's, and Other Tales of Alabama.* Philadelphia: T. B. Peterson and Brothers, 1851.

[Ingraham, Joseph Holt]. *The South-West. By A Yankee.* 2 vols. New York: Harper and Brothers, 1835.

[Irving, Washington]. *A Tour on the Prairies.* Philadelphia: Carey, Lea and Blanchard, 1835.

[Kennedy, John Pendleton]. *Horse Shoe Robinson; A Tale of the Tory Ascendancy.* 2 vols. Philadelphia: Carey, Lea and Blanchard, 1835.

[Longstreet, Augustus Baldwin]. *Georgia Scenes, Characters, Incidents &c. in the First Half Century of the Republic.* Augusta, Ga.: S. R. Sentinel Office, 1835.

Martineau, Harriet. *Society in America.* 3 vols. New York: Saunders and Otley, 1837.

Mayer, O. B. *John Punterick: A Novel of Life in the Old Dutch Fork.*

Edited by James E. Kibler, Jr. Spartanburg, S.C.: Reprint Co., 1981.

Murat, Prince Achille. *America and the Americans*. Translated by Henry J. S. Bradfield. Buffalo: George H. Derby, 1851.

[Paulding, James Kirke]. *Letters from the South, Written During an Excursion in the Summer of 1816*. 2 vols. New York: James Eastburn and Co., 1817.

———. *The Lion of the West; Retitled The Kentuckian, or a Trip to New York*. Revised by John Augustus Stone and William Bayle Bernard. Edited by James N. Tidwell. Stanford: Stanford University Press, 1954.

———. *Westward Ho! A Tale*. 2 vols. New York: J. and J. Harper, 1832.

Porter, William T., ed. *The Big Bear of Arkansas, and Other Sketches, Illustrative of Characters and Incidents in the South and South-West*. Philadelphia: Carey and Hart, 1845.

———, ed. *A Quarter Race in Kentucky, and Other Sketches, Illustrative of Scenes, Characters, and Incidents, Throughout "The Universal Yankee Nation."* Philadelphia: Carey and Hart, 1847.

[Postl, Anton]. *The Courtship of Ralph Doughby, Esquire*. Part 2 of *Life in the New World, or, Sketches of American Society*. Translated by G. C. Hibbe and James Mackay. New York: New World Press, 1844.

[Scott, Sir Walter]. *Ivanhoe; A Romance*. 3 vols. Edinburgh: Archibald Constable and Co., 1820.

Shillaber, B[enjamin] P[enhallow]. *Life and Sayings of Mrs. Partington, and Others of the Family*. New York: J[ames] C. Derby, 1854.

Simms, William Gilmore. *As Good as a Comedy: or, The Tennesseean's Story*. With Introduction and Explanatory Notes by Robert Bush. Text established by James B. Meriwether. Columbia, S.C.: University of South Carolina Press, 1972. Vol. III of *The Writings of William Gilmore Simms: Centennial Edition*. Edited by John C. Guilds.

———. *Atalantis. A Story of the Sea*. New York: J. and J. Harper, 1832.

———. "'Bald-Head Bill Bauldy,' and How He Went Through the Flurriday Campaign!—A Legend of the Hunter's Camp." In *Stories and Tales*. Edited, with Introductions and Explanatory Notes, by

John C. Guilds. Texts established by John C. Guilds. Columbia, S.C.: University of South Carolina Press, 1974. Vol. V of *The Writings of William Gilmore Simms: Centennial Edition.*

———. "The Baron DeKalb." *Southern Quarterly Review,* XXII [n.s., VI] (July, 1852), 141–203.

———. *Beauchampe, or The Kentucky Tragedy. A Tale of Passion.* 2 vols. Philadelphia: Lea and Blanchard, 1842.

———. *Beauchampe, Or The Kentucky Tragedy. A Sequel to Charlemont.* New York: J. S. Redfield, 1856.

———. *The Book of My Lady. A Melange.* Boston: Allen and Ticknor, 1833.

———. *Border Beagles; A Tale of Mississippi.* 2 vols. Philadelphia: Carey and Hart, 1840.

———. *Border Beagles: A Tale of Mississippi.* Rev. ed. New York: J. S. Redfield, 1855.

———. "Bulwer's Genius and Writings." *Magnolia,* n.s., I (December, 1842), [329]–37.

———. *Carl Werner, An Imaginative Story; With Other Tales of Imagination.* 2 vols. New York: George Adlard, 1838.

———. *The Cassique of Kiawah: A Colonial Romance.* New York: J. S. Redfield, 1859.

———. *Charlemont: Or The Pride of the Village. A Tale of Kentucky.* New York: J. S. Redfield, 1856.

———. *Charleston, and Her Satirists; A Scribblement.* Charleston, S.C.: James S. Burges, 1848.

———. "Charleston, the Palmetto City." *Harper's New Monthly Magazine,* XV (June, 1857), [1]–22.

———. *Confession; or, The Blind Heart. A Domestic Story.* 2 vols. Philadelphia: Lea and Blanchard, 1841.

———. *The Cub of the Panther; A Mountain Legend. Old Guard,* VII (January–December, 1869), 11–26, 91–102, 183–200, 255–68, 331–45, 411–23, 491–504, 571–83, 651–65, 731–48, 811–26, 891–99.

———. *Early Lays.* Charleston, S.C.: A. E. Miller, 1827.

———. "Editorial Bureau." *Magnolia,* n.s., I–II (July, 1842–June, 1843).

———. "Editorial Bureau—Agriculture in South-Carolina." *Magnolia,* n.s., II (March, 1843), 200–203.

———. "Editorial Bureau—Correspondence Between Schiller and Goethe." *Southern and Western,* I (June, 1845), 432–33.

———. "Editorial Bureau—Review of *Goethe's Essays on Art.*" *Southern and Western,* II (December, 1845), 423–25.

———. "Ellet's Women of the Revolution." *Southern Quarterly Review,* XVII [n.s., I] (July, 1850), 314–54.

———. *Eutaw: A Sequel to The Forayers, or The Raid of the Dog-Days. A Tale of the Revolution.* New York: J. S. Redfield, 1856.

———. *Father Abbot, or, The Home Tourist; A Medley.* Charleston, S.C.: Miller and Browne, 1849.

———. *The Forayers: Or The Raid of the Dog-Days.* New York: J. S. Redfield, 1855.

———. "From our Literary Correspondent." Charleston *Mercury,* February 27, 1856.

———. *The Golden Christmas: A Chronicle of St. John's, Berkeley.* Charleston, S.C.: Walker, Richards and Co., 1852.

———. *Guy Rivers: A Tale of Georgia.* 2 vols. New York: Harper and Brothers, 1834.

———. *Guy Rivers: A Tale of Georgia.* Rev. ed. New York: J. S. Redfield, 1855.

———. *Helen Halsey: or, The Swamp State of Conelachita. A Tale of the Borders.* New York: Burgess, Stringer and Co., 1845.

———. *The History of South Carolina. . . .* Charleston, S.C.: S. Babcock and Co., 1840.

———. *The History of South Carolina. . . .* Rev. ed. New York: J. S. Redfield, 1860.

———. "How Sharp Snaffles Got His Capital and Wife." In *Stories and Tales.* Edited, with Introductions and Explanatory Notes, by John C. Guilds. Texts established by John C. Guilds. Columbia, S.C.: University of South Carolina Press, 1974. Vol. V of *The Writings of William Gilmore Simms: Centennial Edition.*

———. *Joscelyn; A Tale of the Revolution.* With Introduction and Explanatory Notes by Stephen E. Meats. Text established by Keen Butterworth. Columbia, S.C.: University of South Carolina Press, 1975. Vol. XVI of *The Writings of William Gilmore Simms: Centennial Edition.* Edited by John C. Guilds.

———. "Katharine Walton: or, The Rebel's Daughter. A Tale of the Revolution." *Godey's Magazine and Lady's Book,* XL (February–June, 1850), 107–18, 161–69, 243–51, 320–26, 397–411; XLI (July–December, 1850), 13–27, 89–100, 162–79, 205–19, 286–98, 332–52.

———. *Katharine Walton: Or, The Rebel of Dorchester. An Historical Romance of the Revolution in Carolina.* Philadelphia: A[braham] Hart, 1851.

———. *Katharine Walton: Or The Rebel of Dorchester.* Rev. ed. New York: J. S. Redfield, 1854.

———. *The Kinsmen: Or The Black Riders of Congaree. A Tale.* 2 vols. Philadelphia: Lea and Blanchard, 1841.

———. *The Letters of William Gilmore Simms.* Edited by Mary C. Simms Oliphant, Alfred Taylor Odell, and T. C. Duncan Eaves. 5 vols. Columbia, S.C.: University of South Carolina Press, 1952–56.

———. *The Letters of William Gilmore Simms.* Vol. VI. Edited by Mary C. Simms Oliphant and T. C. Duncan Eaves. Columbia, S.C.: University of South Carolina Press, 1982.

———. *The Life of Francis Marion.* New York: Henry G. Langley, 1844.

———. *The Life of Nathanael [sic] Greene, Major-General in the Army of the Revolution.* New York: George F. Cooledge and Brother, 1849.

———. *Lyrical and Other Poems.* Charleston, S.C.: Ellis and Neufville, 1827.

———, ed. *Magnolia; or, Southern Apalachian,* n.s., I–II (July, 1842–June, 1843).

———. *Martin Faber: The Story of a Criminal.* New York: J. and J. Harper, 1833.

———. *Martin Faber, The Story of a Criminal; and Other Tales.* 2 vols. New York: Harper and Brothers, 1837.

———. *Mellichampe. A Legend of the Santee.* 2 vols. New York: Harper and Brothers, 1836.

———. *Mellichampe: A Legend of the Santee.* Rev. ed. New York: J. S. Redfield, 1854.

———. "Modern Prose Fiction." *Southern Quarterly Review,* XV (April, 1849), 41–83.

———. *Monody, on the Death of Gen. Charles Cotesworth Pinckney.* Charleston, S.C.: Gray and Ellis, 1825.

———. "Mrs. Trollope and the Americans." *American Quarterly Re-*

view, XII (September and December, 1832), 109–33. Rpr. as "Domestic Manners of the Americans," *Views and Reviews in American Literature, History and Fiction*. 2nd ser. New York: Wiley and Putnam, 1845.

———. "A New Spirit of the Age." *Southern Quarterly Review*, VII (April, 1845), 312–49.

———. "Our Agricultural Condition." *Southern and Western*, I (February, 1845), [73]–84.

———. "Our Early Authors." *XIX Century*, I (August, September, 1869), 169–77, 273–83.

———. *Paddy McGann; or, The Demon of the Stump*. With Introduction and Explanatory Notes by Robert Bush. Text established by James B. Meriwether. Columbia, S.C.: University of South Carolina Press, 1972. Vol. III of *The Writings of William Gilmore Simms: Centennial Edition*. Edited by John C. Guilds.

———. *The Partisan: A Tale of the Revolution*. 2 vols. New York: Harper and Brothers, 1835.

———. *The Partisan: A Romance of the Revolution*. Rev. ed. New York: J. S. Redfield, 1854.

———. Review of rev. ed. of *Wilhelm Meister*. *Southern Quarterly Review*, XX [n.s., IV] (July, 1851), 248.

———. *The Revolutionary War Novels of William Gilmore Simms*. With Introductions and Explanatory Notes. Edited by James B. Meriwether and Stephen E. Meats. 8 vols. Spartanburg, S.C.: Reprint Co., 1976.

———. *Richard Hurdis; or, The Avenger of Blood. A Tale of Alabama*. 2 vols. Philadelphia: Carey and Hart, 1838.

———. *Richard Hurdis: A Tale of Alabama*. Rev. ed. New York: J. S. Redfield, 1855.

———. *Sack and Destruction of the City of Columbia, S.C.* Columbia, S.C.: Daily Phoenix, 1865.

———. *The Scout: Or The Black Riders of Congaree*. Rev. ed. of *The Kinsmen*. New York: J. S. Redfield, 1854.

———. *The Social Principle: The True Source of National Permanence. An Oration. . . .* Tuscaloosa, Ala.: [Erosophic] Society, 1843.

———. *The Sources of American Independence. An Oration. . . .* Aiken, S.C.: [Town] Council, 1844.

———. *South-Carolina in the Revolutionary War: Being a Reply to Certain Misrepresentations and Mistakes of Recent Writers, in Re-*

lation to the Course and Conduct of This State. Charleston, S.C.: Walker and James, 1853.

———, ed. *Southern and Western Monthly Magazine and Review,* I–II (January–December, 1845).

———. *Southern Passages and Pictures.* New York: George Adlard, 1839.

———, ed. *Southern Quarterly Review,* XV–XXVI (April, 1849–October, 1854). N.s. I–X (April, 1850–October, 1854).

———. *Southward Ho! A Spell of Sunshine.* New York: J. S. Redfield, 1854.

———. "Summer Travel in the South." *Southern Quarterly Review,* XVIII [n.s., II] (September, 1850), 24–65.

———. *The Sword and the Distaff; or, "Fair, Fat and Forty," A Story of the South, at the Close of the Revolution.* Charleston, S.C.: Walker, Richards, and Co., 1852.

———. "Thackeray's Virginians." Charleston *Mercury,* January 5, 1860.

———. *The Tri-Color; or The Three Days of Blood, in Paris. With Some Other Pieces.* London: Wigfall and Davis, 1830.

———. "The 20th Day of December, in the Year of Our Lord, 1860." Charleston *Mercury,* December 21, 1860.

———. *Views and Reviews in American Literature, History and Fiction.* 1st ser. Edited by C. Hugh Holman. Cambridge, Mass.: Harvard University Press, 1962.

———. *Views and Reviews in American Literature, History and Fiction.* 2nd ser. New York: Wiley and Putnam, 1845.

———. *The Vision of Cortes, Cain, and Other Poems.* Charleston, S.C.: James S. Burges, 1829.

———. *Voltmeier, or The Mountain Men.* With Introduction and Explanatory Notes by Donald Davidson and Mary C. Simms Oliphant. Text established by James B. Meriwether. Columbia, S.C.: University of South Carolina Press, 1969. Vol. I of *The Writings of William Gilmore Simms: Centennial Edition.* Edited by John C. Guilds.

———. *The Wigwam and the Cabin.* 1st and 2nd ser. New York: Wiley and Putnam, 1845.

———. *Woodcraft: Or Hawks About the Dovecote. A Story of the South at the Close of the Revolution.* Rev. ed. New York: J. S. Redfield, 1854.

———. *Woodcraft: Or Hawks About the Dovecote. A Story of the South at the Close of the Revolution*. Edited by Charles S. Watson. New Haven: New College and University Press, 1983.

———. *The Yemassee. A Romance of Carolina*. 2 vols. New York: Harper and Brothers, 1835.

———. *The Yemassee: A Romance of Carolina*. Rev. ed. New York: J. S. Redfield, 1853.

———. *The Yemassee: A Romance of Carolina*. Edited by C. Hugh Holman. Boston: Houghton Mifflin Co., 1961.

Simms, William Gilmore *et al.*, eds. *Album*, I (1825), II (1826).

———. *Cosmopolitan: An Occasional*, I–II (1833).

———. *Southern Literary Gazette*, I [n.s., I] (September, 1828–November, 1829). Final issue titled *Pleiades, and Southern Literary Gazette*.

Smith, Sol[omon Franklin]. *The Theatrical Apprenticeship and Anecdotical Recollections of Sol. Smith*. Philadelphia: Carey and Hart, 1846.

"Southern Literature." *Putnam's Monthly: A Magazine of Literature, Science, and Art*, IX (February, 1857), 207–14.

Thackeray, William Makepeace. *Vanity Fair: A Novel without a Hero*. London: Bradbury and Evans, 1848.

[Thompson, William Tappan]. *Chronicles of Pineville; Embracing Sketches of Georgia Scenes, Incidents, and Characters*. Philadelphia: Carey and Hart, 1845.

———. *Major Jones' Courtship: Detailed, with Other Scenes, Incidents and Adventures, in a Series of Letters, by Himself. To Which is Added, the "Great Attraction!"* Madison, Ga.: C. R. Hanleiter, 1843.

Thorpe, T. B. *The Hive of "The Bee-Hunter," A Repository of Sketches, Including Peculiar American Character, Scenery, and Rural Sports*. New York: D. Appleton and Co., 1854.

———. *The Mysteries of the Backwoods; or, Sketches of the Southwest: Including Character, Scenery, and Rural Sports*. Philadelphia: Carey and Hart, 1846.

Trollope, [Frances]. *Domestic Manners of the Americans*. 2 vols. London: Whittaker, Treacher, and Co., 1832.

Whitcher, Frances M. *The Widow Bedott Papers*. New York: Derby and Jackson, [1856?].

MANUSCRIPT COLLECTIONS

Paul Hamilton Hayne Papers. Manuscript Department, William R. Perkins Library, Duke University, Durham, North Carolina.

Charles Carroll Simms Collection. South Caroliniana Library, University of South Carolina, Columbia, South Carolina.

Secondary Sources

Alden, John Richard. *The South in the Revolution, 1763–1789.* Baton Rouge: Louisiana State University Press, 1957. Vol. III of *A History of the South,* edited by Wendell Holmes Stephenson and E. Merton Coulter. 10 vols.

Appleton, A. I. *et al.*, comps. *The American Catalogue, 1884–1890.* New York: Peter Smith, 1941.

Arndt, Karl J. "Plagiarism: Sealsfield or Simms?" *Modern Language Notes,* LXIX (December, 1954), 577–81.

"The Author of 'Martin Faber,' 'Guy Rivers,' and 'The Yemassee.'" *Southern Literary Journal,* I (September, 1835), 39–49.

Baker, Ernest. *The History of the English Novel.* 10 vols. London: H. F. and G. Witherby, 1924–39.

Barnett, Louise K. *The Ignoble Savage: American Literary Racism, 1790–1890.* Westport, Conn.: Greenwood Press, 1975.

Beer, Gillian. *The Romance.* No. 10 of *The Critical Idiom,* edited by John D. Jump. [London]: Methuen and Co., 1970.

Bell, Michael Davitt. *The Development of American Romance: The Sacrifice of Relation.* Chicago: University of Chicago Press, 1980.

[Benjamin, Park]. Review of *The Yemassee. New-England Magazine,* VIII (June, 1835), 489–90.

Billington, Ray Allen, with James Blaine Hedges. *Westward Expansion: A History of the American Frontier.* 2nd ed. New York: Macmillan Co., 1960.

Blair, Walter. *Horse Sense in American Humor: From Benjamin Franklin to Ogden Nash.* Chicago: University of Chicago Press, 1942.

———. "Inquisitive Yankee Descendants in Arkansas." *American Speech,* XIV (February, 1939), [11]–22.

———. *Native American Humor.* [San Francisco]: Chandler Publishing Co., 1960.

Blair, Walter, and Hamlin Hill. *America's Humor: From Poor Richard to Doonesbury*. New York: Oxford University Press, 1978.

Bluestein, Gene. "'The Arkansas Traveler' and the Strategy of American Humor." *Western Folklore*, XXI (July, 1962), 153–60.

Boas, Ralph P. "The Romantic Lady." In *Romanticism in America*, edited by George Boas. 1940; rpr. New York: Russell and Russell, 1961.

Boatner, Mark Mayo, III. *Encyclopedia of the American Revolution*. Bicentennial ed. New York: David McKay, 1974.

Bode, Carl. *The Anatomy of American Popular Culture, 1840–1861*. Berkeley: University of California Press, 1959.

Bowes, Frederick P. *The Culture of Early Charleston*. Chapel Hill: University of North Carolina Press, 1942.

Breihan, Carl W. *Badmen of the Frontier Days*. New York: Robert McBride Company, 1957.

Bridenbaugh, Carl. *Cities in the Wilderness: The First Century of Urban Life in America, 1625–1742*. Rev. ed. New York: Alfred A. Knopf, 1955.

———. *Myths and Realities: Societies of the Colonial South*. Baton Rouge: Louisiana State University Press, 1952.

Brooks, Van Wyck. *The World of Washington Irving*. New York: E. P. Dutton, 1944.

Bush, Robert. "*Paddy McGann*, William Gilmore Simms's Devil Story." *Bulletin of the New York Public Library*, LXIX (March, 1965), 197–204.

Butterfield, H[erbert]. *The Historical Novel: An Essay*. Cambridge, Eng.: University Press, 1924.

Butterworth, Keen. "William Gilmore Simms." In *Antebellum Writers in New York and the South*, edited by Joel Myerson. Vol. III of *Dictionary of Literary Biography*. Detroit: Gale Research Co., 1979.

———. "William Gilmore Simms." In Vol. I of *First Printings of American Authors: Contributions Toward Descriptive Checklists*, edited by Matthew J. Bruccoli and C. E. Frazer Clark, Jr. Detroit: Gale Research Co., 1977.

Butterworth, Keen, and James E. Kibler, Jr. *William Gilmore Simms: A Reference Guide*. Boston: G. K. Hall, 1980.

Cardwell, Guy A. "The Plantation House: An Analogical Image." *Southern Literary Journal*, II (Fall, 1969), [3]–21.

Cash, W[ilbur] J[oseph]. *The Mind of the South*. New York: Alfred A. Knopf, 1941.

Cauthen, Charles Edward. *South Carolina Goes to War, 1860–1865*. James Sprunt Studies in History and Political Science, XXXII. Chapel Hill: University of North Carolina Press, 1950.

Cawelti, John G. *Adventure, Mystery, and Romance: Formula Stories as Art and Popular Culture*. Chicago: University of Chicago Press, 1976.

Cecil, L. Moffitt. "The Design of William Gilmore Simms's *The Kinsmen*." *Mississippi Quarterly,* XXIX (Fall, 1976), [514]–25.

———. "Simms's Porgy as National Hero." *American Literature,* XXXVI (January, 1965), [475]–84.

Ceremonies at the Unveiling of the Bronze Bust of William Gilmore Simms at White Point Garden, Charleston, S.C., June 11th, 1879. Charleston, S.C.: News and Courier Book Presses, 1879.

Charvat, William. *Literary Publishing in America, 1790–1850*. Philadelphia: University of Pennsylvania Press, 1959.

———. *The Profession of Authorship in America, 1800–1870: The Papers of William Charvat*. Edited by Matthew J. Bruccoli. [Columbus], Ohio: Ohio State University Press, 1968.

Chase, Richard. *The American Novel and Its Tradition*. Garden City, N.Y.: Doubleday and Co., 1957.

Claiborne, J. F. H. *Life and Correspondence of John A. Quitman, Major-General, U.S.A., and Governor of the State of Mississippi*. 2 vols. New York: Harper and Brothers, 1860.

[Clark, Lewis Gaylord]. "Editor's Table." *The Knickerbocker, or New-York Monthly Magazine,* XVIII (November, 1841), 461–62, and XX (August, 1842), 199–200.

———. "Editors' Table." *The Knickerbocker, or New-York Monthly Magazine,* XVI (October, 1840), 364.

———. "Literary Notices." *The Knickerbocker, or New-York Monthly Magazine,* IV (August, 1834), [145]–49, V (April, 1835), 341–43, VII (January, 1836), 91–92, XXII (September, 1843), [265]–67, XXVII (April, 1846), [354]–59.

[Clark, Lewis Gaylord, and Willis Gaylord Clark]. "Editors' Table." *The Knickerbocker, or New-York Monthly Magazine,* VI (December, 1835), 577.

Coates, Robert M. *The Outlaw Years: The History of the Land Pirates of the Natchez Trace*. New York: [Macaulay Co.], 1930.

Cohen, Hennig, and William B. Dillingham, eds. *Humor of the Old Southwest.* 2nd ed. Athens, Ga.: University of Georgia Press, 1975.

Collins, Carvel Emerson. "Nineteenth Century Fiction of the Southern Appalachians." *Bulletin of Bibliography,* XVII (September–December, 1842), 186–90.

Coulter, E. Merton. *Auraria: The Story of a Georgia Gold-Mining Town.* Athens, Ga.: University of Georgia Press, 1956.

Crane, Verner W. *The Southern Frontier, 1670–1732.* 1929; rpr. Ann Arbor: University of Michigan Press, 1956.

Current-García, Eugene. *The American Short Story Before 1850: A Critical History.* [Boston]: Twayne Publishers, 1985.

Daiches, David. "Scott and Scotland." In *Scott Bicentenary Essays,* edited by Alan Bell. New York: Harper and Row, 1973.

———. "Scott's Achievement as a Novelist." In *Scott's Mind and Art,* edited by A. Norman Jeffares. New York: Barnes and Noble, 1970.

Daniels, Jonathan. *The Devil's Backbone: The Story of the Natchez Trace.* New York: McGraw-Hill, 1962.

Davidson, Donald. Introduction to *The Letters of William Gilmore Simms,* edited by Mary C. Simms Oliphant, Alfred Taylor Odell, and T. C. Duncan Eaves. Vol. I of 6 vols. Columbia, S.C.: University of South Carolina Press, 1952.

Dean, Paula Dianne Fix. "Revisions in the Revolutionary War Novels of William Gilmore Simms." Ph.D. dissertation, Auburn University, 1971.

Deen, Floyd H. "A Comparison of Simms's *Richard Hurdis* with Its Sources." *Modern Language Notes,* LX (June, 1945), 406–408.

DeVoto, Bernard. *Mark Twain's America.* Boston: Little, Brown, and Co., 1932.

Dillard, A. W. "William Gilmore Simms and A. B. Longstreet." *XIX Century,* III (October, 1870), 425–30.

Donald, David. *Charles Sumner and the Coming of the Civil War.* New York: Alfred A. Knopf, 1960.

Dorson, Richard M., ed. *Davy Crockett: American Comic Legend.* New York: Spiral Press, 1939.

———. "The Identification of Folklore in American Literature." In "Folklore in Literature: A Symposium." *Journal of American Folklore,* LXX (January–March, 1957), [1]–8.

———. *Jonathan Draws the Long Bow.* Cambridge, Mass.: Harvard University Press, 1946.

———. "Print and American Folk Tales." *California Folklore Quarterly,* IV (July, 1945), 207–15.

Eaton, Clement. *The Growth of Southern Civilization, 1790–1860.* New York: Harper and Brothers, 1961.

———. *The Mind of the Old South.* Rev. ed. Baton Rouge: Louisiana State University Press, 1967.

Ellet, Elizabeth F. *The Women of the American Revolution.* 2 vols. New York: Baker and Scribner, 1848.

Erskine, John. *Leading American Novelists.* New York: Henry Holt and Co., 1910.

Faust, Drew Gilpin. *James Henry Hammond and the Old South: A Design for Mastery.* Baton Rouge: Louisiana State University Press, 1982.

———. *A Sacred Circle: The Dilemma of the Intellectual in the Old South, 1840–1860.* Baltimore: Johns Hopkins University Press, 1977.

[Felton, Cornelius C.]. Review of *The Wigwam and the Cabin* and *Views and Reviews. North American Review,* LXIII (October, 1846), 357–81.

Fichter, Joseph H., and George L. Maddox. "Religion in the South, Old and New." In *The South in Continuity and Change,* edited by John C. McKinney and Edgar T. Thompson. Durham, N.C.: Duke University Press, 1965.

Fiedler, Leslie A. *Love and Death in the American Novel.* Rev. ed. New York: Stein and Day, 1966.

Fisher, Sydney G. "The Legendary and Myth-making Process in Histories of the American Revolution." *Proceedings of the American Philosophical Society,* LI (April–June, 1912), 53–75.

Fleishman, Avrom. *The English Historical Novel: Walter Scott to Virginia Woolf.* Baltimore: Johns Hopkins University Press, 1971.

Foster, Edward Halsey. *The Civilized Wilderness: Backgrounds to American Romantic Literature, 1817–1860.* New York: Macmillan Co., 1975.

Franklin, John Hope. *A Southern Odyssey: Travelers in the Antebellum North.* Baton Rouge: Louisiana State University Press, 1976.

Frye, Northrop. *Anatomy of Criticism: Four Essays.* Princeton: Princeton University Press, 1957.

———. *The Secular Scripture: A Study of the Structure of Romance.* Cambridge, Mass.: Harvard University Press, 1976.

Gaines, Francis Pendleton. *The Southern Plantation: A Study in the Development and the Accuracy of a Tradition.* Columbia University Studies in English and Comparative Literature, LXXVII. New York: Columbia University Press, 1924.

Garden, Alexander. *Anecdotes of the Revolutionary War in America. . . .* 1st ser. Charleston, S.C.: A. E. Miller, 1822.

Gipson, Lawrence Henry. *The British Isles and the American Colonies: The Southern Plantations, 1748–1754.* New York: Alfred A. Knopf, 1960. Vol. II of *The British Empire Before the American Revolution.* 15 vols.

Griswold, Rufus W. *The Poets and Poetry of America.* Philadelphia: Carey and Hart, 1842.

———. *The Prose Writers of America.* Philadelphia: Carey and Hart, 1847.

Guilds, John C. "The 'Lost' Number of the *Southern Literary Gazette.*" *Studies in Bibliography,* XXII (1969), 266–73.

———. "Simms and the *Southern and Western.*" In *South Carolina Journals and Journalists,* edited by James B. Meriwether. Spartanburg, S.C.: Reprint Co., 1975.

———. "Simms as Editor and Prophet: The Flowering and Early Death of the Southern *Magnolia.*" *Southern Literary Journal,* IV (Spring, 1972), [69]–92.

———. "Simms's First Magazine: *The Album.*" *Studies in Bibliography,* VIII (1956), [169]–83.

———. "Simms's Use of History, Theory and Practice." *Mississippi Quarterly,* XXX (Fall, 1977), [505]–11.

———. "Simms's Views on National and Sectional Literature, 1825–1845." *North Carolina Historical Review,* XXXIV (July, 1957), 393–405.

———. "William Gilmore Simms and the *Cosmopolitan.*" *Georgia Historical Quarterly,* XLI (March, 1957), [31]–41.

———. "William Gilmore Simms and the *Southern Literary Gazette.*" *Studies in Bibliography,* XXI (1968), [59]–92.

Hart, James D. *The Popular Book: A History of America's Literary Taste.* New York: Oxford University Press, 1950.

Hauck, Richard Boyd. *Crockett: A Bio-Bibliography.* Westport, Conn.: Greenwood Press, 1982.

Hayne, Paul Hamilton. "Ante-Bellum Charleston." *Southern Bivouac,* n.s., I (October, 1885), [257]–68.

———. "William Gilmore Simms." *Appletons' Journal,* IV (July 30, 1870), 136–40.

[Herbert, Henry William]. Review of *Guy Rivers. American Monthly Magazine,* III (July, 1834), 295–304.

[Hewatt, Alexander]. *An Historical Account of the Rise and Progress of the Colonies of South Carolina and Georgia.* 1779; rpr. in B. R. Carroll, comp. *Historical Collections of South Carolina. . . .* 2 vols. New York: Harper and Brothers, 1836.

Higginbotham, Don. *The War of American Independence: Military Attitudes, Policies, and Practice, 1763–1789.* New York: Macmillan Co., 1971.

[Hoffman, Charles Fenno]. Review of *The Yemassee.* New York *American.* April 18, 1835.

Hoge, James O. "Byron's Influence on the Poetry of William Gilmore Simms." *Essays in Literature,* II (Spring, 1975), 87–96.

Hogue, L. Lynn. "The Presentation of Post-Revolutionary Law in *Woodcraft:* Another Perspective on the 'Truth' of Simms's Fiction." *Mississippi Quarterly,* XXXI (Spring, 1978), [201]–10.

Holman, C. Hugh. *The Immoderate Past: The Southern Writer and History.* Athens, Ga.: University of Georgia Press, 1977.

———. Reviews of *The Letters of William Gilmore Simms. Journal of Southern History,* XIX–XXI; XXIII (February, 1953; August, 1953; November, 1954; November, 1955; November, 1957), 85–87, 389–91, 546–47, 539–41, 544–45, respectively.

———. *The Roots of Southern Writing: Essays on the Literature of the American South.* Athens, Ga.: University of Georgia Press, 1972.

———. "The Status of Simms." *American Quarterly,* X (Summer, 1958), 181–85.

———. *Three Modes of Modern Southern Fiction: Ellen Glasgow, William Faulkner, Thomas Wolfe.* Athens, Ga.: University of Georgia Press, 1966.

———. "William Gilmore Simms." In *Southern Writers: A Biographical Dictionary,* edited by Robert Bain, Joseph M. Flora, and Louis D. Rubin, Jr. Baton Rouge: Louisiana State University Press, 1979.

Hoole, W[illiam] Stanley. "Alabama and W. Gilmore Simms." *Alabama Review,* XVI (April, July, 1963), [83]–107, 185–99.

———. "A Note on Simms's Visits to the Southwest." *American Literature,* VI (November, 1934), 334–36.

Howard, H. R., comp. *The History of Virgil A. Stewart, and His Adventure in Capturing and Exposing the Great "Western Land Pirate" and His Gang. . . .* New York: Harper and Brothers, 1836.

Hubbell, Jay B., ed. *The Last Years of Henry Timrod, 1864–1867.* Durham, N.C.: Duke University Press, 1941.

———. *The South in American Literature, 1607–1900.* [Durham], N.C.: Duke University Press, 1954.

"Intruders upon Indian Lands." New York *American.* October 17, 1833.

Jarrell, Hampton M. "Simms's Visits to the Southwest." *American Literature,* V (March, 1933), [29]–35.

———. "William Gilmore Simms—Almost a Historian." In *Proceedings of the South Carolina Historical Association,* edited by Robert D. Ochs. Columbia, S.C., 1947.

———. "William Gilmore Simms: Realistic Romancer." Ph.D. dissertation, Duke University, 1932.

Johnson, William. *Sketches of the Life and Correspondence of Nathanael* [*sic*] *Greene, Major General of the Armies of the United States, In the War of the Revolution.* Extra-illustrated copy. 2 vols. Charleston, S.C.: A. E. Miller, 1822.

Jones, Alexander E. "A Source for William Gilmore Simms's 'Sharp Snaffles.'" *Journal of American Folklore,* LXX (January–March, 1957), [66]–69.

Kammen, Michael. *A Season of Youth: The American Revolution and the Historical Imagination.* New York: Alfred A. Knopf, 1978.

Kibler, James E., Jr. "*The Album* (1826): The Significance of the Recently Discovered Second Volume." *Studies in Bibliography,* XXXIX (1986), [62]–78.

———. "The First Simms Letters: 'Letters from the West' (1826)." *Southern Literary Journal,* XIX (Spring, 1987), [81]–91.

———. *The Poetry of William Gilmore Simms: An Introduction and Bibliography.* Spartanburg, S.C.: Reprint Co., 1979.

———. "Simms as Naturalist: Lowcountry Landscape in His Revolutionary Novels." *Mississippi Quarterly,* XXXI (Fall, 1978), [499]–518.

———. "Simms' Editorship of the Columbia *Phoenix* of 1865." In *South Carolina Journals and Journalists,* edited by James B. Meriwether. Spartanburg, S.C.: Reprint Co., 1975.

———. "Simms' Indebtedness to Folk Tradition in 'Sharp Snaffles.'" *Southern Literary Journal,* IV (Spring, 1972), [55]–68.

Kolodny, Annette. "The Unchanging Landscape: The Pastoral Impulse in Simms's Revolutionary War Romances." *Southern Literary Journal,* V (Fall, 1972), [46]–67.

Kreyling, Michael. *Figures of the Hero in Southern Narrative.* Baton Rouge: Louisiana State University Press, 1987.

Kyte, George W. "Victory in the South: An Appraisal of General Greene's Strategy in the Carolinas." *North Carolina Historical Review,* XXXVII (July, 1960), 321–47.

Lane, Thomas Darwin. "Two Versions of Simms's *Guy Rivers:* A Record of Artistic Development in Changing Times." Ph.D. dissertation, Texas Christian University, 1972.

Lee, Henry. *Memoirs of the War in the Southern Department of the United States.* 2 vols. Philadelphia: Bradford and Inskeep, 1812.

The Life and Adventures of John A. Murrell, the Great Western Land Pirate. . . . New York: H. Long and Brother, 1847.

Lukács, Georg. *The Historical Novel.* Translated by Hannah and Stanley Mitchell. 1962; rpr. Atlantic Highlands, N.J.: Humanities Press, 1978.

Lynn, Kenneth S. *Mark Twain and Southwestern Humor.* Boston: Little, Brown, and Co., 1959.

McCardell, John. "Poetry and the Practical: William Gilmore Simms." In *Intellectual Life in Antebellum Charleston,* edited by Michael O'Brien and David Moltke-Hansen. Knoxville: University of Tennessee Press, 1986.

———. "Trent's *Simms:* The Making of a Biography." In *A Master's Due: Essays in Honor of David Herbert Donald,* edited by William J. Cooper, Jr., Michael F. Holt, and John McCardell. Baton Rouge: Louisiana State University Press, 1985.

McCowen, George Smith, Jr. *The British Occupation of Charleston, 1780–82.* Columbia, S.C.: University of South Carolina Press, 1972.

McCrady, Edward. *The History of South Carolina Under the Proprietary Government, 1670–1719.* New York: Macmillan Co., 1897.

———. *The History of South Carolina Under the Royal Government, 1719–1776.* New York: Macmillan Co., 1901.

———. *The History of South Carolina in the Revolution, 1775–1780.* New York: Macmillan Co., 1902.

———. *The History of South Carolina in the Revolution, 1780–1783.* New York: Macmillan Co., 1902.

McHaney, Thomas L. "An Early 19th-Century Literary Agent: James Lawson of New York." *Publications of the Bibliographical Society of America,* LXIV (Second Quarter, 1970), 177–92.

———. "William Gilmore Simms." In *The Chief Glory of Every People: Essays on Classic American Writers,* edited by Matthew J. Bruccoli. Carbondale, Ill.: Southern Illinois University Press, 1973.

McIlwaine, Shields. *The Southern Poor-White from Lubberland to Tobacco Road.* Norman, Okla.: University of Oklahoma Press, 1939.

MacKenzie, Roderick. *Strictures on Lt. Col. Tarleton's History. . . .* London: N.p., 1787.

Marshall, Ian. "The American Dreams of Sam Snaffles." *Southern Literary Journal,* XVIII (Spring, 1986), [96]–107.

Meats, Stephen E. "Artist or Historian: William Gilmore Simms and the Revolutionary South." In *Eighteenth-Century Florida and the Revolutionary South,* edited by Samuel Proctor. Gainesville, Fla.: University Presses of Florida, 1978.

———. "Bald-Head Bill Bauldy: Simms's Unredeemed Captive." Paper delivered at annual meeting of the Modern Language Association, 1977.

———, ed. "South Carolina Writers in the *Spirit of the Times.*" In *Gyascutus: Studies in Antebellum Southern Humorous and Sporting Writing,* edited by James L. W. West III. Atlantic Highlands, N.J.: Humanities Press, 1978.

Meine, Franklin J., ed. *Tall Tales of the Southwest: An Anthology of Southern and Southwestern Humor, 1830–1860.* New York: Alfred A. Knopf, 1930.

Meriwether, James B. "Simms's 'Sharp Snaffles' and 'Bald-Head Bill Bauldy': Two Views of Men—and of Women." *South Carolina Review,* XVI (Spring, 1984), 66–71.

Meriwether, Robert L. *The Expansion of South Carolina, 1729–1765.* Kingsport, Tenn.: Southern Publishers, 1940.

Mesick, Jane Louise. *The English Traveller in America, 1785–1835.* Columbia University Studies in English and Comparative Literature, LXXIII. New York: Columbia University Press, 1922.

Miller, Perry. *The Raven and the Whale: The War of Words and Wits in the Era of Poe and Melville*. New York: Harcourt, Brace and Co., 1956.

Milligen-Johnston, George. *A Short Description of the Province of South-Carolina, With An Account of the Air, Weather, and Diseases, at Charles-Town*. 1770; rpr. in *Colonial South Carolina: Two Contemporary Descriptions,* edited by Chapman J. Milling. Columbia, S.C.: University of South Carolina Press, 1951.

Milling, Chapman J. *Red Carolinians*. Chapel Hill: University of North Carolina Press, 1940.

[Moore, J. Quitman]. "William Gilmore Simms." *De Bow's Review,* XXIX [n.s., IV] (December, 1860), 702–12.

Moore, Rayburn S., ed. *A Man of Letters in the Nineteenth-Century South: Selected Letters of Paul Hamilton Hayne*. Baton Rouge: Louisiana State University Press, 1982.

———. *Paul Hamilton Hayne*. New York: Twayne Publishers, 1972.

———. "*Woodcraft*." Paper delivered at "A Conference on William Gilmore Simms and the Revolution in South Carolina," Charleston, S.C., May, 1976.

Morris, J. Allen. "The Stories of William Gilmore Simms." *American Literature,* XIV (March, 1942), [20]–35.

Moultrie, William. *Memoirs of the American Revolution, So Far as It Related to the States of North and South Carolina, and Georgia*. 2 vols. New York: David Longworth, 1802.

Odum, Howard W. *Southern Regions of the United States*. Chapel Hill: University of North Carolina Press, 1936.

[Oliphant, Mary C. Simms, Alfred Taylor Odell, and T. C. Duncan Eaves]. "The Family Circle." In *The Letters of William Gilmore Simms,* edited by Mary C. Simms Oliphant, Alfred Taylor Odell, and T. C. Duncan Eaves. Vol. I of 6 vols. Columbia, S.C.: University of South Carolina Press, 1952.

Parks, Edd Winfield. *Ante-Bellum Southern Literary Critics*. Athens, Ga.: University of Georgia Press, 1962.

———. "The Three Streams of Southern Humor." *Georgia Review,* IX (Summer, 1955), 147–59.

———. *William Gilmore Simms As Literary Critic*. Athens, Ga.: University of Georgia Press, 1961.

Parrington, Vernon L. *The Romantic Revolution in America, 1800–1860*. Vol. II of *Main Currents in American Thought*. 3 vols. New York: Harcourt, Brace and Co., 1927–30.

Penick, James Lal, Jr. *The Great Western Land Pirate: John A. Murrell in Legend and History*. Columbia, Mo.: University of Missouri Press, 1981.

Penrod, James H. "Characteristic Endings of Southwestern Yarns." *Mississippi Quarterly,* XV (Winter, 1961–62), [27]–35.

Phares, Ross. *Reverend Devil: A Biography of John A. Murrell.* New Orleans: Pelican Publishing Co., 1941.

Pictorial Life and Adventures of John A. Murrell. Philadelphia: T. B. Peterson and Brothers, 184[8?].

[Poe, Edgar Allan]. Review of *The Damsel of Darien. Burton's Gentleman's Magazine and American Monthly Review,* V (November, 1839), 283–85.

———. Review of *The Partisan. Southern Literary Messenger,* II (January, 1836), 117–21.

———. Review of *The Wigwam and the Cabin. Broadway Journal,* II (October 4, 1845), 190–91.

———. Review of *The Wigwam and the Cabin. Godey's Magazine and Lady's Book,* XXXII (January, 1846), 41–42.

Porte, Joel. *The Romance in America: Studies in Cooper, Poe, Hawthorne, Melville, and James*. Middletown, Conn.: Wesleyan University Press, 1969.

Pugh, Robert C. "The Revolutionary Militia in the Southern Campaign, 1780–1781." *William and Mary Quarterly,* 3rd ser., XIV (April, 1957), [154]–75.

Ramsay, David. *The History of the Revolution of South-Carolina, From a British Province to an Independent State.* 2 vols. Trenton, N.J.: Isaac Collins, 1785.

———. *The History of South-Carolina, From Its First Settlement in 1670, to the Year 1808.* 2 vols. Charleston, S.C.: David Longworth, 1809.

———. *History of the United States, From Their First Settlement as English Colonies, in 1607, To the Year 1808.* 3 vols. Philadelphia: M[atthew] Carey and Son, 1789.

Reed, John Q. *Benjamin Penhallow Shillaber.* New York: Twayne Publishers, 1972.

Review of *As Good as a Comedy. Godey's Magazine and Lady's Book,* XLIV (June, 1852), 515.

Review of *As Good as a Comedy. Literary World: A Journal of Science, Literature, and Art,* X (March 27, 1852), 222–23.

Review of *Border Beagles. Ladies' Companion,* XIII (October, 1840), 306.

Review of *Guy Rivers.* New York *Mirror.* August 2, 1834.

Review of *Martin Faber. American Monthly Magazine,* IV (February, 1835), 357–58.

Review of *The Partisan. Southern Literary Journal,* I (December, 1835), 284–85.

Review of *The Partisan. Southern Literary Journal,* I (January, 1836), 347–58.

Review of *The Yemassee.* New York *Commercial Advertiser.* April 18, 1835.

Review of *The Yemassee.* New York *Times.* April 16, 1835.

Ridgely, J. V. *William Gilmore Simms.* New York: Twayne Publishers, 1962.

Rogers, George C., Jr. *Charleston in the Age of the Pinckneys.* Norman, Okla.: University of Oklahoma Press, 1969.

Roller, David C., and Robert W. Twyman, eds. *The Encyclopedia of Southern History.* Baton Rouge: Louisiana State University Press, 1979.

Rourke, Constance. *American Humor: A Study of the National Character.* New York: Harcourt, Brace and Co., 1931.

Rubin, Louis D., Jr. "The Romance of the Colonial Frontier: Simms, Cooper, the Indians, and the Wilderness." In *American Letters and the Historical Consciousness: Essays in Honor of Lewis P. Simpson,* edited by J. Gerald Kennedy and Daniel Mark Fogel. Baton Rouge: Louisiana State University Press, 1987.

———. *The Writer in the South: Studies in a Literary Community.* Athens, Ga.: University of Georgia Press, 1972.

Salley, Alexander S. "William Gilmore Simms." In *The Letters of William Gilmore Simms,* edited by Mary C. Simms Oliphant, Alfred Taylor Odell, and T. C. Duncan Eaves. Vol. I of 6 vols. Columbia, S.C.: University of South Carolina Press, 1952.

Schaper, William A. *Sectionalism and Representation in South Carolina.* 1901; rpr. New York: Da Capo Press, 1968.

Scheick, William J. *The Half-Blood: A Cultural Symbol in 19th-Century American Fiction.* [Lexington]: University Press of Kentucky, 1979.

Scholes, Robert, and Robert Kellogg. *The Nature of Narrative.* New York: Oxford University Press, 1966.

Shillingsburg, Miriam J. "An Edition of William Gilmore Simms's *The Cub of the Panther*." Ph.D. dissertation, University of South Carolina, 1969.

———. "From Notes to Novel: Simms's Creative Method." *Southern Literary Journal*, V (Fall, 1972), [89]–107.

———, ed. "The Idylls of the Apalachian." Parts 1 and 2. *Appalachian Journal*, I (Autumn, 1972, Spring, 1973), 2–11, 147–60, respectively.

———. "The Influence of Sectionalism on the Revisions in Simms's Revolutionary Romances." *Mississippi Quarterly*, XXIX (Fall, 1976), [526]–38.

———. "The Maturing of Simms's Short Fiction: The Example of 'Oakatibbe.'" *Mississippi Quarterly*, XXXVIII (Spring, 1985), [99]–117.

———. "Simms's Benedict Arnold: The Hero as Traitor." *Southern Studies*, XVII (Fall, 1978), [273]–89.

———. "Simms's Last Novel, *The Cub of the Panther*." *Southern Literary Journal*, XVII (Spring, 1985), [108]–19.

———. "The Southron as American: William Gilmore Simms." In *Studies in the American Renaissance 1980*, edited by Joel Myerson. Boston: Twayne Publishers, 1980.

———. "William Gilmore Simms and the Myth of Appalachia." *Appalachian Journal*, VI (Winter, 1979), 111–19.

Simkins, Francis Butler. *A History of the South*. 3rd ed. New York: Alfred A. Knopf, 1963.

Simpson, Lewis P. *The Dispossessed Garden: Pastoral and History in Southern Literature*. Athens, Ga.: University of Georgia Press, 1975.

———. "The Humor of the Old Southwest." *Mississippi Quarterly*, XVII (Spring, 1964), [63]–66.

Sirmans, M. Eugene. *Colonial South Carolina: A Political History, 1663–1763*. Chapel Hill: University of North Carolina Press, 1966.

Skaggs, Merrill Maguire. *The Folk of Southern Fiction*. Athens, Ga.: University of Georgia Press, 1972.

Smith, William Raymond. *History as Argument: Three Patriot Historians of the American Revolution*. The Hague: Mouton and Co., 1966.

Stewart, Randall. "Tidewater and Frontier." In *Regionalism and Beyond: Essays of Randall Stewart*. Edited by George Core. Nashville: Vanderbilt University Press, 1968.

Stoney, Samuel Gaillard. "The Country and the People." In *Plantations of the Carolina Low Country.* Rev. ed. Edited by Albert Simons and Samuel Lapham, Jr. Charleston, S.C.: Carolina Art Association, 1964.

Strickland, Betty Jo. "The Short Fiction of William Gilmore Simms: A Checklist." *Mississippi Quarterly,* XXIX (Fall, 1976), [591]–608.

———. "The Short Fiction of William Gilmore Simms: A Critical Description and Checklist." Ph.D. dissertation, University of Georgia, 1975.

Tarleton, [Banastre]. *A History of the Campaigns of 1780 and 1781, in the Southern Provinces of North America.* London: T. Cadell, 1787.

Taylor, Rosser H. *Ante-Bellum South Carolina: A Social and Cultural History.* James Sprunt Studies in History and Political Science, XXV. Chapel Hill: University of North Carolina Press, 1942.

Taylor, William R. *Cavalier and Yankee: The Old South and American National Character.* New York: George Braziller, 1961.

Thomas, J. Wesley. "The German Sources of William Gilmore Simms." In Vol. I of *Anglo-German and American-German Crosscurrents,* edited by Philip Allison Shelley, with Arthur O. Lewis, Jr., and William W. Betts, Jr. Chapel Hill: University of North Carolina Press, 1957. 3 vols.

Thompson, Edgar T. "The South in Old and New Contexts." In *The South in Continuity and Change,* edited by John C. McKinney and Edgar T. Thompson. Durham, N.C.: Duke University Press, 1965.

Thompson, Stith. *Motif-Index of Folk-Literature.* Rev. ed. 6 vols. Bloomington, Ind.: Indiana University Press, 1955–58.

Tomlinson, David. "Simms's Monthly Magazine: The *Southern and Western Monthly Magazine and Review.*" *Southern Literary Journal,* VIII (Fall, 1975), [95]–125.

Tompkins, Jane. *Sensational Designs: The Cultural Work of American Fiction, 1790–1860.* New York: Oxford University Press, 1985.

Trent, William P. *William Gilmore Simms.* American Men of Letters Series. Boston: Houghton Mifflin Co., 1892.

Trowbridge, John Townsend. *My Own Story with Recollections of Noted Persons.* Boston: Houghton Mifflin Co., 1903.

Turner, Arlin. "Poe and Simms: Friendly Critics, Sometimes Friends." In *Papers on Poe: Essays in Honor of John Ward Ostrom,* edited by Richard P. Veler. Springfield, Ohio: Chantry Music Press, 1972.

———. "Realism and Fantasy in Southern Humor." *Georgia Review,* XII (Winter, 1958), 451–57.

———. "Seeds of Literary Revolt in the Humor of the Old Southwest." *Louisiana Historical Quarterly,* XXXIX (April, 1956), [143]–51.

———. "William Gilmore Simms in His Letters." *South Atlantic Quarterly,* LIII (July, 1954), [404]–15.

Turner, Frederick Jackson. *The United States, 1830–1850: The Nation and Its Sections.* New York: Henry Holt and Co., 1935.

"Uses and Abuses of Lynch Law." *American Whig Review,* XIII (March, 1851), 213–20.

Vance, Rupert B. *Human Geography of the South: A Study in Regional Resources and Human Adequacy.* 2nd ed. Chapel Hill: University of North Carolina Press, 1935.

———. "Social Change in the Southern Appalachians." In *The South in Continuity and Change,* edited by John C. McKinney and Edgar T. Thompson. Durham, N.C.: Duke University Press, 1965.

Van Doren, Carl. *The American Novel, 1789–1939.* Rev. ed. New York: Macmillan Co., 1940.

Van Tassel, David D. *Recording America's Past: An Interpretation of the Development of Historical Studies in America, 1607–1884.* [Chicago]: University of Chicago Press, 1960.

Vauthier, Simone. "Une Aventure du Récit Fantastique: *Paddy McGann, or, The Demon of the Stump* de William Gilmore Simms." *Recherches Anglaise et Américaines,* VI (Summer, 1973), [78]–104.

Vineyard, Catherine Marshall. "The Arkansas Traveller." In *Backwoods to Border,* edited by Mody C. Boatright and Donald Day. Texas Folk-Lore Society Publications, XVIII. Austin, Tex.: Texas Folk-Lore Society, 1943.

Wagner, Frederick. "Simms's Editing of *The Life of Nathanael Greene.*" *Southern Literary Journal,* XI (Fall, 1978), [40]–43.

Wakelyn, Jon L. *The Politics of a Literary Man: William Gilmore Simms.* Westport, Conn.: Greenwood Press, 1973.

Wallace, David Duncan. *South Carolina: A Short History, 1520–1948.* Columbia, S.C.: University of South Carolina Press, 1961.

Walton, Augustus Q. *A History of the Detection, Conviction, Life and Designs of John A. Murel, the Great Western Land Pirate. . . .* Athens, Tenn.; George White, 1835.

Waring, Thomas R. "Charleston: The Capital of the Plantations." In

The Carolina Low-Country, by Augustine T. Smythe *et al.* New York: Macmillan Co., 1931.

Watson, Charles S. "Simms and the Beginnings of Local Color." *Mississippi Quarterly,* XXXV (Winter, 1981–82), [25]–39.

———. "William Gilmore Simms: An Essay in Bibliography." *Resources for American Literary Study,* III (Spring, 1972), 3–26.

Watt, Ian. *The Rise of the Novel: Studies in Defoe, Richardson and Fielding.* London: Chatto and Windus, 1957.

Weidman, Bette S. "White Men's Red Man: A Penitential Reading of Four American Novels." *Modern Language Studies,* IV (Fall, 1974), 14–26.

Weigley, Russell F. *The Partisan War: The South Carolina Campaign of 1780–82.* Columbia, S.C.: University of South Carolina Press, 1970.

"William Gilmore Simms." *Harper's Weekly,* XIV (July 2, 1870), 420.

Williams, Stanley T. "Spanish Influences on the Fiction of William Gilmore Simms." *Hispanic Review,* XXI (July, 1953), 221–28.

Wilson, James Grant. *Thackeray in the United States, 1852–3, 1855–6.* 2 vols. New York: Dodd, Mead and Co., 1904.

Wimsatt, Mary Ann. "Simms's Early Short Stories." *Library Chronicle, University of Pennsylvania,* XLI (Winter, 1977), 163–79.

Yates, Norris W. *William T. Porter and the "Spirit of the Times": A Study of the "Big Bear" School of Humor.* Baton Rouge: Louisiana State University Press, 1957.

[Yeadon, Richard, Jr.] "Biographical Sketches of Living American Poets and Novelists. No IV. William Gilmore Simms, Esq." *Southern Literary Messenger,* IV (August, 1838), 528–35.

Index